Reply All

Reply All

A Governor's Story 1999–2007

Jeb Bush

ISBN: 1515149048
ISBN 13: 9781515149040

Table of Contents

Foreword

Like most Americans, I treasure Sundays with my family. For years, Jeb has cooked Sunday dinner—usually Mexican food. He did this even when he was governor. He makes a really great guacamole. (No peas, please!) He likes to go to the grocery store and push the cart through the aisles. Many times I wondered how it could take him so long to shop for dinner, but then I learned why. People I had never met would come up to me at events and say, "You know, I was having a big problem with my child, and I saw your husband in the supermarket and spoke to him about it. He listened and gave me great advice. I am so grateful to your husband."

This little story says a lot about the man with whom I fell in love when I was seventeen, and I have never looked back.

I am very proud to be married to a man who is a great husband, great father, and amazing grandfather. However, he's also a man determined to make life better for every person he meets, and that starts with just one person in a supermarket.

As governor of Florida, he did exactly that—make life better for all Floridians. Yes, there were times when I wished he had been home more, and there were times I wished he had put down his BlackBerry. Then he would read me some of the e-mails he was receiving. They were e-mails filled with concern, frustration, sometimes fear, and once in a while anger—and I knew he was doing exactly what he was born to do: lead.

When he told me some people thought all those e-mails received and answered while he was governor would make a good book, I immediately loved the idea. What a great way to tell his story over those eight years—through what was being written and said at the time it was all happening. I gave the project my enthusiastic blessing.

I know I am not objective. I haven't been since 1971, when this very tall American boy came to my hometown of Leon, Mexico, and changed my life forever.

Jeb put his heart and soul into being Florida's governor, though. It was just as he puts his heart and soul into everything he does, and that includes making guacamole. I watched him for eight years do exactly what he set out to do: make lives better.

So I hope as you read all these e-mail exchanges, you will get to know the man I love. He is someone who is compassionate, determined, honest (no one would ever argue that Jeb doesn't speak his mind), occasionally stubborn, and, of course, passionate. He's passionate about the people he knows and loves, but he's also passionate about everybody he meets along the way. He's passionate about the great state of Florida and about the United States of America, which he believes with all his heart is the greatest country on earth and whose best days are still ahead.

Thank you for taking the time to get to know him.

Como primera dama de la Florida, trabajé con Jeb sobre temas importantes como la violencia domestica y el abuso de drogas.

Siempre he admirado su habilidad de conectar con la población y encontrar soluciones.

Como gobernador, Jeb trabajó con toda su alma y corazón para ayudar a los demás.

Fueron ocho años muy especiales y espero que les guste este eBook sobre sus mandatos.

Columba Bush

Preface

I loved being the governor of Florida.

It was my dream job, and that feeling never changed—not in eight years. Not through the budget debates with the legislature. Not through the hurricanes. Not even through the hanging chads.

As soon as I was sworn in, I was ready to go to work. However, I didn't want to disappear into the governor's office. In my inauguration speech, I said, "Public servants must have the humility to listen to and trust Florida's head, heart, and soul." I meant that. I knew the best ideas didn't come from "Mount Tallahassee"—as I sometimes called the state capital. They came from the human potential of our diverse communities.

How could I keep track of what Floridians were thinking, though? Now that the campaign was over and I was no longer crisscrossing the state every day, I needed a new way to tap in to the energy, passion, and wisdom of the people I was elected to serve.

E-mail. Everyone could e-mail me, and they did.

Millions of e-mails came in through our state website, but it wasn't until I made my personal e-mail—jeb@jeb.org—public that I earned the nickname the "eGovernor."

As much as I could, I e-mailed back. My staff estimated I spent thirty hours a week answering e-mails, either from my laptop or later my BlackBerry. I often did this while on the road. Otherwise I answered e-mails very early in the morning, late at night, or on Saturday. I tried (but didn't always succeed) to reserve Sundays for my family. No one was more supportive or understanding than my wife, Columba, and she never complained about the ever-present BlackBerry. Just like a BlackBerry, however, I needed recharging from time to time, and that was time spent with Columba and our three children—George P., Noelle, and Jebby—when they were home.

The idea of this book is to tell a governor's life story through these e-mails. No day is like the one before it or after. No day ends the way it began. The unexpected becomes the expected.

Every governor from every state will attest to the fact there is no job like being a chief executive. It's truly a twenty-four-hour-a-day, round-the-clock commitment to the people of your state.

Often my favorite part of the day was the strategy session with staff and advisers on how to make our ideas realities. We had a top priority list on which I couldn't wait to cross off items as "done." However, unforeseen challenges (and new opportunities) that arose with little warning frequently interrupted that work. There also were travel, legislative sessions, and interactions with other elected officials—from sheriffs to city council members to members of my cabinet—and all this became part of our daily schedules. There were never enough hours in the day.

After a long day of meetings or travel, answering e-mails was sometimes what actually energized me. E-mails allowed me to stay connected and get firsthand knowledge from Florida's citizens—from the Keys to Cantonment—about what was happening in our communities, in our schools, in our businesses, and with Florida families. In a way reading and responding to e-mails allowed me to be in all sixty-seven counties at once.

Spending time on e-mail also could be quite humbling. On some days, when I thought I had been just brilliant, I would open up my e-mail and see a number of comments about just how brilliant I had not been. I got a lot of advice—some of it very helpful and some that caused me to scratch my head and try to figure out what I had said or done to cause such angst. It was always eye-opening and certainly kept me on my toes.

Then there were the e-mails from the kids. They were my favorites. They told me everything. Who else but a child would confide that his piano teacher smelled like a dead alligator?

Putting this book together was a wonderful trip down memory lane—eight wonderful, challenging, sometimes frustrating, but always fulfilling years. Thank you for taking the journey with me.

Jeb Bush

Author's Note

There are some things that might be helpful to know before reading another word.

- *The e-mails in this book have not been edited for content. That means, much to my sometimes embarrassment, misspelled words and grammatical errors have not been corrected. For the most part, missing words have not been inserted or incorrect words replaced. We did insert a missing word a time or two (using brackets to indicate where we did so), only because the missing word was key to the meaning of the e-mail. However, this was done sparingly and only when absolutely necessary.*
- *We did edit numerous e-mails for length. Otherwise this book would have been thousands of pages long. If part of an e-mail has been deleted, you will see an ellipsis.*
- *Florida has a very open "Sunshine" law. That means the e-mails sent to my personal e-mail address, jeb@jeb. org, were still considered part of the public record if they dealt with state business. The only exceptions were e-mail exchanges of a personal nature, such as those with family members and friends, and those related to political, non-state activity. Since this book is the story of my governorship, I chose not to include personal e-mail exchanges. (I made two exceptions: one e-mail from my mom and one from my dad.)*

Around 2001 I started including this warning on the bottom of all my e-mails to make sure people understood their e-mails could be part of the public record:

```
Please note: Florida has a very broad public records
law. Most written communications to or from state
officials regarding state business are public records
available to the public and media upon request. Your
e-mail communications may therefore be subject to
public disclosure.
```

- *We have included the first and last names of the people who wrote the e-mails included in this book with two exceptions. We only used the first name of any minor (even if he or she is an adult today), and we used only the first name of anyone whose e-mail we felt was of a very personal nature, unless we had permission to use his or her full name. (Sometimes incoming e-mails included first names only and sometimes no names at all.) If someone specifically asked that his or her e-mail be kept personal, we respected his or her request and did not use it in this book. (Again, Florida's public records law does not protect the privacy of these e-mails.)*
- *We deleted e-mail addresses, mailing addresses, phone numbers, and personal or sensitive information.*
- *For the sake of consistency, all e-mails are formatted the same.*
- *In order to save space, we deleted all salutations and closings. Although, someone other than me decided we should leave in all my closings when I signed off as "Jeb" or "Jeb Bush." Maybe that was so you would not forget who wrote the book.*
- *Sometimes it will appear I answered e-mails before I received them. Florida is in two time zones. The part of the Panhandle west of Tallahassee is in the Central Time Zone,*

but the rest of the state is in the Eastern Time Zone. That is why the times of the incoming and outgoing e-mails sometimes appear out of sequence.

- *There are two kinds of people in this world—people who love footnotes and people who hate them. This book likely will irritate both camps. We tried to use footnotes sparingly, but some will think there are too many, and some will think there are not enough. So let me apologize to all of you now.*

- *Each chapter title is taken from one of my e-mails included in that particular chapter.*

- *The sources for most of our facts and figures were from my own records as governor—especially the press releases and statements we issued on the days we signed bills into law, delivered major speeches, or released year-end wrap-up statements. The National Weather Service and National Hurricane Center websites were most helpful on hurricane statistics, but I would be remiss not to thank the newspapers of Florida. Sometimes when we were looking for a key piece of information and just couldn't find it, we did what everyone else does: we Googled it. Often we found what we were looking for in one of our daily newspapers. So thank you. I don't think there was a major daily newspaper in Florida from which we did not glean at least one helpful factoid.*

- Here is a key to the book's formatting:

Georgia 12 italics—current-day editorial comment.
✉Courier 10 bold—my e-mails.
✉Courier 10 regular—incoming e-mails.
[Anything in brackets is explanation/identification inserted in preparation for this book.]
------ Separates e-mail exchanges.

Glossary of Acronyms

I am known to dislike acronyms, but unfortunately they are a fact of life in all levels of government. We have footnoted all acronyms once, but in case you can't remember what "FCAT" stands for the second, third, or fourth time it is mentioned, here is an alphabetical list of the acronyms you'll find in these pages.

AAA—Area Agency on Aging

ACLU—American Civil Liberties Union

ADA—Americans with Disabilities Act

AFSCME—American Federation of State, County, and Municipal Employees

AHCA—Agency for Health Care Administration

AIDS—acquired immune deficiency syndrome

AIF—Associated Industries of Florida

AOL—America Online

AP—Associated Press (news service)

BOG—Board of Governors

BRAC—Base Realignment and Closure

CAT—Hurricane Catastrophe Fund

CBC—community-based care

CEO—chief executive officer

CON—certificate of need

COO—chief operating officer

CQ—Congressional Quarterly Inc.

CSE—Child Support Enforcement

DBPR—Department of Business and Professional Regulation

DCA—Department of Community Affairs

DCF—Department of Children and Families

DJJ—Department of Juvenile Justice

DMS—Department of Management Services

DOEA—Department of Elder Affairs

DOT—Department of Transportation

DUI—driving under the influence

EFI—Enterprise Florida Inc.

EOG—Executive Office of the Governor

EPA—Environmental Protection Agency

ERA—Equal Rights Amendment

ESE—Exceptional Student Education

FAFSA—Free Application for Federal Student Aid

FAMU—Florida Agricultural and Mechanical University

FCAT—Florida Comprehensive Assessment Test

FDLE—Florida Department of Law Enforcement

FDOT—Florida Department of Transportation

FEC—Federal Election Commission

FEMA—Federal Emergency Management Agency

FHA—Florida Hospital Association

FIU—Florida International University

FSU—Florida State University

FTAA—Free Trade Area of the Americas

FTP—Florida Transportation Plan

FWCC—Fish and Wildlife Conservation Commission

GPA—grade point average

GWB—George W. Bush

HSMV—Highway Safety and Motor Vehicles

IBM—International Business Machines

IEP—Individualized Education Plan

INS—Immigration and Naturalization Service

IT—information technology

JNC—Judicial Nominating Commission

JUA—Joint Underwriting Association

KSC—Kennedy Space Center

NAACP—National Association for the Advancement of Colored People

NAEP—National Assessment of Educational Progress

NAS—naval air station

NASA—National Aeronautics and Space Administration

NBC—National Broadcasting Company

NEA—National Education Association

NGA—National Governors Association

NPR—National Public Radio

NRA—National Rifle Association

NYC—New York City

OPB—Office of Policy and Budget

PECO—Public Education Outlay

PIP—personal injury protection

PSA—public service announcement

RCIA—Rite of Christian Initiation of Adults

RN—registered nurse

SFWMD—South Florida Water Management District

SPC—St. Petersburg College

SSG—staff sergeant

UCF—University of Central Florida

UPK—Universal Pre-Kindergarten Education

VCC—Valencia Community College

YMCA—Young Men's Christian Association

Glossary of Names

To help you keep track of the recurring characters in the book, here is a list of their names and titles. Unless otherwise noted, the staff positions were in the governor's office, the cabinet and department heads were all on my team, and the state legislators were from Florida.

Arduin, Donna—Director of the Office of Policy and Budget and budget director, 1999–2003.

Bradshaw, Sally—Chief of staff, 1999–2000; senior adviser to the Bush-Brogan 2002 reelection campaign.

Brantley, Shelly—Secretary of the Agency for Persons with Disabilities.

Bratina, Jill—Communications director, 2002–2005.

Brogan, Frank—Florida's fifteenth lieutenant governor, 1999–2002.

Brown, Brewser—Chief of staff to Lieutenant Governor Brogan.

Byrd, Johnnie—Speaker of the House, 2002–2004.

Canady, Charles—General counsel, 2001–2002; judge—Second District Court of Appeals, 2002–2008; Florida Supreme Court, 2008–present.

Castille, Colleen—Director of cabinet affairs, 1999–2002; secretary of the Department of Community Affairs, 2002–2003; secretary of the Department of Environmental Protection, 2003–2007.

Crowley, Brian—Reporter with the *Palm Beach Post*.

Dana, Pam—Director of the Office of Tourism, Trade, and Economic Development, 1999–2007.

Dáte, Shirish—Reporter with the *Palm Beach Post*.

De La Rosa-Aponte, Berthy—Served on the governor's Developmental Disabilities Blue Ribbon Task Force, 2004; an activist for the developmentally disabled. Her other appointments to commissions and boards are too numerous to list.

Fasano, Michael—State representative, 1994–2002; state senator, 2002–2012.

Feeney, Tom—Speaker of the House, 2000–2002; member of the US House of Representatives, 2003–2009.

Finn, Deirdre—Deputy chief of staff, 2004–2006.

Fugate, Craig—Bureau chief of the Division of Emergency Management, 1999–2001; director of the Division of Emergency Management, 2001–2007.

Gormley, Carol—Deputy chief of staff, 2005–2007.

Griffin, Michael—Reporter with the *Orlando Sentinel*.

Hadi, Lucy—Chief of staff to Lieutenant Governor Toni Jennings, 2003; secretary of the Department of Children and Families, 2004–2007.

Hansen, Mike—Director of the Office of Policy and Budget and budget director, 2003–2006.

Jennings, Toni—Florida's sixteenth lieutenant governor, 2003–2006.

Kaplan, Mark—Staff director of Hurricane Housing Work Group and chief of staff to Lieutenant Governor Toni Jennings, 2004–2005; chief of staff, 2004–2006.

Kearney, Kathleen—Secretary of the Department of Children and Families, 1999–2002.

King, Jim—President of the Senate, 2002–2004.

King-Shaw, Ruben—Director of the Agency for Health Care Administration, 1999–2001.

Lee, Tom—President of the Senate, 2004–2006.

Levesque, Patricia—Deputy chief of staff, 2003–2006.

Levine, Alan—Deputy chief of staff, 2003–2004; secretary of the Agency for Health Care Administration, 2004–2006.

McDonough, Jim—Drug czar, 1999–2006; secretary of the Department of Corrections, 2006–2008.

McKay, John—President of the Senate, 2001–2002.

Moore, Timothy—Executive director of the Florida Department of Law Enforcement, 1989–2003.

Oviedo, Nina—Director of the State of Florida's Office in Washington, DC, 1999–2006.

Pate, Tena—Victims' rights coordinator, 1993–2003.

Plante, Ken—Director of Legislative Affairs, 1999.

Reno, Janet—Attorney general of the United States, 1993–2001; ran for governor of Florida, 2002.

Rodriguez, Raquel (Rocky)—General counsel, 2003–2006.

Shanahan, Kathleen—Chief of staff, 2001–2003.

Silva, Mark—Reporter with the *Miami Herald,* 1979–2001, and the *Orlando Sentinel,* 2001–2004.

Struhs, David—Secretary of the Department of Environmental Protection, 1999–2003.

Stutler, Denver—Chief of staff of the Department of Environmental Protection, 1999–2002; deputy chief of staff, 2002–2003; chief of staff, 2003–2005; secretary of the Department of Transportation, 2005–2006.

Thomas, Mike—Reporter with the *Orlando Sentinel,* 1983–2011.

Thrasher, John—State representative, 1992–2000; speaker of the House, 1998–2000.

Tilley, Cory—Communications director, 1999; deputy chief of staff, 2000–2001.

Wainwright, Tara—Director of scheduling, 1999–2006.

Yablonski, Brian—Deputy director of the Office of Policy and Budget and director of policy, 1999–2001; deputy chief of staff, 2001–2002.

Chapter 1

"This Is Exhilarating."

*I want to thank you for giving me the opportunity
to serve and to lead us in this greatest of undertakings.
This is your journey as well as mine. This is our
call to arms.*

—Inaugural Address, January 5, 1999

*I came into the job as governor of Florida determined to fulfill
my campaign promises. One was rather simple: to make Florida
a better place to live. We felt we had a plan to achieve that goal.*

*As I said in my inaugural speech, we would "unleash the
amazing potential" of faith, family, and friends and "let state government give families and individuals greater freedom—more
freedom to exercise compassion, to keep more of what they earn,
and to make the choices that would improve the lives of their
loved ones."*

We also knew huge challenges awaited us:

- *We had an education system that was not serving our
  children well.*

- *Overtaxation and government regulations were crushing our families and small businesses.*
- *The unfocused state budget was fat with wasteful spending.*
- *Our disabled community had largely been ignored—left both literally and figuratively at the back of the line.*
- *Of immediate concern was a broken foster-care system.*

We got right to work. Before the first month was out, we introduced A+, our plan to reform the public-school system. We also announced our first steps toward restoring the Everglades, one of Florida's—and the nation's—most precious natural resources.

Floridians also wasted no time letting me know what was on their minds. No topics were off-limits. Some people had ideas, some had advice, some needed advice, and some were already not happy with me. Here are just a few samples of some of the early e-mails.

Subject: Inauguration
Wednesday, January 6, 1999 9:41 a.m.
From: Joe Klock

I enjoyed your inauguration and thought that your speech was excellent. It touched on broad values and goals without being a laundry list of projects. I got a really good feeling listening to what you were saying.

…I would offer only one point of practical advice…As a CEO, you need to find a place and a time when you can get away and just think - -
without aides, friends, family, colleagues, or supplicants. Any company gets its top value from its CEO when that individual has break in his or her

schedule when thinking and playing with ideas can take place....

PPS Incidentally, if you are unable to be contacted this way in the future, just let me know. I will not be offended and will simply keep my opinions to myself.

Subject: Inauguration
Wednesday, January 6, 1999 8:53 p.m.
From: Jeb Bush

Joe, I would greatly appreciate your opinions and email is the best way. Since you are a fine writer, I feel I am not losing any value. I haven't figured out the rules of the game about email communication so jeb@jeb.org is OK for now. Please keep writing.

Jeb

———

Subject: ADA[1]
Saturday, January 16, 1999 12:16 p.m.
From: Michael P. Wargin

DON'T MESS WITH OUR RIGHTS ! ! ! !
DON'T MESS WITH THE ADA ! ! !
KEEP THE MOST INTEGRATED SETTINGS ! ! ! !
PLEASE HELP KEEP OUR FAMILY AND OTHERS LIKE OURS TOGETHER. HELP US AFFORD TO KEEP OUR FAMILIES TOGETHER....

---

1 The Americans with Disabilities Act, a federal law my dad actually signed when he was president.

Subject: ADA
Saturday, January 16, 1999 1:25 p.m.
From: Jeb Bush

Thanks for your letter. We are soon to propose a plan that I believe will accomplish the objectives that you desire.

Jeb Bush

———

Subject: school vouchers
Sunday, January 17, 1999 9:41 a.m.
From: David N. Figlio

As an economics faculty member at the University of Florida who was devoted much of the last four years to trying to find examples of effective public schools…I am writing to offer my unpaid assistance in helping you to design, implement, and evaluate the various education reform policies that you are interested in pursuing.

Subject: school vouchers
Sunday, January 17, 1999 6:17 p.m.
From: Jeb Bush

David, thanks for your offer. I have asked Brewser Brown, the chief of staff of the Lt. Governor and our internal point person for our education plan to give you a call to discuss your involvement.

Jeb Bush

———

One of the most urgent tasks facing us was a failed child-welfare system in Broward County. It needed an immediate fix. So on January 11, as one of my first acts as governor, I unveiled our emergency rescue plan. It included measures to reduce the number of children per foster home, improve and enhance foster-care training, and reduce the number of run-away children.

This series of e-mails is about how to fix the problem and how to pay for it. In this first e-mail, I am responding to Brian Yablonski. He was deputy director of the Office of Policy and Budget (OPB) and policy director. He had sent me a draft statement about the plan.

Subject: Final Foster Care
Sunday, January 10, 1999 7:13 p.m.
From: Jeb Bush

Brian, I am assuming that we are fine with the budget on this. Both for this fiscal year and the next. If we are committing to alleviate the deficit for this fiscal year, we have to in the out years as well. In addition, we are talking about annualizing the costs for next fiscal year as well and it must be in the budget.

I keep asking and getting the answer that all is OK. I just don't want to commit to things we aren't going to propose and that we don't have a high degree of chance of getting through the legislature.

Thanks.

Donna Arduin was the director of OPB and budget director. She e-mailed to assure me we had the money in the budget to take care of the problem.

Subject: Final Foster Care
Monday, January 11, 1999 9:02 a.m.
From: Donna Arduin

I looked at the plan before it went out yesterday.…
We have already covered the deficit in the budget.
In addition, we recommend we add $10m to child
welfare (beyond the amount we have been carrying in
the budget) in a lump sum to cover the second phase
of the foster care plan (which has not yet been
determined), legal costs, and other child welfare
costs.

I sent this message to a Miami Herald *reporter whose name was not included in my e-mail.*

Subject: Foster Care
Monday, January 11, 1999 2:17 p.m.
From: Jeb Bush

I just read your article in The Miami Herald today.

**I hope you saw our actions today. Judge Kearney[2]
and I are committed to dealing with the management
and financial problems of our child welfare system,
particularly the challenges faced in District 10. All
we ask is that we are given time to do our job.**

Jeb Bush

---

2 Kathleen Kearney was secretary of the Department of Children and Families.

PS Please call Cory Tilley at 850-488-4802 if you need any information concerning our emergency plan.

———

I was somewhat obsessed with getting a new and improved state website. This is the first of many e-mails I sent on the subject. In this case I was asking Communications Director Cory Tilley for action.

Subject: web page
Monday, January 11, 1999 9:35 p.m.
From: Jeb Bush

We need to get the web page upgraded as a high priority. Use your creativity on how we get this done. Some suggestions...get Adam Herbert[3] to do a competition for the best designed (and maintained) web page for the governor's office. What we have now needs to change and change soon. In addition, we should get rid of the jeb.org web page which has not been updated in a long, long while.

Cory, we have raised the bar and each day of doing nothing, we are not reaching it. If the campaign had the best web page in the country, why shouldn't the Governor's office?

In the immortal words of our friend David Leavitt[4], Why Not????????????

———

3 Adam Herbert, then chancellor of the State University System of Florida, headed up my transition team.
4 David Leavitt was a citizen activist who, among other things, got the law changed so unused school cafeteria food could be used to feed the homeless.

Let us discuss manana.

Jeb

———

I sometimes felt answering e-mails was like taking a pop quiz. This series of e-mails was answered over a few days and illustrates once again that Floridians were thinking about absolutely everything.

   The first e-mail is about my withholding funding for a high-speed rail project. I felt the risk was too great for our already overburdened taxpayers.

Subject: DB/DC, better than ac dc
Tuesday, January 19, 1999 10:23 p.m.
From: Russell Bjorkman

Are things settling down for you a little? The bullet train termination was extremely well reported and received in reports I heard and read.

Subject: DB/DC, better than ac dc
Wednesday, January 20, 1999 9:50 p.m.
From: Jeb Bush

It is still frenetic. I need to force it to slow down or we will all run out of gas.

Jeb

———

Subject: I need your help!!
Wednesday, January 20, 1999 10:31 p.m.
From: Barbara Wilcox

Hillsborough County Crisis Center needs your help!…
We need $900,000.00 to build out the inside and move
4 different locations into one.…Would like a meeting
with you to go over the details and ask that you
include this request in your budget.

Subject: I need your help!!
Thursday, January 21, 1999 7:47 a.m.
From: Jeb Bush

Our budget is at the printer!

Jeb

Subject: semis on the interstate
Wednesday, January 20, 1999 9:06 a.m.
From: Carol Markett

Who do I write about the problems the tractor
trailers are causing now that they are not allowed in
the left lane of I'-75? By the way, are you really
Jeb or a staff member? Just curious.

Subject: semis on the interstate
Thursday, January 21, 1999 7:47 a.m.
From: Jeb Bush

I am jeb. You can write Secretary Barry at the DOT[5]
in Tallahassee.

Jeb Bush

---

5 Department of Transportation.

———

It was almost the end of the month, and still there was no new website. This went to my chief of staff, Sally Bradshaw, and Cory Tilley.

Subject: help request
Tuesday, January 26, 1999 9:45 p.m.
From: Jeb Bush

We need a major upgrade. When will I see the plan to upgrade our web page and how long will it take. How will it be interactive with the rest of Florida. I believe it should be the leader in the nation. If you disagree come and tell me why. If you agree, help me make it so.

Jeb

———

I was blessed with an outstanding staff and more than likely did not tell them often enough what great jobs they were doing. I sent this note to Budget Director Donna Arduin after I saw the package she put together on our proposed $1.235 billion tax cut proposal— the largest in state history. Before leaving office I cut taxes by $19 billion in Florida. So you could say this was just the beginning.

Subject: thanks
Wednesday, January 27, 1999 9:55 p.m.
From: Jeb Bush

The tax cut proposal and the backup material was first class in every way. We will have the high ground on the debate and will have backed it up with solid reasoning. You should be proud of your leadership in this regard. I will confess that I felt a little by myself on the subject of tax relief at the level proposed during the transition but your steady insistence that we were on the right track made me feel comfortable with the proposition.

Good work, Donna and thank you for making it down to Tallahassee to make a difference!

Jeb

——

I received numerous e-mails about Ward Connerly, an African-American businessman and political activist from California who led ballot initiatives in the 1990s to get rid of affirmative action. Our relationship was quite cordial, but his foray into Florida politics set off a firestorm and a lot of anger directed at me. Here is a sample of differing opinions.

Subject: Decision not to back Ward Connerly
Monday, January 25, 1999 8:23 p.m.
From: Douglass R. Pettitt

I was very proud and extremely happy when you became the governor of Florida. I was equally happy when your brother became governor of Texas. However, after reading that you had given the "cold shoulder" to Ward Connerlly and his efforts to end the reverse racism fostered by state sponsored affirmative action programs it has become apparent that the citizens of Florida have simply elected another politically correct coward. It sure would have been nice if you had shown some "back-bone". You leave me utterly disappointed.

Subject: Decision not to back Ward Connerly
Sunday, January 31, 1999 6:43 a.m.
From: Jeb Bush

Thanks for your email. I did not give Mr. Connerly the cold shoulder. Unlike others in Tallahassee, I met with him and was respectful of him. I believe that the issue of discrimination can and should be dealt with in means Other than the initiative process. I will do my part as governor to fight against it.

I think my actions this first month have defied your somewhat unkind comment. Our education plan, the stopping of the bullet train, the proposed largest tax cut in our state's history and going to Federal Court to stop a pending trial concerning our foster care system are examples. The great thing though, is that you can have your own opinion as I know you will. I will keep trying to do what is right in service to Florida.

Again, thanks for expressing your opinion.

Jeb Bush

————

Subject: [None]
Monday, January 25, 1999 5:47 a.m.
From: Bryan Stewart

To put it plainly; people ought to be judged on their merit and charecter, not their color and gender…

you have the ear of many Floridians. You could make
a powerful case for ending "de facto" racism in
this state. People of all colors and creeds would
listen if you speak would from the heart and with
crisp honesty and not gaurded caution. Make no
mistake about it governor, no matter what you call
preferences and quotas, they will always be about the
same thing; taking equality away from some to grant
privilegde to some others. That can never be right,
no matter what the circumstances.

I want to thank you for reading this and for
listening to my opinion. You have the hopes and
prayers of many of us in Florida and regardless of
your eventual decision on this matter, I wish you the
best in your endeavors.

Subject: [None]
Sunday, January 31, 1999 9:46 a.m.
From: Jeb Bush

Well said Bryan.

**I agree with your thesis and oppose discrimination of
any kind. As governor I will do my part to eliminate
quotas and set asides in purchasing practices
and am looking at the admissions policies of our
schools. However, what Mr. Connerly is proposing
isn't the passing of a law. Rather, it is going
through an initiative and referendum process which
will be divisive. It will make it harder for me
to be successful in passing meaningful tax relief
and education reform, two policy areas of great
importance for our state's future.**

Thanks for writing.

Jeb Bush

———

Brian Crowley of the Palm Beach Post *was one of the most respected political reporters in Florida, and he and I had discussed having a regular e-mail relationship to chronicle the life of a governor. We had a flurry of e-mails during the first few months, and then we fell behind. This was our attempt to get started.*

Subject: From: Brian Crowley
Friday, February 5, 1999 5:54 p.m.
From: Brian Crowley

Hi…I'm glad we had a chance to talk briefly about this email project.

So you've been in office a month. What's it been like? What's the biggest surprise? How is being governor different than being a corporate titan? Is the door to the bathroom in the governor's office the smallest one you've ever seen? What's been the most fun? The worst moment? What's the quirkiest thing about the governor's mansion? What's been your toughest decision?…

Anyway, I hope from this random list of questions that you get the idea that I'd like to have your thoughts not just on the making of policy but those things that making being governor different than anything else you've experienced. I look forward to hearing from you weekly and I as I said when we talked, if there is some information that you would feel more comfortable giving me on background please just note that part in your email.…

Many thanks for your help.

Subject: From: Brian Crowley
Saturday, February 6, 1999 8:17 a.m.
From: Jeb Bush

Brian, it has been a joyous experience. I get to eat dinner with my family many nights which we didn't do much of in Miami. Unfortunately, the food at home is verrrrrryyyyy good leaving me with no chance yet to lose any weight. Most important, Columba is happy and so is Noelle. When they are happy, I am as well.

The biggest surprise is the volume of my voice. People listen to what I say and do. I am learning to show more self-restraint so as to not restrict a free flow of thinking that could yield a better decision. That has been hard for me. IN fact, I would say I have a long way to go on this. So far, it has not been a problem since I have known where I want to go on decision but that will change.

I really enjoy the work. It is important and meaningful. Education reform, a drug policy, the largest tax cuts in State history, child welfare and developmentally disabled reform and adequate funding, an ethics package of significance, the Lawton Chiles endowment idea, the end of the bullet train and Powerball and a good solid budget got us off to a good start.

A growing challenge is to focus on the things I need to focus on and slow the pace down for the rest of the team. We got off to a fast and fine start but we need to slow down to follow up and let our partners, the legislature, digest and absorb our suggestions. That will be easier to do with me less visible than I have been.

One of the more interesting events was the one that I saw you at. Talk about "large and enthusiastic crowds" to use a phrase of last year! Yes, I did buy my beautiful wife a music box for about $160 over the QVC web page site. She is gonna love it.

The governor's bathroom door is the smallest in Florida. It requires a sideways twist to make it in.

The water pressure up here is great. Great showers!

The toughest decision has been in the appointments process. Friends who were expecting jobs have not gotten what they want and while I will always do what I think is right, it's not fun to disappoint.

There is much more but I need to move on. Keep prompting me.

Preparing our first budget was one of the biggest challenges we faced when we took office, since we had just one month to get it ready and present it to the state legislature.

We were still hiring staff, so Donna Arduin—who had already been a budget superstar for the governors in Michigan and New

York—leaned on the career state workers, who often labor in the shadows of the political appointees. They loved being asked to actively participate, and our budget sessions tended to be raucous and debate filled. They did an incredible job, and we sent our first proposed state budget to the legislature on February 2. It included five basic principles I outlined that morning in a press conference:

1. *Government cannot grow any faster than our ability to pay for it.*
2. *In times of growth, tax dollars should be returned to Florida's working families and small businesses.*
3. *Government must fund its highest priorities first.*
4. *We must reserve funds for economic slowdowns.*
5. *Community-based problem solving is preferable to government-based problem solving.*

I caught up on e-mails the Saturday after the budget was released, and many were reactions to the budget. I had won a few supporters and lost a few.

Subject: Budget Proposals
Wednesday, February 3, 1999 6:52 p.m.
From: [No name]

Great proposal but do reserve for a rainy day. This state is very dependent on retail & tourism that can dry up quickly. How about supplemental funding for healthcare and immigrant education, South America Trade commission? Can the State attract more sports franchises? This state has got to be the best one other than California for sports?

Subject: Budget Proposals
Saturday, February 6, 1999 9:14 a.m.
From: Jeb Bush

We have proposed reserves of over $2 billion or
roughly 12% of general revenue. We should do more but
that is more than most states in the nation.

Thanks for writing.

Jeb Bush

———

Subject: Thank you
Wednesday, February 3, 1999 10:50 a.m.
From: Georgia

I have never written to a political figure before but I
wanted to write to you. Even though I am a republican,
I voted against you in the last 2 elections. The
reason is, that I didn't believe that a republican
governor would support services for the developmentally
disabled. I have a daughter, her name is Irene, and
she's 11 years old. She has Down syndrome.

She is a joy to us, but it has been difficult
to provide her with everything she needs to live
as normal a life as possible. We want to raise our
children at home. Your proposed budget increase
for developmental services will go a long way to
supporting families in caring for their children.
Thank you. You impress me, and definitely have my
vote from now on. I will also call my legislators to
support this increase.

Subject: Thank you
Saturday, February 6, 1999 12:05 p.m.
From: Jeb Bush

I am sorry that perceptions about our party, unfair in many ways, made you feel compelled to vote against me.

However, I am pleased that wrote and grateful for the encouraging words! I am also pleased that you are going to work on your legislators.

Give Irene a hug for me and thank you for writing.

Jeb Bush

————

Of course Floridians had other things on their minds besides the budget—everything from dental work to broken screen doors. The first e-mail is from my good friend Berthy De La Rosa-Aponte. She became my conscience on the issue of the developmentally disabled since she was raising one of these precious children.

Subject: Donations
Monday, February 1, 1999 7:51 p.m.
From: Berthy De La Rosa-Aponte

Just got a call from Patti Fucille from Kiwanis Horses and the Handicapped (can't stand that name) to let me know that they just received a $5,000.00 check from you. Thank you, thank you.…They really do a wonderful job, and as I told you before they are volunteers.…I do not expect that you do anything on any one individual issue, but I just want to share with you a few concerns. Do you remember Cindy

Benitez and her need for dental services? You are not going to believe it, but we are still waiting for services. Because she needs general anesthesia, we have not been able to find dental services.

Subject: Donations
Monday, February 1, 1999 8:34 p.m.
From: Jeb Bush

I hope that our plan will help with this strange anomaly regarding the dental work. It should.

Tomorrow is the budget day and we are proposing a near 50% increase in funding and reforms to come soon. You should be proud of your "teaching" efforts.

Love,
Jeb

————

Subject: Criminal mischief
Wednesday, February 3, 1999 4:05 p.m.
From: William Tippetts

We have a screen enclosure around our swimming pool. On July 26, 1998, a neighborhood boy threw a baseball through the screen. A neighbor saw it and identified the child. We called the police. The boy fessed up to the St. Petersburg police. The police told us we had two options:

1 - Prosecute the boy for criminal mischief.
2 - Mother (Margret Piszczek) would come down the street to see us in the next hour or so and talk

about paying to get the screen fixed. The police
gave her our name and address and telephone
number.

We chose the latter option.

Guess what. Mother never came down to see us.
Mother never called. We never heard from her.
Meantime, the screen had to be repaired. The bugs
and flies were coming in the hole the baseball had
made. It cost us $40 to get the screen repaired.
A month went by. We never heard from mother. She
never called. She never came by.We called the
police back in late August 1998 and told the police
we wanted to prosecute for criminal mischief. We
hated to do it, but we had no choice. Mother had
never contacted us. A month was more than enough
time for her to do so. The police sent a copy of
everything to the District Attorney in Tallahassee.
The police also sent a copy of everything to a
juvenile department of Pinellas County. The police
advised us we would be hearing from Tallahassee.
To date, we have heard nothing. We want to ask
someone where the case stands. We do not know
who to contact in Tallahassee for a response. All
we want is the $40 reimbursement for getting the
screen fixed. We hated to do it this way because it
means the boy gets some sort of record, but this is
mother's choice, not ours. Can you please redirect
this email to the proper individual for a response?
We want to know where the case stands and when we
can expect a final resolution of the matter.

Subject: Criminal mischief
Wednesday, February 3, 1999 9:59 p.m.
From: Jeb Bush

I am totally confused. I don't understand how a $40 claim is an issue that would make its way up to Tallahassee. You will have to explain how the state government became involved.

Here is my suggestion. Why don't you proactively call the mom up and explain what happened? I don't think the boy should be charged with criminal mischief unless he tried to hurt your property on purpose. You might be surprised that she will respond in a civil way and that will be the end of the story.

Your story reminded me of when I was a boy and we would play baseball all the time after school. One day, I hit a massive homerun over the right center field fence (actually our back yard fence) and the ball crashed through the second story window of the Vanderhoff's home. Mr. Vanderhoof, a nice Christian Scientist reader (I think that is what they are called) called my dad up to tell him what happened. After apologizing, my dad congratulated me on such a fine hit. Yes, I had to apologize to Mr. Vanderhoff (much to the pleasure of the two Vanderhoff daughters who were always fighting with us) and I had to do some work for retribution, but it all worked out in the end.

I guess my point is that we need to try to solve problems amongst ourselves before we ask that our government to intervene.

Now, if I am wrong and the child with malice tried to destroy your property, that is another thing altogether.

Well, that is it...typos and all.

Thanks for writing.

Jeb Bush

———

I would not call this Floridian a fan.

Subject: what are you doing
Thursday, February 11, 1999 1:00 p.m.
From: John Huzzen

Please, please, please stop being so right wing. You are going to screw up this state big time if you do not adopt a more moderate stance on issues that affect each of us. I knew before the election that you where going to be govenor, however, I was hoping all your right wing facist talk was just rhetoric. Now I see you really are a Nazi in disgusise. It is not to late to change. Please, please, please change before it is too late for the rest of us. Otherwise, may God, and all the citizens of this state have mercy on your soul.

Subject: what are you doing
Thursday, February 11, 1999 9:41 p.m.
From: Jeb Bush

Chill out, John. Do you really believe my rhetoric is fascist and Nazi like? Take a deep breathe and relax.

Sincerely,

Jeb Bush

I also found time that Sunday morning to continue my e-mail correspondence with Brian Crowley. I sent him some bullet points of what I had been up to.

Subject: this week as governor
Sunday, February 14, 1999 10:37 a.m.
From: Jeb Bush

* ON Monday, I went to the Governor's lunch at the Florida State Fair. I shook hands with about 500 people before being told to sit down at the head table. It was the first time that the Governor has shaken hands with folks and afterwards walked through the fair itself. I am having a hard time with the entourage factor that comes with my new job. The FDLE[6] guys tolerate me and keep their distance but when you add dignataries with local law enforcement and security, it is very confining. So, I use the tactic of going in my own direction so at least I can get to meet some people without them thinking their about to be hit with a tidal wave.

---

6 Florida Department of Law Enforcement.

*The most interesting person I met was a big man who was in a cage with thousands of ants on a mesh. He created a bee beard (the queen was in a capsule under his neck) and he was proving that bees won't hurt you unless you hurt them which was easy to do with his credit card he was using to keep them from going up his nose and into his eyes. He asked me to join him in the cage. I told him I don't sing or dance and now I can say, I don't go into cages next to bee bearded men…

*I am learning that making news is not a problem in this job. In fact, making too much news is the problem. This week, there were two newspapers fighting over the big story that I try to walk up the stairs to the top of the Capitol twice a day. The practical problem of this is being so accessible means that I am taking positions on things that are not part of my core agenda. Your colleague Charles Elmore's front page story in the Sunday paper is a good example where he talks to me for 30 seconds to get his story finished. That is his agenda and the agenda of your paper not mine. I need to figure out how to deal with this.

* One of the four or so items on my agenda that is important is creating a comprehensive strategy against drugs. The senate put on a very fine drug summit. Our budget proposal and bringing Jim McDonough[7] in from DC combined with the commitment from the legislature gives me great hope that we will begin to see some progress in this area of policy. For the record, the other big items on the agenda are education reform, tax relief and the endowment (with social service funding and reform particularly in dev. dis and child abuse).

---

7 Jim McDonough was our drug czar.

*IN spite of my 16 hour work days, Columba and I are spending more time together than we have in a long while and it is wonderful!

*Yesterday, I canoed down the Oscilla river with some of the office team and it was beautiful. Noelle and I went through some rapids and did not tump over. Tump is dumped and turned in "West tExan".

That is it for this week.

———

There were always reminders that you can't please all the people all the time.

Subject: New Board at SFWMD
Friday, March 12, 1999 8:50 a.m.
From: Joan Cartwright

Does the fact that there were no African Americans appointed to the Board of South Florida Water Management District mean that water is NOT an issue for African Americans? I think you need to rethink these appointment. Hispanics and Whites do not fairly represent African Americans or Asian Americans and Native Americans for that matter.

We've all had enough with White Supremacy in this country. This has got to stop, NOW!

Subject: New Board at SFWMD
Friday, March 12, 1999 9:31 p.m.
From: Jeb Bush

No it does not mean that.

Our appointments to date reflect a commitment to African Americans. I appointed the first African American woman to the Supreme Court. My second judicial appointment was an African American to the Appellate Court. I believe we have appointed more African Americans to the Cabinet and to positions of importance in the office of the Governor than my predecessors.

Thanks for writing.

Jeb Bush

————

We were pulling out all the stops to lobby the legislature to pass our biggest initiatives—especially the A+ education plan and the tax cut package. I was making calls. The staff was making calls. Friends were making calls. We left no stone unturned.

Subject: [None]
Friday, March 12, 1999 3:55 p.m.
From: Brewser Brown

re Tony Knox of Tony's Shoe Shine - I tried to call him, no answer - someone told me he might want a bunch of buttons? Please let me know and I will follow up. Thanks.

Subject: [None]
Friday, March 12, 1999 9:09 p.m.
From: Jeb Bush

Yes. he is the man at the airport who runs the shoe shine business. A great american who is a huge voucher supporter.

The following is another e-mail report to Brian Crowley.

Subject: this week
Sunday, March 14, 1999 8:41 a.m.
From: Jeb Bush

The session is all consuming. First, lots of groups come up and many want to see me so I spend a lot of my time saying hello. I like doing it but I am not taking care of all of my duties as well.

Second, the legislative process is fast moving and I am learning when to intervene and when not to. For an active person, not doing something is hard but I as I said, I am learning.

Getting out of Tallahassee is an enjoyable thing and I intend to do that at least once a week during the session. Monday's trip was fun, kind of a validation of why I am serving.[8]

---

8 I had traveled to Boynton Beach, Miami, and St. Petersburg specifically to meet with small-business owners and senior citizens and talk about my $1.2 billion tax cut plan.

No one tells you about Cabinet when you run for
office. It is a fascinating process dealing with
some of the strangest and most important. This week
we dealt with the Keys and the Miami Circle.[9] For a
generation of time, the State government has been
the "zoning board" for the Keys. AT the cabinet
today, we were dealing with how many building permits
the county could issue. Steve Seibert[10] has been
given the charge to get the state out of this role
in four years. It will be a major challenge and if
successful, a great accomplishment indeed.

The Miami Circle is quite the issue. A work perhaps
as old as old as when Christ gave the Sermon on the
Mount. The combination of Miami-Dade politics (the
county suing the city for issuing what appears to be a
legitimate building permit; etc) with native american
spiritualism and good old property rights. I think we
have created a winning situation. We shall see.

ON Thursday, I ran the Clemency Board. Wow. What
a humbling experience. It is a little unsettling
to have the power to deny or grant clemency, or to
commute a sentence or to restore civil rights. After
five hours of doing this, I was exhausted. The process
is not without its joyous side. Like a wonderful
women who is a special ed teacher who wanted her
rights back so she could teach at a broward county
public school. Her heartfelt presentation made me
want to go down and give her a hug.

---

9 The Miami Circle is an archeological site on the south bank of the
Miami River across from Downtown Miami. The community was trying
to, and did, save it. It's a perfect circle and the only known evidence of a
prehistoric permanent structure cut into the bedrock.
10 Steve Seibert was the secretary of the Department of Community
Affairs.

WE are getting to the end game with the legislature in the next three weeks. We have raised the bar pretty high with the tax cuts, education plan and endowment idea and the underlying spending restraint assumed by our priorities. I think we will get most of what we have advocated for but there is work still to be done.

Jeb

———

Sometimes one-word answers were all that were needed.

Subject: Los Trabajadores Agricolas
Tuesday, March 16, 1999 3:18 p.m.
From: Jose Luis

We need peace betwen the farmers, workers and the clergy. Don't you think ?

Subject: Los Trabajadores Agricolas
Tuesday, March 16, 1999 8:04 p.m.
From: Jeb Bush

yes

———

The A+ bill was making its way through the legislature. The day it passed the House, I wrote to a friend, "Today was very emotional for me. I feel like I have worked a lifetime for this, and now we are getting close."

The progress was not without controversy, though. People were especially nervous about the idea of school vouchers—I called them Opportunity Scholarships. Maybe this was because they were new and innovative. It would be the first statewide program of its kind in the nation, and I was convinced it held the most promise for Florida's kids. Nevertheless, A+ had sparked a spirited debate throughout Florida, as the next few e-mails certainly demonstrate.

Subject: A+ Plan
Friday, March 26, 1999 6:08 a.m.
From: Kim Henriquez

I will be watching closely the out come of this plan as it affects families, students, teachers. We had a chance to make history for public education, and I feel we missed the boat. I am deeply saddened by the partisan spirit that exists. It's sad to know that there are Republican legislators who don't agree with the plan, but are being "bullied" into voting for it.

I have watched and read with great disappointment this whole process which has completely ignored what the teachers have suggested. The educators who have gone to school, and continue to educate themselves through courses and workshops, the educators who have devoted their lives to teaching our young people, are disrespected and told we are not doing our jobs!

Subject: A+ Plan
Friday, March 26, 1999 6:23 p.m.
From: Jeb Bush

Kim, there was no forcing people to vote against their conscious. The only lack of civility that I saw were the accusations by opponents of the bill that the supporters were vampires and mosquitos

and many other things such as that. This will not
be the end of public education. You should not be
depressed.

I am sorry you didn't, but I have had a pretty good
day. Even the union protestors outside the schools
I visited (which by the way are working very well
teaching the so called tough to teach kids) did
not deter me from having one. Most of the union
protesters took sick leave to be away from teaching
to come out and protest. Ironic, huh?

———

Subject: [None]
Wednesday, March 24, 1999 8:01 a.m.
From: Carrie Goldin

As a voting citizen and an educator I feel it is
my civic duty to write to you and voice my views
on your "education plan" for the state of Florida.
Teaching is my first and last career. I practiced law
before returning to the classroom three years ago.
I love what I do and am not here because I have no
other place to go. The day you were sworn in was a
very dark day in my life. I tried to be positive
and believe that you would do the right thing for
education, both morally and intellectually. However,
my nightmare has come true. You insist on going
forward with your racist idea of school vouchers.
Have you read the Constitution lately? I have. Have
you ever set you foot in a classroom, other than for
the purpose of furthering your campaign? I have and I
do each day.

I am a good teacher. I have an extensive education, including an LLM. Is your goal to run good and motivated teachers out of education? Well, you're on your way.

Subject: [None]
Friday, March 26, 1999 7:24 p.m.
From: Jeb Bush

Thanks for writing.

You made some pretty amazing accusations without any basis in fact. If you would like to share your specific concerns, I would be happy to address them.

I have been in hundreds of classrooms and seen the great things that classroom teachers do. That is why I have every confidence that our plan will work to improve all schools.

Jeb Bush

———

We ended March on a high note with the signing of the 10-20-Life law. "Florida just became a very bad place for violent crimi-nals," I said at the signing ceremony. The new law required a minimum ten-year sentence for crimes committed with a gun; a twenty-year sentence for firing the gun during the commission of a crime; and a twenty-five-year to life sentence if the bullet fired caused death or injury. We invited victims of violent crime to join the signing ceremony. The e-mail below from Tena Pate—the victims' advocate in the governor's office—meant a great deal to me.

Subject: victims - todays bill signing
Wednesday March 31, 1999 4:31 p.m.
From: Tena Pate

The victims that were present for today's 10/20/
Life bill signing ceremony were so impressed with
your sensitivity to their issues, especially Thomas
Balbone. He was very nervous as it was his first time
participating in such an event. He was amazed with
your ability to put him at ease. He mentioned to me
that he should have brought his colored photos of his
gun shot injuries…he thinks you would have liked to
see them. Imagine that! He can't wait to get his copy
of the photo you had made with them.

Again, thanks for caring. It's a pleasure to work
with you.

Subject: victims - todays bill signing
Wednesday, March 31, 1999 8:00 p.m.
From: Jeb Bush

**Tena, when you see an opportunity where I can help a
victim, lift their spirits, give them hope, etc. I
hope you will email me and I will give them a call or
send them an email. I have a responsibility to help.**

**You are doing a great job and I am appreciative of
your service. Have a wonderful Easter week.**

Jeb

———

One sidenote about the signing ceremony. It was one of the first bills I signed as governor and one that meant a great deal to me. I was so excited that I forgot to take the bill out of the clear-plastic folder in which the staff had so carefully placed it. Sharpies don't work too well on plastic.

———

I had fallen behind on the once-a-week e-mail exchange with Brian Crowley. We caught up in early April.

Subject: hi
Friday, April 2, 1999 1:30 a.m.
From: Brian Crowley

Happy Easter.

On April 15 you will have been governor for 100 days. So how does it feel? What are you learning? Are you surprised that even Democrats seem to be praising your work so far? How do you see the session ending? What are your plans for the summer? What will you try to accomplish in the months ahead? Enjoy your weekend. And thanks for taking the time to do this.

Subject: hi
Saturday, April 3, 1999 11:45 a.m.
From: Jeb Bush

The job is intense but fun. It is important and I take it very seriously but it is joyful as well. I feel the weight of responsibility but I don't recall being as happy as I am now.

I think the session will end with more substantive things being done than most sessions allow. A budget that funds education at record levels, the creation of an Endowment for social services, real school reform including private options for parents whose kids are going to chronically failing public schools, significant tort reform, the creation and funding of a drug control policy, the passage of 10-20-LIFE, the largest tax cut in the State's history, beginning to rebuild the dev. disabled and child welfare delivery systems and funding them adequately I think will all happen. I have been fortunate to have legislative leadership that has been supportive of my agenda.

In all honesty, the one element of the session where the outcome is in doubt relates to member projects. I am not in sinc with the legislature on this as of yet.

Post session, I am going to try to get everyone to slow down a bit. I know I have a weakness of needing to have my time full of work and it impacts everyone around me. Come mid May, we will need to regroup, reflect, and recharge.

———

By "member projects" I was referring to spending earmarks included in the budget by state representatives and senators. The problem was many of these projects didn't meet a statewide need or merit taxpayer support. As always reporter Shirish Dáte from the Palm Beach Post *had a lot of questions. In the subject line, you'll see the word "turkeys." This was the nickname used in Tallahassee for the more commonly called "pork" projects put in budgets by lawmakers at all levels of government.*

Subject: turkeys
Thursday, April 8, 1999 10:43 a.m.
From: Shirish Date

Mr. Plante[11] and Ms. Arduin appeared before Sen. Childers' committee this morning (committee members surprisingly were much less fiesty about member projects in their presence…), but I don't believe the legislature yet thinks you will deal any more harshly with member projects than previous governors. If you have an opportunity to talk today, I am still interested in getting your views on this matter. My latest tally of the budgets shows $464 million of member projects in the House budget, ~$420 million in the Senate.

Specifically, I would like your answer to this: Legislators say their projects meet the needs of their communties, new health clinics, for instance, in poor counties that would be unable to build them on their own. My understanding of your budget presentation was that your concern was that these projects should be determined on a rational basis, competing against similar programs in the state or service district. (Why, for example, should Taylor county get a clinic but not Suwannee or Bradford or Baker?) More simply: money ought to be allocated based on objective criteria, not on the political savvy of an area's legislator or the connections of a community or non-profit entity's lobbyist.

---

11 Ken Plante was the director of legislative affairs.

Subject: turkeys
Thursday, April 8, 1999 10:23 p.m.
From: Jeb Bush

I am overwhelmed by emails these days. I guess I have
told too many people that it is the way to get in
touch with me. So, I am sorry I didn't get back to
you any sooner.

Member projects are not all bad. But many of them
have had little scrutiny, aren't part of any
statewide review, don't have performance criteria
attached to them and have little community support.
In addition, they crowd out programs that go through
the state government process that do have to meet
performance criteria.

This is a question of good government. I am
respectful of the role of the legislature to create
priorities and policy. However, the plethora of
member projects, which has occurred in the last few
years in record numbers, invades into the prerogative
of the executive. It has to change.

I sincerely and respectively believe that member
projects should go through a thorough review and the
ones that don't pass that review, no matter who the
sponsor is, will be vetoed. I am confident that the
legislature will understand that my position is one
based on principle not politics.

Jeb Bush

———

I loved hearing from students, which I did quite a bit. I couldn't help them with all of their issues—getting what they felt were unfair grades, for example—but I loved when they asked questions.

Subject: Student from Manatee Middle
Friday, April 9, 1999 4:57 p.m.
From: Danielle

I am one of the students at Manatee Middle school that showed you around the TV Production room. I wanted to ask you a few questions about your job. You gave me your E-Mail address and told me to write to you. I know you have a tight schedule so please write back only if you have time. Here are my questions...

1. What exactly does your job require?
2. Describe your job on a daily basis and what you have found as being the hardest part of being governor?
3. What are your goals or things you would like to change and make better while you are in office?
4. Can you explain what a what a student voucher is and why you are in favor of them?
5. How does it feel to be the son of a former president and what do you admire most about your father?

Subject: Student from Manatee Middle
Friday, April 9, 1999 8:17 p.m.
From: Jeb Bush

thanks for writing. Here is going:

39

1. It requires lots of energy, lots of work. lots of passion and lots of humility. I have to always remember that I represent 15 million diverse people and always struggle to be true to my beliefs and always strive to do what I think is right.

2. I go work at 7 am and work to 6 pm normally, then I go home and start working again at 7:30 pm until 11:00 pm when I sleep. I have lots of meetings, most of them short and try to stay connected with people outside of Tallahassee. I am now spending lots of time with legislators since they are in session and it is very important to work with them. I normally travel outside Tallahassee once a week like I did today when I met with you. The hardest part of my job is staying focused on my agenda and maintaining patience in a very intense legislative process.

3. I have many goals but the top three would be a) reforming and funding public education so kids that aren't learning get a chance to do so and the ones that are, learn even more; b) building the best business climate in the country so Florida is the place where more high wage jobs are created than any other state; and c) that we take care of the most innocent, the most frail and the most vulnerable far better than we do today. Fighting crime and protecting the environment and fighting drugs are all other priorities as well.

4. A voucher (I call them opportunity scholarships) is simply a scholarship to allow a parent to choose more than the option that the school system currently allows them, including a private option. In my plan, parents would only be given the

opportunity scholarship when the public school has failed and failed again to provide a years worth of knowledge in a years time for the students.

5. I am very proud of my dad. I admire his gentleness, decency, and respect for everyone whether they be a waiter or a king. He is the man who most exhibits integrity, courage, determination and compassion that I have ever met. I love him more than life.

Again, thanks for writing!

Jeb Bush

(un-proofed)

———

We were still working on that state web page. I sent this e-mail to Sally Bradshaw on a Saturday night.

Subject: spend thirty minutes
Saturday, April 10, 1999 9:02 p.m.
From: Jeb Bush

Spend thirty minutes looking at the eog[12] web page and link to some of the other pages in our departments. I think we should ask that each secretary review their web pages to see how they can be more user friendly, how they reflect our priorities and how we can use the web page better than we do now. I would like to know how many hits each page gets and I am sure that the secretaries would as well.

———

12 Executive Office of the Governor.

What do you think?

Jeb

PS Our kids page needs some work and so does our web page. Can we discuss?

———

In the meantime I was still trying to get the Senate to pass A+. We were nearing the end of the session, and it was nail-biting time.

Subject: Opportunity Scholarships
Monday, April 19, 1999 9:08 p.m.
From: Roberto Martinez[13]

I want to commend your wisdom, determination and courage in pressing so vigorously for the opportunity scholarships. I think that this is one of the most significant domestic policy initiatives in this country in a long time. It is very important that we affect a fundamental improvement in our system of public education. The children who cannot afford to attend a private school are nevertheless entitled to a quality public school education, and not to the mediocrity that many are now getting. We cannot continue to fail them. Your courage in placing so much "political capital" on this issue is unselfish and courageous – a sign of true leadership. I pray that you are successful on this issue, and that get what you want.

---

13 Bobby had been a classmate of mine at Andover. I eventually appointed him to the State Board of Education, not because he was a friend but because he felt so passionately about education issues and demonstrated great leadership in the area.

Good Luck!

Subject: Opportunity Scholarships
Monday, April 19, 1999 9:37 p.m.
From: Jeb Bush

thanks so much for writing me on this. I feel beaten down on this. I know our position is right. It hurts to get hammered by people who sincerely wish the best for students but are blinded to the catalytic impact opportunity scholarships will provide. About a month ago, I kind of gave up on fighting the p.r. battle and am focusing on the legislative battle. My hope and prayer is that we will win the p.r. when people see the concerns are minimized and see the benefits in front of them.…

You are a great friend.

Jeb

———

A+ passed, and I had the great privilege of signing it into law on June 21. I still believe now what I said then at the signing ceremony: "This is a historic day for education reform in Florida and the nation. By signing this plan into law, we are honoring our commitment to ensure that every child in the state can learn." Here were the key provisions of the bill:

- *Grade all schools on an A to F scale.*
- *Expand the Florida Comprehensive Assessment Test (FCAT) to all third through tenth graders.*
- *Reward successful and improving schools.*

- *Increase funding for Florida's public schools by $750 million.*
- *Provide unprecedented support to improve failing schools.*
- *Raise teacher standards.*
- *Increase parental choices and encourage innovation by providing Opportunity Scholarships to children in chronically failing schools.*
- *Provide financial rewards for superior teachers.*

———

E-mails from people lobbying me to sign the bills that would fund their favorite projects inundated my in-box. These projects included everything from soccer parks to performance arts centers, airport improvements, crises centers, and mosquito control. It was more than one thousand bills and/or projects in all. For the most part, I would tell everyone, "Thanks for writing," and, "We are studying the feasibility of your project." This exchange was with Florence Rivas, former head of the Florida ACLU and one of my more liberal friends. We enjoyed a lively e-mail relationship, and I always appreciated her perspective.

Subject: I couldn't believe it!
Tuesday, April 20, 1999 9:51 a.m.
From: Lawyer Flo

the times[14] is editorializing today that $3mil
for the Florida Museum for a JFK exhibit is NOT
a turkey! talk about tap dancing---haven't seen
anything like this since Shirley Temple and Bill
Robinson!

———

14 The *St. Petersburg Times.*

Subject: I couldn't believe it!
Tuesday, April 20, 1999 8:45 p.m.
From: Jeb Bush

This is an interesting one. The supporters of this are several big supporters of our campaign and very, very fine people. However, it will get the ax. Being against turkeys wins no friends. I am not looking forward to the hunt but I would feel miserable not doing it. With few exceptions, I believe we kill what the legislature has done.

Jeb

————

One of Florida's most famous residents—singer and songwriter Jimmy Buffett—came to personally lobby for funding to save the manatees in Florida waters. That visit prompted this e-mail exchange with Shirish Dáte.

Subject: buffett
Wednesday, May 19, 1999 3:40 p.m.
From: Shirish Date

So what does Jimmy Buffett want?
Do you own any of his albums? Fruitcakes? White Sportcoat and a Pink
Crustacean? A1A?

Subject: buffett
[No date/time]
From: Jeb Bush

He wanted to become a Republican :)

**I own the Pirate Looks at Forty which I think I
bought before I was 40.**

Subject: buffett
Wednesday, May 19, 1999 5:39 p.m.
From: Shirish Date

I'm pretty sure A Pirate Looks at 40 is a song on the
album A1A (all sailors are required to know this;
it's on the Coast Guard master's exam).

So, for my story tomorrow: Any thoughts on your
meeting?

Subject: buffett
Wednesday, May 19, 1999 8:50 p.m.
From: Jeb Bush

**For the story: We are looking at the member projects.
I am committed to improving the chances of survival
of the manatee. The preservation of the manatee
deserves a greater focus on a statewide level than it
has received in the last eight years.**

Jeb

———

*The first round of vetoes was announced on May 27. More than
$300 million was cut out of the budget, and this earned me
the nickname "Veto Corleone." Of course, disappointed e-mails
flooded my in-box. They came from citizens and legislators, and
several even threatened to sue. And those were the Republicans.
One man e-mailed and said I made his wife cry. I even let down
Jimmy Buffett.*

Subject: Cockroach attack on Buffett
Thursday, May 27, 1999 7:37 a.m.
From: Jimmy Buffett

Thanks again for taking the time to see us in
Tallahassee. I did think that when the Palmetto bug
(alias roach) sprang out from behind the leather
chair that Johnny Tanner[15] might leap from behind the
curtain and capture him and drag the startled bug
back to his ranch in Christmas. I hope you noticed
that in my comments to the press after the meeting,
that I avoided mentioning the attack of the Palmetto
Bug on the environmentalists in the Governor?s office.
Your secret is safe with me.

Turning to our larger and more endangered Florida
creatures, I feel pretty passionate that the well
being of the manatee is a litmus test on the larger
quality of life in Florida. I was happy to discover
your knowledge of the issue, your sense of personal
commitment to our entire save the manatee effort, and
your willingness to work with us on this problem. We
both know that sometimes when environmental interests
collide with government bureaucracy, both groups can
get frustrated.…

Thanks again for your time and interest. I am also
forwarding a signed copy of my book. It?s not P.J.
O?Rourke, but it?s the best I can do as a Democrat.

---

15 I believe Johnny Tanner was a friend of Jimmy Buffett. If I have the
right person, he was the lead singer of a group called the "5" Royales.

Subject: Cockroach attack on Buffett
Saturday, May 29, 1999 3:31 p.m.
From: Jeb Bush

Thanks for writing. As you may know, we did veto the
two projects along with a few others. David Struhs
and Colleen[16] are at work on the manatee issue and
will be back to the potential litigants soon.

Finally, thanks in advance for the book and I hope
you have a great tour

Jeb

———

There were some positive responses as well. This note came from Elaine, a businesswoman from Broward County who cochaired my campaign there in 1998.

Subject: You show them
Friday, May 28, 1999 7:02 a.m.
From: Elaine Micelli

WOW! When you mean business…you mean business.
Florida finally has a principled Governor CONGRATs on
sticking to your guns. Now I don't want you to think
life is easy here in Broward. I went to the Miami
Herald dinner last night being honored by the Jewish
Federation. I took the entire blame personally for
your Broward Cuts.…

---

16 David Struhs was secretary of the Department of Environmental
Protection. Colleen Castille was head of cabinet affairs and specialized in
environmental issues. She was appointed because of the cabinet's central
role in state land preservation and acquisition.

Geeezzz...I didn't know these people had such tempers and no sense of humor. I told t hem to get used to a new leadership and learn to legislate like they were taught in Politics 101.

Our Guv who means what he says. You added an all new meaning to the phrase "Read My Lips."...Besos to Columba

Subject: You show them
Saturday, May 29, 1999 3:25 p.m.
From: Jeb Bush

Elaine, Broward County did pretty good compared to other places. Social service operating expense were not vetoed which was a reflection that there was no good system in place. Finally, the overall budget in the important areas of education and social services grew dramatically. It is never enough for some.

You are a good friend.

Jeb

———

This veto inquiry came from a reporter.

Subject: Policy and Priority
Monday, May 31, 1999 10:49 p.m.
From: [No name]

Recently you vetoed over 300 million in funding projects that you considered inappropriate by the Florida Legislation. Please give me your examples of what priorities and broad policies the Florida Legislation should be developing for Florida's future. Also include how you would define the proper role of our legislators.

Subject: **Policy and Priority**
Wednesday, June 2, 1999 10:49 p.m.
From: **Jeb Bush**

My policy priorities are fixing our ailing public education, child welfare, developmental disability and aging-in-place systems; restoring fiscal responsibility to state government and reducing taxes; reducing crime, particularly drug crime; preserving our environment; and revitalizing our urban core neighborhoods.
The way it best works is how it did this session (but for the proliferation of member projects). I laid out an agenda that reflected the items mentioned above. The legislature responded to that agenda by passing laws and a budget that reflected their priorities. Sometimes these priorities come in conflict but in this session they did not. The executive branch carries them out.…
We have a program/performance budget structure that requires the legislature to decide what we need to accomplish through these programs. This can not work if the legislature is also micromanaging how we get there.

Thanks for writing.

Jeb Bush

———

I probably would have been smart to ignore this e-mail from an Associated Press reporter. After it was published, my e-mail in-box exploded! Her questions seemed reasonable, though.

Subject: email story
Tuesday, June 1, 1999 2:59 p.m.
From: Jackie Hallifax

AP would like to do a story on how you use e-mail
_ and I'd like to interview you for that story via
e-mail. I've got a few questions but I'll start with
just one in this note: How do you use e-mail to help
you do your job?

Subject: email story
Tuesday, June 1, 1999 7:00 p.m.
From: Jeb Bush

**I am sitting in a parking lot in front of Boeing in
Seal Beach [California] and have twenty minutes.
I have answered fifteen emails, most supporting
my veto decisions on the budget, several from
Karen Unger[17] regarding appointments we are
about to announce, one from Cecil Rush[18] about my
wife. I have received and sent over 100 messages
today while traveling by car throughout Southern
California. In short, email helps me work hard and
with a focus without losing sight of the people I
am trying to serve.**

**Email allows me to stay connected with all sorts of
people who otherwise wouldn't get to do so with a
Governor.**

---

17 Karen Unger was my appointments secretary.
18 Cecilia Rush was Columba's aide, and she also managed the governor's mansion.

Some people abuse that accessibility, most do not.

Thanks.

Jeb

———

I try every single day to emulate my father, who is the finest person I know. I am, however, my own man. Unlike him, I don't jump out of airplanes. This e-mail was from Robin Higgins, executive director of the Department of Veterans Affairs.

Subject: Fundraiser
Tuesday, June 8, 1999 7:59 a.m.
From: Robin Higgins

For our WWII fundraiser, would you jump out of plane for us?

Subject: Fundraiser
Tuesday, June 8, 1999 11:58 p.m.
From: Jeb Bush

Nope. no way. no.

———

On June 11 I made history by signing a bill into law live via the Internet. It seemed appropriate since the legislation created the Information Service Technology Development Task Force. The task force's job was to make Florida more high-tech.

Subject: Internet Bill Signing
Friday, June 11, 1999 10:37 p.m.
From: Bill Justin

Must have been a lot of people watching your internet bill signing as bandwidth kept dropping down and I had to reconnect the real audio a few times.…

Keep up the good work, governor. It was very innovative to be the first governor in Florida's history to sign bills into law on the Internet. Were you also the first governor to sign legislation into law in the US?

Hopefully your dad and mother watched online. If not you need to get them online.…I've always liked the saying "you're never to old to learn."

Subject: Internet Bill Signing
Sunday, June 13, 1999 1:59 p.m.
From: Jeb Bush

Thanks Mr. Justin. I believe I was the first Governor to do sign a bill over the internet.

Yes, my parents are computer literate and access the internet regularly!

Jeb

———

One of the hardest parts of being an elected official is that all aspects of your life become public. This means there is little to no room for mistakes. However, since we are human, we make them anyway. To this day Columba regrets a mistake she made. After returning from a trip to Paris, she failed to declare all her purchases. She paid a $4,100 penalty and learned a difficult life lesson. Most people were understanding—but not all.

Subject: Shopping in Paris
Sunday, June 20, 1999 1:42 p.m.
From: Harry Rabb

How is it that you can claim a place as an everyday
Floridian, sensitive to the plight of the inner city
and the plight of public schools, when you sanction
a shopping trip in Paris for your wife that exceeds
the salaries of many real Floridians? To top it off,
your wife makes a weak attempt to smuggle her Parisian
goods into the country by not paying the duty that is
owed. Is this the family values and new morality that
you and your administration are trying to communicate?
The Mac Stapanovich attitude of "I got mine!"? The
classless attitude of "It's not a foul unless you
get caught"? Your actions in sanctioning this obsence
shopping spree and your wife's smuggler mentality are
deplorable given your's and your brother's concept of
"compassionate coservatism." The message here seems to
be, in the words of George Orwell, "We are all equal,
but some of us are more equal than others."

I welcome and look forward to your response.

Subject: Shopping in Paris
Sunday, June 20, 1999 2:48 p.m.
From: Jeb Bush

**My wife made a mistake for which she is suffering more
than you will know. I love her dearly.**

**I will continue to advocate policies that place
the interests of Floridians in the forefront. Some
people will appreciate my work, others like you,
won't.**

I hope you have a good father's day and thanks for writing to express your views.

Jeb Bush

———

Subject: [None]
Friday, June 25, 1999 2:26 p.m.
From: Rob Clark

Just a quick note to tell you what a great job you are doing! Keep it up! Also tell your wife that she has a lot of friends in this state.

I'm the senior minister in a church that has over 2,000 in attendance every Sunday. Barry Banther, who I believe worked with you campaign, is a member here and one of my closest friends. Because of the size of our church, and our being conservative both morally and politically, we get hammered by the press all the time. (especially the st. pete times) I reached a point several years ago where I began to refuse all interviews. That's a luxury you and your wife don't have.

Just remember that when the press goes after you and your wife as they have lately, it's a good sign that you're succeeding, and that makes you a threat to them.

Your wife is a very gracious and dignified person. There's not a person in this state (including those who write and report the news) who hasn't made an error in judgement at one time or another. I know I have. Both of you just hang in there and keep doing what you are doing.

Ps-The St. Pete Times couldn't wait to report that you had received a majority of negative e-mail. Maybe this one will help toward balancing that out.

Subject: [None]
Sunday, June 27, 1999 11:46 a.m.
From: Jeb Bush

Thank Rob for writing. Actually, I have had more positive emails to me directly but I guess they didn't count those. In any case, what my wife did was wrong and she has accepted responsibility for her actions. I love her dearly and know that the many good things she does and will do will win out in the end.

I am very grateful for your support. Your prayers for Columba and me would be appreciated. And for Frank and Mary Brogan.

Have a blessed Sunday.

Jeb Bush

———

Lieutenant Governor Frank Brogan's wife, Mary, died a few hours later of cancer. She was a remarkable woman and loved by everyone. Like Columba and me, she and Frank had been high-school sweethearts.

What were Floridians thinking about during the dog days of the summer of 1999? Everything.

Subject: Highway Safety
Thursday, July 22, 1999 2:44 p.m.
From: Buck Roberts

The vehicle speeds on our highways have become dangerously excessive. Specifically, traveling on Interstates 10/75/275 anymore is a harrowing experience. It is my observation that our Highway Patrol does not enforce the speed limits. Even though the stated limit is 70 MPH, vehicles generally travel 80 MPH and higher and our Patrol seem to allow it. To me, this is allowing the law to be broken. If the "limit" is 70 MPH, then 71 is speeding.

Subject: Highway Safety
Wednesday, August 4, 1999 7:50 p.m.
From: Jeb Bush

thank you for writing. I am passing on your email to the head of the Department of Highway Safety and Motor Vehicles for his response. I agree with you that we need to enforce the speeding laws of the state.

Jeb Bush

Subject: "No" to sodas
Wednesday, August 4, 1999 2:10 p.m.
From: Belinda Aubuchon

I read with great interest an article in todays
paper regarding a decision to be made soon regarding
the increased availability of sodas in our public
schools. I realize you are faced with many decisions,
perhaps,more critical than this one. As a former
Home Economics teacher, a yearbook representative
who spends most days in schools, and mostly as a
nutrition-informed mother - it is my definite and
emphatic view that this is a move in the wrong
nutrition direction for our children. My informed
belief is that soda machines have NO business in
schools at all (and the day-to-day cafeteria offerings
need to be radically changed as well — a topic for
another email).

Subject: "No" to sodas
Wednesday, August 4, 1999 8:55 p.m.
From: Jeb Bush

Thank you so much for writing. Here is my view.…This
is a local decision. Too many things are decided in
Tallahassee and too little is decided at the local
level. I think local school districts should decide
whether or not to allow sodas and the restrictions if
they are allowed to do so.

Jeb Bush

———

Subject: a question and statement
Thursday, August 12, 1999 10:40 p.m.
From: Robin Vandevoir

I am writing to you as Mr. Bush because from my standpoint right now you are not a govenor. You are in all legal sinces of the word but from a percpective aspect I do not see you as a govenor. I see you as a man and not a very good one at that. Personally you may be a great guy, i really do not know because I have not had the good fortune of meeting you. However, from a political standpoint I see you as a bad guy. You have done a few things that I trully disagree with.

First on my list is allowing the right to life license plate. I take no standpoint on aborstion. Yes, i have my opinion but that is not what I am discussing. My problem is with the fact that this is a very touchy issue. The discussion about aborstion is not even really touched on in school, because of teachers' fears of even bringing up such an issue. Yet, for some reason you found it proper to indorse a license plate on such an issue. From what I have learned so far it is the governments job to stay away from religious affilation.…

I did not contribute to your campaign and I do not hold any position that would make me of any importance to you. I am simply a person, one of your loyal subjects of the state. (loyal, what a word) I attend a public school, Boyd Anderson's Internatioal Baccalaurte program to be exact. I have always attended public school, a true product of the system. I come from a middle class family. I work as a computer consultant and play classical guitar. Now in this short paragraph I have told you more about me then I know about you and you represent me, and everyone else here in Florida. There is something wrong with this. As our figure head shouldn't we at least know who you are. You must be more then a sound bite on TV. You must have some purpose.

More things wrong with your office. I hope you don't mind all this criticism, i mean it with the utmost respect. I am mad at your choice for school votures. This is silly. Everyone should be allowed the same educational oppurtunity. In a great country such as are, should we rely on private education. Should one of our goals not be to raise the educational acheivement of everyone. What does a private school trully offer.…

P.S. Note: I know that Jeb Bush himself, even though this is his email address will probably never read this. I hope that the aid that is reading this will note what I have said, and maybe even show Jeb. I know it is all just a silly idea, writing and all. It doesn't really matter. Nobody probably listens, but I have hope that someone will. I guess hope is all that I have left. Feel free to reply. It would trully mean something if I got a response, but a real response, not just a form letter that is sent to everyone on the issues I have stated.

Subject: a question and statement
Saturday, August 14, 1999 9:44 p.m.
From: Jeb Bush

I appreciate your writing although I am sorry you
see me as a bad guy. I am working hard to earn the
respect of Floridians by advocating tough changes in
our education system to improve student achievement;
lowering violent crime and drug use through first time
comprehensive strategies; making government work for
our citizens through the use of technology and other
businesslike efforts; enhancing economic opportunities
for Floridians and helping the most vulnerable. I
think we have had a pretty good start on our agenda.

I would like to meet you one of these days. Maybe you
would not think I was such a bad guy then. Who knows?

To close, let me promise you that this is me, not a
staff person. I work very hard to answer the thousands
of emails I get. It helps me understand the work I
have to do to implement my agenda.

Have a wonderful weekend.

Jeb Bush

PS A little bit about me. I am 46, have been married
for 25 years and am blessed with three kids. My oldest
is George who was a high school teacher last year and
now is working as an intern for a law firm in Mexico
City. My daughter goes to Tallahassee Community
College...My 15 year old boy goes to school in
Jacksonville. I have worked in all sorts of jobs since
graduating from college in two and half years when I

turned 21. I love Florida (I have lived here for 20 years), and I love serving Floridians as Governor.

———

Improving Florida's business climate was another top priority. As the former secretary of commerce under Governor Bob Martinez, I felt strongly that governors should lead in recruiting businesses into the state. That was why I had traveled to California earlier in the year—to visit with businesses that might be interested in opportunities in Florida.

Subject: Recruiting companies to Florida
Tuesday, August 31, 1999 6:18 p.m.
From: Bea Garcia

I'm a business columnist with the Miami Herald. In the course of reporting a column last week on the Florida Manufacturing Technology Centers, a state official mentioned that you have made a commitment to call an average of 5 to 6 out-of-state companies every week and inviting them to come to Florida. I understand it has been one of your initiatives since you took office.

I find it very unique that you have undertaken such a mission. Of course, there is no better spokesman for the state of Florida than the governor himself.

Could you tell me more about your initiative and your success with it? Why did you feel you had to be the one to call? Could Lt. Gov. Frank Brogan or John Anderson from Enterprise Florida make the calls? Have any companies followed up on your phone call, asking for more information or coming to Florida to check out the state for themselves? Any company convinced it should relocate here? What kinds of companies have you been approaching - have they been in any particular industry? What kinds of reaction have you gotten to your calls? I'm sure calls from the Governor of Florida are not the norm for most CEOs. Has any secretary or assistant ever hung up on you, thinking the call was a hoax? Thanks for your assistance.

Subject: Recruiting companies to Florida
Saturday, September 4, 1999 8:32 p.m.
From: Jeb Bush

I make a call a day on average to businesses inside and outside the state. Most of the time, it is to find out what we can do to help them make a positive decision to invest in Florida. Many are prospects of communities across the state. For the in state companies, the calls are to thank them for their commitment to our communities and find out what they want their governor to be doing.

People receiving the calls appreciate the fact that the Governor considers it a priority to here from them. I enjoy the calls since I learn about current trends in business.

I have put deals back on track where there have been misunderstandings. I have spoken to a businessman from California who was looking at a facility in the Tampa Bay area while I called him on his portable. He wrote me afterwards saying that it made the difference in coming to the state.

Not all deals work out. I have called businesspeople who have decided to go to other states. Sometimes learning why we weren't successful is valuable information.

On rare occasion, the caller doesn't believe that I am who I am but in the end, it works out.

Jeb Bush

———

The following illustrates one of the best parts of my former job.

Subject: Help with a school project?
Thursday, September 9, 1999 8:04 p.m.
From: Drew

I am a fourth grader at Landmark Christian Elementary School in Haines City, Florida. After Christmas we will be studing Florida in our Social Studies class. My class and I have been asked to collect things about Florida over the next few months. I thought it would be cool to share a letter with my class from you. Would you please send me a letter telling me about the things you like to do in Florida and about your job? I would really like that. Thank you very much for helping me with my school project.

PS. Could you use your influence and get the Lt. Governor to write me a letter also? Thanks!

Subject: Help with a school project?
Friday, September 10, 1999 8:23 p.m.
From: Jeb Bush

Thank you for your email.

I have the best job in the world. I get to serve
an incredible state of fifteen million people. My
priorities for our state are 1) to see increased
student achievement through our A plus plan;
2) cut drug use by 50% in five years through a
comprehensive plan which includes prevention,
treatment and enforcement; 3) make government work
as efficiently as possible through budget reform,
the use of technology and sound business practices;
4) improving how we take of the most needy in a
more compassionate way; 5) building a world class
business climate and finally 6) protecting the
natural environment for the next generation of
Floridians.

I wake up each day and try to advance one or two or
all of these priorities. I get to do it inside and
outside of Tallahassee. As I said, I have the best,
the most awesome job in the world.

I am ccing my buddy, Frank Brogan so you will have
his email address.

Jeb

PS if you are interested in what we are doing, you
can check it out at www.eog.state.fl.us

———

Then came Floyd. He was my first but unfortunately not my last hurricane. I got this report from Deputy Chief of Staff David Rancourt.

Subject: FLOYD
Sunday, September 12, 1999 8:37 p.m.
From: David Rancourt.

This thing is as big as Hugo and as fast as Andrew. Lots of things could happen at this point, and virtually all of them are bad.

We will get a 10:50 p.m. update tonight from the national hurricane center. If major changes occur, I will call Sally - but I presume this will maintain a steady course for Florida. It is traveling around 12 miles per hour.

All our agency heads were to be notified by Steve[19] today and asked to have a high level official there tomorrow morning. Corrections, Health, AHCA (nursing homes), DOT, HSMV, etc., in particular.

This has the potential to keep us busy for quite some time.

Subject: FLOYD
Sunday, September 12, 1999 10:03 p.m.
From: Jeb Bush

Let us make sure that we all take this seriously. Please tell Steve to call me after the 8 am meeting

---

19 Steve Siebert's Department of Community Affairs included emergency management.

if there is not high cooperation from other
department heads. I am sure there will be but if not,
let me know.

Jeb

———

Subject: How are you doing Governor?
Monday, September 13, 1999 7:12 p.m.
From: Adriana

We are doing the best as far as preparations and
the rest is in God's hands. We must pray for one
another.

Subject: How are you doing Governor?
Monday, September 13, 1999 10:27 p.m.
From: Jeb Bush

**I am praying very hard. This is going to hurt many of
the people I try to serve and it hurts a lot.**

Jeb

———

*Millions of Floridians evacuated our east coast as the storm bar-
reled our way. In the end it pounded the Bahamas at its peak,
skirted our eastern coast, and came ashore as a much weaker
Category 2 in North Carolina. Phew! I was very proud of the
work our team did, and with every storm we learned lessons to
be applied next time.*

Subject: Floyd...
Wednesday, September 15, 1999 7:23 p.m.
From: Shelley

I would like to compliment you on the fine manner in which you handled the Floyd crisis. I am grateful that Florida received less catastrophic damage than we feared. My family and I did evacuate off of the beach where we live...across the river to the mainland. I was so traumatized by this thing...fearful...terrified by the size and strength of it....

You know things are pretty nuts when a captive (hurricane news) audience around the television started placing bets on the color of [your] next shirt when you'd appear in a live tv broadcast! I really liked the dark green one and am now told that I must have missed the purple one. I know, I know....We did have cabin fever. (Better known as looney bin.)

Subject: Floyd...
Wednesday, September 15, 1999 7:48 p.m.
From: Jeb Bush

I am so pleased that you are back at home safe and sound. We are truly fortunate!

Jeb

———

While I had to fight hard against the teachers union to pass my education reforms, I never lost my optimism that I would convince every single principal, teacher, parent, and student

*that the A+ plan was exactly what we needed to fix our schools.
I was willing to talk to or write to every single Florida resident.
It's possible I did. I did enjoy the give and take and learned a
great deal. Announcing which schools received cash bonuses for
improving their grades prompted this e-mail exchange.*

Subject: [None]
Wednesday, September 29, 1999 9:27 p.m.
From: George W Drake

I still don't get it.

The white middle class and above schools get the
extra money, your A,B,C schools. The poor low class/
minority schools get nothing.

What am I missing here? Does it take a rocket
scientist to figure this out. It is not the schools or
the teachers, it's the populations.

All I ask you to do is think. Hello, average and rich
kids compared to poor minority kids. The population/
make up of the students.

Why do I even try???? And we can't figure out who the
problem is???

The problem is in Tallahassee, from the top, down.

Subject: [None]
Friday, October 1, 1999 9:09 p.m.
From: Jeb Bush

**Not all the schools were white middle class schools.
Schools that showed improvement got the same amount**

of money. Schools that are F rated get more money as well to give them a chance. What is there not to get? You appear to want to have two standards, one for poor minority kids and one for white kids. I want to have one high standard for all and then work to make sure that all can achieve that standard. Which idea is the better one?????

Jeb Bush

———

I spent the evening of the first Sunday of October catching up on e-mails. That included numerous staff missives. This e-mail went to Sally Bradshaw, Karen Unger, Brewser Brown, and Tara Wainwright, my scheduler.

Subject: a plus
Sunday, October 3, 1999 6:41 p.m.
From: Jeb Bush

I have not heard if we are following up on my belief that I need to meet with a group of superintendents, a group of teachers, a group of principals to discuss the grading system. Can you let me know how we are doing?

Jeb

This e-mail went just to Sally Bradshaw. I won't explain what it all meant. All these years later, I am not sure I remember the exact details. However, the to-do lists always got longer—never shorter.

Subject: things to discuss
Sunday, October 3, 1999 9:35 p.m.
From: Jeb Bush

The list has grown. I hope we will have a chance to go through these things when life gets moving at a pace below the speed limit. As I am sure you can tell, I am frustrated about lots of things. Talk to you on Tuesday or during down time tomorrow.

1. film commission plan
2. my tax return
3. Senior Escorts DOEA[20]
4. Depositions for drug cases.
5. Family literacy initiative timing
6. Pope letter
7. Public corruption task force
8. Wages transportation/ FAMU[21] issue
9. Russell Bjorkman
10. Law Enforcement group
11. Liza McFadden/Mentoring initiative
12. IDEON/Frist
13. NEA/FTP/Stephanie King meeting
14. Southern Command letter
15. Education governance structure
16. King Shaw lunch
17. Black Enterprise convention
18. Gates Foundation
19. Veronica Anderson
20. Gema's thoughts on AAA and the older American act.

———

This e-mail exchange was with a St. Petersburg Times *columnist who wrote me a rather lengthy e-mail inquiring about the appointment process for judges. The issue was not without controversy. Among other things, I was accused of using a litmus test*

---

20 Department of Elder Affairs.
21 Florida A&M University.

to make sure my appointees agreed with my thinking, not being diverse enough, and appointing friends.

Subject: Judges
Thursday, October 7, 1999 9:13 a.m.
From: Martin Dyckman

In short, precisely what values do you hope to apply? The answer would satisy more people coming from you than through people purporting to quote you.

Subject: Judges
Thursday, October 7, 1999 2:27 p.m.
From: Jeb Bush

Martin, I have no biases built in about the selection of judges. We have done more than our predecessors in terms of interviews and research on their qualifications. I would be happy to provide you with backup on this fact.

I am committed to diversity which is evidenced by the fact that I have appointed women and minorities in significantly higher numbers than what the JNC[22] has sent to me. I would be happy to provide you information to back this up as well.

---

22 Judicial Nominating Commission. The governor and the Florida Bar each appointed three people to this commission, and then those six appointed three more. The nine-member commission presented potential judicial candidates to the governor. The law was amended in 2001 to change the role of the Florida Bar—much to its members' disapproval. The governor now appointed all nine members, but four of them had to be from a slate of nominees presented by the Florida Bar. Six of the nine members have to be members of the bar. As governor I had the power to veto the bar's nominees—a power I never exercised.

There are no litmus tests. No one is being
precluded from service based on their professional
experience. Why don't you look at the judges I have
appointed to date as an indication of what I will
do in the future rather than speculate about what I
will do based on yours or other people's fears? We
would be happy to provide you with that information
as well.

Thank you for writing.

Jeb Bush

———

Another Sunday afternoon was spent e-mailing the staff. This one
went to Tony Villamil, head of the Office of Tourism, Trade, and
Economic Development.

Subject: update
Sunday, October 10, 1999 2:13 p.m.
From: Jeb Bush

I need an update on:

1.   contracts
2.   followup on defense initiative
3.   plan for film commissioner
4.   Israel acceptance list
5.   Enterprise Florida board chair search
6.   followup on Mexico trip (prospects, actual sales,
     State governors etc)

7. **FTAA**[23]
8. United Technologies proposal
9. I Four corridor study (or is it the semiconductor plant in Orlando)

Given my apparently difficult schedule this week, I may brief Sally and get her to follow up with you.

Jeb Bush

———

This note went to Frank Brogan, Sally Bradshaw, Donna Arduin, and Brian Yablonski.

Subject: water and juvenile justice
Sunday, October 10, 1999 2:38 p.m.
From: Jeb Bush

I spoke to senator Jennings yesterday and told her we were going to follow up with Senator Burt to set up a process for juvenile justice issues. Do we have a proposed structure? If not, we need one before we begin to speak to the members. I would like a timeframe for this to happen. My suggestion is that it be mid November but I am open to your suggestions.

As it relates to water, how to do you envision getting our threshold criteria established? Who is

———

23 Free Trade Area of the Americas. In 1994 thirty-four leaders in our hemisphere launched negotiations to create a free-trade zone. I was pressing to make Miami the permanent headquarters of the FTAA secretariat, but the trade agreement was never completed.

in charge of getting the names ready for our five appointees?

Let us keep the momentum moving on the fine work you all have done.

Jeb

———

I also was catching up on e-mails from constituents.

Subject: Update & School voucher comments
Friday, October 8, 1999 11:35 p.m.
From: Taurii Nishiyama

As to the school voucher issue - I've been watching the press coverage in Tampa, and wanted to encourage you to hold the line. You're doing the right thing - but it's hard to articulate the "why" in a way that the majority of adults can comprehend. I've been a sole-supporting single mother of one for going on 16 years now. When my daughter was four, I researched all I could to learn about education opportunities, and made the decision that she would go to Catholic school. We are catholic, but the deciding factor for me was the statistics on outcomes for those educated in catholic vs. public schools, particularly when you look at the long term numbers. I had to work three jobs while paying for K- 3rd grade; by 4th grade I was able to build my career to the point where I only had to work two jobs; by 6th grade just one job. Now my daughter is a sophomore at Tampa Catholic in the honors program, pulling a 4.1

GPA, with academic and sports awards too numerous to list (my favorite is probably the Presidential Award of Academic Excellence with the obvious catholic school listed and bearing Clinton's signature just below it - that's because I find the dichotomy so humorous), and she intends to go to Notre Dame. Tuition, tithing and books combined for her attendance at Tampa Catholic total more than my mortgage payments - and it's the best investment I'll ever make.

Parental priorities are truly tested when you have to choose between making a tuition payment, buying food or paying the light bill - when you can pay two of those bills but certainly not three - and you try to suppress the knowledge that you're paying tax dollars for public school, because that kind of negative thinking is unproductive, and you really can't change it. Basically, you eat less, and beg the power company to give you some time or let you pay late, and you hope someone (like a Governor Bush) comes along to change things. Meanwhile, your credit rating takes a tumble, because when you're living paycheck to paycheck and the tuition must be paid, any unbudgeted expense - such as a car problem, an ear infection - makes the whole financial house of cards collapse.…

The point of this long email is perhaps just a message to you to please hold the line on vouchers.… It must be very, very difficult. And if you can imagine any way anyone can help you with this, please let me know.

Subject: **Update & School voucher comments**
Sunday, October 10, 1999 5:56 p.m.
From: Jeb Bush

As I read your email, I started to cry. Your
testimony filled my heart with emotion. I will stay
the course. My hope and prayer is that all children
will get a quality education and moms like you won't
have to make such a big sacrifice in doing so.

I will pass on your email to Tara Wainwright to see
if I could visit should there be some time. I think
I did it already once a while back so this will be a
reminder.

Jeb Bush

———

*Our war on drugs was another hot topic in Florida. We hoped to
send the dealers to prison and stop drugs from coming into the
country. Our plan, though, focused heavily on prevention and
treatment. After a town-hall meeting in Fort Myers about our
drug problem, my e-mail in-box once again exploded. Most e-mails
were from people who were grateful for what we were trying to
do, but others were not. They also did not agree with each other.*

Subject: **DRUG ABUSE**
Tuesday, October 12, 1999 12:11 p.m.
From: Chuck Atwood

CONGRATULATIONS ON YOUR IDEA TO ATTACK THE DRUG
PROBLEM BY SOLICITING THOUGHTS FROM THE PUBLIC. I'M

SURE SINCE ALCOHOL REPRESENTS THE VAST MAJORITY OF
ABUSE CASES; PROHIBITION AND MANDATORY JAILING OF
ANYONE PARTAKING OF ALCOHOLIC SUBSTANCES WILL BE #1
PRIORITY. THINK OF THE DECLINE OF SPOUSAL ABUSE, THE
TOTAL ELIMINATION OF DRUNKEN DRIVING AND ACCIDENT
TRAGEDIES, MISSED DAYS OF WORK DUE TO HANGOVERS
ETC....NEXT WE GET TO WORK ON ELIMINATING THE TOBACCO
INDUSTRY. I BELIEVE WE ALREADY HAVE SUFFICIENT
STATISTICS ON THE HEALTH DEVASTATION THAT DRUG HAS
CAUSED. ONCE THESE TWO KILLERS HAVE BEEN ELIMINATED
AND THE PUBLIC EDUCATED, WE CAN TURN OUR ATTENTION TO
THE OTHER PROBLEMS WE HAVE.

WHAT DO YOU THINK GOVERNOR? TIME TO SET DOWN THAT
BEER,MARTINI,WINE COOLER,CIGARETTE,CIGAR,SPIT OUT
THAT CHAW AND OPEN OUR EYES TO THE REAL PROBLEMS, OR
SHOULD WE KEEP ON THE COURSE THE POLITICAL BANDWAGON
HAS CHARTED? I THOUGHT SO, HYPOCRITE.

Subject: DRUG ABUSE
Tuesday, October 12, 1999 10:15 p.m.
From: Jeb Bush

**thank you for your interesting but misguided email.
I don't smoke or take drugs and take an occasional
drink. However, I don't rob anyone for my addiction.
I don't hurt my wife or my child because I am abusing
alcohol or drugs. I hurt when families hurt from the
agony of a member destroying themselves and their
family members from drug and alcohol abuse. Don't you
hurt as well?**

Jeb Bush

———

Subject: Town Hall Meeting
Monday, October 11, 1999 11:27 p.m.
From: April

I was at the Town Hall Meeting tonight in Ft. Myers and was next in line to ask a question when it was time to stop. Maybe this is better because I had such a hard time deciding which question I wanted to asked or which area I wanted to comment on and this way I can address them all.

First, I suppose the best place to start is, I like many others, have a family member addicted to drugs. She has been on crack cocaine for 15 years. I listened to how many people talked about the family being a big factor on the war of drugs and I agree. However, in our case, my niece is an adult and therefore our hands are tied as to what we are allowed to do.…The last time we saw her was in the emergency room after a drug overdose in an attempt to take her life, the second attempt in a week.

Second, Education is great but do you know that every single year and I mean that literally, every single year the threat of the Dare program being dropped is in the headlines. Our sheriff uses it as a leverage for his budget. The program always get saved but it is always threatened. If that program saves just one child then it is worth every penny it cost.…

Schools.…My daughters tell me that they can get anything, anytime they want. As far as I am concerned, put the drug dogs in there. It wouldn't bother me one little bit if they were there every day checking lockers. If there are parents that

don't like it, too bad. It saddened me to see that
there were schools that did not have a teacher or a
principal at the town meeting.…

We talk about enforcement of underage drinking? Do
you realize how many kids relate sports to beer?
If cigarettes cannot be advertised, why do we as a
society allow most sporting events advertise beer? I
can walk into a 7-11 almost any Friday night and see
underage people buying beer with fake ID's.…

Thank you for taking the time to read this. I get
frustrated because I am never sure if I can convey
what I want to say with the passion of what I feel.

Subject: Town Hall Meeting
Friday, October 15, 1999 10:51 p.m.
From: Jeb Bush

**thank you so much for writing me. I am so very
grateful for your attending the town meeting.**

**First, let me tell you how I admire your concern for
your niece. Having gone through the pain of a loved
one suffering with drug abuse, I know how hard it is
to know that the next call could be from a police
officer or a hospital about someone you love.**

**Secondly, I am absolutely, completely committed to
reducing drug use in our state. I think we can do it.
Your niece needs treatment and if need be, she needs
to be forced to accept it. That is why the drug court
concept is a good one.**

**Thirdly, I am sending your email on to Jim McDonough
so he can suggest how you can get involved.**

Again, thank you for writing.

Jeb Bush

———

Then we had to deal with Hurricane Irene. Unlike Floyd it did come ashore. Thankfully it was as a Category 1, but Irene still caused heavy damage in Florida.

Subject: Flooding Due to Irene in the 8.5 Square Mile Area
Sunday, October 17, 1999 11:35 a.m.
From: Madeline Woodward

My family and I saw you on the news today visiting Miami and commenting on the flooding. Have you forgotten the 8.5 Square Mile Area like everyone else seems to have done? The farmers in our area have had their crops flooded out, our roads are impassable due to the flooding.…I IMPLORE YOU GOVENOR TO DECLARE THE 8.5 SQUARE MILE AREA A DISASTER AREA so our area can receive the necessary help. Thank you for you consideration.

Subject: Flooding Due to Irene in the 8.5 Square Mile Area
Sunday, October 17, 1999 12:02 p.m.
From: Jeb Bush

We have declared the entire South Florida area a disaster area. I have sent emails from residents in the area to the appropriate people for their action. Thanks for writing.

Jeb Bush

———

I started holding cabinet meetings in different locations around the state. At this point we had been to Jacksonville and Fort Lauderdale. I sent this idea to key members of my staff.

Subject: cabinet for a day
Sunday, October 17, 1999 7:16 p.m.
From: Jeb Bush

I think we should build on the cabinet for a day
idea. Why not have a town meeting the night before.
An ask Jeb event. It could be sponsored by the public
television station or the Sunshine Network or a local
affiliate. It could be about one of our priorities or
a "let the big dog eat, anything goes" event.

In addition, I like very much the idea Justin[24]
proposed recently which we have discussed previously
of scheduled meetings with people as well. I suggest
we publicize the fact that the Guv will be available
to meet with citizens for five minutes at a shot on
anything on their minds and do 100 appointments.

I know I am crazy so I won't be offended if I am
making stupid suggestions.

Jeb

The staff likely thought I was crazy, but we continued to hold cabinet meetings around the state for all eight years. We held office hours in those cities where people could line up and present their problems to the governor, cabinet members, department heads, and staff.

---

24 Justin Sayfie was a member of my communications team.

———

Finally I received an easy question from a reporter:

Subject: [None]
Friday, October 22, 1999 3:57 p.m.
From: Alicia Caldwell

Greetings. I'm Alicia Caldwell, a reporter for the
St. Petersburg Times. We met last month when you were
at Operation Par to unveil your drug plan.
I have a question for you. It may not be a pressing
policy matter, but judging from the phone calls we're
getting around here it nonetheless is of some import.
It's about Halloween. It falls on a Sunday this year.
People want to know whether to send the kids out
trick-or-treating on Sunday or a different day. You
can thank Bernie McCabe and Dave Fischer for this
e-mail. Both suggested I call you when I posed the
question to them.

Please know that my search for an arbiter of Halloween
is something of a light-hearted story. Thank you in
advance for taking a moment to type up a response.

Subject: [None]
Friday, October 22, 19999 5:36 p.m.
From: Jeb Bush

you know that I believe in community problem solving.
In Tallahassee, Sunday is the day. Columba and I are
going to the local hospital to give candy out to the
children. It may be different in St Pete. Another
reason why we live in a great state!

Jeb

———

*I sent this to all the department heads. I hated acronyms (still do)
and banned their use in staff meetings.*

Subject: Government acronyms
Saturday, October 23, 1999 5:30 p.m.
From: Jeb Bush

I am writing you with a simple request. Could you
check your web pages and vet them for acronyms and
"non-english" words. Put yourself in the shoes of a
Floridian who is trying to access information from
your web. Then, put your information in a form that
would be useful and understandable.

Thank you for your help on this. This is not some
wacky and weird obsession of mine. It is important to
remember who we serve and think of them in all we do,
including our forms, our contracts and our web pages.

Jeb

———

*I announced a statewide mentoring program. This encouraged
all Floridians who could to donate a few hours a month to mentor
a student. I was a very happy participant, as I had been mentoring a seventh grader for one hour a week since January. I
encouraged the more than 125,000 state employees to join me,
and I encouraged those in the private sector to do the same. I
truly believed we could change the course of history—one child at
a time. The reaction was huge. I often wrote friends—and sometimes strangers—and encouraged them to sign up. I wrote this
e-mail to several university presidents.*

Subject: Mentoring
Friday, October 29, 1999 10:13 p.m.
From: Jeb Bush

One hour a week with a child. It can make a difference. Leaders lead by example. Imagine if the leaders lead and thousands upon thousands followed spending an hour a week with a child. Imagine helping a child by giving guidance on life's journey, helping them read, understand math and teaching them to write.

I spend an hour with a 14 year old boy and it is the best hour I spend each week. I humbly ask that you consider doing the same. If each of you do so, others will follow and children will have a better chance to gain a year's worth of knowledge in a year's time.

What say you?

Jeb Bush

PS if you are interested, you can write me and I will get Liza McFadden[25] to get in touch.

———

On November 9 I announced One Florida, an initiative to end the divisive and discriminatory use of racial and gender preferences, quotas, and set-asides. At the same time, this initiative expanded access to higher education and state contracts for an increasingly diverse population. I didn't want to just end affirmative action. I wanted to transcend it. The initiative's provisions provided:

---

25 Liza McFadden ran the mentoring program.

- *Guaranteed college admission to the top 20 percent of seniors in every Florida high school.*
- *A $20 million increase in need-based financial aid.*
- *Reform of the state's procurement process to open the doors to minority vendors.*

The plan was, of course, not without controversy.

Subject: Afirmative action
Wednesday, November 10, 1999 2:25 p.m.
From: Loida Salicrup

You know I believe that everybody should be equal, but I know for a fact that if I did not have afirmative action in my favor I would not have a job as a mechanic with DOT. The reason was not that I was not qualified the main reason because I was a woman in a male dominated job. I believe sometimes that people turn what afirmative action law is and applied in a way that was not written. I do not believe in quotas either. But then again you have a ignorant white sector because they do not have something or can't get a job because of qualifications use this issue as a main excuse. As you might know whites expect to be in the upper echelon in everything including in the oportunities in jobs and other related issues. Raising in a ignorant family environtment is a another issue, weird that this country fight a civil war for the ending of slavery but today's we continue have a country divide by ignorants in the issue of race.

Today I saw in FSU[26] a guy practicing his right to express himself. The sign he was walking around

26 Florida State University.

said " I support afirmative action, F...k Jeb Bush"
I call him an idiot specially if you want to say
something spell it out complety and another is
the ignorancy of the person in the subject. really
irritates me. Yes I been discriminate many times
in the past, by whites and guess what blacks why,
I have three strikes against me, I am a woman, I
look white and I am puertorican but just because
of that I can't be bitter the rest of my life. You
know what sometimes I asked to people Did you serve
your country? If you don't I did, and they did not
ask me where I come from or tell me go back to your
country, so shut off.

read the law you signed but actually what it suppose
to do. Just the erradication of affirmative action
in goverment, etc. What are you planning to do to
the business that now might use this new to actually
discriminate against people?

Have a nice day.

Subject: Afirmative action
Wednesday, November 10, 1999 8:36 p.m.
From: Jeb Bush

We are not ending affirmative action. We are
transcending it and moving to a new system where we
embrace diversity but not through divisive and unfair
means.

Again, you are good to write.

Jeb Bush

Subject: Proposed Program
Wednesday, November 10, 1999 1:04 p.m.
From: Vi Ella Balloon

I have researched and read about your proposal to
end race-based admissions to universities and racial
set-asides in state contracts. I must say, with a
little apprehension, that I believe your intentions
are well and I somewhat understand how you would
like to "lead Florida to unprecedented diversity
and opportunity -- but without laws mandating it".…I
tend to be skeptical about how this all will turn
out.…

The issue of racism is not going away. Things will
never be equal among the races no matter what you
may try to implement. I have worked extremely hard
for everything that I have accomplished or obtained
in my life. Much of what I have accomplished was not
made possible by affirmative action or race-based
criteria's. I wonder what would happen to several
persons if they could be black for just one day. I
don't think many of them could handle it for even a
day. But we must endure all that comes our way day
after day, month after month, year after year; all
the intentional mistreatment and abuse that we often
encounter just because of the color of our skin. Is
that fair?

I don't ask for much. I just want to be able to
receive all that I have worked for and deserve.
I want an equal opportunity to live the type of
life that any other American can live. I have
never asked for, nor do I want any hand outs. It

just hurts when you are deprived of something simply because of your race or skin color, and no matter how many times you are knocked down you are expected to get right back up. Gov. Bush, why get back up if there is a very slim chance that you will succeed or progress?

Gov. Bush, I guess I felt like "venting". I know you are busy. There is no need to respond to my email. I will try to support your efforts and I am putting my trust, first of all in God, and secondly in you. Do not hurt a people who are continuously struggling overall. We still have a long way to go, but we have made much progress. Remember, there is good and bad in every race. We are all God's children and we must learn how to live together as one.

Subject: Proposed Program
Thursday, November 11, 1999 5:30 p.m.
From: Jeb Bush

Thanks for writing.…Racism is still alive in Florida but laws that discriminate won't eliminate it. We need to enforce civil rights laws and punish discrimination at every turn. If you want to get the whole plan you can go to www.flgov.com and read our plan. I would love to get your opinion.

Jeb Bush

———

All you can do is try to make good policy that everyone understands and supports.

Subject: [None]
Sunday, November 28, 1999 11:23 a.m.
From: [No name]

If you have the guts to read your own email, let
this sink into you brainless mind - $10 Million to
fund your christian value ideas of sex eduction is
outrageous! You can take that plan, long with your
fetus license tags, & any other brainless ideas &
STICK IT UP YOUR FAT ASS!

Before I allow my tax dollars to go to fund your
christian ideas & will move out of the state of
Florida & take my money with me!

Subject: [None]
Sunday, November 28, 1999 1:05 p.m.
From: Jeb Bush

Have a wonderful restful day. You appear to need it.

Jeb

––––––

*This e-mail exchange was a great way to end a year's worth
of sometimes very tough back-and-forth. It begins with an
e-mail that a very happy mother wrote to my good friend
Berthy.*

Subject: Thank you!!!!
Wednesday, December 29, 1999 2:13 p.m.
From: Kathi

Dear Berthy,

As you know, raising a child with a disability is extremely challenging and difficult.

I have some extremely good news. The other day I got a call from my case worker, at Department of Children and Families, who said she realized that I had been waiting a long time for help. She said that she was requesting the medicaid waiver for me and that I would be receiving diapers (since Christopher is 8 years old and still in diapers) on a monthly basis.

As you know, I was at that town hall meeting in Orlando and I believe Governer Bush has helped us in so many ways. He has changed the way developmental services is operating. Finally, for the first in Christopher's life, we are getting the help we need. I hope it continues like this.

Berthy forwarded the e-mail to me, and I forwarded it to my staff.

Subject: Support Coordination
Thursday, December 30, 1999 2:46 p.m.
From: Jeb Bush

if you ever get frustrated about the challenges of the jobs you have, remember Kathi and her boy Christopher. Thank you all

Jeb Bush

———

Wow. What a first year. It truly was exhilarating—and we were just getting started.

From day one I knew it was important to get a fast start and make good on my campaign promises. I went into 2000 confident we had done just that.

We still had a lot work to do, and as you can tell from some of the e-mail exchanges, I still had a lot of people to convince we were on the right track. Ever the optimist, though, I was confident the second year would bring us even closer to our goals.

In our first year, we had:

- *Implemented the A+ education-reform bill.*
- *Made significant improvements to services for developmentally disabled Floridians. The e-mail Kathi sent my friend Berthy was like a late Christmas present.*
- *Cut taxes by $1 billion.*
- *Signed into law Florida Forever, a ten-year land-acquisition program to continue Florida's leadership regarding conserving and preserving land and natural resources.*
- *Signed into law a provision requiring parental notification for minors seeking abortions.*
- *Passed a new crime bill.*
- *Introduced One Florida.*

We were ready for the New Year. So was the great state of Florida.

"I Will Do My Best..."

*Do we have it within us to take us where
we need to go?*

—State of the State Address, March 7, 2000

As any governor can testify, you don't always get to choose the path where you need to go—much less want to go. Life chooses it for you. That was certainly the case in 2000.

We will begin with a little boy named Elian Gonzalez.

Elian's saga actually began on Thanksgiving Day 1999. On that day fishermen anglers found him and two others floating on inner tubes off the coast of Fort Lauderdale. His mother and ten others had died when the boat they used to flee Cuba capsized.

The federal Immigration and Naturalization Service (INS) turned six-year-old Elian over to relatives living in Miami. The problem was his father, Juan Miguel Gonzalez, lived in Cuba and wanted his son back. The relatives in Miami felt his mother had sacrificed her life to get her son out of Cuba, and he should stay put.

The case exploded early in 2000 when the INS ruled his father had custody. This meant Elian would be returned to Cuba. What followed was five months of court battles, protests, and heated rhetoric on both sides. I thought the case belonged in a state family court, and at first the federal government agreed. However, Attorney General Janet Reno changed her mind, and it remained an issue for the federal government.

Nevertheless, the e-mails flowed into my in-box.

Subject: Did anyone ask?
Friday, January 07, 2000 07:54 a.m.
From: Michael J. Gibbons

Did anyone ask Elian where HE wanted to live? I know it's easy to forget the actual issue while tied up in rhetoric and red tape, but shouldn't this boy have had a major part in the decision? Why are we so worried about Cuba's opinion anyway? Are they really any major threat to us anymore. Does Fidel Castro still tell us what to do? Sorry; I hate rhetoric!

Thanks for listening;

Subject: Did anyone ask?
Friday, January 7, 2000 10:03 p.m.
From: Jeb Bush

Excellent question. I have been told that the boy wants to stay here with his relatives. I don't know that for a fact. I hope that a custody hearing would shed some light on this issue. You have hit the hammer on the head.

jeb Bush.

PS All i know is that when i see him on television, i want to hug him and tell him that many people love him.

Subject: Cuban Boy
Saturday, January 8, 2000 9:49 a.m.
From: Matt Conroy

Good for you to make an appeal to Janet Reno. I only wish I could believe it will do that little boy some good.

Clinton and Reno talk about law--what about one of the corner stones the foundation this country was founded on--freedom from oppression and tyranny?

Clinton and Reno talk about family values-since when has Fidel Castro given a damn about family values? Why don't we turn the table on Fidel and find the Dad a job, a home and request Fidel give the father his FREEDOM to come to Miami and join his son? Now that is compassion! Not returning a boy to a father the mother was running from in a communist country (not to mention dying in the process). I know you can't do that (or can you?)-- it is just a shame the President of the United States behaves like a spineless jerk, instead of acting like the leader of the free world. One of the presidential contenders on Russert[27] the other night, I think Hatch, said the boy is a human sacrifice from Bill Clinton to Fidel Castro--I think he is right.

I think a lot of people appreciate the fact you have tried to do something.

---

27 He is referring to the late Tim Russert, moderator of NBC's *Meet the Press.*

Keep up whatever pressure you can--maybe it will work? Good luck!!

Subject: Cuban Boy
Saturday, January 8, 2000 2:47 p.m.
From: **Jeb Bush**

thanks for writing. He should be given a custody hearing like anyone else. ONce that is decided, then a determination can be made about whether he should go back to Cuba. Like you, i believe his dad should come to the US given the extraordinary circumstances that got Elian to our country.

Jeb Bush

———

Subject: The new year; and Elian Gonzales
Saturday, January 8, 2000 9:24 a.m.
From: Jeff Pattinson

Elian Gonzalez: I have to tell you that I am very surprised and disappointed to see you weigh in on the side of trying to detain this child here, against the wishes of his father. In all respects (except perhaps political expediency, for which I have no time or inclination in such a case as this) you must know this is WRONG; and as a Christian and a strong 'family man', I fail to see how you could possibly attempt to justify your public position. THIS CHILD BELONGS WITH HIS FATHER AND THE SOONER HE'S RETURNED TO HIM, THE BETTER.

```
Subject: The new year; and Elian Gonzales
Saturday, January 8, 2000 2:53 p.m.
From: Jeb Bush
```

```
Jeff, thank you for writing.
```

```
Regarding Elian, would you say the same if a mom
tried to escape East Berlin with her six year old
child by climbing over the Berlin wall and was shot
and the boy made it across? Should that boy go back
to East Berlin without a hearing? That is what the
INS proposed and they did so against their own rules.
I am asking for a hearing in state court to determine
what is in the best interests of the child.…
```

```
Jeb
```

———

Elian was not the only controversy making headlines. On January 18 Senator Kendrick Meek and Representative Anthony Hill conducted a sit-in in Lieutenant Governor Frank Brogan's office—in the same suite of offices as mine—to protest the One Florida plan, which was about to go into effect. I was confident the initiative would expand opportunities for minorities to achieve success on their merits. Obviously not everyone agreed. The two legislators declared they would not leave until I rescinded the order. When word got out, about one hundred people joined them outside my office. Sometimes they sang "We Shall Overcome." A few managed to get inside and spent the night with the two senators on Frank's couch. After a very loud and disruptive twenty-four hours, I agreed that before proceeding with One Florida, we would have hearings in Miami, Tampa, and Tallahassee. I was confident One Florida was right for Florida, but I didn't want to ask police to end the sit-in. It was obvious I still had some convincing to do.

Subject: Affirmative Action
Wednesday, January 19, 2000 7:44 a.m.
From: Don Bowen

I was suprised to read this morning about the protest in your office suite. I know that you have a lot of resolve and support on your One Florida Initiative. Just wanted to reaffirm for you that there are many people and leaders in the black community who do "get it", who are not afraid of change, and who are willing to give your plan a chance. I wrote a column in the most recent Urban League newsletter which I will give to Windell Paige[28] which speaks to this issue. I will make sure you get a copy. I don't need to tell you…but hang tough anyway.

Subject: Affirmative Action
Wednesday, January 19, 2000 8:00 a.m.
From: Jeb Bush

thanks Don. I would love to see the newsletter. I am going to use this an opportunity to advance the cause of economic and education opportunity for African Americans and other minorities. We will keep you apprised. If you have any thoughts, please let me know.

Jeb Bush

---

28 I had just named Windell Paige head of the Florida Minority Business Advocacy and Assistance Office. Its mission was to increase diversity in state contracts.

Subject: The sit-in
Wednesday, January 19, 2000 5:45 p.m.
From: Mike Griffin[29]

I'm trying to understand what's happening there.

I know your intention with One Florida was sincerily intended to bring people together. But, given the events in the last 24 hours, I have to ask you if you have miscalculated on this issue. Is the racial divide in Florida even greater than you suspected? Did you move too fast?

If the purpose was to bring people together, how does what happened today fit within that goal?

The average Floridian likely isn't going to care about removing the reporters.…You're more popular than any newspaper.…But under these unusual circumstances, wouldn't it have been better to let them stay? It would have given Floridians a third party perspective of the 40-minute meeting you held with the lawmakers.

Subject: The sit-in
Wednesday, January 19, 2000 8:09 p.m.
From: Jeb Bush

Mike, the purpose of one florida is to increase minority purchasing opportunities and increase minority admissions to the university system. I intend to make that happen with the help of many people.

---

29 Mike Griffin was a reporter for the *Orlando Sentinel.*

I had more than one forty minute meeting and would not have been able to resolve this issue with 15 press people in the room. It was not a public meeting and the press did not have to be there.

jeb

_____

Subject: **AFFIRMATIVE ACTION**
Monday, January 24, 2000 9:50 a.m.
From: Marilyn and Charlie Waldron

REF.AFFIRMATIVE ACTION,YOU ARE ABSOLUTELY CORRECT WHEN YOU SAID RACIAL PREFERENCES DONT WORK.WE ARE COUNTING ON YOU NOT TO WAVER IN THE FACE OF THIS LAST DITCH CLINTONIAN ATTEMPT.THANK YOU FOR YOUR CONTINUED STRONG LEADERSHIP.

Subject: **AFFIRMATIVE ACTION**
Monday, January 24, 2000 1:13 p.m.
From: Jeb Bush

i will stay the course. We can achieve diversity and opportunity for people without discriminating by race or nationality.

Jeb Bush

_____

I should mention that at one point during the sit-in, I lost my temper. In the heat of the moment, and not knowing I was speaking into a live microphone, I asked a staffer to remove the reporters covering the sit-in. "Kick their asses out" were my exact words. I apologized the next day and made the point my mother would not have approved of my choice of words. In any event I should not have spoken in that way.

Subject: Society of Professional Journalists
Wednesday, January 26, 2000 9:26 p.m.
From: Chris Miller

There is no need for you to apologise to any reporter who was at the scene of the sit-in in the Lt. Governor's office. When journalists start behaving like professionals there will be enough time for apologies. Please continue with the policies you have been pursuing to date. You have my whole-hearted support.

Subject: Society of Professional Journalists
Thursday, January 27, 2000 9:11 p.m.
From: Jeb Bush

I apologized for the use of bad language and losing my temper. I did not apologize for asking them to be escorted out. Thanks for your support.

Jeb Bush

———

In the meantime I wanted to make sure One Florida would indeed help more than students when implemented. I was adamantly opposed to set-asides of any kind, but I was determined to expand the pool of minority businesses considered for state contracts. At the same time, I wanted to improve the state's outreach to those businesses. I knew we could do better. I sent this note to Tom McGurk, secretary of the Department of Management Services (DMS).

Subject: One Florida
Tuesday, February 1, 2000 9:11 p.m.
From: Jeb Bush

Tom - I'd like a personal update on the progress DMS
has made in implementing the contracting side of One
Florida. I know your staff prepared an implementation
plan, which was delivered to me today, but there
are many unanswered questions. Would you be able to
answer these questions by Thursday afternoon?

1. How are our agencies doing in certified minority
   business spending fiscal year-to-date? Are we on
   track to exceed last year's spending with certified
   businesses? What are we doing to ensure that we
   exceed last year's spending? I'd like an agency-
   by-agency analysis.

2. What support is DMS providing to agencies to
   increase their spending? How is it helping each
   agency to identify and pursue minority business
   spending opportunities? What are we doing to
   change the culture and mindset at the agencies?

3. When will all of the state's minority vendors be
   registered under our new registration system? I
   need a date certain. I thought this was to be done
   in Janauary.

4. How much will it cost to implement our new
   registration system? Who will pay the costs and
   how?

5. I know every agency has supplied DMS with a
   list of contracts coming up in the next 90 days.

What will DMS do with this information? What is the plan to convert this information into real opportunities and more contracts for minority businesses?

6. What has been done to pave the way for moving the Minority Business Office to DMS? Has sufficient office space been identified? What are we doing to recruit staff who have the matchmaking skills necessary to advance the new focus of the office?

7. I know legislation is needed to make the certification process easier and to include locally certified firms in the state database. Once this legislation passes and we have more state-certified firms, what is the plan to make sure these firms are actually used and don't just sit dormant in our database? How quickly will it take to get the local certified businesses into our system?

One Florida's successful implementation is very important to me. You and your department are on the front lines and I appreciate your leadership on this.

Jeb

The controversy surrounding One Florida didn't end with the sit-in. When the legislative session opened in the first week of March, an estimated ten thousand people marched on the capitol to protest the end of affirmative action. The critics who said we had moved too fast were right. I had failed to communicate the mission of One Florida to the people who would be affected the most. That was my failure.

Despite the unfortunate rollout of the plan, One Florida proved hugely successful. When I left office in 2007:

- *Minority enrollment in state universities had increased by 44 percent. African-American enrollment increased from 33,011 to 39,528 students, and Hispanic enrollment increased from 32,776 to 48,821 students.*
- *State spending with certified minority- and women-owned businesses hit a record $761.2 million. That was an increase of 189 percent since the 1998–1999 fiscal year.*

———

I received many heartbreaking e-mails while I was governor, but the one below was one of the sadder stories. All these years later, it's impossible not to wonder what happened to Virginia and her grandson. My staff shone when it came to outreach and follow-up, but more often than not people tended to get on with their lives, and we lost touch. There will be other similar e-mails in these pages where unfortunately we won't be able to give you the end of the story.

Subject: I am writing you in desperation
Monday, February 7, 2000 2:19 p.m.
From: Virginia

I'm just a parent seeking advice. Through my search, I was advised to contact you for advice.

I am writing you in desperation, with hopes that you might be able to advise me. For the past 39 years I have cared for my grandson, Errol who is autistic. His mother died the morning he was born. During his birth, she had suffered 3 cardiac arrests, causing deprivation of oxygen to the baby's brain. My son, the baby's father, abandoned all responsibility for the baby, leaving me and my husband to the task of raising him. Eventually we officially adopted Errol and raised him as our own.

Now, after nearly 40 years of raising him, I find that I simple cannot cope with the horrendous task of continuing his care. I am 80 years old. My husband is very ill, in the advanced stages of Parkinson's Disease. I am not only caring for Errol with his terrible disability (Autism), but I am also the sole caretaker of my husband. I am just physically and mentally drained.

I wonder if you could direct me to some type of group home, or other facility for a man with Autism, where he would be cared for properly. I love Errol, but I know that I will not be around forever, and he will need to be placed in a home where he will not be just "warehoused" or neglected or abused. If you know of an istitution that specificly cares for Autistic individuals, that will take his Social Security Suplemental Income, and his Medicare, I'd be so grateful if you would let me know.

We live in South Daytona, Florida. If Errol could be placed somewhere in the South end of Florida, it would be ideal, as I plan to move south to be near my daughter who lives in Ft. Lauderdale soon. This way we would be near Errol and able to visit Him regularly. I don't know where to begin my search for a list of homes. Could you please help me if you know of some?

Subject: I am writing you in desperation
Monday, February 7, 2000 3:10 p.m.
From: Jeb Bush

Yes, i will try to help. I first want to tell you
how much I admire families and loved ones who take
care of special people like Errol. We are committed
to providing more support than used to exist (a 60%
increase in the last two years) so I hope we can be
of help.

I am sending this to kate Kearney and asking her
to get someone from your area to contact you to
see what can be done. Kate is the head of the
Department of Children and Families, the department
which provides services for the developmentally
disabled.

Do you have a phone number?

Jeb Bush

PS Please email me anytime.

———

I sent this e-mail to Steve Case, the founder and CEO of America Online (better known as AOL). I invited him to be part of my State of the State speech. He said yes and was terrific.

Subject: a favor
Saturday, February 12, 2000 10:42 a.m.
From: Jeb Bush

This may be out of line but I was wondering if you
could go on film for thirty seconds to a minute to

explain the importance of Florida's state government
embracing technology to serve its citizens and
creating fertile ground for the new economy. I am
giving my state of the state speech on March 7th and
I would like to include four or five people via video
as part of the speech. One would be an adult with
developmental disabilities, another a single mom
whose two children go to a new school because of our
A Plus plan and another would be a person pleased
that we are committed to building more roads. We
would get a film crew to film you at your convinience.

I understand if you can't do it, but it would be a
great help in my quest to get our state prepared for
the exciting changes in which we are living.

Jeb

————

*Capital punishment is a tough issue for any governor. Nobody
wants to be responsible for deciding whether someone lives or
dies. However, my Catholic faith made my decisions even more
complicated. In this e-mail to a constituent, I thought it was
important to explain my position from the perspective of both the
law I was sworn to uphold and my personal faith.*

Subject: Death Penalty & Catholicism
Thursday, February 3, 2000 8:30 p.m.
From: Connie Barron

First, let me congratulate on your governorship. I
was in Florida visiting my dad when you first ran for
office, and followed the election when I returned home
to Indiana. I now am a resident of Florida and had
the pleasure of casting my vote for you this time.

As an RCIA[30] candidate at St. Cecilia's in Ft. Myers, I am approaching my confirmation and official acceptance into the Catholic faith. It's been a long journey back, but I have arrived to my God's doorstep.

I know you converted to Catholicism, and I have to wonder how you have resolved in your mind the Catholic teachings of "right-to-life" with the political realities of the death penalty here in Florida. I realize that Cardinal Bernadin made the issue simple by explaining that every life has an "intrinsic value." But it's hard sometimes to see that value in a person who has taken the life of another human being, or in some cases, several human beings.

How do you make the decision between following the path of least political resistance or adhering to the teachings of your Catholic faith? If God's teachings, according to the Catholic religion, say that no person has the right to take the life of another, how can you, as a true Catholic and not a governor, not follow those teachings? (I'm not being critical… just asking.) And if you truly believe in your faith, how could you sign a bill that reduced the appeals process in order to expedite these executions? Yes, that was a politically popular decision (and I have been close to politics for many years -- I worked for Mayor Goldsmith for three years in the Public Information field and do the same work down here in the City of Cape Coral). But it just appears that you closed your eyes to your faith to further your political ambitions. As someone in the RCIA process,

---

30 Rite of Christian Initiation of Adults is a process through which adults are received into the Catholic Church.

that disappoints me. My faith has to be the highest priority in my life, and if I'm not going to embrace the religion and its teachings, and live those teachings, then why should I bother?

Subject: Death Penalty & Catholicism
Saturday, February 19, 2000 9:33 p.m.
From: Jeb Bush

First and foremost, let me apologize for not responding to you sooner. If you have been reading the paper, you know that I have been a little busy!

Secondly, congratulations on your decision to seek to become a Catholic. In 1993, I promised myself and my wife that I would take your same RCIA journey after the election in 1994 win or lose. I lost, and I now know that God had a plan for me that included my conversion to Catholicism. My faith has been strengthened because of this journey and I am thankful to God for the chance to serve Him.

I am at peace with my decision to ask the legislature to reform the incredible delays in the appeals process. It should not take 20 years to implement the death penalty in our State. Our plan will shorten the sentence of people who should not be sentenced to death in the first place.

The death penalty has become a big deal over the last year for a variety of reasons. That heightened awareness has given me a chance to reflect on my views and feelings in a deep and profound way. Signing a death warrant is not an easy thing to do. Calling the Warden of the Florida State Prison when someone is to be executed is the most difficult thing I have done as Governor. This is an issue of great personal importance to me both in a public policy context and, more significantly, in a moral context given my beliefs about the sanctity of life and my Catholicism.

I am aware that many spiritual leaders, including the Pope, have called for the abolition of the death penalty and that 10 states have abolished capital punishment. However, any many years of deliberation on this subject, I am also convinced that Florida's capital punishment law is just because it is applied so rarely and only in the most horrific cases. I have not reached this conclusion with any personal pleasure or satisfaction, but with a deep sense of humility and understanding that reasonable people may disagree, and in fact, be correct in their beliefs.

According to the Catechism of the Catholic Church, preserving the common good of society requires rendering the aggressor unable to inflict harm. While the Catechism states that bloodless means are preferred to defend human lives and protect public order, it also says that "the traditional teaching of the Church has acknowledged as well-founded the right and duty of legitimate public authority to punish malefactors by means of penalties commensurate with the gravity of the crime, not excluding, in cases of extreme gravity, the death penalty."

After briefly reviewing state records, I found that in 1996, there were more than 1,000 people murdered in the State of Florida, with 985 persons arrested for murder. Only 25 capital criminals were sentenced to death in 1996, and significantly, only 2 convicted criminals were actually put to death.

While the issue is so delicate, these numbers suggest to me that Florida law has been very carefully developed to ensure that the death penalty is applied very sparingly and only in cases of extreme gravity. I suspect that are those in my faith who will disagree with this interpretation, and I solemnly respect and value their opinions. I take very seriously my belief in the sanctity of life and any decisions that I may have to make relating to capital punishment will be exerted with great weight on my heart and soul, both as a public servant and as a human being.

Connie, one of the great joys of my life was my conversion to the Roman Catholic Church. It added a dimension to my life that was lacking. I encourage you to learn of the great mysteries of the Church. The Easter Sabbath will be one of the most important days of your life.

Respectfully,

Jeb Bush

———

I do not think of myself as a micromanager. I hope I'm not, since it's not a style I admire. However, I did enjoy being a hands-on governor. I found that reading about what was happening in Floridians' classrooms, in their neighborhoods, and in their homes was extraordinarily helpful and inspiring.

Sometimes hearing what people worried about was just plain interesting.

Subject: Hang Tough
Monday, March 6, 2000 8:31 a.m.
From: Frank and Ruth Montelione

Are you aware of the unisex rest rooms (called family rest rooms) at the rest stop on I 10 just west of I 75? Not a good message for a moral Florida.

Subject: Hang Tough
Wednesday, March 8, 2000 8:20 p.m.
From: Jeb Bush

No I am not aware of unisex bathrooms at the rest stops. I will check into it.

Jeb Bush

———

I asked Tom Barry, secretary of the Department Transportation, to explain the issue of unisex bathrooms.

Subject: Family Restrooms at Interstate Rest Areas
Thursday, March 9, 2000 1:56 p.m.
From: Tom Barry

We have what we call family restrooms at our rest areas. They are designed primarily for physically disabled users, but are also used by families traveling with small children. We were made aware a number of years ago about situations where travelers of opposite sexes may be using our facilities. If one

was disabled, it was difficult for their companion to
assist them in a discrete manner. The solution was
these family restrooms.

The sign on the door has the symbol for a man, a
woman, and the wheelchair symbol for the physically
disabled. Newer signs also have the words "Family
Restroom" on them. In the restroom are full disabled
access facilities as well as diaper changing tables.

------

*Our team was very disappointed on March 14. A local Tallahassee
judge ruled tax dollars could not be used to fund Opportunity
Scholarships for students whose schools had received a grade
of F. We immediately appealed the ruling, which began several
years of courtroom battles over the program.*

Subject: Opportunity Scholarships
Wednesday, March 15, 2000 8:50 a.m.
From: Sandy Faulkner

I was disappointed to hear about the ruling regarding
opportunity scholarships/vouchers. As you know, I
have always been an ardent supporter of vouchers
and will do whatever I can to help restore this
opportunity to our children. I had hoped that all
children would have this chance, but I felt that the
current method was a step in the right direction, and
am discouraged by this setback.

I can only imagine how bad an "F" school must be. I
removed my daughter Lisa from a "B" school because I
felt she wasn't getting an adequate or appropriate
education. We chose home school as our alternative.

Once we began I was shocked that a child who
had received all "A's" in a 6th grade Honors
Language Arts class couldn't distingquish between
an adjective and an adverb, couldn't identify
a prepositional phrase, and difficulty with some
reading. Added to that, I realized that she couldn't
identify the capitals of our states, and lacked
a basic understanding of the history, geography,
and government of the USA. I am still amazed that
without this basic knowledge, this child received an
"A" for her final grade in all subjects in the 6th
grade.

I absolutely agree with you that no child should have
to attend one of these failing schools. Please let me
know what I can do to help.

If it becomes necessary to raise private funds to
protect the children already in the private schools,
count on me for a donation. While I cannot donate a
lot, I will definately give to the best of my ability.
Every child deserves the opportunity to achieve to
the best of their personal ability.

Jeb, I can't thank you enough for staying the
course you promised us during your campaign.
The past 8 yrs have made it so difficult to have
faith in our government and our leaders, but your
continued efforts to move forward with your ideas is
helping restore it. Keep the faith -- our country
needs you.

Subject: Opportunity Scholarships
Saturday, March 18, 2000 6:32 p.m.
From: Jeb Bush

Thanks, Sandy, for your uplifting email. I get tired and depressed sometimes with the struggle. Then, I read an email or get a call or meet someone who lifts my spirits. We are on the right track. I really believe it.

Yes, we will need to raise money for all the parents and children who would have gotten an opportunity to choose after being in a f rated school for two years. If you have any thoughts how we can make this a movement for fairness, equity and a moral imperative, I would love to hear from you.

It was great seeing you last Sunday. Your precious older daughter has grown up! Wow!

———

This note came from a state legislator.

Subject: Opportunity Scholarship Program Ruling
Wednesday, March 15, 2000 6:29 a.m.
From: Mike Fasano

It's sad Governor when the wishes of the people of our state are ignored and in fact overturned by a judge. I am confident that you and the vast majority of the people of this state will prevail - b/c what you are doing for the children of Florida is the right thing to do!

I heard on the radio this morning you were going to raise funds privately to help pay for the children's schooling in the Panhandle who are taking advantage of the Opportunity Scholarship. I will be glad to

assist in anyway I can. In fact, if the Lord keeps an
opponent out of my race this year, you are more than
welcome to use some of our unused campaign dollars to
assist those students.

Keep up the good work my friend and FIGHT ON!!
God bless.

Subject: Opportunity Scholarship Program Ruling
Monday, March 20, 2000 9:39 a.m.
From: Jeb Bush

**Mike, thanks for your email. We will need some
private money to sustain the program through the
court case and your offer is great!**

**Subject: Opportunity Schlorships and Judicial
Activism**
Monday, March 20, 2000 3:51 p.m.
From: David Biddulph[31]

Last week I was asked at Grover's[32] meeting of some
50 conservative organizations how our governor was
doing. I stated, "In my opinion Florida has the
best governor in the country. Leading the country
with Opportunity Scholarships, fighting to have a
real death penalty, cutting tax burdens, reforming
the tort system, and ending preferences. But, his
great reforms may be lost to judicial activism
as demonstrated by the recent judicial decision

---

31 David Biddulph was an antitax activist from Volusia County.
32 Grover Norquist, the founder and president of Americans for Tax
Reform.

potentially ending Florida's great Opportunity
Scholarship program."

Are you considering a constitutional amendment
this term that would "inoculate" the Opportunity
Scholarship against the likely adverse Supreme Court
decision?

Also, should citizens be able to recall judges in
Florida to curb judicial activism?
Is it acceptable to you to win the battle of
reforming public policy and than lose the war to
judicial activists? Isn't it time that judges be
held accountable to the people for interpreting
the law as it was intended by our elected
representatives and the constitution as it was
intended by its ratifiers?

Keep up the good work. We live in a great
state with great elected representatives. All we need
now are judges who understand that making public
policy is not in their job description.

**Subject: Opportunity Schlorships and Judicial
Activism
Monday, March 20, 2000 10:50 p.m.
From: Jeb Bush**

**thanks Dave. I have to admit that I am frustrated but
still respectful of the judiciary.**

Jeb

PS I hope you are doing well.

———

Funding for the scholarships stayed in place until the Florida Supreme Court struck it down in 2006. Fortunately in 2001 we established the Florida Tax Credit Scholarship program, which provides an income-tax credit to corporations that contribute money to scholarship funds. It has been enormously successful. In 2015 69,846 students received these scholarships, making it the largest voucher program in the nation. Another 29,776 students are on scholarships through the McKay Scholarships for Students with Disabilities Program,[33] which gives students with special needs the opportunity to attend private or public schools of their choice.

Although I disagreed with the court's decision, the private sector stepped up to the plate to keep scholarship opportunities available for Florida's underserved students.

———

Sometimes the more mundane concerns were a relief. Did she inadvertently use the word "ribbing"?

Subject: proposed bill embarrases state
Friday, March 31, 2000 7:31 p.m.
From: MARIAN BAILEY-GODOWN

a proposed bill by rep. george albright of ocala authorizing you to appoint a commissioner of barbecue makes florida look ridiculous. it has already gained national ribbing in the 3-27 issaue of nnewsweek. if it passes, i urge you to veto it.thank you for your consideration.

---

33 The state legislature enacted the McKay Scholarship Program in 1999. I don't think the courts wanted to mess with a program for students with disabilities, so that funding stayed and remains in place. It was named for then Senate President John McKay. He has a disabled daughter and in many ways was the godfather of this program.

Subject: proposed bill embarrases state
Friday, March 31, 2000 8:39 p.m.
From: Jeb Bush

don't fret about this. it will not pass.

Jeb

———

Subject: THE AMERICAN LANGUAGE
Thursday, March 30, 2000 9:55 a.m.
From: CRYSTAL C CHEVELIER

YOU MAY HAVE IMPRESSED SOME VOTERS AT YOUR ST.
PATRICK'S DAY APPEARANCE BY SPEAKING SPANISH TO THE
GROUP OF SPANISH-SPEAKING FARM WORKERS. HOWEVER,
AS REPORTED IN FLORIDA TODAY: QUOTE: "I WAS VERY
HAPPY TO HAVE DONE THE INTERVIEW WITH LUCAS[34] AND HIS
COLLEAGUES IN SPANISH BECAUSE I HAD THE CONFIDENCE
OF KNOWING THAT NO ONE IN THE PRESS UNDERSTOOD A
SINGLE WORD OF THE CONVERSATION. YOU HAVE NO IDEA HOW
LIBERATED THAT MADE MEFEEL," HESAID.

WELL, WE'RE HAPPY IT MADE YOU FEELS SO GOOD. BUT
LET ME ASK YOU THIS, WE ASSUME THESE FARM WORKERS
ARE ALL AMERICAN CITIZENS? THEN, WHY ARE THEY NOT
USING THE NUMBER 1 AMERICAN LANGUAGE, WHICH IS
ENGLISH? THE MERE FACT THAT THEY HAVE COME TO OUR
BEAUTIFUL COUNTRY SHOULD SET OFF A BURNING DESIREAND
A MOTIVATION TO SPEAK ENGLISH AND LIVE UNDER THE
AMERICAN RULE OF LAW, AND CERTAINLY NOT BE ENCOURAGED
TO DO OTHERWISE. OUR ANCESTORS WERE REQUIRED TO LEARN
ENGLISH AS A NUMBER 1 PRIORITY UPON ARRIVAL IN THIS

---

34 Lucas Benitez is the founder of the Coalition of Immokalee Workers.

WONDERFUL COUNTRY, AMERICA. ARE WE CHANGING THE RULES FOR A FEW NOW?? OR IS THERE ANOTHER MOTIVE???

Subject: THE AMERICAN LANGUAGE
Saturday, April 1, 2000 9:20 p.m.
From: Jeb Bush

Thanks for writing.

The quote was a joke. Didn't the reporter report it as such since it was on him?

I believe that the men that came to see me were legal residents. As such they had the right to see their governor. I spoke spanish with them because I am fluent in the language and they are more comfortable in Spanish. Most of them spoke english as well.

I hope this clarifies what happened.

Jeb Bush

———

No. We could not solve every single problem of every Floridian, but we loved trying.

Subject: Federally Backed School Loan
Tuesday, April 11, 2000 12:29 p.m.
From: Karan Lee Freeman

Back in 1977 or 78, i took out the first of several Federally backed college loans from a now defunct bank in Miami. After defaulting briefly, I finally

paid these loans off in (i believe the year was) 1986.
Now, 14 years later, I am receiving a bill from a
collection agency for $25,000 in penalties & late
fees. Without cancelled checks proving i've paid
these loans off, "they" (a collection agency on behalf
of the US Dept of Education) say I owe them the money
and have threatened to lien bank accounts/ property,
etc.

When i have asked to speak with someone directly
at the Department of Eductation, I am told that
"they" are the ones responsible for handling the
account & that there is no one at at the Dept. of
Ed. for me to speak with. All attempts to acquire
specific information regarding the loans, recorded
payments, etc. (from the collection agency) have
been rebuffed.

I am trying to locate any information i can regarding
anything that may have been recorded per these
loans and have contacted several banks i was dealing
with at the time as well as Dade County's Records
Management Dept. to that end. Thus far, i have turned
up empty handed. Banks don't keep these records for
so long & i don't have account numbers, etc. from so
far back.

I cannot believe that in 14 years no one has tried
to contact me about this & now, all of a sudden they
expect me to come up with cancelled checks, pay
$25,000 or have my credit & finances ruined. It sounds
like legalized extortion.

Outside of hiring expensive attourneys (i cannot
afford to do this), what are my options?

Subject: Federally Backed School Loan
Tuesday, April 11, 2000 9:54 p.m.
From: Jeb Bush

Jeez, if what you say is true, this is a little
scary. I will seek some guidance from our team and
someone will be back in touch.

Jeb Bush

————

I then sent this challenge to some of my top staff.

Subject: Federally Backed School Loan
Tuesday, April 11, 2000 9:57 p.m.
From: Jeb Bush

Every state employee should help a citizen a week,
minimum. Here is one of your chances. How can this
be? How can we help Karen Lee Freeman? Let me know.

Jeb

————

*The fate of Elian Gonzalez was still being debated in the courts,
in the media, and on the streets of Miami and Havana. This
inquiry came from a former Florida reporter who was with*
Congressional Quarterly *when he wrote this e-mail. Now he is
with the* Washington Post.

Subject: cubans
Monday, April 3, 2000 2:44 p.m.
From: Peter Wallsten

I'm plugging away here at CQ, trying to come up
with unique angles on national politics. This is an
interesting year in Washington, what with the control
of the House hinging on just a few races.

Thought that, if you had a couple of minutes, you
could add something to a piece I'm doing this week on
the role that Cuban-Americans will play in state and
national elections this year.

I'm exploriung: How does such a small group have
maintain such a loud, unified voice? In addition to
Elian, what issues remain vital to that community? Is
there now some support for lifting certain elements
of the embargo, such as food sales?

Just as Democrats are divided over these issues, it
seems that Republicans in Congress are not unified on
Cuba. Some, such as Sen. Hagel, support loosening the
embargo. Some, such as Rep. Steve Largent, want to
send Elian back to Cuba.

Do you have any thoughts on these issues? I ask you
not as the brother of the presidential nominee, but
as the governor of Florida. I would really appreciate
anything you could add.

Again, I hope you are doing well. Please give my
regards to Lt. Gov. Brogan.

Subject: cubans
Monday, April 3, 2000 10:29 p.m.
From: Jeb Bush

Peter, my thoughts are that this should not be looked at from a political perspective. Or at least, we should look at Elian from the perpestive of what is in his best interest. Janet Reno and I presume President Clinton are rigidly clinging to the law in this instance. But the fact is that the law gives the INS enormous discretion on these matters and administrations have used that discretion in the past. Why not now?

Elian disserves a custody hearing. Such a hearing was what the INS was prepared to give until the big feet from DC decided to overrule that position. What a shame since we would not be discussing little Elian if the initial policy was kept.

This is what I believe. I believe it from the bottom of my heart. Elian should not be on ABC. Elian should not be the subject of yet another Castro imposed rally. Elian should not a tool of politics in Miami. He is a six year old child who has lost his mom seeking freedom and we should be more respectful of that.

Jeb Bush

————

In a predawn raid on April 22, armed federal agents entered the home of Elian's relatives, removed him from the home at rifle-point, and returned him to his father, who had arrived in Miami on April 6. This e-mail also went to our two Florida US senators, Bob Graham and Connie Mack.

Subject: Cuban Anarchy
Sunday, April 23, 2000 4:08 p.m.
From: Brigadier General and Mrs. Fred L. Knight

The media is aiding and abetting Cuban Anarchy in America. These people from Miami do not speak English, fly the Cuban flag and break the laws of their host country. The media is having a feeding frenzy over a subject that deserves no more than a mention in the back pages. We have become the laughing stock of the world over this. We have received letters from friends from India, Australia, Europe and Qatar etc. who are appalled that we allow these outlaws to make their own laws and given all the free publicity they want 24 hours a day. The media is salivating over every crumb of this disgusting story. Everyone who is involved in giving voice and camera/newspaper/magaine time to these people should be ashamed!!! One oasis in media madness. Washington Week in Review on PBS did NOT mention the Elian subject ONE time on their Friday April 21 program. They have been commended by us for sanity in the midst of madness. Comments made today in our Sarasota Herald Tribune by Governor Bush and Senator Mack did not surprise us but we find it very disappointing that you two have joined the enemies of democracy and condone their illegal behavior. A sad day in Florida history

Please don't continue to pander to these people just for votes. They are trying to take over our state with their lawlessness. Where will it stop? They have a war to fight. Let them go home and fight it in Cuba!!! They aren't Cuban Americans…they are Cubans, first last and always and they are using their freedom in the worst possible way.

P.S. For heaven's sake don't send us one of those thank you for you comments letters/emails. We know you aren't going to read this or care if you did read it. So save your time.

Subject: Cuban Anarchy
Sunday, April 23, 2000 7:36 p.m.
From: Jeb Bush

this is Jeb Bush and I am not writing you to give you a formal "thank you for writing" email.

I thank you for writing but respectfully disagree with you on the matter of Elian. I am from Miami and I have worked and lived with Cuban Americans. They are, in their great majority, god fearing, patriotic Americans who I would imagine share your values. Many have served in the military of our country. They don't break the laws of our great country. Please don't fall prey to the national media stereotype of this group since it is not monolithic.

As it relates to Elian, I find it shameful that US Marshalls entered into the home as though this child was a hostage. It was not necessary and a peaceful less traumatic solution was within the grasp of the mediator. Atty General Reno was not truthful with the folks she agreed should act as intermediaries.

Again, I appreciate your writing and I hope you have a joyous Easter.

Jeb Bush

———

Subject: elian case for Miami Herald story
Wednesday, April 26, 2000 6:00 p.m.
From: Manny Garcia

Manny Garcia here from The Miami Herald. I'm working on a story about the Elian negotiations and my colleague Steve Bousquet said I should email you.

I know you spoke with President Clinton last Friday at 7 p.m. to discuss the Elian case, and I wanted to find out more about that conversation.

My questions are:

1) A federal judge signed a search warrant at 7:20 p.m. Friday to enter Elian's house.
2) Were you aware of this?
3) Did the President Clinton mention the warrant or any discussion about using force to remove Elian?
4) What did President Clinton say about trying to come up with a peaceful settlement?
5) It seems President Clinton was well aware of the negotiations that were going at the time involving Aaron Podhurst et al. What did the president say about these negotiations?
6) What were your feelings about the negotiations?
7) Did you talk to the Miami lawyers and/or representatives for the Miami family about the

negotiations? And what did they tell you? Were you under the impression - if you know - that any deal required the Miami family to hand custody of Elian to his father? Did the Miami representatives make that clear to you?

8) Did Eric Holder[35] from Justice tell you that they were going into the house when he first call you?

9) Finally, now that all is said and done and you can reflect back on everything that happened? Have you come up with any conclusions about what went wrong? Also, if there is anything I have forgotten to ask and you feel is relevant that I know, please let me know.

Subject: elian case for Miami Herald story
Wednesday, April 26, 2000 8:48 p.m.
From: Jeb Bush

1 and 2: No I was not aware of the search warrant. In addition, I might have spoken to president Clinton at 8 rather than 7. That was an estimation.

3 and 4 and 5: No he didn't mention it. He stated that they were trying to reach an agreement with the mediators and it looked pretty good that an agreement would be reached. The President did not mention names of who was involved.

6) The purpose of my call was to encourage mediation as was suggested by the Federal Appellate Court.

---

35 In 2000 Eric Holder was US deputy attorney general. In 2009 President Obama appointed him attorney general.

7) I spoke to Kendall Coffey and Jose Garcia Pedrosa[36] regarding the issue and they said that there was significant progress made. When I said I was going to speak to President Clinton, they encouraged me to do so. They thought the areas of disagreement were minor and that a deal could be reached.

8) No, the first time that Eric Holder called me, which was from 5:00 to 5:10 am; he said that the AG had mobilized the agents but not given the final order. He said that there were negotiations underway that were encouraging.

Jeb Bush

———

Subject: [None]
Tuesday, April 25, 2000 5:49 p.m.
From: Jackie

HELLO MY NAME IS JACKIE. I AM 11 YEARS OLD.IM JENNIFERS SISTER.ADREANNA IS MY COUSIN.ANYWAY.WHAT I SAW ON THE NEWS WITH ELIAN WAS NOT TO HAPPY. FOR ME THAT WAS A DISGRACE AND THERE COULD'VE BEEN LESS COMMOTION.I THINK JANET R. COULD HAVE THOUGHT A LITTLE HARDER ALL SHE NEEDED TO USE WAS 50 PERCENT OF HER BRAIN.I THINK IF THAT WAS ME I WOULD HAVE DIDED I AM SORRY .

JACKIE

---

36 Kendall Coffey and Jose Garcia Pedrosa were attorneys for Elian's Miami relatives.

Subject: [None]
Saturday, April 29, 2000 3:27 p.m.
From: Jeb Bush

Thanks Jackie. I agree with you on how Washington has handled the Elian case. It is very disappointing and now we have many people hurting and many wounds to heal.

Jeb Bush

———

Back to the business of the state, which in springtime centered on the closing weeks of the legislative session. The opinions, advice, and pleas were pouring into my in-box.

Subject: so called tax break??
Wednesday, May 03, 2000 12:32 a.m.
From: Keith A. Green

I will address this to you since you have final say on these kinds of breaks? I seen on the evening news that AGAIN the Legislature has made the proposal to give special sales tax relief to the Parents to help them to buy school clothes for the CHILDREN! Why is my question is it that only PARENTS get this special legislation? I thought that if there was a surplus in State revenue all people who pay sales tax should enjoy relief. Nor only PARENTS. I cannot see where this is anything but a ploy to curry favor with the PARENTS who seem to enjoy some special consideration in the Florida Constitution that Legislators know about but anyone else who reads it can't see. What happened to equality, one man one vote etc. Being a Senior I don't have that much cash to buy $400.00 or more in clothes in August! Where is the standard of equal justice for all. Why not send a check for $25.00 or whatever is determined to be fair and send it out to all loridians? Or is it just good publicity to say here is a tax break & when you really know the majority will not benefit!! But the special few get another favor! Who decides to have CHILDREN ? Why does that qualify a person for special treatment under a supposedly equal rights & opportunity Government? Is this stud fees? You should not have CHILDREN if you can't afford to provide for them. Why not a tax break on Dog food Or car parts or soda or medicine? I really don't see where this tax break is Constitutionally legal. Isn't this outright discrimination?

Subject: so called tax break??
Wednesday, May 3, 2000 9:42 p.m.
From: Jeb Bush

Mr. Green, I support tax relief that is broad. The irony is that when proposed, the liberals then say that the amount is not enough to make a difference. So, the legislature migrates to the targeted relief efforts. My view is that we should strive to give back to the taxpayers monies when times are good. It starts adding up after $6 billion over four years which is where we are now with this year's budget.

Thanks for writing.

Jeb Bush

Subject: Legislative session
Tuesday, May 9, 2000 4:18 p.m.
From: Dr E. T. York

This is a communication that I would normally not
send to the Governor, but I send it to you, a person
I have developed great respect for in the six years
or so that I have known you.

In the beginning, let me apologize if this offends
you, but at times a person in your position needs
to receive the very candid views of friends and
supporters who are outside the ?palace guard,? and who
are willing to provide you their honest opinions.…

I am genuinely concerned, however, over what has
transpired in the past legislative session, led by
Republican legislators and supported, in the main,
by a Republican governor. I have heard many say that
this was the worst, most mean spirited Legislature in
our state?s history.

A state newspaper referred to the fact that this
Republican Legislature spent money like ?a bunch of
drunken sailors.? In fact, I have never seen more
irresponsible spending by any Legislature before.
This has included support for every kind of ?turkey?
imaginable, including $15 million in start-up money
for the Florida Center for Arts and Education in
Orlando which was a special interest of the President
of the Senate. This also included a $50 million
initial expenditure for John Thrasher?s college of

medicine at his alma mater, FSU, which has been his announced priority for the last two years.…

The big question that many are raising is why did the Governor allow all of this to happen.

And, of course, a big concern that people all over the state have had is a move to abolish the Regents, supported by both houses of the Legislature and, apparently, supported by the Governor. In my 37 years in Florida I have never seen an important piece of legislation pushed through the Legislature and endorsed by the Governor with essentially no hearings or input from the public of any kind. This proposal has been thoroughly condemned by every major newspaper in the state, liberal and conservative, by all ten university presidents and by many other prominent citizens of Florida. And to date, nobody has indicated what is wrong with our current governance system that would be fixed by this legislation. Apparently, the only ones pushing this legislation were those legislators who were mad with the Chancellor and the Regents for opposing some special project they favored.…

Certainly you can exercise your veto power to get rid of the most ?turkeys? that I have ever seen in an appropriation bill. To do so would be consistent with good, conservative, Republican philosophy. Although you said publicly that you would allow the education reorganization bill to become law, I urge you to reconsider and veto this bad legislation. There is likely to be a successful challenge of the constitutionality of this legislation. There is still

adequate time to develop a ?seamless? organizational
plan for education in the next Legislature without
this very undesirable provision relating to
university governance.

Let me assure you, Jeb, that I write you as a friend
and strong supporter who wants nothing but the best
for you, your brother George and the Republican Party.

Subject: Legislative session
Saturday, May 13, 2000 4:42 p.m.
From: Jeb Bush

Thanks Dr. York, for your email. I am not offended
by the content of your letter and appreciate your
writing it. It has given me the opportunity to clear
up some misunderstandings and to concur with some of
what you wrote.

First, let me give you some of the good news of this
legislative session.

- K—12 Public education received over a 8% increase
  in funding. Teachers will receive more training and
  significant bonuses for serving in underperforming
  schools and in shortage areas. Accountability
  was maintained in spite of efforts of the loyal
  opposition to eliminate consequences from results.
- Universities received a 10% increase. (there
  was an explosion of capital outlay dollars not
  included in that amount but I will have the
  opportunity to veto part of that)
- Social services such as Kid Care, Developmental
  Disabilities and our Child Welfare system received
  20% + increases. As Republicans we can be proud

that services that have languished for the truly
needy are no longer in the back of the line.

- We created a reserve so that the surplus of the
Florida Retirement System can't be taken down too
fast. This was a hugely important accomplishment
since it will allow future policy makers needed
flexibility.
- We now have a Defined Contribution alternative for
state workers.
- We now are in the process to securitize the $450
million of payments from the tobacco settlement so
the state is not dependent or vulnerable to the
financial status of a handful of tobacco companies.
- We were allowed to reorganize outmoded departments
and use technology more effectively.
- We passed historic Everglades legislation, funded
it historically and also funding a major increase
in water projects across the state. These efforts
will do much to protect our state's heritage and
long term economic development future.
- we passed Mobility 2000 which speeds up many
bottleneck road projects.
- Florida now has the toughest statewide building
code in the nation but also the efficiency that
comes from one code.
- We have dramatically altered our workforce
development organizational structure to
significantly better meet the needs of business.
- We cut taxes by $500 million. Over the four years
I will serve as Governor, our cummulative tax
relief now totals over $6 billion.

E.T., you didn't read much about the good things that
happened but believe me they did and it wasn't done in
a mean spirited way from what I could tell. When the

Democrats controlled the legislature and governor's office, they seldom did as much during a session.

On the medical school, $50 million is not being appropriated this year. It is much less than that. I believe there are pretty strict criteria that the med school must adhere to for it to make it into existance. I will support the law schools for the same reason.

On the education governance question, the Board of Regents and State Board of Community Colleges sunset in two years, they are not abolished. As you know, many institutions are reauthorized under the sunset review process and the work of the transition commission should not be prejudged by the opponents of the bill. I assure you that I will put men and women on the Commission of the highest caliber who will have an open mind about the best way to organize our education system for the new and exciting world we are moving toward. However, I will not be intimidated into defaulting to doing things the same way because we have been doing them that way without an honest review of the other possibilities.

Finally, you are correct about the spending habits of the legislature. It is my duty to continue to advocate for fiscal responsibility. I must admit that it is a tough part of my job but I accept the responsibility.

Thank you for writing. Please do so anytime. I respect you and look forward to a continuing dialogue.

Jeb Bush

PS I must also defend my friend John Thrasher[37]. He is a principled and courageous man.

———

I signed the new budget on May 30, which managed to fund all our top priorities—education, transportation, and programs for our underserved. At the same time, it gave Florida taxpayers a $500 million tax cut. "Veto Corleone" reappeared when I used the line-item veto to cut $313 million in "turkeys." The state reserve fund was at an all-time high: $2.9 billion. As I said at the signing, the new budget reinforced "my commitment to sound, conservative fiscal policy."

———

On May 26 a seventh-grade honors student at Lake Worth Middle School shot and killed a popular schoolteacher, Barry Grunow. In situations like this, there are no words that really can convey the depth of one's sorrow, but you have to try. Tena Pate sent me this note.

Subject: school teacher–Lake Worth Middle School
Saturday, May 27, 2000 12:16 p.m.
From: Tena Pate

I spoke with Barry Grunow's wife this a.m. Her name is Pamela. She is a former school teacher who quit teaching to stay home with her children (6 months and 5 years of age). Barry rode his bike to school/work so she could have the one family vehicle for her and the children during the day. They lived on one salary and according to family representative and school

---

37 At this time John Thrasher was speaker of the House. He's now the president of Florida State University.

secretary, they live a very non-materialistic/meager to moderate existence.

The school secretary says Barry was the kind of teacher who reported to work early and stayed late with his students who needed his extra attention. The school secretary, and of course Barry's wife, says he was a truly remarkable person always willing to help any student and that he was well-loved by the student body.

I spoke with the school resource officer, Matt Baxter, and a detective with the Lake Worth Police Department. Crisis response counselors are already on scene for students and faculty. I advised the victim's wife about crimes compensation to assist them with loss wages, burial expenses and crisis counseling for her and the kids. We will follow up with written information because I know she is likely to forget a lot of what I said.

I inquired from the school secretary how the student, Nathaniel Brazill, who did the shooting was doing and how his family was holding up. Not much was known. I have their phone number if anyone needs it. According to CNN reports, it is thought he used his grandfather's gun. From the reports at this time, everyone is saying Nathaniel was a good student and everyone is shocked he did this. He resides with his mother, step-father and a little sister. His mother's name is Polly Josie Whitefield. I have not talked to his family.

This is a serious case of secondary/vicarious victimization. The ripple effect will be felt for some time. I have no information on how the faculty is holding up but I do not counselors are on hand.

Subject: School teacher-Lake Worth Middle School
Monday, May 29, 2000 7:20 p.m.
From: Jeb Bush

i have spoken to the principal and to the wife. How sad. I told the wife of the murdered teacher that I would call her in a month to see how she was doing after the support had gone away. I wanted to help her since she and her husband made the noble commitment for one of them to be with their kids rather than work and it would not be fair to stop that now because of the murder. She was grateful for the call....

Jeb

———

Based on incoming e-mails, one of the most popular programs we got approved in the budget was Mobility 2000, which provided more than $4 billion for much-needed improvements to Florida's roads and bridges without raising taxes. It's been said my e-mail answers were sometimes succinct, so it should be no surprise I appreciated incoming e-mails that were the same.

Subject: Mobility 2000
Monday, June 12, 2000 5:52 p.m.
From: Matt Conroy

Wow--way to go. I just read about the Mobility 2000. Congratulations!! Keep on jamin' Jeb.

Subject: Mobility 2000
Monday, June 12, 2000 7:36 p.m.
From: Jeb Bush

i shall.

jeb

———

Although we carefully monitored our programs and initiatives after they were implemented to ensure they were getting the intended results, there was nothing quite like an e-mail from the field saying something we did was working.

In this case it was the 10-20-Life law. We had decided passing the law was not enough, and we launched a big public-service campaign. We went into the jails and interviewed inmates serving time. Between their powerful testimonials and the campaign's tag line—"use a gun and you're done"—the campaign had made an impression.

Subject: 10-20-Life Is Working
Wednesday, June 21, 2000 11:43 a.m.
From: Timothy C. Taylor, Sr.

Several Months ago, I was involved in a minor traffic accident. This young man scrapped my vehicle while driving rather reckless. He became so angry until he wanted to get physical.

After leaving the scene, he approached me again at a traffic light. The young man said that he was about to get his <u>gun</u> but he thought about the"**10-20-Life**" **law.** I told him that I commended Governor Bush for pushing such a law; which proves we don't need new

gun laws just enforce the ones we have on the books.
After talking with the young man about life, we
departed.

Governor, keep-up the good work.

Subject: 10-20-Life Is Working
Wednesday, June 21, 2000 9:45 p.m.
From: Jeb Bush

is this a true story? Wow!

Jeb Bush

Subject: 10-20-Life Is Working
Thursday, June 22, 2000 7:01 a.m.
From: Timothy C. Taylor, Sr.

sure is. as an ordained deacon and chairman of said
board, i wouldn't make it up. let's keep the governor
in office.

———

Here's another "report card" report.

Subject: You did two good things!
Tuesday, July 11, 2000 7:07 a.m.
From: Bea Fowler

1. 25% reduction in state employees in 5 years--
   (about time!)
2. Orlando Sentinel-July 11th editorial-- Educational
   progress--Florida fell mid range in the nation.
   (that's big improvement) Florida does a better job

than the nation in increasing the number of children in preschool. Also done well in setting standards.

Jeb, it's to your credit! You did it!

How do you feel about Florida leading the nation in education?

Subject: You did two good things!
Tuesday, July 11, 2000 7:46 a.m.
From: Jeb Bush

It is my aspiration.

Jeb

———

The 25 percent cut in the number of state employees prompted a reporter from the Florida Times-Union *to send this e-mail to Budget Director Donna Arduin.*

Subject: 25% cut in Govt
Monday, July 17, 2000 3:47 p.m.
From: [No name]

when you are budget director for the president in Bush Administration II, Jan. 21, 2009, i hope you will raise your sights and go for 50 percent instead of a paltry 25.

Donna forwarded the note to me, and I answered.

Subject: 25% cut in Govt
Monday, July 17, 2000 10:33 p.m.
From: Jeb Bush

Donna, I won't be President but you and I can cut 25% and we will if we are really smart about it.

Subject: 25% cut in Govt
Tuesday, July 18, 2000 4:47 p.m.
From: Donna Arduin

We can and we will!! We had an all day training session on the Long-Range Planning instructions for hundreds of agency staff today and I started them out with my cheerleader/inspirational/think-outside-the-box speech.…I thanked everyone on your behalf for going the extra mile to dramatically change the way we plan and provide information to policymakers and taxpayers.

Subject: 25% cut in Govt
Tuesday, July 18, 2000 10:22 p.m.
From: Jeb Bush

i am ready to do battle.

————

This inquiry came from a San Francisco Chronicle *reporter. I believe the son to whom she was referring was George P.*

Subject: quick questions for the E-governor
Monday, July 17, 2000 5:40 p.m.
From: Carla Marinucci

Nicolle Devinish[38] suggested I drop you a quick line in hopes of hearing your quick thoughts on the impact

---

38 Nicolle Devenish was the communications director for the Florida State Technology Office. You might know her as Nicolle Wallace, one of

of the Internet in politics -- and at the upcoming GOP Convention. Knowing that you've been dubbed the "E-governor," I'd like to understand how your own work in office, and outreach to voters, has changed with the Internet. Also, how much you use it daily, and for what (news, messaging constituents, political websites).

Finally, do you think the Internet Alley firms (like Nicolle's Grassroots.com) will change the way we in the "traditional" media cover what politicians do? Do they cover politics differently -- or better?

I know you're very busy, and even a few sentences would be much appreciated. The San Francisco Chronicle is the biggest paper covering Silicon Valley; I'm covering the presidential race and the conventions (your son is a BIG hit out here, in addition to his uncle), and I know our tech-savvy readers will love hearing from you on this.

Subject: quick questions for the E-governor
Tuesday, July 18, 2000 9:57 a.m.
From: Jeb Bush

Thanks Carla for writing.

The internet is reshaping everything in society so it should be no surprise that it is having an impact on politics. I am more focused on the use of the internet in role as Governor rather than candidate although we used the internet extensively in 1998.

---

the hosts of ABC's *The View.*

In my job, I receive about 300 emails a day and look at half of them and respond daily to over 100. As I write this, I am in Sao Paulo, Brazil[39] and have corresponded with my chief of staff, with about ten constituents, with my communications director and a variety of other folks this morning. The internet allows my to be incredibly more productive in pursuit of serving Florida.

We use the internet to communicate with thousands of Floridians on a regular basis. This helps us get our agenda in front of people in an direct and unbiased way.

The internet connects ordinary people to their governor. Those ordinary folks have extraordinary ideas and needs. I learn from them and seek their advice even if it comes in forms that sometimes is crude.

We are revolutionizing the use of technology in state government. This year we will have a single portal for citizens to access services. It is one of many initiatives we have undertaken to transform government into an enterprise focused on service. It is fun!

Jeb

PS I did not proof this since I have to go give a speech at the American Chamber of Commerce!

PPS Yes, my son is quite the star. I love him very much and am proud of him!

---

39 I was on a trade mission that proved very successful. It generated an estimated $65 million in sales from Florida to Brazil.

I agreed on a Saturday morning to participate in a "Bikes for Tykes" dunk-tank fund raiser. It was a nice change of pace.

Subject: dunking booth
Saturday, July 22, 2000 8:29 p.m.
From: Cynthia Byrd

In observing the dunking booth action at the Toys for Tots drive, I think the dunkees had the best deal. It was hot out there, and I imagine it got hotter before the end. I abandoned ship and headed into Lowe's to dream. I am preparing to add on a family room with adjoining bath and screened in porch, so have items to choose. I just wanted to let you know that it is refreshing to see a man who so easily communicates with children. Even when he is standing soaking wet in his clothes! I personally think you enjoyed the dunking part.

Subject: dunking booth
Saturday, July 22, 2000 8:35 p.m.
From: Jeb Bush

cynthia, if I could spend my entire time with kids, I would do so. I love children. I love their intelligence, their innocence, their humor and their funlovingness.

Thanks for coming by.

Jeb

Finally there was a report on the state website. On July 24 we broadcast live via the Internet and unveiled www.MyFlorida. com—a portal that would allow Floridians to access information on more than 150 state agencies on one website. Yes. I was excited. However, I was not completely satisfied.

Subject: MyFlorida.com
Monday, July 24, 2000 10:21 p.m.
From: Jim Grantham

Just wanted to drop you a line to say that I am
so glad that someone (YOU) finally created a portal.
My office has always wanted to create a one stop site
for citizens with access to any and all information
they may need. Both you and Roy[40] have my support
and I look forward to watching Florida grow into a
E-Government with access by all it's citizens.

Subject: MyFlorida.com
Tuesday, July 25, 2000 7:04 a.m.
From: Jeb Bush

**Jim, MyFlorida.com is work in progress. Let us know
how we can improve it.**

Jeb

————

The same day I was very excited to announce some preliminary results from One Florida. This included that fifteen state agencies had increased spending with minority businesses by more than 85 percent during the previous fiscal year. Overall, state spending with minority-owned businesses, including the noncertified ones,

---

40 Roy Cales was Florida's chief information officer.

totaled a record-breaking $1.03 billion. So why did I send this grumpy e-mail to my friend Florence Rivas? I had sent her a staff report about the almost nonexistent press coverage of the results.

Subject: AP
Wednesday, July 26, 2000 10:15 p.m.
From: Jeb Bush

this is so typical. I have given up worrying about it but thought you would be interested in knowing how an 85% increase in procurement in my departments is not worthy of news after all of the front page stories and editorial pontificating over the last months against what we were doing. It is hard not to be cynical about the "fairness" of the press.

It was wonderful seeing you today.

Jeb

Despite letting down Jimmy Buffett a year earlier, I was a big fan of the Florida manatees and wanted to make sure they were protected. We were planning the first ever Manatee Summit for October to discuss how to cut down on boat-related manatee deaths. In the meantime we were waging a public awareness campaign and asking boaters to observe the speed limit.

Subject: More bouquets!
Wednesday, July 26, 2000 3:01 p.m.
From: Richard Pettit

It is with TREMENDOUS DELIGHT I send yet another email to congratulate you for your courageous stand

for our manatees!! I have stood helpless many times
and watched as boats sped thru the Venice and Casey
Key jetties (where I have SEEN manatees present!)
with NO concern for anything but themselves and their
pleasure. (I have given a few THUMBS DOWN to their
thoughtless disregard for no wake rules). If we
turn down the requests for increasing the number of
marinas, I know that will certainly cut down on the
threats to manatees endangered by speeding boaters.
Thanks again for not allowing BIG MONEY to be the
bottom line in "all-things-Florida"!!!!

Subject: More bouquets!
Wednesday, July 26, 2000 9:56 p.m.
From: Jeb Bush

Thanks so much.

**We can have boaters and manatees enjoy our waters with
proper planning. I hope our actions at the Cabinet
will be able to be a catalyst for that to happen.**

Jeb Bush

I sent the exchange to staffers Tara Wainwright and Colleen Castille.

Subject: More bouquets!
Thursday, July 27, 2000 7:53 a.m.
From: Jeb Bush

**We need to have a meeting late next week. Friday
to be exact on our plan for the manatees. Can you
bring all of the players? I would like to discuss
the summit, the enforcement ideas, the psa plans,**

get briefed on each of the unfinished manatee plans, etc.

What say you, Tara and Colleen?

Jeb

———

Here is an exchange with St. Petersburg Times *reporter Howard Troxler, who had golf on his mind.*

Subject: In the 80s?
Friday, July 28, 2000 2:59 p.m.
From: Howard Troxler

High or low 80s?
No mulligans, one per side, or none?
Didn't you just start playing a couple of years ago?

Subject: In the 80s?
Friday, July 28, 2000 4:31 p.m.
From: Jeb Bush

I am a 10 handicap. Low 80s and high 80s. I started playing in earnest about 12 years ago. Jeez, I think I am going to launch an initiative so that idle SPTimes reporters get back to work and stop writing about golf.

Jeb Bush

———

Here's another "report card" e-mail that made my day—this one about the new state website. This e-mail actually came to Mike

Moore, head of the Department of Corrections, and he was good enough to share it with me.

Subject: My compliments
Tuesday, August 8, 2000 10:13 a.m.
From: Lisha

I reside in NC and have been using your website to track the release of my ex-husband so as to provide my 3 children with the information as well as to keep Child Support Enforcement informed. Your new 'supervised population' link has now enabled me to provide the CSE office with the ability to track his address and even enabled me to locate his PO. I have found it amazing that this public site has provided me with information that the CSE office was unable to obtain. Years of experience has taught me that without this kind of information, pursuit of child support arreage would be almost impossible. If this information has helped my situation, I can only imagine how this site has helped crime victims. I must commend the State of Florida and the Department of Corrections for making this information available to the public. I only wish more states would follow your lead. Thank you.

Subject: My compliments
Wednesday, August 9, 2000 7:35 a.m.
From: Mike Moore

Governor thought you would like to see this email. These types of comments make it all worth it.

———

I sent this note to all the agency heads. I was looking for good people just like them.

Subject: ten good men and women
Friday, August 11, 2000 8:05 a.m.
From: Jeb Bush

I would like you to come up with ten names of people
who would be ideal candidates to serve in Tallahassee.
I would appreciate a brief description of their
talents and what they would be suited for. They can be
capable of serving at all levels of government.

Can you get this done for me by the next agency head
meeting?

Thanks.

Jeb Bush

———

*My e-mail project with Brian Crowley had fallen by the wayside,
but we stayed in touch.*

Subject: hi
Wednesday, August 30, 2000 5:34 p.m.
From: Brian Crowley

So when I got done meeting with your brother in
Austin, as I was shaking his hand goodbye I asked him
with smile "so who got the better mansion?" He says
he hasn't spent much time at yours but he knows his
is more historic. (I guess Sam Houston does beat out
Claude Kirk[41]).

———

41 Claude Kirk served as Florida governor from 1967 to 1971. Sam
Houston was governor of Texas from 1859 to 1861.

I pointed out, however, that you have a pool and he doesn't.

"Really, well then he got the better deal."

Now if your brother wins the White House, I won't ask that question anymore.

Subject: hi
Wednesday, August 30, 2000 9:35 p.m.
From: Jeb Bush

you got that right.

———

I loved this joyous e-mail from a teacher from Trenton Middle School—even if he was a little premature in calling me a brother of a president. He was so committed to raising student achievement. I remember he promised to dye his hair pink if his school received a certain grade.

Subject: [None]
Friday, September 8, 2000 10:35 p.m.
From: Gordon Dasher

Thanks for making our F-CAT celebration an exceptional day. I can assure you, our kids will never forget that Governor Jeb Bush, son and brother of US presidents, visited their school and thanked them for a job well done.

And while I'm at it, thanks for making us accountable for how well we educate our community's children. Let the teacher unions whine and complain — we aren't obligated to them anyway. One hundred and eighty days out of each year I look my obligation in the eye. The only problem is, they are having trouble looking back at me. Something about the glare from the pink hair.

Subject: None
Friday, September 8, 2000 10:36 p.m.
From: Jeb Bush

It was so cool to be with you. it was truly one of the highlights of my tenure as Governor. Thank you.

Jeb

———

Here is another nonbeliever that I really did read and answer e-mails.

Subject: [None]
Thursday, September 21, 2000 2:40 p.m.
From: Just Jane

Is this really you answering my e-mail or is this one of your staff? This may sound as a little strange, but I would very much like to ask you a question but I really need to know if I am writing directly to you. I know that you are a busy person, but this would mean so much to me if I could directly ask you. Thank you for taking the time to consider my e-mail. A reply would be most welcomed.

Jane in St. Cloud FL

Subject: None
Thursday, September 21, 2000 8:06 p.m.
From: Jeb Bush

Jane in St. Cloud, FL, this is me. Scouts honor.

Jeb

I am not sure she ever wrote back!

The presidential election between George W. Bush and Vice President Al Gore was headed into its final stretch. When I could I campaigned for my brother, but my time was limited. For the most part, Floridians seemed excited about the connection between one of the candidates and their governor—but not everybody.

Subject: your campaigne is over!
Wednesday, August 30, 2000 4:12 p.m.
From: [No name]

i would like you to do what we pay you to do, run the state of florida. You said the other day you would be out getting votes for big brother. you are an employee of the state voted in by people who expect a days work for a days pay. besides that your brother will loose all by himself he ain't the brightest bulb in the string.

Subject: your campaigne is over!
Thursday, September 21, 2000 5:15 a.m.
From: Jeb Bush

Thank you for writing. I work about 80 hours a week in my capacity as governor. You are getting a days

work for a days pay. In my limited spare time, I
will work for my brother and other candidates that I
believe in and the taxpayers won't pay a penny.

Jeb Bush

————

Subject: 5 percent budget cut
Friday, September 15, 2000 10:19 a.m.
From: Michele

I sent the following email to the Tallahassee
Democrat after reading about your efforts to reduce
"waste" in the budget.

When our Governor is traversing the state and the
country to support his brother's presidential campaign
while cutting the state budget, one wonders is he using
state resources? Does the Governor take vacation time
while campaigning? With the governors policy of cutting
"waste" such as extra employees and big projects, I
would be curious to know how much value to place on the
resources he is spending to assist his brother.

Thank you for reading my email.

Subject: 5 percent budget cut
Friday, September 22, 2000 12:39 p.m.
From: Jeb Bush

**Thanks for writing. I take personal time to campaign
for my brother and other candidates. This is not at
taxpayers' expense. Additionally, I continue to work**

very hard in my capacity as Governor (normally 60 to 80 hours a week).

Finally, we are not cutting the budget but identifying savings that can be used to fund our priorities which are education, the developmentally disabled, drug treatment programs, community care for the elderly, transportation, the environment and targeted tax relief.

I hope this clarifies any misunderstandings you may have.

———

I was happy to tackle some other questions and concerns. Although, this one also concerned the election.

Subject: Environment
Thursday, August 17, 2000 11:18 a.m.
From: Wofford Johnson

As a loyal republican who also feels we should do everything possible to protect our environment I urge you to take positive steps with some environment issues immediately. It will help me to feel better about our republican party and will help George W. in the election. Among my friends, most of whom are also republicans, the concern I most often hear is a perceived view that the republican party favors developers to the detriment of the environment. This is a growing concern among the general population and will have an ever growing impact on future elections.

Subject: Environment
Saturday, September 23, 2000 4:09 p.m.
From: Jeb Bush

1. Everglades funding
2. actively working on passage of federal everglades bill.
3. advocating the taking down of the rodman dam.
4. fighting against offshore drilling in Florida waters.
5. $38 million appropriated to clean up Lake O.[42]
6. Growth management commission
7. Manatee protection initiative

These are a few of the initiatives of the last year.

Thanks for writing.

Jeb Bush

———

One of the issues of great importance to me in 2000 was a comprehensive plan to save the Everglades. The plan would restore the flow of water to the famed River of Grass. This would protect the natural habitat of sixty-eight threatened or endangered species. It also would replenish the underground water supply for eight million Floridians. I had announced the ten-year project on January 18. Half the funds were to come from the federal government, and the state legislature had approved our part of the funding.

Getting the bill through Congress was an interesting challenge. I went to Washington and testified before the US Senate

---

42 Lake Okeechobee feeds into the Everglades. It's that big lake in the middle of Florida that is very prominent on all state maps.

Committee on Environment and Public Works to plead our cause—really America's cause. The latest hiccup was the insistence of Minnesota Congressman Jim Oberstar that the rules of the Davis-Bacon Act applied, which regulated wages on federally funded projects. Needless to say, this would drive up the cost of the project. My patience was wearing thin. The bottom line was so important. We needed to save an incredible national and Florida treasure. However, red tape and politics were dragging us down. Nina Oviedo, head of our Washington, DC, office, sent me this note.

Subject: everglades update
Friday, September 29, 2000 8:29 p.m.
From: Nina Oviedo

Apparently Oberstar is requiring that Davis-Bacon apply to Everglades state and water management construction projects, not just federal projects.…
Meaning that union wages would be required.

I will call Charles Canady[43] and see if his Committee can do some research on a federal wage practices imposed on states.

Subject: everglades update
Friday, September 29, 2000 9:08 p.m.
From: Jeb Bush

I am ready to let the big dog eat. You have not let me unleash as of yet but I promise I will do so.

---

43 At that time Charles was a congressman. He joined our team as my general counsel when he fulfilled his promise to serve only eight years in the US Congress. He's now on the Florida Supreme Court and served as its chief justice from 2010 to 2012.

Davis Bacon is a stupidity. We should abolish it
rather than expand it. That is what will say. the
cost to Florida taxpayers will blow up the deal
partnership.

Jeb

———

*Columba led the effort to create the most comprehensive drug
strategy in the country—prevention, treatment, and enforcement.
She did so without seeking attention. I appreciated this note from
our drug czar, Jim McDonough.*

Subject: Counterdrug Update
Thursday, October 19, 2000 8:29 a.m.
From: Jim McDonough

The first lady did an excellent job in Pensecola on
Tuesday. She spoke three times: at a coffee thanking
drug free workplace businesses (these were all small
businesses) for their involvement; to a middle school
red ribbon assemblage at the city's convention
center, with about 3000 children present; and to the
Pensecola Rotarians, with about 200 present. Press
the next day was very laudatory of the first lady's
presence and remarks.

Subject: Counterdrug Update
Thursday, October 19, 2000 10:06 p.m.
From: Jeb Bush

thanks Jim. I am proud of my wife.

———

Congress gave us the funding we needed to help save the Everglades!

Subject: Everglades funding
Friday, October 20, 2000 7:23 a.m.
From: Jerry Fernandez

Congratulations on the Everglades Funding !!

It would not have been possible without your hard work.

Subject: Everglades funding
Friday, October 20, 2000 2:24 p.m.
From: Jeb Bush

thanks Jerry. It is a huge victory.

Jeb

———

I had no idea when I answered this e-mail how much I would appreciate—just a week later—questions about the simpler issues of the day.

Subject: Ending Daylight Savings Time
Monday, October 30, 2000 1:31 p.m.
From: Becky Mariotti

Thank you for the wonderful things you are doing
for this great State. I would like to know your
thoughts on ending Daylight Saving Time in the State
of Florida. In other words, if a bill came before
you, would you be likely to sign it? If would like

to know more about this subject, please visit www.
standardtime.com.

Subject: Ending Daylight Savings Time
Monday, October 30, 2000 5:38 p.m.
From: Jeb Bush

I don't have a position on the subject but will look
at the webpage when I get some time to breathe!
Thanks for writing.

Jeb Bush

———

*What happened next certainly was a great example of a path I did
not choose but one that was chosen for me.*

*I was in Austin, Texas, with my family on November 7—the day
of the presidential election. Our extended family was having an
early dinner with George and Laura when the most amazing thing
happened. The networks called Florida for Vice President Gore,
which meant George would lose. However, they did so before the
polls closed in the heavily Republican Florida Panhandle, which is
in the Central Time Zone.*

*I went to my brother, gave him a hug, and told him I was
sorry I had let him down. I told Don Evans, George's campaign
chairman, I was going upstairs to my room to make calls to talk
radio and encourage people out west to vote for George. In a couple hours, the networks changed their minds and said the race
was too close to call. Columba and I went to the governor's mansion to be with my parents, George and Laura, and a few others.*

*Way after midnight the networks called it for George! Vice
President Gore called to concede, and George prepared to declare
victory in front of tens of thousands. I was on the phone to Miami
and trying to get a sense of what precincts were left to be counted*

in Dade County. I realized the vote was still too close. I reluctantly told George I did not think he should go out yet and declare victory. Within minutes the vice president called to withdraw his concession.

Thus began a six-week roller-coaster ride, which included recounts, lawsuits, court rulings, overturned court rulings, contradictory court rulings, and accusations of wrongdoing on both sides. The entire country developed a case of whiplash while waiting to see who would be the next president.

Because of my obvious conflict of interest, I stayed completely out of it. One of my first moves was to recuse myself from the Elections Canvassing Commission—whose job it was to confirm the election results. It was made up of the governor, the secretary of state, and the director of the Division of Elections. Agriculture Commissioner Bob Crawford, a Democrat, replaced me.

As George's brother I was beyond frustrated for him. As governor I was somewhat embarrassed about how difficult the recount became. Who had ever heard of "hanging chads"?

As you can imagine, the e-mails poured in.

———

Subject: Florida needs it's Governor back!
Monday, November 13, 2000 12:59 p.m.
From: Ken and Ana Davey

I know you are doing everything possible to end this fiasco. I would hope that all Republicans elected will support the Secretary of State[44] before the democrats destroy her. This is War.

Best of luck and thanks for being a great Governor.

---

44 Florida Secretary of State Katherine Harris, who had been elected in 1998, had jurisdiction over election laws. She came under great fire from the Democrats.

Subject: Florida needs it's Governor back!
Monday, November 13, 2000 2:58 p.m.
From: Jeb Bush

**Hopefully, the courts will allow for the election
laws to be applied and we can have a decision on who
won by Friday. then, we will have to heal deep wounds
on both sides.**

Jeb Bush

———

Subject: Your Sec'y of State
Monday, November 13, 2000 5:35 p.m.
From: Bill Williams

I know you are covered up with emails with many
diverse opinions. However, I hope you reserve a
special place for your Secretary of State for standing
up for the legal process of the Great State of
Florida. The Gore people are after her big time, I
know she has support from your camp. Damn, I further
know these strange people from the Gore Planet have
you painted in some kind of corner since you are
George W's bro. Stand tall sir, your Sec'y of State
absolutely deserves some kind of medal. Please know
there are many of us that appreciate you, George
W, and your Sec'y of State. Those Gore people will
continue to press for counts until their man wins; go
figure.

Subject: Your Sec'y of State
Monday, November 13, 2000 10:33 p.m.
From: Jeb Bush

Thanks Bill. Secretary Harris did the right thing, she followed Florida law.

———

Subject: Recounting in Florida...
Tuesday, November 14, 2000 6:38 a.m.
From: Gwen Raker

I certainly hope that the 5 P.M. deadline today for recounts holds up.

This is getting absolutely ridiculous. I agree that everyone should have their vote count, but not counted and recounted and recounted until the election turns out like you want it too. The local TV station here in Orlando, Channel 9, created a ballot that looked like the ballot used in the Palm Beach area and distributed it to a class of 1st and 3rd graders and asked them to vote for their favorite Disney character and the first graders couldn't read the names, but when they were read the names allowed all of the 1st and 3rd graders except 1 marked the correct bubble. The one who got it wrong voted for Mickey Mouse rather than Minnie so they weren't even sure if it was bubbled incorrectly or if the student just couldn't tell the difference in the names. Now come on if elementary students can figure out then the voters down there sure should have been able to.

This is getting out of hand. I have been a registered Democrat in the state since becoming voting age and this is the type of shenanigans that turned me against the Democrats in the beginning. I certainly have been happy with my vote for you as governor and hoped that since you have been so active and involved in Florida that maybe your brother would do the same for the country, but I am not sure Gore will allow him the opportunity.…I hope that this resolved soon as it is making Florida look like a mockery. I am sure it must put you in an awkward position where you will be accused of favortism by some, just because it is your brother involved, but please try to hold with the stance and keep the pressure on to end it as soon as possible.

A concerned & registered Democrat Florida voter –

Subject: Recounting in Florida…
Tuesday, November 14, 2000 6:50 a.m.
From: Jeb Bush

My position has been consistent. I want the rule of law to prevail. We have pretty clear laws about certifying this election. Where there is confusion a swift and concise judicial ruling should provide guidance. I hope and pray the winner will be determined on Friday for the sake of our country.

Jeb Bush

———

Subject: Voting
Monday, November 20, 2000 11:44 a.m.
From: Don Collins

I think Florida has been embarrassed enough by its antiquated IBM card voting technology. It's time to modernize and go with an electronic system !!

Subject: Voting
Monday, November 20, 2000 3:22 p.m.
From: Jeb Bush

we will be looking at changes after this is said and done.

Jeb Bush

———

Subject: NEW SLOGANS FOR FLORIDA
Wednesday, November 22, 2000 7:03 p.m.
From: Tom Bennis

Both of you[45] have a stake in this but I know you really don't care that Florida is now the butt of all the jokes and after the so called Supreme Court proceedings were shown live (I think they were live it was hard to tell sometimes) we look even dumber. Hell the Chief Justice had to ask twice what the date would be 6 days before the 18th. DUH I think it might be the 12th. DUH Am I right?

Subject: NEW SLOGANS FOR FLORIDA
Wednesday, November 22, 2000 9:49 p.m.
From: Jeb Bush

Mr. Bennis, with all due respect, it upsets me more than you will know that Florida is the brunt of the jokes I have seen.

Jeb Bush

———

45 This e-mail also went to US Senator Bob Graham.

Subject: please help
Wednesday, November 22, 2000 2:26 p.m.
From: Adam Tatum

I was told that you could call the Florida legislators
back from break to overide the Florida Supreme Court.
I know some people would not agree that you should get
involved but enough is enough. The supreme court has
stepped out of their boundaries and is creating law.
Please do something to stop the chaos.

Subject: please help
Thursday, November 23, 2000 10:37 p.m.
From: Jeb Bush

**The leadership of the legislature can call a special
session and that is under consideration.**

Jeb Bush

**Subject: Does the voter have any (legal)
responsibility?**
Thursday, November 23, 2000 10:46 p.m.
From: Greg Pratt

My wife and I have been looking (incredulously) at
the mess in this state and have continuously asked
why there is no accountability on the part of the
voter in all of this. Are there any laws on the books
that say (in essence) that the voter is responsible
to make sure that the ballot is properly punched or
otherwise filled out?

It seems to me that if there is such a statute,
no one has brought it up. And if there is no such
statute, perhaps that should be an immediate order of
business for the legislature to undertake (in Florida
as well as all other states).

Voting is clearly a right, but it should also be
the voter's responsibility to do it correctly - or
relinquish their right to 'be heard'. If there is
such a 'voter responsibility statute', could you
please let me (and the media, and the canvassing
boards) know about it?

**Subject: Does the voter have any (legal)
responsibility?**
Friday, November 24, 2000 7:11 a.m.
From: Jeb Bush

**Greg, I don't know of a law but it is clear that
there is a responsibility that comes with the
right and privledge of voting. Thanks for
writing.**

Jeb Bush

———

Subject: [None]
Tuesday, December 5, 2000 3:56 p.m.
From: Jerry Payne

I understand you having stayed out of the limelight
during the recent election and the ensuing mess. That
for the most part is behind us and I hope it is time for
you to get out and visit with Florida citizens. After
all that is why you were elected. KEEP PUSHING AHEAD!

```
Subject: [None]
Tuesday, December 5, 2000 5:49 p.m.
From: Jeb Bush
```

I have been out visiting Florida citizens. By staying out of the limelight, I have been doing my job! I appreciate your writing.

———

At 10:00 p.m. EST on December 12, in a complicated and divided ruling, the US Supreme Court stopped the recount and effectively made George W. Bush the president-elect of the United States. Vice President Gore conceded that night. Although, he disagreed with the court's ruling. A post-election analysis by several newspapers, including USA Today, *the* Miami Herald, *and the* New York Times, *showed that if the recount had been allowed to continue, George would have won the state by 1,665 votes.*

The night of the ruling, Columba and I went to Mass in rural Gadsden County to celebrate the feast day of the Virgin of Guadalupe. We heard about the Supreme Court decision on the radio on the way home. I then thanked God the ordeal was over and that George would be our next president.

Ironically, the day before I had been in Washington, DC, in the Oval Office with President Clinton for the signing of the Water Resources Development Act, which authorized the federal funding for Everglades restoration. It was an awkward moment, given we both were anxious to see whether my brother or his vice president would succeed him.

Finally, though, we could all move on. As you can see from this e-mail exchange with Barbara Walters, that didn't mean I wanted to talk about it!

Subject: [None]
Thursday, December 14, 2000 5:57 p.m.
From: Barbara Walters

Congratulations. Now, finally, you and your family can get some sleep. The President-elect made a wonderful speech on Thursday night, and I think the whole country feels gratified and relieved. As an old friend of your mother and father, may I personally add my warmest wishes.

May I put on my other hat now, to request an interview with you, which I hope would be the first one you give on television. The interview would not be a rehash of chads, pregnant or otherwise, nor of the decisions of the Florida and U.S. Supreme Courts. It would rather be about how you saw your own role, both as the governor of a great state and as a much loved and loving brother. What have these past weeks been like for you? How do you now put away the past and get back to the business of governing your state. There are many other areas of substance to cover, including your proposal to reform Florida's election system, which could prove a model for the rest of the country.…

I hope to hear from you. In the meantime, I wish you and your family the happiest of holidays and a chance to relax and enjoy a well-deserved victory.

Subject: [None]
Friday, December 15, 2000 10:40 p.m.
From: Jeb Bush

I am not a big fan of the national limelight. I am really only interested in serving my state. I

appreciate your interest in interviewing me but I
will have to take a pass.

I will pass on your regards to my parents.

Jeb Bush

PS I hope you and your family have a peaceful and
joyful holiday season.

———

After a year that began with Elian Gonzalez and ended with hanging chads, I planned on taking Barbara's advice to enjoy the holidays. Life had indeed forced us to go down several unexpected and difficult paths.

Between the controversies, though, we had accomplished a lot:

- *Signed a $5 billion tax-relief bill over four years.*
- *Increased funding for child-welfare programs, which enabled Florida to move to a community-based care model of child welfare where the focus could be on prevention rather than just crisis management.*
- *Expanded Florida's KidCare program, which was created to provide health insurance for uninsured children under the age of nineteen.*
- *For the first time ever, provided enough funding to serve the entire waiting list of persons with developmental disabilities.*
- *Signed into law the largest transportation funding increase in state history. Floridians were ecstatic with Mobility 2000 and that much-needed repairs and improvements were coming to our heavily traveled highways and bridges.*

I am sure it will not surprise you that one of my last acts as governor in 2000 was to sign an executive order creating a task force charged with recommending an overhaul of the state's elections procedures.

The election recount had been tough on the entire nation but especially Floridians. As one e-mailer pointed out, we had indeed become fodder for the late-night comedians. In the closing days of 2000, I decided to address the state and try to rally the troops for better days ahead. As I admitted in the speech, "There were nights when I prayed that the controversy would end, and I wondered out loud, 'Why Florida?'"

Here are the last few paragraphs of that address, which was in my heart as the holidays approached.

Over the last few weeks, I've traveled to Lecanto, Melbourne, Marianna, and Miami. What I saw, and what many of the national pundits have missed, is a vibrant and dynamic state where no one—Democrat, Republican, African American, white, Hispanic—is afraid to tackle the toughest challenges. Our potential is limitless if we work together.

Tonight I call upon all of us to reach out and rebuild. And I ask for your prayers as I seek to fulfill the trust you have placed in me. I pledge that I will work with leaders from both parties to heal the events of the past several weeks.

Together we will do much more than simply weather this storm—we will be better. We will show the nation and indeed the world that Florida is the best place on Earth to live, work, and raise a family.

God bless each of you this holiday season, and God bless Florida.

Chapter 3
2001

"Pray for Our Beloved Country."

They have indeed hurt us, but they will never humble us.

—Address to the State, September 11, 2001

After the drama of hanging chads, all of us were hoping for a less controversial 2001, and for a good part of the year, it was.

For me it was great to get back to the business at hand—being the governor of the great state of Florida.

I was thrilled to start the New Year talking about one of my favorite topics: technology and how we could use it to make life better for all Floridians. Chris Cobbs, a reporter for the Orlando Sentinel, *sent these questions through a member of my communications team.*

Subject: Interview with the Governor
Thursday, January 4, 2001 4:01 p.m.
From: Chris Cobbs

* how often he uses the Web and e-mail, how he uses
e-mail to gauge voters' views on policy, how he
handles a vast number of e-mails

174

* how technology will make government more efficient
and responsive (thru delivery of online services,
like tax collection, license renewals)

* how the web can make citizens more plugged
into government (by watching webcasts of county
commmmission meetings, etc)

* thoughts on electronic voting machines and online
voting.

Subject: Interview with the Governor
Thursday, January 4, 2001 10:51 p.m.
From: Jeb Bush

I use the web daily to check newspapers and
MyFlorida.com to see how it is progressing. I do use
email to gauge citizens' views on policy but since
I am a heavy receiver, I discount the mass mailing
emails organized by groups. I have to work very hard
to read the volume of email that I get but I still
find the reward worth the effort.

Technology is the greatest tool for limited
government and for improvement of services that we
have in the public sector today. In state government,
we have a whole array of projects underway including
the MyFlorida.com portal, the online license renewals
for around 1.8 million professionals, the revamping
of our accounting, purchasing, human resources and
budgeting systems and much, much more. In the end,
hundreds of millions will be saved and citizens will
get much better services. The challenge is to finance
the hundreds of millions of dollars to generate the
above mentioned savings and efficiencies.

Web enabled services offer great possibilities. Next week, our IT town hall meeting in Jacksonville will be broadcast live over the internet. Most of my press conferences are done so as well. A citizen can watch the Cabinet, the Board of Regents and many other entities over the internet when they would like to do so. With www.MyFlorida.com folks will be able to access the service they require, be prompted to the next step along the path (for example, if you need to start a business, it might require a couple of forms to be filled out) and go to a call center if they need additional information from a live person. Our child protection services is being enhanced by remote viewing by trained professionals over the internet of the abused child. I could go on and on with a multitude of projects already underway.

I have not seen the online voting systems but would be wary of something that provided inequities in access to the technology.

Jeb Bush

———

Speaking of technology, one of the reasons I felt so strongly about staying in touch through e-mail is that the most common complaint I hear from people about the government—local, state, and federal—is that it doesn't care about them. For the most part, people feel disconnected from the leaders who represent them.

So this e-mail from a single mom who was seeking our help to find her ex-husband and make him pay child support made my day. She even included a photo of herself and her son. In this case the hero was Karen Kellum. She worked in the Department

*of Revenue and was my point of contact on child-support enforce-
ment and constituent requests. There are many, many Karen
Kellums at all levels of government who don't get the credit they
deserve. I am happy to be able to give a little credit here. With
the help of Karen and some reforms we passed, we were able
to increase child-support enforcement collections by 90 percent
during my governorship.*

Subject: Thank You
Saturday, January 13, 2001 3:23 p.m.
From: Tina

The picture did not come out, as well as I wanted but
I at least wanted to put a face with the name.…

I would like to start out by saying Congratulations
on your brother's victory. I wanted to write sooner
but with the problems with the election I knew you
were extremely busy. I was truly shocked that you
responded to my letter and most of all followed
through. This was the first letter I have ever written
to a politician. I wanted to be able to say I tried,
but I never anticipated anything to come of it.
Karen Kelum has been amazing, she calls regularly to
keep me informed. The really good news is Patrick
was found and arrested and I have a court date in
Jacksonville on the 18th of this month. I know this
is only the beginning but I am reassured that the
system does work.

I can't thank you enough. This was way beyond my
expectation. The best thing about it is the reassurance
in knowing you (the government) do care. I am just one
person but I do want you to know if you ever need my
help don't hesitate to ask. Well I would not say I am

just one person my entire family and circle of friends are indebted to you for the help you've given.…

Good luck, and if you ever run for Presidency or for that matter any office I would be honored to lend a hand because this country needs politicians who care. Tell your brother congrats and that I am so so glad he is our President elect.

Subject: Thank You
Saturday, January 13, 2001 8:19 p.m.
From: Jeb Bush

tina, I am so happy that some progress has been made. But you don't have to thank me. You are deserving of support and the State has a responsibility to help. You are very kind to write and I hope you will keep me apprised of how the case develops.

Jeb

PS You and your son look great!

PPS I was moved by your story because of your obvious love for your son and what a creep Patrick is. I can never understand how a father can abandon without any remorse his child.

————

Of course, if it was January, it was budget time. On January 17 I sent my budget to the state legislature. For the third year in a row, improving student achievement was my top priority, so my budget asked for a 5.4 percent increase in funding for K–12 public *schools. The new budget also included a $313 million tax cut. How is that possible? You begin by cutting the size of government.*

Subject: Budget focuses on job cuts
Thursday, January 18, 2001 8:07 a.m.
From: Bob

Congratulations for having the courage and insight to undertake such a program but be patient because most people in government won't understand the concept.

Budget focuses on job cuts
JOE FOLLICK
of The Tampa Tribune

"Fewer state jobs will allow the state to increase spending and provide a few selected tax cuts," Gov. Jeb Bush said Wednesday as he revealed his budget proposal for the next fiscal year.

In his plan for 2001-02, Bush adds $1.1 billion in new spending - most of it in education and transportation - while eliminating thousands of positions in state government."

Subject: Budget focuses on job cuts
Thursday, January 18, 2001 12:25 p.m.
From: Jeb Bush

patience is a virtue!

Jeb

———

As you can imagine, the idea of a smaller state bureaucracy made many state workers very nervous. I sent this e-mail to some of my top staff. That included my new chief of staff, Kathleen Shanahan. Sally Bradshaw was now a stay-at-home mom for her newborn girl, Helen. Although she was just a phone call away, I missed her daily advice and leadership. She had been at my side since the beginning, including through the campaigns. However, I respected and applauded her decision to put her family first.

Subject: workforce
Friday, January 19, 2001 12:03 p.m.
From: Jeb Bush

I would like to make a presentation to the Tallahassee Chamber of Commerce and to the Tallahassee Democrat on workforce issues and their impact on the Big Bend economy. I think we should not allow the debate to be defined as it will be by our passive silence.

In order to do this, we need at least the following information:

The number jobs reduced to date and what part of the state they were located in.

How many of those "jobs" were vacant positions and how many were filled?

- What happened for the folks that lost their jobs?
- If the functions were outsourced, who is doing those services now?

- Going forward, how many jobs will be lost, where are the located in the state, how many are vacant versus filled?
- We should get a sense of the increases in the offices of the consulting firms that are seeing an increase in their business because of the outsourcing activities and the technology projects. Is their some benefit to the community because they are private sector based?

It continues to be imperative that we develop an internal communications strategy for the workforce. This is of the highest priority. Kathleen should coordinate the creation of the strategy.

———

We are overdue for an update on the state website. This e-mail was from Justin Sayfie, who was now the communications director.

Subject: Web Visits
Friday, January 19, 2001 1:44 p.m.
From: Justin Sayfie

Just wanted you to know that the myflorida.com web site had the most visitors it's ever had on Jan. 18, the day after the e-budget release, primarily due to the publicity resulting from the e-budget, and our own efforts to distribute the e-budget hyperlink.

On Thursday, myflorida.com had 120,364 visitors, (while the average for January is 47,047 visitors per day). We had 90,892 visitors on Wednesday.

Subject: Web Visits
Friday, January 19, 2001 6:30 p.m.
From: Jeb Bush

awesome

––––––

These kinds of e-mails to the staff members—who were ter-rific at following up—were quite common after I met with heads of organizations or community members. This note went to Kathleen Shanahan; Ruben King-Shaw, secretary of the Agency for Health Care Administration; Alison Hewitt, who headed the Front Porch initiative (an inner-city project designed to better connect residents to their communities); Bob Brooks at the Department of Health; David Struhs, sec-retary, and Denver Stutler, chief of staff, at the Department of Environmental Protection; and Arlene DiBenigno, head of external affairs.

Subject: William McCormick
Monday, February 5, 2001 4:40 p.m.
From: Jeb Bush

Today, I met with William McCormick, the new head of the Ft. Lauderdale NAACP, and the publisher of the Sun Sentinel. I promised to work with the NAACP on issues of common interest and you all were volunteered to followup.

• Ruben, if you could call William (he is in the health care business) to discuss the efforts we are making to think differently in the medicaid program, I would be grateful.

- Bob, if you could brief him on our minority health initiative, i would appreciate it.
- David, please discuss with him the Wingate matter[46] and get James Blount to call him about South Florida water management district procurement policies.
- Alison, can you call Mr. McCormick and see how he can help with our Front Porch Ft. Lauderdale effort?
- Arlene, we need the setting the record straight on minority outreach and one florida asap.
  The publisher (at least I believe it was the publisher) of Florida's third largest paper was surprised of our results and so was William. If you can get me the information, I would like to write them with it as an attachment. I promised it would be forthcoming.

thanks, all.

Jeb

———

Reporters were already asking if I was going to run for reelection—even though it was almost two years away. This inquiry was from Mark Silva, political reporter for the Orlando Sentinel.

---

46 Wingate was an incinerator site near Fort Lauderdale where contaminated ash and soil were found and eventually removed as part of the federal EPA's Superfund cleanup program.

Subject: Democrats amassing
Thursday, February 8, 2001 3:37 p.m.
From: Mark Silva

Hi, I am writing an article for Saturday's paper about many Democratic fundraisers and some of their potential candidates in 2002 assembling for a three-day retreat at the Biltmore, Friday evening through Sunday morning.

I know your stance on waiting til spring to state your own intentions, but I wonder if you might offer up a few thoughts on what you make of the Democrats gearing up now for the governor's race, whether the closeness of the 2000 contest hear causes you any pause about the GOP's prospects in 2002, that sort of thing.

Here is my answer, which had no date or time in the e-mail file.

Mark, I am completely focused on the next legislative session and fulfilling my duty to the people of our state. The politics of the next election will have to wait. In my political life, I have lived by the credo of saying what I will do and then fighting hard to do what I said I would do. No amount of posturing by potential opponents will change my commitment to my job or to my timetable for making up my mind whether I will be a candidate in the next election cycle.

Jeb

———

I was amazed to get this note from Deputy Chief of Staff Frank Jimenez. When we proposed civil-service reform—the first in nearly fifty years—I asked that a website be set up where state employees could send in their ideas. We received approximately ten thousand e-mails, and some of the ideas did indeed make it into the reform bill. However, not everybody was happy about being asked for input.

Subject: AFSCME Lawsuit
Saturday, February 10, 2001 12:12 p.m.
From: Frank Jimenez

AFSCME[47] has filed a complaint charging that our efforts to gather employee input on civil service reform constitute an unfair labor practice. It is seeking an emergency injunction to block these efforts. Our outside counsel on labor matters, Mike Mattimore, is handling. Our lawyers do not believe the complaint has much merit. It's a stretch, to put it mildly, to claim that we're negotiating directly with employees.

Subject: AFSCME Lawsuit
Saturday, February 10, 2001 12:48 p.m.
From: Jeb Bush

this is amazing. We are trying to hear the views of workers and we get sued!

Jeb

---

47 American Federation of State, County and Municipal Employees.

Subject: [None]
Monday, February 12, 2001 9:17 a.m.
From: Mark Wells

As a hard working state employee I would like to tell Governor Bush that you can't run all of state government like a private business. The majority of my office tasks are routine task. Everybody does the same thing. Everybody works together to get the job done. How are you going to decide who is performing better than someone else? Giving out bonuses the way you suggest will promote favoritism in the workplace. The workers who are not rewarded will resent this and the once productive group will now start working against each other. I feel that the best way to reward good performance in state jobs is to reward the whole section for the work that they do.

Also, how does the Governor expect anybody to be productive with the looming threat of losing his or her job in the future? The Governor says on one hand how he is proud of state workers, but then on the other hand he still wants to cut back a state government that has already been cut back and trimmed.

Subject: [None]
Monday, February 12, 2001 9:52 p.m.
From: Jeb Bush

thanks for writing. Many enterprises, both public and private, provide bonuses for attaining objectives. In fact, it is being done on a small scale in State

Government. I agree that paying for team effort is
a good idea and nothing that we have suggested
would preclude that. I hear from many state workers
concerning their fears of favoritism. Perhaps the
workers themselves should decide who gets performance
pay bonuses as is done at the Department of Revenue?
What do you think?

Jeb Bush

PS I fully appreciate that state government is not a
business but common sense principles can apply to any
organization. Rewarding for effort is just one common
sense suggestion.

———

Over the objections of the public-employee unions, I did sign civil-service reform into law in May. It moved sixteen thousand state workers out of protected civil-service jobs so they could be hired and fired more easily.

———

Earlier in February four flags that had historically flown over Florida were permanently removed and sent to the Florida State Museum: British, French, Spanish, and Confederate. It was done very quietly and without fanfare. In fact they were taken down during a renovation project on a fountain on the capitol grounds. Georgia had recently undergone a divisive debate about the Confederate flag flying over its state capitol, and given that I knew that flag was an offensive symbol to many Floridians, I made the decision that the flag belonged in a museum and not on state government grounds.

Not everyone agreed. This is one of just several e-mails I received on the removal of the Confederate flag.

Subject: flags
Sunday, February 11, 2001 4:12 p.m.
From: Carole Shelton

I am terribly upset that you have chosen to sanction the removal of the 4 flags, one of which is the venerated confederate flag. You are not from the South. You have no right to impose your northern prejudices and misconceptions on the people of Florida and to snub your nose at its history. I demand that the flags be returned to their original place, around the fountain or in front of the old capitol. My father was a legislator for 10 years; I was a page in the House. It sickens me to see and hear how you are doing everything you can to wipe out our heritage in the name of "inclusion" and political correctness. I am a conservative Republican, but I will not support you in the next election if these flags are not put back. Carole Shelton

Subject: flags
Sunday, February 11, 2001 4:21 p.m.
From: Jeb Bush

Carole, soon you will be able to see the flags in the Florida History musuem. They will be respectfully displayed.

Jeb Bush

PS I am a Floridian born and raised in Texas.

———

My team had an exciting yet daunting task ahead of us. We were about to change how the state colleges and universities were governed. I had appointed a commission to study how to best reorganize into a seamless system—covering pre-K through graduate school. They had made their recommendations to me and to the state legislature. Although the new legislation was still pending, we needed to get to work. We needed to find candidates for the now-appointed state board of education,[48] which would then select an education commissioner. We also need to find candidates for boards of trustees, subject to Senate approval, for every public university. There were lots of opportunities to do good. There was also lots of work. We needed to find more than five hundred good people. I sent this note to the key staffers working on this important project.

Subject: Education Reorganization
Saturday, February 17, 2001 3:50 p.m.
From: Jeb Bush

Thanks to the great work of the commission, we have
a wonderful opportunity to build a 21st century
education governance structure. But there is going to
be a tremendous amount of work necessary to meet the
proposed deadlines the commission is recommending.
AS soon as is possible, I would like to speak to you
about:

---

48 Florida voters had approved a constitutional amendment that changed the State Board of Education from a seven-member board of statewide elected officials to a governor-appointed seven-member board. I selected the first appointed board that officially began its duties in January 2002.

- legal considerations. How do we craft legislation that makes moot or minimizes the chances of legal challenges. This is important to have ready very soon.
- selection of board of trustees for all of the universities. This is a huge undertaking and we should consider setting up a separate structure to identify candidates.
- selection of Board of Education. This group needs to be ready to work on July 1st.
- selection of the Commissioner of Education. We need to better understand the transition period and when a commissioner should be selected. In addition, how do we go about the search?

I know we will have to begin this work prior to the legislature passing a law but who is going to do the work?

We need to gather soon.

Jeb

———

It appeared the "turkey hunt" was going to be more interesting than ever this budget year. This e-mail came from my budget director.

Subject: special projects
Friday, February 23, 2001 4:44 p.m.
From: Donna Arduin

Member project requests total over $7.6 billion (including some duplications between house and

senate), and average over $44 million per house
member and $58 million per senator!

Subject: special projects
Friday, February 23, 2001 9:08 p.m.
From: Jeb Bush

you have got to be kidding me.

Jeb

————

*One of my top priorities in 2001 was to create an elder-friendly
Florida for our greatest generation and generations of seniors to
come. Our budget proposal included $46 million in new funding
to improve the quality of nursing-home care and an additional
$52.4 million for community-based options.*

*However, getting the most attention was a proposal to control
the large number of lawsuits being filed against nursing homes.
Florida had three times the national average of these lawsuits.
That part of the measure was also part of my overall goal of comprehensive tort reform in Florida. Here is a sample of some of the
e-mails I was getting.*

Subject: Our nursing homes.
Tuesday, March 13, 2001 10:42 a.m.
From: Dick Rogers

There is the most alarming news that some of our
elected elite wish to affect the quality of life in
our nursing homes, and to take away the few remaining
rights that these unfortunate folks have. Sounds like
callous greed, to me. Please use whatever powers you

have to protect the residents of nursing homes. They are not able to protect them selves, but require our compassionate help.

Subject: Our nursing homes.
Saturday, March 17, 2001 3:09 p.m.
From: Jeb Bush

We will protect the rights of patients to sue but we also need to lessen the huge cost of litigation, we need to improve quality and expand community based alternatives.

Jeb Bush

———

Subject: Nursing homes legislation
Tuesday, March 27, 2001 2:10 p.m.
From: Mary Anderson

Please do all you personally can to protect the rights of people unfortunate enough to have to be put in nursing homes. They need your support and help just as much as your parents would if they were to have to be put in a nursing home.

Subject: Nursing homes legislation
Tuesday, March 27, 2001 9:47 p.m.
From: Jeb Bush

thanks for writing. I think we can balance the rights of patients and control the excessive costs of litigation that hurt quality.

Jeb Bush

_____

On February 25, 1990, a twenty-six-year-old woman named Terri Schiavo suffered massive brain damage after going into cardiac arrest. More than ten years later, I received this desperate e-mail from her father. It was many months before I realized this letter was only the beginning of a very long, complicated, and controversial journey for her family and me.

Subject: Terri Schiavo "Right to Die Case"
Thursday, April 5, 2001 10:06 a.m.
From: Robert Schindler

Allow me to introduce myself. My name is Bob Schindler, Terri Schiavo's dad. In a Florida Court of Law, Terri has been sentenced to die of starvation. The process could take place as soon as April 20, 2001, unless we receive a "stay of execution."

There are many frustrations our family has experienced regarding my daughter Terri's nutrition food removal trial. Terri's husband's attorney could very well have been an advisor to Lawton Chiles 1994 distorted political campaign allegations you personally experienced. He has spun a tale of propaganda, which is exemplified by a false characterization of my daughter's hopeless condition. He has walked a fine line mixing partial truths with fabrications. Hopefully the deceit will be exposed before it is too late.

Terri is falsely depicted by her husband's attorney as a hopeless vegetable. To the contrary, Terri is not "brain dead." Terri is not being kept alive by any mechanical devices nor is she connected to any machine. Although Doctors believe Terri can swallow, she receives her nutrition via a nutrition feeding tube. Terri is responsive to family and friends.

Challenging this inaccurate portrayal with a neurological assessment is presently not permitted. The prospect of an independent neurological opinion is barred by a court order along with any type of video tape or photograph, which would display Terri's true condition.

As Governor of this state, it is imperative that you are aware of the manner in which the legal system has been manipulated to serve an individual's personal agenda. The reality is that Terri's legal story is interlaced with suspicious events which contradict any reasonable explanation. Terri's story contains serious moral issues, such as "Marriage Infidelity" and legal issues, such as "Clear and Convincing Evidence" that have been totally disregarded or minimized.

Terri's story also demonstrates unbridled Guardianship legal powers. In addition to making Terri's "Life and Death Decisions," Terri's husband and legal Guardian, is endowed with the legal authority to:
*** Deny Terri's rehabilitation and medical care.
*** Deny Terri independent medical examinations.
*** Deny Terri's family access to Terri's medical records.
*** Use Terri's medical fund to pay her death trial legal costs.
*** Control biased medical diagnosis for personal advantages.

Terri's husband is openly engaged and has been living with his fiance for the past 5 years. He professes he will marry this woman after his wife (my daughter) dies and as Terri's husband, he will inherit the balance ($750K).of Terri's original $1+ million medical fund

The money was awarded by a jury in a medical malpractice suit explicitly for Terri's long term care and rehabilitation. Within months of the receipt of the award money, her husband made his first of two attempts to end Terri's life. To date, her husband has not honored his rehabilitation commitment. These events should shout out a message to people as to what is motivating this man to kill Terri. That's for starters. There is plenty more, that makes his marriage infidelity almost mild by comparison.

Governor Bush, I am very sensitive about encroaching on your time limitations, however I desperately need your help. I would like to see you personally to discuss this travesty of justice. Terri's case may be beyond your realm of authority, but I sincerely believe you could be helpful, if only to prevent a reoccurrence of this atrocity to future vulnerable individuals.

If you do not object, I would like to call your secretary to arrange an appointment to see you. I am hopeful you will be agreeable to my visitation request.

I thank you for your consideration.

Subject: Terri Schiavo "Right to Die Case"
Saturday, April 7, 2001 7:54 p.m.
From: Jeb Bush

Mr. Schindler, thank you for writing. I am asking that Charles Canady look into your daughter's case.

Jeb Bush

———

A top priority in 2001 was the retention and recruitment of good teachers. With a rapidly growing population, Florida was facing severe teacher shortages. I received several e-mails from teachers on the subject. This included the one below. The frustrations she expressed echoed those of so many others.

Subject: Meeting with your teacher in residence
Tuesday, April 10, 2001 7:12 p.m.
From: Helen Rowland

I teach at Johnson Middle School in Melbourne, Florida. Today your Teacher in Residence made a visit to my school to discuss issues that teachers felt were important to Florida's educational system.

Governor Bush, I know you are very busy, but I hope that you are reading this personally and will take the time to not only read but also give thought to what I have to say. Please don't pass this along to one of your assistants to placate another constituent and then forget about it tomorrow.…

I became a teacher because I loved working with children. I had the patience, the talent, and the

196

desire to make a difference in the lives of children. Over the past several months, I have seriously considered changing careers- a problem that education is facing much too consistently and to the detriment of the children and our educational system. Good teachers- dedicated teachers- quitting and moving into other careers.

Why would I do such a thing? Why would I give up a career in which I'm so successful? One of the answers is quite simple. I can barely survive on the salary that I am paid.

I am a single mother of two children. With my extensive educational background, I am now making $33,044 a year. Think about that for a moment, sir. I'm not sending you this message because I expect a great change in teacher pay. I am under the impression that you want to know why good teachers leave their profession. The fact that we can't survive financially on what we are paid is a big reason. It will be my reason.

Of course, I am told that I can always go back to school, get my master's degree in Educational Leadership and go into administration. Governor Bush, as I've previously stated, I am a single mother of two children. How do I afford not only the expense but the time to go back to school?

A majority of the problems with today's youth is that there is no parental supervision at home. I can not and will not sacrifice my children for money. There are some things which count more. That is what many people do, and we in public education are faced with the reprocussions of that on a daily basis. Parents

who leave their children alone or to be raised by
daycares.

I believe in family values. I believe that my
time with my children while nurturing them to be
responsible adults is more important, yet because of
this, I am punished.

I have served in the capacity of acting dean at my
school for the past 3 years. I am very good at this
job. I will never be allowed to move up the ladder
into this position however until I get that degree
in Educational Leadership. That is unfair. I know
many people that graduate with degrees who are quite
imcompetent. I, on the other hand, have proven myself
over and over again in that position, but I will
never be an assistant principal or dean because I do
not hold that degree. That is sad, sir. Doesn't work
experience and knowledge count for anything anymore?
Our system says a resounding,"No"!

Faced with little chance for advancement in my
career, I think again about moving into another
area that will offer me more financially and
professionally.

How can you help me and others with that?

Finally, I have seen many changes in the classroom
and school environments over the past 12 years.
Unfortunately, schools are no longer a safe haven for
learning. Teachers are faced daily with disruptive
and violent students. Too many children than one
would care to admit are sitting in our schools on
community control, probation, etc....

I have always wondered as a teacher and a parent why children who want to learn are forced to pay for their education while those who only wish to disrupt the learning environment continue to do so at the public's and taxpayer's expense.

As a parent, sir- do you ever wonder the same thing?

Subject: Meeting with your teacher in residence Saturday, April 14, 2001 8:30 a.m.
From: Jeb Bush

Thank you for writing.

I have read your email (i read about 300 a day to stay connected to concerned and committed Floridians) and first commend you for your commitment to teaching and learning.

Teacher pay will have to go up if in order to retain and recruit the teachers needed for the next decade. Over the last three years (including the budget year starting july 1st), the State has appropriated over $2 billion or an increase of 17%. In addition, Florida now has the second highest number of Nationally Certified teachers and we have increased funding for teacher development programs.

Now here is a problem. Not all of that increase makes it to the classroom and into increased teacher salaries. It is frustrating for everyone here in Tallahassee i can assure you. Secondly, the collective bargaining process doesn't help the aspiring productive teachers either. These are constraints that can be overcome but they make it harder.

On school safety, incidents of violence are down but I think you are right that disruption of classroom activity places an unfair burden on teachers and students that want to learn. I believe we need to expand alternative schools to get the disruptive kids out of the classrooms so you can safely teach and kids can learn. There should be a change of culture at schools to have less tolerance for the kind of behaviour that we would not accept off campus.

Helen, changing a system that resists change at all costs is hard work. I believe in building a new system that is student centered and not "system" centered, we can create the kind of professional climate that will motivate you to stay and flourish. I wish I could wave a magic wand to make it so but I don't have one. All I can do is challenge and advocate and lead as best I can.

I hope you are having a restful, joyful and reflective Easter weekend with your children.

Jeb Bush

———

Florida residents along the Gulf Coast—specifically in the Pensacola area—were nervously watching the federal government's deliberations about selling drilling rights of 5.9 million acres in the Gulf of Mexico. Most Floridians, including myself,

*were opposed to drilling off the Florida coast—the only oil rig-
free coast on the Gulf. Was I lobbying my brother? Absolutely.*

Subject: oil
Friday, April 20, 2001 9:20 p.m.
From: [No name]

People are going nuts here over this possible oil
drilling deal.…While campaigning, the President
stated that he was not going to drill off the Florida
coast.…I remember the news article, because I
brought it into headquarters here. I grew up in
Galveston [Texas]; after drilling was permitted, the
beaches were RUINED. After a visit to the beach, you
got petroleum products and tar all over your feet,
swimsuit, shoes, and subsequently, your car. Please
tell me GWB is not serious about this.…We will never
carry Florida in '02 if off shore drilling starts up.
A lot of people are asking me how to email or fax
the President on this issue. Any advice?? Fight on,
Jeb!

Subject: oil
Friday, April 20, 2001 10:23 p.m.
From: Jeb Bush

we will fight to win on this one.

Jeb

––––

*We were in the final days of the legislative session, so Floridians
were weighing in with their concerns, congratulations, and advice.*

Subject: budget-C.A.F.E.[49]
Saturday, April 21, 2001 8:21 a.m.
From: David Engels

Trust this finds you well.

On the face of it, the Senate is looking more
responsible than the House. Why is there the "need"
for tax cuts when revenue is down and the "need"
for services provided to the people is up? You have
championed an increase in social services in the
past 2 years, bringing our state from near last
to somewhere in the middle when compared with the
other 49. The Texas legislature, both Republican and
Democrat, lament now their tax cuts of the last 3
years. Once flush with revenue, they now don't have
enough to meet their needs.

Rep Feeney appears to be playing a game. Senator
Mckay[50] will sit down to talk. Both men do not
know me, yet only the Senator's office would return
my calls to discuss the budget. I'd love to hear
from you. If I can be of any assistance,pls call.
Brokering a compromise would be my honour.

P.S. I am open to learn why the House's position may
have more merit.

---

49 CAFE stands for Collaboration, Advocacy, Friendship, and
Empowerment. I helped launch this group and the Family Café Annual
Conference, which brings together disabled individuals and their families
with state agencies to connect them to their service providers. I tried to
attend every year. I am not sure why "CAFE" was in David's subject line
since we didn't discuss it in the e-mail.
50 Tom Feeney was speaker of the House. John McKay was Senate
president.

Subject: budget-C.A.F.E.
Saturday, April 21, 2001 1:03 p.m.
From: Jeb Bush

David, the revenue to the state is up not down. The senate budget grows by 5.9%, the house by around 5%. There is money for tax relief, fund education with an increase in real terms and increase funding for important social service policy areas. The senate budget has $400 million in member projects with a ton of them never having gone through any review.

This can be resolved and I believe it will. The President and the Speaker are fine public servants and want to do what they think is right. I believe compromise is in order.

Jeb Bush

PS If we had not done the tax cuts of the last two years, the money would have been spent and we would be in a serious mess now which thankfully we are not.

———

Subject: turkeys
Monday, April 23, 2001 7:52 a.m.
From: Fred Eisinger

I am shocked by a report in Sunday's Palm Beach Post that describes the behavior of legislators in terms of their "turkey" demands. I want you to know that, while I am very disappointed in what lies ahead for social service delivery in this state truly

believe that prioritization is as much to blame
for threatened cuts to social service funding as
the decrease in projected revenues, I support you
in granting no turkeys this year. Governor, it may
be politics, but it just isn't right to bleed off
millions from an anemic budget to satisfy a few. You
set the rules from the beginning, and now you have
got to stand firm. Failure to do so would certainly
undermine this budget and cause you a great deal of
criticism and challenge on the turkey issue next
year.

Subject: turkeys
Monday, April 23, 2001 2:30 p.m.
From: Jeb Bush

Thank you Fred!

Jeb Bush

Subject: Budget & Tax cuts
Wednesday, April 25, 2001 7:05 p.m.
From: Lorraine Grigsby

Although I haven't written you in ages, I have been
following the legislative session fairly closely.
You are on target, especially with intangibles tax
cuts,[51] JNC appointment reform, civil service merit/
accountability reform, and trial lawyers v. nursing

---

51 The intangibles tax was imposed on investments such as stocks,
bonds, and money-market funds. I called it the "insidious intangibles
tax" since it mainly punished seniors and savers. Getting rid of it was one
of my top priorities.

homes tort reform. I've been sending lots of emails to legislators.

I like what Speaker Feeney has to say. Finally, it seems, President "Buddy" McKay (er, I mean John Mckay, but their positions are so easily confused!), is getting the message on the importance of tax cuts and accountability to the principles of conservative, republican (small r intended) governance.

Best regards. As the leader of our State and a man with informed views, a moral conscience, principled purpose, and a kind heart, you are in our prayers. God Bless.

Subject: Budget & Tax cuts
Wednesday, April 25, 2001 7:59 p.m.
From: Jeb Bush

I love you Lorraine!

Jeb

———

Yes. I loved these e-mails. Who wouldn't?

Subject: thank you for your attention recently
Saturday, April 21, 2001 12:33 a.m.
From: Daughtry Maher

recently my child and her entire class visited tallahassee. you were kind enough to come out of your office and meet the children. i was impressed. you had NO thought about meeting the parents and pumping hands for votes, you were very focused on the children. you made them all feel special.you actually bordered on flirting with my daughter.(her cheeks were very red and you commented on how cute you thought it was.). it was an experience she will never forget.

we were also fortunate enough to meet the LT. gov. ,,,,he was cute.

i have been exposed to lots of swarmy type politicians in my life....you are an exception....good for you.

Subject: thank you for your attention recently
Wednesday, April 25, 2001 8:39 p.m.
From: Jeb Bush

Very cool email.

to tell the truth, I like hanging out with kids. It is the best part of my job. Adults can be so stupid! :)

Tell your precious daughter to study hard and have fun in life!!!!

Jeb

I was delighted on April 23 to announce Florida's lowest crime rate in twenty-eight years. Particularly gratifying was the 26.4 percent decline in violent gun crimes since the enactment of 10-20-Life.

Subject: Crime Rate
Wednesday, April 25, 2001 8:53 a.m.
From: Mike Gallo

Congratulations Governor on the latest crime rate
figures. I am also excited that your brother's
approval rating after 100 days is at 64-65%. I really
like his way of getting things done, yours too.
Hopefully your travels have you in the Orange-Brevard
County area soon. Take care Jeb.

Subject: Crime Rate
Wednesday, April 25, 2001 11:47 a.m.
From: Jeb Bush

thanks Mike. Life is good.

Jeb

———

*On May 1 I signed a bill that prevented local governments from
suing gunmakers. As I said at the signing, I believe strongly that
people who commit crimes with guns need to be punished—not
the companies that make them.*

Subject: Gun Bill
Wednesday, May 2, 2001 10:16 p.m.
From: Maurice Hernandez

Thanks, Jeb for signing this bill into law. I'm
ecstatic to know that you have the same reasoning I
do on this - Guns don't kill people, criminals kill
people!!!

I cannot agree with you more that we do not need more laws on this issue but we need to ENFORCE the laws that rare on the books!

Good goin' sir.

BTW - I don't even own a gun, myself. Its a matter of principle.

Subject: Gun Bill
Wednesday, May 2, 2001 10:31 p.m.
From: Jeb Bush

i don't either and you are correct, it is a matter of principle.

Jeb

———

On May 9 I signed into law election reform. It passed the House 120–0 and by 39–1 in the Senate. (Why is there always that one person who just can't quite see the light?) It was truly a joyful moment. As I said at that signing ceremony, our election process was "now the envy of the nation." Among its many provisions, the new law provided for better registration procedures and prohibited punch cards or other antiquated voting systems. There would be no more hanging chads. I promised Floridians we would never have another election like 2000, and we haven't.

This e-mail exchange was short but oh so sweet.

Subject: Election Reform Bill
Saturday, May 5, 2001 8:38 a.m.
From: [No name]

are you going to sign the election reform bill into
Law

Subject: Election Reform Bill
Saturday, May 5, 2001 9:04 a.m.
From: Jeb Bush

yes!

Jeb

―――――

*Even the political reporters were ready to wrap up legislative
business. This exchange was with Mike Griffin of the* Orlando
Sentinel *in the closing days of the session.*

Subject: You get a deal on growth, or what?
Friday, May 4, 2001 6:42 p.m.
From: Mike Griffin

So what's the deal? Is it soup yet?

Subject: You get a deal on growth, or what?
Friday, May 4, 2001 6:49 p.m.
From: Jeb Bush

The soup is still being made. It is a struggle!

Jeb

Subject: You get a deal on growth, or what?
Friday, May 4, 2001 6:52 p.m.
From: Mike Griffin

Can't you call out the state police or something?

Subject: You get a deal on growth, or what?
Friday, May 4, 2001 8:49 p.m.
From: Jeb Bush

I wish I could.

Jeb

Subject: You get a deal on growth, or what?
Friday, May 4, 2001 9:15 p.m.
From: Mike Griffin

Hang in there.

Subject: You get a deal on growth, or what?
Friday, May 4, 2001 9:32 p.m.
From: Jeb Bush

we got election reform, nursing home reform, teacher recruitment and retention, career civil service reform, and hopefully, educational governance. Not bad!

Subject: You get a deal on growth, or what?
Friday, May 4, 2001 10:30 p.m.
From: Mike Griffin

Better than a poke in the eye with a sharp stick.

Subject: You get a deal on growth, or what?
Friday, May 4, 2001 11:48 p.m.
From: Jeb Bush

much better than that. Look at previous sessions.
this is an historic one in terms of big things
happening. We can do much of our bill in terms of
growth management by DCA[52] rules and we intend
to do so.

Jeb

————

I signed the new budget on June 15, and I declared, "This is the budget that will lead Florida into the twenty-first century." I was particularly excited about the tax relief included in the budget. Here are the statistics we released that day.

- *The burden of state-based taxes would be reduced from 6.4 percent of personal income to 6.1 percent by fiscal year 2001–2002—the lowest level since 1991.*
- *State tax revenues had continued to grow, averaging 4 percent annually over the past three years. This was despite substantial tax cuts.*
- *After three years of intangible tax cuts, seven hundred thousand taxpayers, mostly seniors, would no longer have to pay taxes on their savings.*
- *Over the past two years, we had enacted almost $1.5 billion in tax cuts. This reversed the tax increases from the eight years prior to the Bush/Brogan administration. In fiscal year 2001–2002, an additional $180 million in tax was granted. That brought cumulative tax relief over four years to $5.7 billion.*
- *We enacted a sales-tax holiday on clothing for the third straight year, which took place during the back-to-school shopping period. It was expected to reduce taxes family*

---

52 Department of Community Affairs.

paid by $30 million and generate additional economic activity in the form of extra sales.

Other budget highlights included:

- Florida's K–12 system would receive a 6.3 percent increase—even higher than my budget proposal—along with additional resources for instructional materials, teacher recruitment, and teacher retention bonuses.
- New funding for health and human services would support a variety of critical services for Florida's most vulnerable.
- For seniors new funding would focus on community-based care options, ensure the care provided in nursing homes was of the highest quality, and improve the quality of nursing.

Last but not least, I used the line-item veto to eliminate more than $290 million in special projects—the infamous turkeys—in the budget.

It was a productive session.

———

With the legislative session over, it was time for me to decide whether to run for reelection. The answer was "of course." Being governor of Florida was the best job in the world. On July 5 my great friend Berthy De La Rosa-Aponte—once an avowed Democrat—and her daughter, Lucy, filed the required papers on my behalf.

Subject: Thanks
Thursday, July 5, 2001 12:59 p.m.
From: Paul

Thanks from all your friends from the Broward Special Olympics for continuing to understand the needs of the Developmentally disabled. How appropreate that you selected a parent of a child with special needs to file your papers. Our children will continue to not only be the best that they can be because of your committment, but to hold their heads high in their community because they know their Governor cares about them.

Subject: Thanks
Thursday, July 5, 2001 2:57 p.m.
From: Jeb Bush

thank you Paulie!!! You are a great friend.

Jeb

———

Columba and I then went to Maine to spend some time with my parents and other family members. This e-mail exchange was with Lucy Morgan, then the Tallahassee bureau chief for the St. Petersburg Times.

Subject: dempsey barron[53]
Saturday, July 7, 2001 11:35 a.m.
From: Lucy Morgan

Dempsey Barron died this morning.…I'm doing the obit from the mountain top.…If you check in and hve something to say, I'd love to include it.…
ps hope you've had fun in maine and managed to defeat W in a game of golf!!!

---

53 Dempsey Barron served in the Florida Senate from 1961 to 1988.

Subject: dempsey barron
Saturday, July 7, 2001 5:18 p.m.
From: Jeb Bush

jeb and i are family champs in horse shoes beating 41
and 43[54] two days in a row.…

On Dempsey. I admired him greatly.

Jeb

Subject: your fingers
Monday, July 9, 2001 5:51 p.m.
From: Lucy Morgan

A little bird that flew over the mountains this
afternoon tells me I'm not the only one with a war
wound today - so what did you do to yourself????

Subject: your fingers
Tuesday, July 10, 2001 8:41 p.m.
From: Jeb Bush

the news is out. A boating accident has put in my
middle finger temporarily in the "Rocky salute",
unless I hide it.

jeb

---

54 I think by now just about everyone knows my dad is called "Forty-One," and George W. is called "Forty-Three." They were, respectively, the forty-first and forty-third presidents of the United States. Someone once joked that if you were talking about both of them, you would say "Eighty-Four."

In the meantime we won our fight with Washington about keeping drilling away from the shores of Florida. President Clinton, Secretary of the Interior Bruce Babbitt, and my predecessor, Lawton Chiles, originally negotiated the six-million-acre lease. Parts of that lease put the drilling only sixteen miles from Florida's coastline. As a result of our negotiations, the US Department of the Interior reduced by 75 percent the size of the tract to be made available for offshore drilling, which meant no drilling within one hundred miles of our shores.

Subject: Thanks for being a great governor!
Sunday, July 15, 2001 7:24 p.m.
From: Neal

Congratulations on winning the fight to save our states beaches from oil drilling in the Gulf of Mexico! This is a tremendous victory for our state, and it shows how much clout you have with the administration in Washington.

Even the previous Democratic Governor could not get the kind of concessions from democrat President Clinton, that you have been able to extract from President Bush. This will not be lost on the voters in November 2002!

Also, thanks for your crime fighting efforts. The sinking of the three drug smuggling vessels in Miami was well covered by the news media, and sends a clear message to the criminals out there that 'Miami Vice' will not be tolerated. I know the sinking is symbolic, but that symbolism has a great psychological impact on the tourists that come to this city. As you know, South Beach is one of the hottest destinations in the world right now.

Governor, I am so very proud to have you as the Chief Executive of our state. I know there is going to be no stopping you from achieving loftier goals in the future.

Subject: Thanks for being a great governor!
Sunday, July 15, 2001 11:39 p.m.
From: Jeb Bush

Thank you Neal!

Jeb

———

I was about to fall in love for the second time in my life.

Subject: Wireless email
Saturday, September 1, 2001 12:30 p.m.
From: Rob Heyde

I am writing this from a minature remote device called blackberry. It would be a great device for you. You can receive and send email and it is the size of a palm pilot. I'm sitting in a restaurent sending this to you. Check it out, I think you would like it.

Ps it is wireless and has many other features also.

Subject: Wireless email
Saturday, September 1, 2001 3:34 p.m.
From: Jeb Bush

i am going to get one soon.

jeb

———

Yes. It had been a comparatively easy year so far. I had a budget deal that included more tax cuts for Floridians. I had a great vacation with Columba and the family. I had my new BlackBerry. I was ready for the fall season and to tackle all the usual challenges that make being governor the best job in the world.

Then our world changed forever.

On September 10 I flew to Jacksonville to meet the president of the United States. We did an event together at the Justina Road Elementary School and then flew to Sarasota, where we had dinner with friends. I went back to Tallahassee that night, as I had a cabinet meeting the next morning. George stayed in Sarasota. He was going to visit another school the next morning.

On September 11 I was getting ready for my meeting. At 8:46 a.m. American Airlines Flight 11 crashed into the North Tower of the World Trade Center in New York. United Airlines Flight 175 followed at 9:03 a.m. into the South Tower. A half hour later, American Airlines Flight 77 crashed into the west side of the Pentagon, and then United Airlines Flight 93 crashed into a field in Somerset County, Pennsylvania.

Two thousand nine hundred ninety-six people were killed.

My immediate reaction, like all Americans, was shock, anger, and grief. However, as the governor of a state, I needed to put emotions aside and get to work. My first focus was on what we needed to do to protect our state in case these were not isolated incidents. I headed to our emergency operations center and convened the heads of all the relevant agencies. We shut down the state capitol and sent all state employees home. We coordinated among local, state, and federal agencies to share intelligence. We especially focused on some high-profile potential targets such as Disney World and the Kennedy Space Center.

I placed calls to the governors of New York, Virginia, and Pennsylvania to see if there was anything Florida could do to help.

I had a brief conversation with my brother—just long enough to tell him I loved him and was thinking of him. None of us will ever forget the look on his face and the calm he maintained as White House Chief of Staff Andy Card whispered in his ear what was happening as he listened to a child at Emma E. Booker Elementary School joyfully read a story to the president of the United States.

I addressed Floridians and told them I felt confident our state was safe. I asked them to fly the American flag. I asked them to pray for the victims, their families, and our country.

About nine o'clock that evening, I started answering e-mails. It seemed like the next best thing I could do to help. People were scared and confused. I did what I could to offer reassurance, advice, and support.

Subject: Public School closure
Tuesday, September 11, 2001 6:22 p.m.
From: Stephen Windhaus

I am told the St. Lucie County School District will be open tomorrow. I am told this is done according to State policy. I strongly urge the closing of the public school system in this entire state tomorrow. Our children, and the inconvenience it creates for the parents are the least we can do to insure our children understand this something more than just some realistic extension of a movie, which, today, is evident.

Those of us in positions of power and influence need to insure the U.S. population understands the gravity the loss of 10,000+ Americans means to the history of this country and the future of our system of Democracy.

Subject: Public School closure
Tuesday, September 11, 2001 9:08 p.m.
From: Jeb Bush

Steve, if we allow the terrorist to paralyize our
country, they win.

jeb bush

_____

Subject: Hey
Tuesday, September 11, 2001 8:29 p.m.
From: Briana

Hey my name is briana im 13 years old can you
please send me some more information about the
attack is it going to turn into a war? i heard it
was going to be bigger then pearl harbor is that
true? please please please write me back when u get
a chance

Subject: Hey
Tuesday, September 11, 2001 9:15 p.m.
From: Jeb Bush

Briana, you can be sure that our country's government
will do everything to protect you. It was an act of
war and we will respond accordingly. Pray for our
country.

jeb bush

_____

Subject: god be with you
Tuesday, September 11, 2001 9:48 p.m.
From: Daisy

jeb…I am shocked but am glad that you are our governor during this time. I trust your leadership.…I will pray for you and may god be with you during this time.

Subject: god be with you
Tuesday, September 11, 2001 10:41 p.m.
From: Jeb Bush

Pray for our beloved country.

———

Subject: Thank You Jeb!
Tuesday, September 11, 2001 10:02 p.m.
From: Roberto Martinez

I appreciate your strong presence and leadership during your press

conference this afternoon. It was very important to me and many others to hear their Governor and other political leaders address the citizens to reassure us that as Americans we will once again rise to the occasion and be able to confront this latest tragedy. I encourage you to continue to address the public repeatedly during the next few days. Your strong and articulate presence is important to the people of the State of Florida. We need to see you and our other strong leaders during this time of crisis. It is very reassuring.

Please let me know what this private citizen can do to assist the State of Florida during this time of crisis. During the next few days Miami-Dade Community College will be organizing a blood drive in each campus to gather blood to transmit to New York City. I heard in the news tonight that New York City is already low in its blood supply.

Subject: Thank You Jeb!
Tuesday, September 11, 2001 10:42 p.m.
From: Jeb Bush

you are a good man, Bobby. I will be giving blood tomorrow as well. God bless our beloved country.

jeb

———

Subject: Our Arab-American FRIENDS
Wednesday, September 12, 2001 10:22 p.m.
From: Gwen Meehan

Please let Floridians know that we must not harrass our Arab-American counterparts who are citizens or guests of this country! It is imperative that we maintain our dignity and respect the legal status of these people. We were all in their shoes at some point in our history! All people who LOOK Middle Eastern are neither terrorists nor Islamic. They routinely suffer indignities based on how they look…does that bring to mind our black brothers and sisters, and our hispanic brethren? They cannot help that.

You and all other leaders in the United States must stress the need to use restraint. I don't need to say anymore. I'm sure you and your brother can come up with strong words to encourage people to think before they speak or act! We must remember how we treated the Japanese-Americans during WW II…despicably! We are considering reparation now many years later. Let's not do it again to our Arab-Americans.…

Subject: Our Arab-American FRIENDS
Thursday, September 13, 2001 7:58 a.m.
From: Jeb Bush

Gwen, I agree with you completely. I am concerned about this and have already made one statement about it.

Jeb

I sent this note to the commanders of all the military installations in Florida.

Subject: Thank you
Friday, September 14, 2001 10:25 p.m.
From: Jeb Bush

I am writing on behalf of all Floridians to thank you for your leadership in this moment of crisis for our wonderful country. We are blessed to have the best armed forces in the world. The men and women who protect our freedom will be put in harms way in the upcoming months and Floridians are thankful beyond words for their sacrifice.

God Bless America.

Jeb Bush

I received this answer from US Air Force General Charles Holland, commander of the US Special Operations Command headquarters at MacDill Air Force Base near Tampa.

Subject: Thank you
Tuesday, September 18, 2001 6:40 p.m.
From: Charles Holland

Thank you for your superb support of our people in uniform. We'll continue to be worthy of your trust and confidence. Our people have a clear understanding of why they serve and when that is reinforced by our senior state and national leaders they just stand that much taller. We're proud to be serving in your state.

Subject: Thank you
Tuesday, September 18, 2001 8:16 p.m.
From: Jeb Bush

you are most welcome. God bless America.

jeb bush

————

Unfortunately there was a connection between the terrorists and Florida. Many had taken flying lessons here and used our state as a training ground for their atrocious attack on our nation. This inquiry came from a St. Petersburg Times *reporter.*

Subject: Florida
Saturday, September 15, 2001 1:19 p.m.
From: Steve Bousquet

Sorry to interrupt your weekend. As you know, most
of the suspected hijackers had Florida driver's
licenses and/or ID cards issued by the state. Do
you, as one of those overseeing Highway Safety, have
any concerns as to whether the state ought to review
the procedures and requirements for obtaining such
a license in our state? Is it too easy to get a
Florida license? Or, conversely, is such a question
completely irrelevant?

Subject: Florida
Saturday, September 15, 2001 4:44 p.m.
From: Jeb Bush

We are reviewing everything, Steve.

Jeb Bush

———

I sent this note to my chief of staff, Kathleen Shanahan.

Subject: [None]
Saturday, September 15, 2001 8:59 p.m.
From: Jeb Bush

i am very, very worried about the economic impacts of
911. I think our worst fears will come true. If my
instincts are wrong, we still need to be prepared.
We need to work on worst case scenarios for this
fiscal year and next. This should be done in the next
several weeks.

I hope you are hanging in there. Kathleen, I am so grateful for you being in Tallahassee. I know your heart is elsewhere and my heart aches for you now with all of your friends that died or are suffering up in NYC.[55] I want you to know how much I appreciate your leadership. You are one of the most talented people I have ever met.

Will you let me know if I can ever be of help to you in any way?

Jeb

———

I was receiving e-mail complaints that some homeowners associations had rules against flag flying. On September 15 I had to issue a statement strongly suggesting the times overruled the rules.

Subject: Thanks for Your Stand on The American Flag
Tuesday, September 18, 2001 2:00 p.m.
From: Jo Ann Hutchinson

Thanks for standing up to groups who will not allow the display of our American Flag. It was the first thing me and my husband did on Tuesday and it means so much to everyone. Our thoughts are with your brother on the difficult burden he carries at this time. Thanks for your leadership as well.

GOD BLESS AMERICA!

———

55 Kathleen had lived in New York City for a time and lost twelve friends on 9/11.

Subject: Thanks for Your Stand on The American Flag
Tuesday, September 18, 2001 9:18 p.m.
From: Jeb Bush

strange isn't it, that this would have to be an issue? God bless America!

Jeb Bush

———

Besides the immediate task of making sure Florida was safe, there was a growing crisis with our economy. Here are some statistics my office released a few weeks after 9/11:

- *Fifty thousand Floridians applied for unemployment after September 24. Forecasts predicted a loss of 120,000 jobs by June 30, 2002.*
- *Planes were arriving at 35 percent capacity at first then slowly grew back to 60 percent capacity, which was still low.*
- *Florida's very large aviation industry lost $700 million in September. Almost 80 percent of the aviation companies we surveyed predicted they would have to lay off thirty thousand to fifty thousand employees by the end of the year.*
- *Hotel occupancy was at 40 to 50 percent. This was compared to a normal average of 75 percent occupancy. Many conventions had been canceled.*
- *Attendance at Florida's major tourist attractions was down 50 to 70 percent.*

In a state where tourism is the largest industry, these numbers were devastating. I worried about Floridians being able to put food on their tables and keep their homes. I knew our state revenues were going to take a huge hit.

Once again the e-mails of concern and ideas poured in.

Subject: FL budget
Monday, September 17, 2001 9:59 p.m.
From: David Johnson

You may have heard that US Air and Continental have
laid off 25% and 20% of their employees. Can Delta
or even Southwest be far behind? This, together
with other economic factors--not to mention fear--
augurs poorly for tourism and consumer spending for
at least the next six months, and probably longer.
The rainy day fund is like spent already. You know
this; even the public knows. Everybody knows. I saw
Sen. McKay on Sunday tv calling for a broadening of
the sales tax base. The point in e-mailing you is
to suggest that you use events of the past week to
call for an emergency legislative session to deal
with the problem. Don't wait for the 1.5% trigger.
It's already come and gone. Citizens want a fairer,
more understandable, tax base. Broaden it. Include
internet sales. Then reduce the rate to what you
think you need to get thru the next fiscal year. Then
see what happens. Leading here will deprive the
opposition of a major issue next yr.

Subject: FL budget
Tuesday, September 18, 2001 7:18 a.m.
From: Jeb Bush

Dave, raising taxes is not the answer. We do have a
serious problem caused by september 11th. There is no
denying it and we are working on solutions.

Jeb Bush

———

Subject: [None]
Tuesday, September 18, 2001 8:11 a.m.
From: David Colburn

I write as a result of last weeks events to make a suggestion to you. If it is a bit presumptuous, then just ignore it.

In the aftermath of these developments, Florida may face a difficult time in the next several months because tourism is likely to suffer significantly. I think most Floridians understand this. But it may be helpful to you to have a bipartisan group of distinguished Floridians working directly with you as we address this national crisis and the financial one we are likely to experience at the state level. My proposal to you is to establish such an advisory group of Floridians - perhaps with Bob Martinez and Reubin Askew as co-chairs and folks from cities, like John Delaney, and folks from the business community. I would think you would want a relatively small working group. If you think this idea is worthwhile, I hope you will also include one or two of us from higher education to be part of this working group. I think you would want people who can think big, understand what is fundamentally important to the future of this state, and who also enjoy statewide respect.

Subject: [None]
Tuesday, September 18, 2001 9:33 p.m.
From: Jeb Bush

Thank you David. I am worried that the emergency is too in the here and now. I am on the case working

with the agency for workforce innovation, Visit
Florida, the airport folks, the cruise industry,
the hotel and motel industry, the restaurant
association, the Florida Chamber, Tax Watch, AIF and
others to see what we can do to protect and defend
our economy. The impact will be felt in the next two
months and a commission as you describe, which is
a good idea for a long term situation, won't help.
Anyway, that is my current thinking and I appreciate
your views.

Jeb

PS My life is focused on the threats of terror, the
budget impacts and how to boost our economy.

———

Subject: From Susan Lewis
Wednesday, September 19, 2001 6:18 p.m.
From: Susan Lewis

I haven't written since this awful thing has
happened to our country. I know you are as upset
as al of us. I know this is an unusual question,
but I thought you would give me a straight answer.
I'm getting really scared as far as our business
goes. We've had our retail gift store since 1986
and since the beginning of last year and expecially
since the election dragged on during our most
important retail selling season…our business is
way off. And then all of this, we've hardly done
anything since Sept. 11. Do you think the retail
business will pick up during all of this? I hate to
have to think about it, but we were already barely

hanging on and then this. I feel so bad, I wish I could give to the Red Cross, help, anything.…I can't even get caught up. I don't know whether to cancel my orders for giftware and Christmas for the store. I know this is not your expertise, but I thought you might be able to advise me re: if business is going to improve.

I know the President says to continue our lives.…It is so hard when you own your own business and it is your paycheck…other people spending. The airlines, etc. are hurting on a large scale, but it will kill us who have small businesses. I'm not one to panic nor ever ask anyone for anything.…Always worked hard my entire life. I just want to work for the President, the state. Any jobs available for a business owner or RN in government.? Your brother has done great and we are very proud of him. I feel so useless to help.

Subject: From Susan Lewis
Thursday, September 20, 2001 8:16 a.m.
From: Jeb Bush

Susan, I am so sorry about the impacts this will have on our economy and on Floridians. I think we will rebound economically but some sectors will take time. Tourism is one that is of particular concern. Hang in there and let me know if you think I can help.

Jeb Bush

———

I sent this "thinking out loud" e-mail to Kathleen and some other top staff members about possible action items.

Subject: ideas on how to stay out front on the security, economy and budget. your additional thoughts?
Saturday, September 22, 2001 4:39 p.m.
From: Jeb Bush

- conference calls with chambers of commerce coordinated with efi[56] after they develop a plan of action for retaining business.
- invite business editors up to tally for lunch to discuss the economy.
- going on radio in the morning more.
- floridians visiting florida plan
- get my mom and dad on a cruise.[57]
- meeting with general aviation industry
- visit dade health dept. to highlight defense against biological terrorism.
- ads around country encouraging people to fly to florida (ric cooper)
- aviation fuel tax plan
- take a loved one out to eat night.
- laura bush flying commercial to florida
- savings bonds
- travel agent conference call
- call five companies or associations that did not cancel convention each day
- call five companies or associations that did cancel convention each day and ask them to reconsider.
- develop small business assistance plan.

---

56 EFI is Enterprise Florida, Inc., a public-private partnership with business and industry to recruit and retain businesses in Florida.
57 Mom and Dad did not go on a cruise, but Dad took a Continental Airlines flight from Boston to Houston just a few days after commercial airliners started flying. NBC anchor Tom Brokaw met him at the gate at Logan Airport in Boston and interviewed him before he boarded the plane. It was huge news and a huge help.

- budget requests anti terror pro security plans.
- AirTrans
- Get president to jawbone tv execs to resturn to normal news coverage.
- get superbowl to Florida.
- student letter writing campaign (liza McFadden)
- televised town hall meeting
- visit miami dade firefighter while in nyc
- we will rebuild briefing with Guliani
- use myflorida.com more effectively to communicate about the economy and security issues
- homeland defense person
- selling the budget cuts
- call non tourist businesses each day.
- workforce development issues
- pray a lot

E-mails like the next few kept me going.

Subject: A Grateful American
Saturday, September 22, 2001 8:41 p.m.
From: Tim Leadbeater

On June 6, 1973, I became an American citizen in Miami, Florida. Nine years earlier, in 1964, my parents and six siblings entered the United States of America through the Port of New York as emigrants from Canada. My youngest sister was just two months old. We came with limited resources but bountiful spirits and full of hope. As we sailed into New York, I was struck by the awesome presence of the Statute of Liberty. At that time I could not fully appreciate her majesty. After clearing immigration, our family traveled from New York by train to Deerfield Beach, Florida to live the American dream.

Today, September 22, 2001, I received word that I, as an Army Reservist, would be mobilized in response to the events of September 11, 2001. Since arriving here 37 years ago, I have come to more fully understand the majesty of America as symbolized by the Statute of Liberty. The events of September 11, 2001, and America's response to those horrific events have solidified that understanding and stirred my heart. I am so grateful that I have been given the opportunity to serve this great country…my country. God Bless America!

Subject: A Grateful American
Sunday, September 23, 2001 11:22 a.m.
From: Jeb Bush

God bless you for your service to our country.

Jeb Bush

———

Subject: From your Holy Name Middle School studets
Wednesday, September 26, 2001 11:36 a.m.
From: [All fifty-three students signed this note]

We are "Proud to be Floridians" and Americans!! Thank you for your good leadership.

Subject: From your Holy Name Middle School studets
Wednesday, September 26, 2001 8:13 p.m.
From: Jeb Bush

thank you as well. I hope you have a great school year. The way you can show the terrorists that they are wrong is to gain at least a year's worth of knowledge in a year's time.

Jeb

———

Subject: Pres. speech today
Thursday, September 27, 2001 1:33 p.m.
From: Dinah Voyles Pulver[58]

Wow, not bad when you can get the President of the United States to get on live TV and tell people to go to Disney World in Florida! Nice work.

Subject: Pres. speech today
Thursday, September 27, 2001 9:01 p.m.
From: Jeb Bush

he did it on his own!

Jeb

———

I hit the road to promote Florida's vital tourism industry. In Boston I met with representatives from New England-based travel agencies, Amtrak, and rental-car companies as well as hoteliers. In Chicago I met with a group of tourism-industry leaders at a Disney store. I received this note from the vice president of government relations for Walt Disney World.

---

58   Dinah Voyles Pulver was a reporter for the *Daytona Beach News-Journal*.

Subject: Saturday's event in Chicago
Monday, October 1, 2001 1:37 p.m.
From: Jane Adams

We cannot thank you enough for your recent support
of tourism and Walt Disney World -- particularly
the event in Chicago. Unfortunately, I was not able
to be there this weekend, but I understand it was a
wonderful success.

We appreciate the effort you made to go there and to
generate so much favorable media coverage for our
resort. And, our cast members and guests were excited
to see you and participate in the festivities. That's
the most excitement we've had at a Disney Store in
some time!

We also appreciate your efforts today to produce PSAs[59]
in support of our industry.

Thank you again for all you are doing to help us
through this challenging time.

Subject: Saturday's event in Chicago
Monday, October 1, 2001 8:24 p.m.
From: Jeb Bush

**Thank you Jane. it was a wonderful event. Lots of
kids going to disney this winter from Chicago!**

Jeb

---

59 PSA stands for public service announcement. PSAs are used to educate the public rather than sell products.

In the midst of all the challenges, it was very nice to get this note from the CEO of Yahoo! about the state website and my great team. However, I still managed to bring up our tourism crisis.

Subject: MyFlorida.com
Friday, October 5, 2001 7:55 p.m.
From: Terry Semel

I wanted to personally reach out to you to indicate how excited we at Yahoo! are about the partnership between our company and the State of Florida. Over the years, your efforts have placed Florida at the forefront of state's that are leading in technology and e-government.

At Yahoo!, we take this opportunity to work with you to deliver on your vision of providing many of the states services on-line very seriously. We know from working with some of the world's largest corporations, like McDonald's, Honeywell and Pfizer, that the cost savings opportunities associated with aggregating information into a portal are exceeded only by the improvement in the "user experience" associated with personalized, multi-lingual access to relevant information.

As we have worked on this project my team has been impressed with your staff; particularly those at the State Technology Office. I would like to thank you for the performance and professionalism of your staff in working to make this project happen. From the initial encounter that Yahoo! has had with your team, we are confident that this is a relationship that will continue to grow and prosper.

We all recognize what a trying period these last several weeks has been both emotionally and economically. We at Yahoo! are particularly sensitive of the impact that the reduction in travel and tourism could have on the State of Florida. As part of this project, let's discover ways Yahoo!'s vast reach to over 200 million users can stimulate tourism in Florida. I think you will find there are many ways in which we can help you.

Again, thank you for this ground-breaking opportunity to work with your great state. If you have any needs, or would like to broaden our discussion, I urge you to call me.

Subject: MyFlorida.com
Friday, October 5, 2001 9:15 p.m.
From: Jeb Bush

Thank you Terry. I was excited to learn that your enterprise was helping us with our myflorida.com portal. My aspiration is to make state government the most accessible, the most efficient and the most service driven organization in the nation. Your help is greatly appreciated. I hope you team has a sense of urgency about this. I do. I hope you can use us as a model to sell to other governmental entities.

Any thoughts you have to make my aspiration come true would be greatly appreciated.

For example, right now, Floridians are suffering because folks are concerned about flying. it is killing us temporarily. Is there a way to launch a email/internet campaign with strong discounts to get people to come to paradise? This is one of many ways that we are anxious to work with you and others.

Again, thank you for writing.

Jeb

———

After another round of e-mail exchanges between Terry and me, we wisely turned this over to our respective teams to work out a partnership between Florida and Yahoo! They did a great job helping us get the word out about the great state of Florida.

———

The state legislature went into special session to address the budget crisis and consider an economic recovery package I had unveiled on October 12. I sent this note to my top staff the day before.

Subject: [None]
Thursday, October 11, 2001 7:55 a.m.
From: Jeb Bush

a few random toughts:

WE need to start making daily progress on the special session.

The first place where I think we can get agreement is security. We should try to do so this week. I will see the Speaker this afternoon and see if we can expand the call to include a set number of recommendations.

Economic development may be more illusive since there are more ideas out there but we need to push for a deal.

Daily progress on the budget is critical. I need to know what the last day we must have an agreement in order to get the session ended on time.

I suggest that the Lt. Governor look at his schedule so as to spend more time with members either on the phone or in person.

We need to include the democrats in the process.

we need to make this our highest priority for the next few weeks.

Jeb

————

Subject: Would you give me a list of prayer needs for the state?
Thursday, October 11, 2001 8:32 p.m.
From: Pam Olsen[60]

Would you give me a list of the top prayer needs to focus on for our state as the legislators go into special session. I know the obvious:safety and budget needs. Are there certain areas that I can cover in prayer that you are concerned about? Hundreds

----

60   Pam Olsen is the president of the Florida Prayer Network.

of prayer leaders from across the nation will be gathering in Orlando Oct.24-26 to pray for our nation and state. I know this is a very difficult time for the nation and for Florida. We are praying for south Florida and for people not to be filled with fear. Please let me know the burdens on your heart so that I can stand with you in prayer. Send my love and prayers to Columba. You already know this, but you are covered in prayer! Hope you both have a wonderful weekend!

Subject: Would you give me a list of prayer needs for the state?
Saturday, October 13, 2001 9:40 p.m.
From: Jeb Bush

- **pray for the unemployed who worry about making ends meet.**
- **pray for the families who are fearful of the breadwinners in the family losing their jobs**
- **pray for the first responders who are working to keep us safe**
- **pray for the members of the legislature that they put aside some of their differences to get the job done in the weeks ahead.**

Thank you Pam.

Jeb

———

The following e-mail from Michael Eisner, then head of Disney, shows just how nervous people were. There were rumors in and out of the press that Walt Disney World was among the next ter-rorist targets.

Subject: From Michael Eisner at The Walt Disney Company
Saturday, October 13, 2001 1:05 p.m.
From: Michael Eisner

Bob Iger[61] just talked to Collingwood at the FBI who said they had no evidence about Disney being a target, not did they have an information about Disney being surveyed by anybody anytime. I think the FBI is going to put out a strong statement. We will make sure it gets to the right places. I hope the CIA doesn't have other information. Do you know if they do?

If Bob get anymore information from ABC News or anybody else he will e-mail both of us.

———

Subject: From Michael Eisner at The Walt Disney Company
Saturday, October 13, 2001 9:23 p.m.
From: Jeb Bush

I know of no evidence that Disney is a targete. I will follow up through our chennels. I troed to call you just give minutes ago on your portable My number is 850-488-1809.[62]

---

61 Bob Iger was president and COO of Disney. He succeeded Mike Eisner as CEO and chairman.

62 I do hope Michael forgave my pathetic spelling in this e-mail and wrote it off as stress. As for the phone number, it's no longer active.

———

*In the meantime e-mails from worried Floridians continued to
flood my in-box.*

I didn't mind. I was glad to help provide answers when I could.

*The next e-mail was about a new workforce initiative called
Operation Paycheck, which I had announced on October 4. It was
a public-private partnership, and the idea was to direct displaced
workers toward high-demand employment opportunities, connect them with the job-skill training they needed, and then help
them find jobs. Ideally all this would happen in twenty-six weeks
or less—before unemployment compensation ran out.*

Subject: Operation Paycheck!
Monday, October 15, 2001 6:18 a.m.
From: Karen Lynn Tate

As a life long Florida Resident and a displaced Tourism
employee I am very interested in Operation Paycheck,
and how others might partnership with the State.

Thank you for your Time, Efforts and the Results that
are Sure to Come when Together Everyone Achieves More!.

Subject: Operation Paycheck!
Monday, October 15, 2001 7:19 a.m.
From: Jeb Bush

**Thank you Karen. I am asking that tom MCGurk, the
director of the Agency for Workforce Innovation, have
someone to get in touch with you.**

Jeb Bush

———

This e-mail was from an elementary school principal.

Subject: Saving Schools from Budget Cuts
Monday, October 15, 2001 9:58 a.m.
From: Gary Mogensen

In the crisis that has followed the terrible events
of September 11, 2001, we have been challenged by
those who believe that they can bring the United
States to its knees. We must meet this challenge
with a resolute determination to maintain the
high standards of education for our children. Only
with young people prepared to take an active,
knowledgeable and creative role in our society can
we resist the debilitating forces of fear, insecurity
and anti-Americanism.

Please do all you can to maintain the funding of
our public schools at the present level. In a lean
budget year, we have already been cut to the bone
and any further reductions will cause losses in
staff that will undermine our ability to provide for
student needs. I would like to suggest that under
the financial crisis conditions of today, that school
districts be allowed to move money from where it
exists in capital outlay and categorical funds to
where it is needed in operations. I would also like
you to consider seriously rescinding the tax cut of
last Spring which primarily assisted our more affluent
citizens and rechannel those lost funds into the
areas that need it most, our public schools.

Subject: Saving Schools from Budget Cuts
Monday, October 15, 2001 7:34 p.m.
From: Jeb Bush

Thank you Gary for writing. I have advocated protecting direct classroom instruction and giving school districts flexibility to make the cuts. It is hard for me to believe that you have had to cut to the bone given the fact that there has been a 22% increase in funding in the last three years. To put the tax cut mentioned in perspective, it is $130 million. The adjustment downward to the budget will be $1.3 billion. I have stated that if to reach a consensus we need to defer the intangible tax reduction, then I would be prepared to do so.

Jeb Bush

PS on the intablibles tax, raising the exemption from $100,000 to $200,000 certainly isn't a boon to the "wealthy". The great majority of the benificiaries would be elders on fixed income who rely on their savings to get by.

———

Subject: budget cuts
Friday, October 19, 2001 4:44 p.m.
From: Bob Maltz

I attended a meeting a few days ago where a Florida Congressman spoke about the fiscal problems with the State of Florida. It would appear that budgeting problems started to occur prior to September 11th and of course a major change had taken place since that time. The State, therefore has decided to take steps to solve this problem of a deficit by reducing all spending with the State. Therefore many programs will be cut or reduced.

In my opinion, this is not the solution. The amount of reductions or shortfall is over 1.5 billion dollars. Instead of reducing all programs, why not try to increase revenues. This increase of revenue could be achieved in the following manner:

1. Increase the sales tax from 6% to 6 ½%.
2. Change the real estate $25,000 exemption from the first $25,000 to the second $25,000. This will be fair to all, as everyone enjoys all of the benefits of the State. Poorer individuals could be dealt with by welfare if need be or by some other helpful way for those that cannot afford this.
3. Since, major revenues to the State come from Tourism we must think of ourselves in Florida. We should establish an area of large size that can be developed into a special area for gaming casinos. We keep trying to pass bills to allow gaming and it is those people that eliminate it each time that might be in the poorer categories. Gaming, if done right will help Florida while making it extremely pleasant for Floridians to eliminate the travel to the Islands. Keep the money here. Also, most people going to the Islands etc. travel through Florida. So, if gaming brings in money through hotels, shows and gaming, it is all for the better. We need a large area for this where travel is easy. Miami, might be okay but it is too difficult and congested.

These are three ways in which we could earn enough revenues without reducing State benefits. Keep our school classes small and lets develop income.

Subject: budget cuts
Friday, October 19, 2001 7:36 p.m.
From: Jeb Bush

Thank you for writing. I respectfully disagree that we should raise taxes as the way to deal with our shortfall. Remember, we are talking about cutting the growth in the budget from 6.6% to half of that in terms of growth. We have adequate reserves to deal with half of the shortfall and the rest should be handled by cutting some the growth in the current budget.

Jeb Bush

———

You might remember that a week after 9/11, letters containing anthrax spores were mailed to several US Senate offices and media organizations. This included American Media, publisher of the National Enquirer, *in Boca Raton, Florida. On October 5 Bob Stevens of American Media died. He was the first victim of anthrax in the United States in twenty-five years.*

Members of my team and the Florida Department of Health worked closely with federal officials to determine the protocols of how to deal with this new threat.

There was no connection to 9/11, but it certainly scared everyone for a while. Five people died. The other victims lived in Washington, DC, New York City, and Connecticut. Seventeen others were infected. A man who worked in a biodefense lab was the main suspect, but he died of a drug overdose as the Department of Justice was poised to file criminal charges against him for the attacks.

This inquiry came from a reporter for the Palm Beach Post.

Subject: Your health
Monday, October 22, 2001 6:43 p.m.
From: Jim Ash

I noticed on "Face to Face" and in your presentation
today to the House working group, that you appear
to suffering from a cold or the flu. Given the recent
discovery of anthrax spores in Gov. Pataki's[63] office,
wonder if you haven't considered _ or if you haven't
been advised _ to be tested for anthrax exposure.

Subject: Your health
Monday, October 22, 2001 7:53 p.m.
From: Jeb Bush

**i haven't considered it since there is no reason to
be concerned. I am sick cause i have worn myself out
over the last month.**

Jeb

PS nice haircut!

———

Subject: taxes
Wednesday, October 24, 2001 4:57 p.m.
From: Elizabeth Gulitz

Please consider a one year "victory tax" (.5%
increase in sales tax)!

---

63 George Pataki was the governor of New York.

Gutting our budget now shows the terrorists that they have won. Our most vulnerable populations will be the victims of a budget reduction thereby reducing our capacity to respond to terrorism and to rebuild.

Subject: taxes
Wednesday, October 24, 2001 8:53 p.m.
From: Jeb Bush

thank you for writing. To be honest with you I'm opposed to increasing taxes during these tough times.

Jeb Bush

———

The special session ended abruptly when the House and the Senate, both controlled by Republicans, could not reach consensus on several issues and passed a plan I did not want to sign. "It's much easier to spend money rather than cut," I said in frustration when the legislators went home without finishing their business. They did approve $20 million for a tourism ad campaign and $1 billion for road and school construction, which would mean nearly thirty-three thousand new jobs. Both were critical to jump-starting the sluggish post-9/11 economy.

Subject: [None]
Wednesday, October 31, 2001 11:18 a.m.
From: Bob Levy

My little personal note - Speaker Feeney says you called the legislature without having a consensus before you brought them here. I don't know what book that is written in - but the bottom line is they are not supposed to leave until they've reached consensus and that's far more aggregious than what you've been accused of!

My second consider it piece of advice - act quickly - to not do the economic stimulus or security measures will haunt this legislature - it's irresponsible. Act before you leave for Spain[64] and lay down the mandates - and distance yourself as far as you can from the legislature - I believe they've done themselves as a body serious damage - D and R alike.

You know that we care about you and the job you're doing and have the utmost respect and admiration for you and your family - so please take my comments in the manner in which they're offered -- just my 25 years of working in this process and my sensibilities about the public pulse and politics.

Subject: [None]
Wednesday, October 31, 2001 1:52 p.m.
From: Jeb Bush

Thank you Bob.

Here is the good news. The security and economic stimulus packages were funded. I can do the security issues by the executive order. The aviation fuel tax airport flexibility bill was passed. We can do all of the contruction acceleration. We got the $20 million for the ad campaign.

The other good news is that the legislature made $800 million in recurring cuts and the budget is balanced.

---

64 Columba and I were leaving on November 4 on a trade mission to Spain.

The bad news is that the job needs to get completed.

Jeb Bush

———

On November 6 Senate President John McKay and House Speaker Tom Feeney joined me to announce we had agreed on a set of budget principles to "guide another special session" of the legislature. They would reconvene November 27. In the meantime the debate continued in my e-mail in-box—especially about a proposal to delay the intangibles tax cut.

Subject: Intangible Tax
Tuesday, November 6, 2001 4:18 p.m.
From: Bob Johnson

I have been asked to say on behalf of some friends on the barrier island that they will find it hard to support you or the Fl GOP if the intangible tax goes the way you want. (It is being reported that you want to postpone the latest tax change for a couple of years.

Subject: Intangible Tax
Tuesday, November 6, 2001 7:40 p.m.
From: Jeb Bush

Yes I do. The democrats support a repeal, as did the Senate 39-1. The compromise is to defer for 18 months. The cummulative effect of our tax cutting efforts are close to $5.5 billion over four years. My opponents want to raise taxes. So how can your

friends support Reno[65] and the liberals. That is
ridiculous.

Jeb

―――――

*On November 9 I visited the Miami-Dade County Health
Department and regional laboratory and the Turkey Point
Nuclear Plant in Homestead. Special apparel was required at the
health department, which got the attention of this* St. Petersburg
Times *reporter.*

Subject: haz mat suit
Friday, November 9, 2001 5:56 p.m.
From: Julie Hauserman

I can't believe you wore a haz-mat suit and I
wasn't there to give you a hard time about it.
Doesn't that violate your no-funny-looking hats
rule?

Subject: haz mat suit
Friday, November 9, 2001 7:14 p.m.
From: Jeb Bush

rules are made to be broken at the appropriate time.
How did I look?

Jeb

―――――

―――――――

65 Former Attorney General Janet Reno was running for governor on
the Democratic side.

Subject: A quick question
Friday, November 9, 2001 11:43 a.m.
From: John Geyer

I am helping a very close friend prepare for a day at her alma mater (University of New Haven) where she is being honored as an example of someone who has risen from a modest background and has achieved great things. She will be making comments to various groups throughout the day including undergraduate classes, graduate classes, a group of professors, the board of governors and a general session with the student body at large.

She is gathering a number of direct messages from the other side (meaning, outside the world of academia, some might say the "real > world") and would appreciate your thoughts on the following:

If you were talking to a group of students - what's the number one message you would leave them with

If you were talking to a group of professors - what's the number one message you would leave them with?

Subject: A quick question
Friday, November 9, 2001 8:40 p.m.
From: Jeb Bush

I would tell students to dream big unconventional dreams and pursue them with passion, intensity and integrity.

I would tell professors to encourage students to dream big unconventional dreams and pursue them with passion, intensity and integrity and give them the real world tools to do so.

Jeb Bush

———

Subject: Budget
Tuesday, November 27, 2001 1:37 p.m.
From: Thomas E. Woods

I wish you luck on the special session. So far it does not look good from the statewide ink I have seen to date and that is sad.

The Legislature just needs to understand we do not have a money problem. We have a financial challenge and everyone needs to think more creatively to find the solution.

If they are still trying to "think out side of the box" - they are

dinosaurs. In today's technology world we are "beyond the box". There are no boundaries.

The impossible is made possible on a daily basis.

Subject: Budget
Tuesday, November 27, 2001 8:47 p.m.
From: Jeb Bush

we will get through this and do so better than most
of the 50 states having to do the same thing.

Jeb Bush

———

*Sometimes it was a relief to get e-mails about the problems with
which we were dealing before 9/11.*

Subject: here's that story
Tuesday, November 27, 2001 10:16 a.m.
To: Rebecca Eagan

KNOW you have your hands full, but please read this
article when you get the chance. If what the St.
John's Water Management District says is true---that
we will run out of water in five years!---then this
presents another sound and urgent argument for a
statewide growth management plan. Bless your heart, I
don't mean to dump new "horrors" on you willy-nilly---
but this problem could be dire in our area in 5 years.
(They originally projected that we had 20 years before
"crisis" occurred.) Growth isn't just a problem of
aesthetics or socioeconomics, obviously, now.…
Thank you for at least considering it in your bundle
of priorities!

Subject: here's that story
Tuesday, November 27, 2001 9:33 p.m.
From: Jeb Bush

Rebecca, thank you for writing. Yes, we have a huge
challenge regarding our growth. Growth is good but
only if we organize it in a way that allows for a

commitment to infrastructure (schools, roads, water
resources, natural environment) that allows us
to sustain a quality of life we aspire to. growth
management reform is a high priority because of
this and I will work for next session to make it a
reality.

Jeb Bush

————

However, some problems were even too big for a governor.

Subject: Proper pronunciation of "nuclear"
Saturday, November 17, 2001 1:05 p.m.
From: D. Lynn Keith

I am a great fan of both you and your brother.
What I especially love about the President is
his sense of humor and willingness to poke a
little fun at himself. This trait has endeared him
to the country. Which brings me to the point of my
email.

Being married to a transplanted Texan myself, I know
how difficult it can be to tell a Texan something he
does not want to hear (namely, any criticism at all!)
That is the ONLY reason I can figure for why Laura has
not corrected the President's pronunciation of the word
"nuclear." It should be pronounced new-clee-ur, not
new-q-ler. I can assure you that millions of people
around the country shudder everytime he mispronounces
this word. It is just like a fingernail on a blackboard.
It gives people the wrong impression of his educational
level. I know it shouldn't, but it does.

Since he has been reaching out in so many ways
to the schoolchildren of this country, and is
becoming a role model for and a hero of them, I
think it is important that he not mislead them on
the pronunciation of a word which may figure so
prominently in their future.

Apparently all of his aides are reluctant to tell him
he is pronouncing it incorrectly as well. I'm hoping
that, brother to brother, you will not be afraid to
tell him, and he will be receptive to your doing so.

I think it would be a wonderful opportunity for him to
again poke a little fun at himself -- because, believe
me, millions of people around the country would be so
delighted to know that he's finally been told!

Thank you very much for taking care of this matter.

Subject: Proper pronunciation of "nuclear"
Tuesday, November 27, 2001 9:45 p.m.
From: Jeb Bush

As a former Texan, I can appreciate the President's
dilemma. I hope you give him a pass. If Laura can't
help him, I can assure you his reformed "bro' " won't
be able to.

Jeb Bush

———

It wasn't easy, but the legislature passed a new balanced budget
that addressed our post-9/11 reality. Calling it a "statesmanlike
effort," I signed it into law on December 13. We were able to cut

$1.3 billion in state spending to close the budget gap. Some of the highlights included the following:

- *The budget reflected a deferral of the third step in eliminating the intangibles tax. This resulted in an additional $128 million to help meet the state's needs. Still Florida residents would benefit from tax relief totalling $5 billion over four years.*
- *Universities, community colleges, and school districts were given the autonomy to transfer money from one fund to another in order to protect classroom instruction.*
- *After the special session, total budget reserves stood at $2.8 billion—up from $1.3 billion three years before.*

I was proud of all Floridians and how we had responded to 9/11. Across the state people had come together for love of their country and their state.

That included my superb team, who did an amazing job addressing our immediate issues of security and our longer-term issue of economic stability.

That included all the branches of law enforcement who worked together to make sure our state was safe.

That included the state legislature, who overcame their differences to pass a budget that got our state back on the right track.

Above all it included the great people of Florida and the United States of America. One of my favorite e-mails after 9/11 came from Brian Paone, who wrote in part:

It is simply amazing how all peoples in the U.S. came together since the attacks. All squabbles and issues that were all so important at the time passed from our view. We responded quickly, and our efforts are showing in the way we have mobilized as a nation. I am a conservative/

libertarian by nature, and I usually question everything I hear in the media, but, this crisis has shown that all of the petty concerns of September 10th are gone...BY the display of spirit we have seen lately, I know I'm not alone. We are an American family...and it is good to know we're together in this. I know you and your brother will help us find peace again, just remember that YOU are not alone, you have the citizens of Florida to look to for support. Call on us, and we're there 110%!

Yes. All these years later, we have gone back to squabbling—often about petty issues. However, with all my heart, I still believe now what I said to Floridians on September 11, 2001:

"They will never humble us because Americans have always risen to the occasion when our liberty has been threatened and when liberty must be defended. America's leadership, strength, and history will lead us not only to survive this terrorist attack but also to remember why we are the greatest country on the face of the Earth."

Chapter 4

2002

"I Am One of the Worker Bees."

We in this room have the privilege of serving the people of Florida. In the coming weeks, let us serve them well. Let us serve them so that when our children look back on this time, they will see the moment of change...There are sixteen million Floridians. There is but one destiny.

—State of the State Address, January 22, 2002

What better way to start 2002 than with a little humor?

As Florida's tourism season was about to go into full swing, we were determined to convince our northern neighbors to come on down. A St. Petersburg Times *reporter went on NPR and did a wonderful, satirical essay about the joys of visiting Florida. She stole a quote from me from a 2001 press conference about Florida's severe drought.*

"When I decided to run for governor, they didn't have it in the playbook that we'd have to spend a lot of time dealing with storms, the fires, the drought, and the plagues and the pestilence. There's a price we pay for living in paradise."

I really only meant that last part.

Subject: radio spoof
Wednesday, January 2, 2002 5:42 p.m.
From: Julie Hauserman

Hope you had a good holiday.

If you want to hear your quote about the "plague
and pestilence" state in my radio spoof on Florida
tourism, you can go to npr. org, pick the Weekend
Edition Sunday show off the pull-down bar and type
in my name. You can listen on real audio, and it's
about two minutes long. It aired nationally on Dec.
30 with the lede - come down to Florida this winter
- Please?

I tell you this because you say real Republicans
don't listen to NPR.

Subject: radio spoof
Wednesday, January 2, 2002 8:36 p.m.
From: Jeb Bush

**i am on the case. Don't let anyone know but the
entire office listens to NPR. It will ruin our
collective reputation. thanks, Julie. Happy New year.**

Jeb Bush

———

After I listened to her piece, I sent her this note.

Subject: radio spoof
Wednesday, January 2, 2002 9:05 p.m.
From: Jeb Bush

I love Florida and now I know that you do as well…I
think :). Plagues and pestilence aside, this is
the best damn place in the world and only getting
better.

they are coming back, our friends from other places.
And yes, thank God for air conditioning!!!

Jeb Bush

———

Another great way to start a New Year is to visit a classroom.

Subject: Classroom visit today 1/8/02
Tuesday, January 8, 2002 12:28 p.m.
From: Sally Feehrer

Thank you so much for your interest in our students'
future, they are precious to us all. I know you value
education and now my students know it first hand! I
am giving you their names and they want to add some
brief comments.…

Here are their comments:

I want to be a governor to help people with the
groceries. Sharodrick
I want to help other people get help like a good
education. Brianna
I liked being on TV. Tia
I like you very much and I will be a good reader.
Teresa
I hope you come back soon. Quinton
I love you you are a good governor. Dakota

I want to tell you I saw you on the news. ArKeem
Governor Bush-I love you JaShawna
I loved the way they took pictures of us today when
you came here.
Tamyra
I was on the camera. I will watch on the TV channel.
Laura
I liked all of the cameras when you were here.
Jacarri
I like you for saving the school. LaTonya
Bush-I liked how you wrote your e-mail on the board.
Jasmine
I wish I was a governor just like you! Charlie
Thank you for helping people nicely. I love you.
Alisha
I am glad you came to our class. Ashley
I love you Governor Bush, you have helped us.
Nakedra

Subject: Classroom visit today 1/8/02
Tuesday, January 8, 2002 1:36 p.m.
From: Jeb Bush

**Wow, that was quick. It was a joy to be in your
classroom, Ms. Feeher!**

**SHARODRICK: YOU ARE THE VERY BEST TO WANT TO HELP
OTHERS!**
BRIANNA: YOUR GOAL IS A GREAT ONE!
TIA: TELEVISION IS OK BUT READING IS THE BEST!
TERESA: I AM SO HAPPY YOU LOVE READING!
QUINTON: I HOPE TO SEE YOU AGAIN SOON AS WELL.
DAKOTA: I LOVE YOU TOO!
ARKEEM: MAYBE I WILL SEE YOU ON THE NEWS TONIGHT!
JASHAWNA: I LOVE YOU TOO!!!!

TAMYRA: AREN'T THE PRESS FUNNY????
LAURA: I HOPE YOU SEE YOURSELF ON THE NEWS!
LATONYA: IT WAS SUCH A JOY MEETING YOU!
JASMINE: THANK YOU FOR WRITING TO ME AT MY EMAIL
ADDRESS!
CHARLIE: MAYBE YOU WILL BE GOVERNOR???
ALISHA: I LOVE YOU TOO!!!!
ASHLEY: IT WAS A BLAST TO VISIT YOUR CLASS!
NAKEDRA: THANK YOU FOR YOUR KIND WORDS!

Ms. Feeher's wonderful class, thank you for writing
me.

Jeb Bush

———

*I also loved reminding a self-proclaimed cynic there are plenty of
"profiles in courage" in our world.*

Subject: political courage ?
Wednesday, January 9, 2002 9:19 p.m.
From: Jay Ayres

My daughter Ashley, a high school senior, needs
a political subject (person) to write about
concerning a "profile in courage" sponsored by the
JFK Library, for the purpose of a scholarship.
The "profile in courage" person must be an elected
political figure, local, State, or National, in
the US, who has acted courageously concerning a
political issue either current or no earlier than
1956. I suddenly realized how cynical I am. Any
suggestions?

Thank you for your thoughts.

Subject: political courage ?
Thursday, January 10, 2002 2:06 p.m.
From: Jeb Bush

Thanks for writing.

How about black republicans such as JC Watts and Clarence Thomas[66] **who risk ostracism from the minority community to stand by conservative principles —**

How about Adam Herbert who, as an african american, helped lead charge to ban quotas and preferences in florida university system?

How about the Class of 94 Congressional crew, including Charles Canady, who said they would only serve 8 years in Congress and held true to their word?

How about Ronald Reagan who went eye ball to eye ball with the soviets on defense build up/star wars and didn't blink?

Jeb Bush

———

Speaking of cynics, some of my toughest opponents were in the media, and I do believe they got tougher in election years. We'll begin with a nasty op-ed column in the St. Petersburg Times.

---

66 J. C. Watts, a star quarterback for the Oklahoma Sooners, was a congressman from Oklahoma. Clarence Thomas is a US Supreme Court justice appointed by my dad.

I sent this note to my communications team.

Subject: Opinion: Florida sliding back to its Old South ways. St. Pete Times 1/12/02
Saturday, January 12, 2002 6:58 p.m.
From: Jeb Bush

this is worth responding to.

Jeb Bush

Florida sliding back to its Old South ways
By DIANE ROBERTS
© St. Petersburg Times
published January 12, 2002

TALLAHASSEE -- William Faulkner once said, "In the South, the past is never dead, it's not even past." Faulkner, Mississippi's second-best product (after the Delta Blues), knew what he was talking about....

Progressive Democratic governors such as LeRoy Collins, Reuben Askew and Bob Graham did much to lead the state out of the torpid and hateful days of Jim Crow, fighting for integration, fair courts, equal rights, access to quality education and health care. But now for all its superficial New South patina, the state is sliding back to its Old South ways....

Now what the rulers of Florida care most about is the "right" of the affluent to pay as few taxes as possible, no matter who suffers. It wasn't just the recession or the attacks of Sept. 11 that hurt the state's economy, it's two years of tax cuts, sponsored by Gov. Jeb Bush and the Republican-controlled Legislature. In this failure of responsibility, you could say that Florida has seceded from a commitment to a just society.

We have seceded from decent education funding. In the recent budget-slashing frenzy of two special sessions, our Republican-led government has zeroed-out money to recruit and retain new teachers. Florida used to want to compare itself to New York, Michigan, Massachusetts and California in the quality of its public education. Now we do worse than Georgia and North Carolina. And we are losing teachers to better-paying jobs in Alabama.

We have seceded from a serious university system. By junking the Board of Regents in favor of politicized boards of trustees, we will have warring tribes competing for each pitiful higher education dollar. Tuition will go up, making it even harder for lower-income students to afford a four-year degree.

We have seceded from responsibility for the poor and the old. The Legislature cut prenatal care to women who will never own stocks and bonds and so aren't too bothered by the intangibles tax -- now they just have to worry about bringing a healthy baby into the world. And 23,000 elderly people will have to find a way to pay for their own prescription drugs because of the budget cuts. Many of them will just do without. This coming legislative session, there's no telling what Florida will secede from.…

Jeb Bush and Tom Feeney (John McKay, the senate president, actually has ideas for tax reform, making him a bit of a freak in the party) seem convinced that they are taking Florida forward. But forward to what? Some kind of banana republic where the rich get richer, the poor get poorer, and everybody who can goes to college in Georgia?

———

My advice to the staff charged with drafting a response was the following.

Subject: Opinion: Florida sliding back to its Old South ways. St. Pete Times 1/12/02
Sunday, January 13, 2002 11:43 a.m.
From: Jeb Bush

i wouldn't focus on just taxes. this was a mean spirited column equating me to racists policies of the past. we lead the nation in job growth, increased funding for schools by 25%, drug treatment by %, foster care by x %. Rising student achievement, more care for the vulnerable, lower crimes rates, lower drop out rates etc is the result.

Jeb Bush

———

Then there was this St. Petersburg Times *editorial.*

Bush puts on best face for budget

published January 11, 2002

Gov. Jeb Bush and a cast of dozens commandeered a
Tallahassee elementary school Tuesday to boast that
the budget he'll propose next week will recommend
"nearly $1-billion in new funding for education."
What he didn't say is that the money will do little
more than restore the cuts he and the Legislature
made just last month.

Give the governor credit for acting so quickly
to repair at least some of the damage he and the
Legislature did to the education budget a few weeks
ago. But it's still not clear how much new money he's
really offering, or where it's going to come from.
When a reporter asked how much the public schools
would get in new state money, Bush refused to say.
"I'm not going to go there," he replied.

The reason he doesn't want "to go there" is that, once
again, he is practicing budgetary sleight of hand. To
finance a large portion of his proposed $726-million
increase in K–12, he is planning to use increased
local property taxes and "surplus" retirement fund
contributions that the counties will be told to spend
on classrooms instead. It may be new money for the
classroom, but it won't be new money from the state.…

As the budget is likely to bear even worse news
for health care, children's issues and other human
services, Bush wanted the headlines to first record
that education is his priority. That was the purpose
of the event, which had as much to do with his re-

election campaign as with persuading the Legislature
to adopt the budget.…

The only alternative, the fairer one, is to raise
revenue somewhere, whether from raising local taxes
or state support. Conceptually, that's not difficult.
It's how to raise the courage that boggles the mind.

*My communications director, Katie Baur, sent Phil Gailey at the
Times an exasperated e-mail explaining our numerous factual
issues with the column. I then added my two cents.*

**Subject: editorial "Bush puts on best face for
budget"**
Friday, January 11, 2002 10:03 p.m.
From: Jeb Bush

**Phil, let me add my voice on this. Katie did not
tell me she was going to write to you but I agree
with her and would like to speak to you personally
about this. You guys have every right to advocate
higher taxes and more government to advance
education improvement but it does not give you the
right to mislead your readers about the realities
of the last few years. Can we discuss this over the
phone?**

Jeb Bush

———

As you can see, I was a firm believer in supporting the economy.

Subject: Girl Scout Cookies
Tuesday, January 22, 2002 9:38 p.m.

From: Jennifer

I'm 13,and I'm a girlscout in troop 95 which is
located in Bradenton,FL. I was wondering if you would
like to buy some girlscout cookies. There 3 dollars
a box and come in 8 flavors: Trefoils,Samoas,Thin
Mints,Do-si-dos,Tagalongs,Ole'Ole',Aloha Chip,and
All Abouts. My order form has to be in by Febuary
28,2002. So please reply to my letter. Thank You and
God Bless America.

Subject: Girl Scout Cookies
Wednesday, January 23, 2002 5:38 p.m.
From: Jeb Bush

I will buy 4 boxes. Tell me where to send the money?

Jeb Bush

———

*One night before calling it quits for the day, I sent this note to my
office staff. I didn't do it often enough.*

Subject: [None]
Tuesday, January 29, 2002 8:45 p.m.
From: Jeb Bush

**After a long day, all I can say is how truly blessed
I am to have such fine co workers. I love you all.**

Jeb Bush

———

I spent Friday evening catching up on e-mails. I read and answered e-mails from people worried about a change in the sales tax, malpractice insurance, an upcoming clemency hearing, and rights for the disabled—just to name a few. So I was excited to write to a student about one of my favorite projects.

Subject: hi, I'm a fifth grader…
Wednesday, February 6, 2002 6:44 p.m.
From: Rachel

I attend Morikami Park Elementary School. In fifth grade we have to do an Exhibition Project. This project lasts the whole year. We get split up into groups and get assigned topics for the project. My group got National Parks used for Tourism. Our group discussed this and came to the conclusion that all types of pollution effects National Parks. I know you help people with disabilites (I've gone to every Family C.A.F.E.) but can you suggest how we can help our parks?

Subject: hi, I'm a fifth grader…
Friday, February 8, 2002 8:35 p.m.
From: Jeb Bush

Rachel, thank you for writing. The most important National Park in Florida, in my opinion, is Everglades National Park. We are working hard to improve the quality and quantity of water flowing into the park. As Governor, I have helped pass legislation in Florida and Washington to secure funding for the restoration plan which will take a generation of time to complete. It is one of the efforts of which I am most proud.

Again, I appreciate your writing.

Jeb Bush

———

If only I could have convinced more teachers I was on their side as well. The union leaders in Tallahassee did everything they could to fight my reforms. However, education remained my number-one priority, so I never minded answering questions about what we were doing and trying to do.

Subject: A conservative teacher in a liberal kingdom!
Wednesday, February 6, 2002 4:04 p.m.
From: Joe Laughlin

I just walked out of a faculty meeting during which you and Mr. Brogan were trashed by the NEA[67] union rep. I asked for time to speak and was told "no". When the meeting ended, I stood up and asked for attention so that I could make positive statements about your efforts. It felt like being Daniel in the lion's den.

You have to continue to find ways to communicate to the teachers of Florida about your work. Maybe requiring all counties with staff e-mail to forward your weekly newsletter would be a start.

The union is currently telling people that you have a secret plan to totally privatize the public school system (which may not be so bad). You do not care about students, teachers, or anyone other than

———

67 National Education Association.

your friends and colleagues. You are intentionally promoting "white flight".

Subject: A conservative teacher in a liberal kingdom!
Thursday, February 7, 2002 5:31 p.m.
From: Jeb Bush

thank you Joe for your support. I am amazed at the lies being spread by the NEA representatives at schools.

Jeb Bush

———

Subject: Too many tests
Friday, February 8, 2002 10:27 a.m.
From: Linda Young

Im here addressing the subject of too many tests.I think that kids are having trouble taking tests. If I practice the night before a test for a hour, when I get ready to sit down and take it it just washes out of my brain. I wish there was a way to show my skills without a tests am asking you to try and see what you can do about too many tests.thre is good reasons for tests, when you take them it teaches the teachers what levels your on and what teaching you need. Thank you for your time.

Subject: Too many tests
Friday, February 8, 2002 9:07 p.m.
From: Jeb Bush

There is only one test that is required, the FCAT test, which is alligned to the Sunshine State Standards developed by teachers and educators from

across the state. How do we know how our students are
doing if we don't measure it by testing?

Jeb Bush

———

*Senate President John McKay was proposing to expand the state
sales-tax base, which I opposed. Specifically he wanted to lower
the sales tax from six cents to 4.5 cents but expand it to apply to
services. The net effect would have been a tax increase—one that
would have hit small businesses hard and eliminated jobs. I had
a lot of respect for John, but we sparred quite often—including
over this idea. He could call his plan what he wanted; it was still
a tax hike.*

Subject: Chamber Meeting
Thursday, February 7, 2002 11:55 p.m.
From: Charles Caulkins

I enjoyed chatting with you this am. Your
speech was really perfect. I sat on the plane
ride out of Tallahassee next to Senator Dan
Webster. He seemed tired but "pumped" by your
public position on the McKay tax plan. Keep up the
good work!

Subject: Chamber Meeting
Friday, February 8, 2002 7:33 a.m.
From: Jeb Bush

Thanks Charles. The retribution has already started
but we will get through the session and protect
Florida's taxpayers.

Jeb Bush

———

Subject: We oppose changes in Florida's tax system
Monday, February 11, 2002 12:03 p.m.
From: Chuck and Beth Riley

We are opposed to the proposed changes to the Florida
tax system. Raising taxes is never a good idea.
Specially when it means increasing the bureaucracy.

It would be better to drop tax plans, and reunite as
Republicans for the good of the party.

Subject: We oppose changes in Florida's tax system
Monday, February 11, 2002 8:13 p.m.
From: Jeb Bush

I agree with you.

Jeb Bush

———

McKay's sales-tax plan was defeated.

———

*Ending the practice of social promotion (promoting students
based upon their ages versus their abilities to read) for third
graders who were functionally illiterate was a core component
of my education strategy. Studies showed that children who
couldn't read by the time they entered fourth grade experienced
problems throughout the rest of their education in our K–12*

system—and would likely drop out. It was a controversial policy but a key reason we saw strong gains in student achievement in Florida.

Subject: retention policy
Tuesday, February 12, 2002 11:23 a.m.
From: Nancy Revell

I've been very interested in your education proposals - in particular the vouchers. My in-laws run a private school in Ormond Beach and are doing a great job with children who are using vouchers there. However, my letter is in response to the retention policy. I am sending it to you via email and snail mail.…

[From the attached letter:]

"The issue of retaining children who can't read by fourth grade is a tough issue to balance. Retention can discourage a child but promoting them will do the same thing if they can't handle the work. On top of it all, if there's no money for smaller size classes, there's no way a struggling child will get the attention he needs. All of this doesn't even factor in the home situation—something that can't be legislated! What a mess!!"

Subject: retention policy
Friday, February 15, 2002 8:13 p.m.
From: Jeb Bush

Thank you nancy for your very thoughtful and insightful letter.

Social promotion is a very tough issue. But here is the deal.…It is not right that only 3% of our students are held back when 32% of those same students are reading at level one (below basic) in fourth grade. I think the answer is to start before fourth grade with diagnostic tools, with a command focus on reading (even at the expense of other things) and a tighter social promotion policy. We are not doing students any favors if they are not getting the skills they need because they can't read.…

Jeb Bush

———

Every family has challenges, and mine is no different. As I have mentioned before, though, a loss of privacy is one of the greatest sacrifices the families of elected officials must make. I never ran for office without my family's permission and full support, but that didn't make the limelight any easier—especially for my daughter. She had been arrested in January for trying to buy prescription medicine with a fraudulent prescription. She was going through a very tough time.

I would like to add that Noelle's courage inspires me every day. She is a fighter and is determined not to let her struggles define who she is. I am very proud of what she has accomplished.

Subject: [None]
Thursday, February 21, 2002 6:43 p.m.
From: Ron Berry

I saw in the paper the other day that your daughter was doing very well in rehab. As a father myself, I am happy that she is doing better, but quite frankly, it is none of my business. I just wanted to let you know that I think, it is a shame that your family is not off limits to the media. Maybe if the next time someone from the media asks you how your daughter is doing, you should reply "fine how is yours?". See if they want to talk about their kids.

Subject: [None]
Thursday, February 21, 2002 9:59 p.m.
From: Jeb Bush

Ron, thank you so much for your concern about my precious daughter.…

Jeb Bush

My mom likes to quote Lady Bird Johnson, who talked about the power of the first lady's platform to do good. Lady Bird used it to beautify our country. My mom used it to promote literacy. In fact, at age ninety, she still is! As governor I loved being able to use my bully pulpit and my tremendous and resourceful staff to help people who felt they had nowhere else to turn.

Subject: School
Thursday, March 7, 2002 8:34 p.m.
From: Shane

Last July I wrote you a letter asking for your help to find me a school. I received a phone call from Tallassee a very informative man. I also received a phone call from Susan Bailey (I believe superintendent of schools for Pinellas county) She hooked me up with James Natelle, PTEC TEAM Program. I called Mr.Natelle in August (2001) He within a week

helped me enroll into school. He said how did you hear
about the Program I explained to him as I have to you,
I said I wrote a letter to Mr. Bush and I told him
how GREAT you were helping me out! Mr.Natelle, came
across shocked that I had a response from my letter.
I told him how helpful you were. He has talked about
my situation so much I am known as the Jeb Bush kid.
That's a good thing, shows that you care.

I graduate high school in June, I have a 4.0 GPA, I
still work 40 hrs a week. I owe a lot of this to you,
for being their to help me out!

Mr.Bush, If their is ANYTHING I can do to help you
on your re-election please let me. I had faith in
you to help me out with school that's why I wrote
you. (last July) I know you are the best man for the
job!

I start SPC (ST. Petersburg College) in June. I have
sent in my FAFSA form (Financial aid) I am only
receiving 600.00 dollars per semester because I made
16,888.00 last year but I made that amount because I
half to in order to make ends meet.…

Please if you have any information,suggestions please
let me know what is available to help me with college
as I am supporting my self on my own as I am only 18,
I will turn 19 on May 22. (trying to do the best I
can on my own)

Subject: School
Saturday, March 9, 2002 5:11 p.m.
From: Jeb Bush

**Shane, thank you so much for the update. Man, am
I proud of you. I am going to see if there is
scholarship monies available for you. given your GPA,
there might be.**

Jeb Bush

Speaking of Mom, this note came from Mark Silva at the Orlando
Sentinel.

Subject: String of Pearls, I'm humming it
Thursday, March 14, 2002 10:30 a.m.
From: Mark Silva

Having just jumped off a little red truck[68], or at
least the chase van, it's nice to be home. Even nicer
to see your mom coming to town today. I probably will
be covering her tongiht at the civic center. Can you
please answer me today, for use in tonight's story:

Q: Do you hope to have your mother and father in
Florida a lot this year? And your brother, of course?

Q: Seriously, your successful and warmly received
parents and brother will contribute what to your
campaign for reelection this year, in terms of the
strength of the family y'all portray to the public?

PS: Reno's reply: "Say hi to the governor.''

Subject: String of Pearls, I'm humming it

---

68 Mark had been covering Janet Reno's campaign for governor. She
traveled the state in a red truck.

Thursday, March 14, 2002 9:21 p.m.
From: Jeb Bush

My mom is here for a speaking engagement not arranged
by me. We added an event for all of the women's
event in Tallahassee. In addition, my mom and dad are
coming back for the family literacy event[69] which is
in its second year. They want to help in the campaign
and they will get a chance to do so.

Jeb Bush

Subject: String of Pearls, I'm humming it
Thursday, March 14, 2002 9:26 p.m.
From: Mark Silva

Thanks, and as I'm sitting here receiving your email
and replying I am listening to your mother speak.
It's a nice night, 550 at dinner. She is very warm.
She also says she spanked you.

Subject: String of Pearls, I'm humming it
Thursday, March 14, 2002 9:31 p.m.
From: Jeb Bush

she sure did. And I am sure I deserved it.

Jeb Bush

---

69 This refers to Celebration of Reading, an annual event we started
when I was governor to raise money for a statewide literacy program I
founded in partnership with the Barbara Bush Foundation for Family
Literacy. We are still holding Celebration of Reading today and raise
more than $1 million every year for literacy.

Columba had accompanied a Florida delegation on a trade mission to Japan.

Subject: Japan visit
Saturday, March 23, 2002 11:39 a.m.
From: Dan Richey

I returned Thursday from Japan on Citrus Commission business. It was great to have Columba there. She is a wonderful person and a great ambassador for the State of Florida. The Japanese customers were very impressed with her and having her there was a huge benefit for the Citrus growers in Florida.

Subject: Japan visit
Saturday, March 23, 2002 8:45 a.m.
From: Jeb Bush

thanks Dan. I am glad the trip went well. I hope to have colu home tonight!!!

Jeb Bush

———

I loved this student's very specific "this is why you know me" subject line.

Subject: hi im from Clay Springs Elementary you saw us a couple of weeks ago
Wednesday, March 27, 2002 2:42 p.m.
From: Ashley

Hi I just wanted to say hi, Im from Clay Springs Elementary. The group you met with like 4 weeks ago]. I wanted to ask you If you are doing anything for the endangered animals,Do you like being the Governor and Do you want to become the President? Well I just want to thank you for your time and im sure that you have like a THOUSAND other e-mails so I will go Bye

Subject: hi im from Clay Springs Elementary you saw us a couple of weeks ago
Wednesday, March 27, 2002 8:07 p.m.
From: Jeb Bush

thank you Ashley. Yes we are working hard and spending tons of money to protect endangered species like the panther, the Florida bear and the wonderful manatee. I love being Governor and have little interest in being President. You are great to write me. Onward!

———

I was glad to see the press pay attention to the best lieutenant governor in America. Like many number twos, the people he served underappreciated him. Frank Brogan was having a tough legislative session wrangling all the ins and outs of what the legislators wanted—not to mention what I wanted! I had just sent him an e-mail telling him, "Don't let the bastards get you down. We will prevail."

This inquiry came from Julie Hauserman of the St. Petersburg Times.

Subject: frank brogan
Thursday, March 28, 2002 2:37 p.m.

From: Julie Hauserman

I am working on a profile of your Lt. Governor. I wonder if you might be able to answer a few questions?

1. How did Frank come to your attention after Mortham[70] left the ticket?

2. Why did you give him the legislative liason responsibility?

3. Would you like to see him succeed you as governor?

Thanks in advance for your response.

Subject: frank brogan
Thursday, March 28, 2002 8:56 p.m.
From: Jeb Bush

1. **I never thought that Frank would be interested in being my running mate. He was cruising to reelection as Commissioner of Education based on his excellent first term. I called him in one of those "light bulb" moments and he said he would consider. A week later, he agreed to be part of the ticket which was a true blessing.**

---

70 Sandy Mortham, a former state representative and Florida's secretary of state, served briefly as my running mate in 1998. Two nonprofit foundations overseen by the Department of State ran into some ethical issues, and she had to resign. She is a good person and has remained a friend and colleague.

2. **After Ken Plante moved back to the private sector, we needed to have someone who had the respect of the members and Frank agreed to do the job. The last two regular sessions have been extrtraordinary in that the leadership of the Senate and House have relied on Frank to be the go between. this is a job that goes beyond legislative liasion and he does it very,very well.**

3. **Yes.**

Jeb Bush

———

In the next few e-mails, I once again tried to set my record straight. Because it was an election year, the naysayers always said, "You have lost my vote."

In this first e-mail, HB261 was a transportation-related bill. It was specifically about turnpike governance. It was nuts-and-bolts type legislation, so this unhappy citizen surprised me.

Subject: Miami Herald calls for VETO on HB261
Friday, April 12, 2002 1:06 p.m.
From: Rich Walker

I hate to say this but my family and I will not be voting for you in November and we are active workers for the Republican Party. We have made this decision because you have not done anything to protect the environment in Florida in any significant way; you have only helped the special interest groups (i.e., developers) get their way! The FINAL straw was the signing of the**HB261 last night.**

I personally will work with Democrats this year so that we can remove you and your staff from office. I am very sorry for this but the environment is more important to my family and I than the Republican Party!

Subject: Miami Herald calls for VETO on HB261
Friday, April 12, 2002 1:33 p.m.
From: Jeb Bush

Nothing in this bill will damage the environment. I will run on my record of doubling the funding of water restoration projects in three years, of the everglades restoration plan and record funding, of a steadfast opposition to offshore drilling, and of enforcing environmental laws.

I am sorry you have not been following our successes.

Jeb Bush

———

Agriculture was one of Florida's most important industries, so the threat of citrus canker was a major issue impacting growers throughout the state.

Subject: Citrus
Saturday, April 13, 2002 6:19 p.m.
From: Dawn Catherine

I heard you on Y100 the other day. I had to get to work, so I didn't hear the entire show. Did you get around to explaining how you could support the taking of our citrus trees, especially the healthy ones? If this isn't too much government, I don't know what is.

I thought Janet Reno was the only one who cornered the market on invasion of private property. I was wrong.

If the citrus industry needs our trees, let them negotiate with us. We are reasonable people. That's why companies keep legal staff. Let us determine what is a reasonable price to replace our shade trees and become totally dependent on the citrus industry since now we cannot grow our own.

You're only hurting the people who voted for you.

Sincerely,
Former Bush Supporter

Subject: Citrus
Sunday, April 14, 2002 4:09 p.m.
From: Jeb Bush

I appreciate your writing me. I was not asked that question but am happy to do so through this email. The Federal Department of Agriculture told us several years ago that if a contaminated tree was found, any tree within a certain radius had to be eradicated as well. the possibility of an quarantine loomed ahead of us. We had to act and had the State Department of Agriculture been able to complete the job without court injunctions (finally won by the Department), many trees would have been saved.

I wish there was another way to have deal with citrus canker.

Again, I appreciate your writing.

Jeb Bush

———

High-speed rail continued to be a thorn in my side and an unnecessary burden on the hardworking taxpayers of Florida. After I zeroed out funding for it in 1999, proponents put forward a ballot measure that received voter approval. I eventually succeeded in passing my own initiative in 2004 to finally get rid of this boondoggle.

Subject: Tax Day-----taxes, schmaxes
Monday, April 15, 2002 10:05 p.m.
From: Kelly Layman

Gentlemen: "What's doing" in signing the high speed rail authority bill? Why commit us to billions in a boondoogle project still largely unproven (in both need and logistics)?…It surely didn't help the enviro/conservation mantra.…Teddy Roosevelt would have been "all over it" slowing down and/or killing high-speed rail. Approving yet more money is to going to overshadow and dilute any positive enviro moves by GOP in the next decade…and maybe then some. Keep to getting the Glades cleaned up. That's enough of a chore. I cannot believe, with all the science and abdication of finding the TRUE cost of high-speed rail, that this is being allowed to continue. Governor, what happened to the courage you displayed when you vetoed the bullet train within weeks of taking office? What a bold, common-sense move back then! It stopped everyone in their tracks, pardon the pun (as well it should have). You said then that the need doesn't come near justifying the cost, basically, and that we were in uncertain economic times and couldn't afford to pay for this 2- or 3-decades long project! Isn't that an even truer, clearer statement ---to uphold ----today?? High-speed rail is not a solution; it's exacerbating the problem(s). That money for FOX that's now being used to explore so-called high-speed rail (which travels barely more than current Amtrak trains---the whole thing's a misnomer, anyway) well that should've been turned on to education, the mentoring initiative, state park improvements, whatever.…Not a continuation of the same ol' (30-year) saga.

Subject: Tax Day-----taxes, schmaxes
Monday, April 15, 2002 10:22 p.m.
From: Jeb Bush

Kelly, you have been gone from Tallahassee for a while and what we do up here in terms of conservative governance doesn't get to the people because of the filter. I withheld money that was not spent last fiscal year for high speed rail. I have said that I won't support High Speed Rail unless it is financially feasible and the Government's cost is finite. I have pledged to veto all high speed rail funding next year unless the tax exemption issue attached to the transportation bill is eliminated and I have a commitment that this will happen. I have stated publicly that I will propose going back to the people with a

referendum to kill the high speed rail if the
taxpayer's cost is too high.

Kelly, what else would you like me to do?

Jeb Bush

———

*Education was the big issue in my reelection campaign. My
Democratic opponents and the teachers union pulled out all
the stops to discredit my A+ reforms. If I remember right, this
included the union mortgaging their headquarters to support
my opponent. As a result the media focused a lot on education
in 2002, which resulted in an in-box full of e-mails about school
reform.*

This e-mail was about a piece in the Orlando Sentinel *by Mike
Thomas.*

**Subject: Jeb's Education Effort Fails Those Most In
Need-Orlando Sentinel April 18—B-1**
Thursday, April 18, 2002 7:57 a.m.
From: Ed McLean

This guy Mike Thomas hates your guts and takes a shot
at you everytime he can. My property line backs up to
Dommerich Elementary school and my children all went
there. It is a great school because of the parents of
the children who attend there. Yes, there are a lot
of portable classrooms there because everyone want's
their children in this school. This is a school that
proves that children can learn in portable classrooms
if they come from good families and have good teachers.
This school sits in probably the strongest Republican
voting precinct in Orange county. It might be a school

that you should visit sometime when you are in Orange county. You can invite Mike Thomas to visit with you.

Subject: Jeb's Education Effort Fails Those Most In Need-Orlando Sentinel April 18—B-1
Thursday, April 18, 2002, 10:10 p.m.
From: Jeb Bush

Mike's hatred won't change. Nothing I can do about it. I am resigned and sleep well at night. The fact is that we have increased funding more than my predecessor. 27% in four years. Did Mike get upset about Lawton? If he did, then he is consistent. If he didn't then hypocrisy is the word which should be no surprise. Such is life as a republican. Again, in twenty minutes I will be asleep like a babe.…

Jeb Bush

At the time Mike worked for the Orlando Sentinel. *He now works for the Foundation for Excellence in Education, which I founded. He has written numerous pieces defending the A+ plan after years of studying the results. He's a true convert! I was wrong to say Mike had hatred in his heart.*

———

No one ever knows where the next controversy might come from. In this case the Associated Press was trying to add a little fun during a not-so-fun legislative session. They sent these two drafts of the same story to my communications team, trying for a reaction.

Bush lacks leadership: Can't decide between milk and cream

TALLAHASSEE, Fla. _ Gov. Jeb Bush was criticized by Democrats for failing to make a clear choice in what he puts in his coffee, choosing half-and-half instead of opting for milk or cream.

"We need a governor that can choose one or the other," said Florida Democratic Party Chairman Bob Poe. "Graham was a cream man, Chiles used milk. But half-and-half, give me a break? Even just going black would be a stronger show of leadership."

Bush responded to the criticism in a way that makes him look intellegent, thus the comments will not be included in this story.

Bush decisions hurt Florida's agriculture industry

TALLAHASSEE, Fla. _ Florida is the nation's largest cane sugar producing state, yet Gov. Jeb Bush each day chooses to put Sweet 'N' Low in his coffee.

"The governor needs to do more to help the state's agriculture industry and his decision to use Sweet 'N' Low is just one sign that he doesn't care about Florida farmers," said Florida Democratic Party Chairman Bob Poe.

Sweet 'N' Low is a sugar substitute manufactured by a Brooklyn-based company. Other people known to use the pink-packaged powder include former Enron Chairman Kenneth Lay, Osama Bin Laden and Texas Rangers pitcher John Rocker.

It was assumed that Bush would not comment, so he wasn't asked about his Sweet 'N' Low consumption.

My response follows:

Subject: Coffee

Wednesday, April 17, 2002 12:17 p.m.
From: Jeb Bush

Fake sugar fake cream real coffee.

For the record today I take my coffee with milk.

———

While funding education was one of my core commitments, my critics in the media and teachers union criticized me throughout my governorship for underfunding education and cutting taxes too much. I firmly believe I struck the right balance. While I was governor, we had strong job growth in Florida, and we balanced eight straight budgets while cutting taxes for Floridians every year. Yet we ushered in major education reforms that led to significant gains in student achievement. Having to respond to the constant criticism of neglecting our schools was frustrating, therefore, to say the least.

Subject: EDUCATION !!
Friday, May 3, 2002 8:45 a.m.
From: Cathy Wright

262 million tax savings for corporations. Yes, by all means, let's give Big Business more money.

It's a pity that money couldn't go into education, creating more teaching jobs to help get funding back to where it was before you became governor. I am a teacher in a Title 1 school - I've been here for 28 years and I'm not going anywhere - but if I was just starting out I sure wouldn't go into teaching. Last year you said Teachers in the state of Florida are doing a lousy job. Well, I think we perform miracles

every day - and we will continue to - but the more
children in each class, the harder it will be to give
each and every child the attention he needs.…

Education funding in Florida is in the bottom 5
states on money spent per student. I can't imagine
how anyone could give himself the title "Education
Governor" & spend so little on education!! Seems to
me that title should be earned.

Subject: EDUCATION !!
Friday, May 3, 2002 9:16 a.m.
From: Jeb Bush

Ms. Wright, I have no clue who is providing you with
information but let me set the record straight.

I have never said teachers are doing a lousy job. I
fully understand the challenges you face which is why
we continue to increase funding for programs like
the national board certification for teachers (we are
approaching the number state in the country).

Funding is higher today than it was prior to me being
governor. For the upcoming budget year, we will see
close to a 9% increase, which is equal to 6% per
student and over $1 billion. For the four years, the
total increase will be 27% and over $3 billion. These
increases are greater than my predecessor's first
or second term. Taking into consideration student
population growth and inflation, the numbers are
higher than before.

We are not in the bottom five states in terms of per
student funding and that funding is increasing.

Finally, the corporate tax issue is not a tax cut but a tax deferral which only will come into play if a business invests which will increase the chance of job creation. The money will come back to government.

Thanks for allowing me to correct the record. I appreciate your writing.

Jeb Bush

———

This very brief e-mail is the beginning of one of the most painful incidents of my eight years as governor of Florida and the worst example of how governments too often fail the people they are supposed to protect.

I sent this note to Kate Kearney, secretary of the Department of Children and Families, cc'ing Kathleen Shanahan and Deputy Chief of Staff Laura Branker.

The e-mail is in response to news reports that a little girl named Rilya Wilson, a foster child under the care of the state, was missing in Miami-Dade County. What was worse was it appeared she had been missing since 2000 from her foster home, and no one knew. How could that be? She was four years old. The foster mother claimed someone from the state had picked her up for a doctor's appointment but never brought her back.

Subject: [None]
Thursday, May 2, 2002 7:18 a.m.
From: Jeb Bush

I would like a report of the events regarding the Wilson child. Please match what we believed happened to what should have happened.

Jeb Bush

———

Then the story exploded.

Subject: DCF
Wednesday, May 8, 2002 9:34 a.m.
From: Louise Palmier

I just loved your initial reaction to the news
of the Wilson girl's plight. You tried so hard
to blame everyone but your department. You have
underfunded it as well as nearly every other
department that deals with the poor. You and your
brother detest the poor and it shows in oh so many
ways.

Subject: DCF
Wednesday, May 8, 2002 9:22 p.m.
From: Jeb Bush

**Ms. Palmer, you need to get your facts right. In four
years, we will have doubled funding for the child
welfare system. We have increased funding for the
developmentally disabled by 75%. Drug treatment by
40%. 86% of the kids eligible will have insurance
compared to around 50% four years ago. Those are the
facts. You can believe otherwise to fit your beliefs
but you are incorrect.**

**I have not blamed anyone else about the Riyla case
and won't do so. I have said that we are making
progress in getting kids out of foster care,
preventing abuse to begin with, lowering case loads,**

etc. However, the situation that occured with Riyla is not acceptable.

Jeb Bush

––––––

Subject: Rilya Wilson
Friday, May 10, 2002 1:16 p.m.
From: Jonas Walton

I think that you should be brave in terms of politics and public policy regarding Rilya Wilson and tell the truth. Little Ms. Wilson did not go missing because of your "failure to adequately fund social services" (although I do feel that you need to spend more money in that area as well as transportation and even more so in education.…If that isn't the role of government what is?)

No, Rilya Wilson is missing solely because her guardian handed her to a stranger. Whatever her fate is, it was for all intents and purposes sealed when that was done, even had the police been called immediately (which they were not). You can make that statement clearly and without demonizing her guardian.

Why did Rilya Wilson go missing for so long? It is true that there was negligence in this case, but the true reason is because DFACS is overburdened. Why is DFACS overburdened? Again, not because of your "neglect" of social programs or "failed state bureaucracy," but because there are so many children in its care. Why are there so many children in its

care? Because of family breakdown. Drugs, AIDS,
crime/incarceration, unemployment, etc. compound
the problem, as does poor educational systems. They
should be referenced as causes contributing to the
problem and be addressed.

But the primary cause of this overwhelming of
state resources with hundreds of thousands of
children is the culture of so many people having
children for which they have no capacity of ever
supporting, specifically teenage pregnancy, men who
abandon their children and women having children
out of wedlock. I would wager large sums of money
that the vast majority of children under the care
of DFACS and the state's many other noneducational
social welfare programs (as well as those in
the juvenile crime system) are products of this
culture.…

If you fail to show courage by taking on the real
underlying root issues that led to this tragedy in
public speeches and public policy, it would be a
failure of leadership. You have to do it not because
of politics but rather because no one else will.
Thank you.

From: Jeb Bush
Friday, May 10, 2002 4:52 p.m.
Subject: Rilya Wilson

Jonas, you are right that family breakdown is the
cause of the need for a government run child welfare
system that can't replace loving wholesome families.
I say that everytime I speak about this case. Your

number on 25% of the children being out of wedlock is sadly low. The number is about 33%.

Having said that, the negligence in handling this case is cause for concern and we have a responsibility to improve the system until their is a societal change that lessens the demands placed on government.

Thank you for writing.

Jeb Bush

One of the immediate steps I took was to ask John Walsh, host of the television show America's Most Wanted, *to feature Rilya's disappearance, which he did on May 4.*

On May 6 I appointed a blue-ribbon panel to review the state's child-protection system.

———

In April I also appointed a blue-ribbon task force to study how to help developmentally disabled students participate in the FCAT without compromising the test itself. I did so because of students like Kirsty, who will be introduced for the first time below. She was having trouble passing the test. She had excellent literacy skills—as you will see in her notes—but her developmental issues made math very difficult.

As a side note, I visited with Kirsty on one of my personal days. I had asked my staff to set aside a few unscheduled days a month to allow free time for spontaneity, drop-in visits, or coffee with cabinet members or legislators. Making sure I had time for people such as Kirsty is exactly why I loved and protected those days. In this case she rode with me in the governor's car on my way to somewhere so we could visit.

Subject: Thank You
Tuesday, May 14, 2002 7:49 p.m.
From: Kirsty

I just wanted to say thank you once again for the wonderful opportunity that you gave me today. I have struggled and fought for my rights but no one has ever really cared. I was just some non-existent entity that people thought nothing of. Words can not describe how much my visit with you meant because you are one of the few who actually wanted to hear what I had to say. This is America and because I am in the land of opportunity, I am entitled to my freedoms. I am entitled to be myself, to soar like the eagle and pursue my highest dreams and aspirations. I am different and I am unique but I deserve the same opportunity to have equal benefit and equal access to my education as my non-disabled peers have. A strong believer and follower of the American dream, I will do whatever it takes to succeed in life and I have seen that my hard work has paid off. Thank you from the bottom of my heart for taking the time to meet with me. It's like I said before, I agree wholeheartedly with your brother that in education, no child should be left behind. Please, don't let kids like myself be left behind. We too deserve a bright future.

Subject: Thank You
Tuesday, May 14, 2002 8:00 p.m.
From: Jeb Bush

Thank you Kirsty. It was a joy spending time with you tryoing to learn about your unique issues. I will inquire about you appeal and we will be back with you.

Again, I appreciate you riding with me. I am sorry you were nervous. You shoildn't have been!

God's blessings!

Jeb

_____

The search for Rilya continued.

Subject: Missing girl
Tuesday, May 21, 2002 10:55 a.m.
From: Gwen Holz

I'm so sorry that you are taking so much "heat" from the media etc. You are not responsible for every person that is kidnapped.

This obviously was well planned. The person who kidnapped Kilya knew her well, where she lived and that she was under the care of the child welfare system to be able to fabricate the story to make it sound legitimate.…This child did not just "fall through the cracks".

Stick to your guns!!!.

Subject: Missing girl
Tuesday, May 21, 2002 10:39 p.m.
From: Jeb Bush

thank you Gwen. The heat goes with the job in which I joyfully serve in.

Jeb Bush

———

There was a $25,000 reward—eventually increased to $100,000—for information on Rilya's whereabouts. This note came from Tim Moore, executive director of the Florida Department of Law Enforcement.

Subject: 5/31/02 Status Briefing for Rilya Wilson Case
Friday, May 31, 2002 9:15 p.m.
From: Tim Moore

Governor...here is a sample of the type and kind of leads the $$ is generating. This is the list for the last 24 hours.

Each lead is farmed out to an agent and/or Miami Dade Pd for follow up and a briefing is held in Miami every afternoon at 3pm with all involved.

Still nothing extremely strong.

Subject: 5/31/02 Status Briefing for Rilya Wilson Case
Friday, May 31, 2002 9:26 p.m.
From: Jeb Bush

thanks, Tim. I hope and pray we find this child.

Jeb Bush

———

Subject: Children in Crisis
Wednesday, June 5, 2002 5:22 p.m.
From: Diane Richardson

Please address the needs of the many children in
Florida that are abused and beaten. We can't ignore
them. Our state has a crisis. Please show your
leadership by taking action to fund programs that
work and fix those that don't.

Subject: Children in Crisis
Wednesday, June 5, 2002 9:05 p.m.
From: Jeb Bush

**thank you for writing. You will be glad to know that
we have doubled the funding of our child welfare
system in four years. We are on the right course and
I hope you can get involved in the community based
efforts in your area.**

————

*The legislative session was ending, which meant it was time to
shoot turkeys. I am including this e-mail exchange with a legislator to show just how heated the discussions were and how tough
the decisions could be. He was right about at least one thing—I
am not proud of my first answer. In general I sound a little testy.
Mike is a good and loyal friend, and we decided in the end to
agree to disagree. I think we need more of that kind of discourse
in government and politics.*

Subject: [None]
Wednesday, June 5, 2002 10:26 a.m.
From: Mike Fasano

Just got a phone call from one of your staff people to tell me about the vetoed Pasco Projects. As I said to you in the past, Veto all my projects, but I ask that you and your administration be consistent. Why do McKay and Feeney get to keep their capital outlay projects?

Subject: [None]
Wednesday, June 5, 2002 10:30 a.m.
From: Jeb Bush

When you become President or Speaker, we will talk, my friend.

Jeb Bush

Subject: [None]
Wednesday, June 5, 2002 10:43 a.m.
From: Mike Fasano

Not a good answer, my friend.

What happened to principals first? The Speak sold those out on the last day of regular session when the deal was made to push for tax reform (tax increases) something you, I and everyone opposed. Now I see we have to give up a few more principals to complete the deals made with the two gentlemen.

What a sad day, indeed!

God bless.

Ps—you were supposed to veto the 200K for the Sheriff's office. Hayden was told that the Sheriff disbanded the program and he was expecting a veto…

Subject: [None]
Wednesday, June 5, 2002 10:10 p.m.
From: Jeb Bush

Mike, check the vetoes and you might want to revaluate your statements.

Don't lecture me about principles. If you were interested in principles, which I have adhered to, you wouldn't be upset about member projects that you knew from the get go were not going to be kept in the budget. We will not have a tax increase because of the tax reform initiative. Would you have preferred to have complete gridlock allowing for your opponent to beat you which would have happened because of the revulsion of the people we serve?

Jeb Bush

———

Subject: [None]
Thursday, June 6, 2002 8:17 a.m.
From: Mike Fasano

Smile, my friend. You are doing a great job. However, that does not mean I am not allowed to complain once in a while.

God bless.

Subject: [None]
Thursday, June 6, 2002 10:04 a.m.
From: Jeb Bush

complain all you want, my friend.

Jeb Bush

———

Here is another note from my new friend Kirsty:

Subject: [None]
Monday, June 17, 2002 9:56 p.m.
From: Kirsty

Tonight I started work again after taking some
time off to prepare for finals and go on vacation
with my family. Over at Disney we have a college
program where college students from all over are
allowed a chance to learn and work in a certain
position at a Disney theme park. Tonight I was
talking to some of those students and after I did,
I wanted to cry, which is exactly what I did when
my mom picked me up from work. Just thinking that
all of these kids are going to be able to pursue
their dreams breaks my heart. One of the students
I talked to is majoring in Criminalistics, which is
a subject that I am very much interested in.
Yet because I can't pass the FCAT, I won't even
be able to have a chance to pursue this area of
interest.

I can't even begin to tell you how horrible it is to wake up every morning and go to sleep every night just wondering if I'll be able to graduate next year. Because of my disabilities worrying about graduation has now become a part of my life that is hindering my everyday activities. It is the first thing on my mind when I wake up in the morning and the last thing on my mind when I go to bed. That is of course, if I can even get to sleep, sometimes I can't because I'm so worked up and stressed over this entire issue that it just wont let my mind rest.

Another thing that happened tonight at work is during our closing procedures, I was asked to close the bumper cars. Part of the closing procedure is to drive the cars to the other side of the pen and line them up. The problem was that I didn't really know how to do that because I've been working on learning to drive a car for two years because of my defects in visual-spatial perceptions while everyone else has been driving for two years. Yet, Disney has absolutely no problem taking time to teach me what I need to learn in order to be able to do the job and make me feel comfortable with it. That is something that my school and my state have completely denied me. I just find it incredibly sad that my own workplace is more accommodating than my school and the state I live in. If I had a physical disability then I know that the school and state would accommodate me but because I have a mental disability and no one can "see" it, then they just deny that it might even exist. That is something that I find to be degrading and discriminating.

Governor Bush, I just don't understand. If I cannot get my diploma, what was the point of all the struggles, pain and tears? What was the point of even attending school for twelve years of my life? Was it just to be told that no matter how hard I work I will never amount to anything? Is that what it is? I can only pray to God that it isn't and I also pray that no child like myself will ever have to hear that or go through what I have gone through. I want to learn to lobby for disabled students rights because kids like me have been ignored and discriminated against long enough. I want to help and since no one has stood up and taken the job, perhaps I can. How do I do it? I want to aid others in the hopes that they will at least get a fair chance to do something they love even though I might not. I am sick and tired of being looked at like I'm some sort of freak because I learn differently and need special accommodations. I am disabled Governor Bush, not stupid, and not a quitter.

Subject: [None]
Tuesday, June 18, 2002 9:10 p.m.
From: Jeb Bush

Kirsty, you are not sick and I know you are not a quitter. Don't lose faith. the FCAT commission may offer some hope. The challenge for us to keep standards and have some flexibility for students like you. I remain confident that we can find some common ground.

Jeb Bush

———

It's impossible to give enough credit to the work our entire law enforcement team does. I received this report from Jim McDonough.

Subject: Significant Seizure - 2 Kilos of Cocaine 07-09-02
Wednesday, July 10, 2002 12:40 p.m.
From: Jim McDonough

Operation Sudden Storm, to which this is credited, continues to get a number of seizures, small in comparison to the tonnages seized in Operation River Walk, but meaningful as they accumulate over time, eventually, I would hope, sreving as a deterrent to running drugs into Florida on the highways.

What's intesting about this particular seizure is that it was done by the same two troopers you recognized with a certificate of achievement at the Drug Summit. They also seized $70,000 drug money concealed in a gas tank (18 wheeler) about 3 weeks ago. They have been the steadiest producers of the various teams involved in Sudden Storm.

Altogether we have seized several hundred pounds of marijuana, as well as smaller, but significant amounts of cocaine, methamphetamines, club drugs, and precursors, and are pushing up towards a quarter of million dollars in drug cash. The operations continue.

Subject: Significant Seizure - 2 Kilos of Cocaine 07-09-02
Wednesday, July 10, 2002 9:33 p.m.
From: Jeb Bush

good work, Jim. How can I applaud the work of the Troopers?

Jeb Bush

_____

I appointed Raoul G. Cantero III to the Florida Supreme Court. He was the first Hispanic in our state's history to serve on our highest court. He resigned in 2008 because of his family's desire to return to Miami.

Subject: Cantero
Wednesday, July 10, 2002 6:18 p.m.
From: Anthony Morejon

Way to go!!!!!!!!!!!!!!!

next open an office of Hispanic Affairs.

seriously thank you.

Subject: Cantero
Wednesday, July 10, 2002 8:26 p.m.
From: Jeb Bush

i am the office of hispanic affairs.

Jeb Bush

_____

Again the following is to set the record straight.

Subject: Partial-birth Abortions
Sunday, July 21, 2002 8:43 p.m.
From: John Baxstrom

This is concerning partial-birth abortions, please
hear me. I am greatly troubled that our countrymen
would pass a law to kill our nations most presses
resource, our children. I would love to help you
stop this murdering that is happening in our nation.
Everyone I have talked with about the subject has
been surprised and outraged that it is going on.
I think most people do not know what is happening
(I did not know for some time). Being a father I
know you now my Paine. Please let me know what is
happening with this subject.

Subject: Partial-birth Abortions
Monday, July 22, 2002 2:31 a.m.
From: Jeb Bush

**I oppose partial birth abortions. My first year
as Governor we passed a bill that abolished the
procedure but it was overturned in the courts.**

Jeb Bush

———

Subject: Are you awhere of Medicaid
Thursday, July 25, 2002 11:58 a.m.
From: David Feltner

They say that "elephants are near sighted, donkies
are not that much brighter. "Have you herd about the

new Medicaid rumor cutting prescription drugs leving
the elderly And disabled with the bill?

With the Bushes leading the state of Florida and the
nation, Andrew Jackson would flip. If he'd lived. I
like you, your polices we all can do without! Please
share this with your Brother.

Subject: Are you awhere of Medicaid
Thursday, July 25, 2002 3:34 p.m.
From: Jeb Bush

There are no cuts in perscription drug benifits. In
fact we have expanded benefits for the elderly. Andrew
Jackson would be proud!

Jeb

———

Still there was no news on Rilya Wilson. I sent this note to Tim
Moore. Even though I knew if he had news, he would have told
me, it was hard not to ask.

Subject: [None]
Friday, July 26, 2002 3:43 p.m.
From: Jeb Bush

Any news on Riyla case? Any leads? Any news on the
"grandmother and aunt"?

Jeb Bush

———

Hollywood was threatening our manatees! My mission was to protect both the manatees and the jobs the film industry brought to our state.

Ken Haddad of the Florida Fish and Wildlife Conservation Commission sent this e-mail to Denver Stutler, who had left the Department of Environmental Protection to become my deputy chief of staff.

Subject: Bad Boys II update/manatees
Sunday, July 28, 2002 9:47 a.m.
From: Ken Haddad

Denver, I spoke with the Exec. producer (Barry Waltman) late Friday. Apparently he is coming up to meet with the Gov Monday. He is really pushing to film the boat chases starting Thursday Aug 2. I told him I would do what I can but he must bring the Save the Manatee Club on board. My lawyers are very concerned about the use of an emergency variance and that is the only tool available for being able to waive speed zones even if everyone agrees to a solution that would allow it. Is it possible for a lawyer in your office listen to our interpretation of the rules and statute and help with the interpretation of "emergency" and "severe hardship"? If the lawyers can come to grip with this and all parties agree to protection measures then it is doable. I told this to Barry and he accepted but of course big dollars and threat to production occur if the shooting is delayed. He seems willing to bend over backwards and has admitted that the current emergency is due to the failure of the production team to give enough notice on their intentions and request. They could easily have handled this over a month ago but did not contact the Gov film office in a timely manner.

Denver sent me this note.

Subject: Bad Boys II update/manatees
Sunday, July 28, 2002 10:44 p.m.
From: Denver Stutler

As an update…we will continue to work with FWCC and ask legal to also look into.

Bottom line - Columbia (filming Bad boys II) needs to shoot about two days in the Miami River. This a manateee protection zone. Columbia is offerering a very impressive plan to watch for manatees and if present will not shoot. FWCC attorneys are claiming that this does not warrant an exemption but they will give a variance (14 day notice instead 30). Problem: Columbia is hoping to shoot next Thursday.

Subject: Bad Boys II update/manatees
Monday, July 29, 2002 6:21 a.m.
From: Jeb Bush

my perspective is we should do what we can to help columbia. it would look bad if we could not get it done. Why does the Save the Manatee Club have to sign off. Certainly they should be notified, briefed, be part of the process, etc. But sign off?

Jeb Bush

Colleen Castille weighed in with her concern. The next time you see Bad Boys II, *remember all this as you watch the boat chase scene.*

Subject: Bad Boys II update/manatees
Monday, July 29, 2002 9:09 a.m.

From: Colleen Castille

Governor, if they don't sign off, they can sue and bring a halt to the whole thing anyway.

Subject: Bad Boys II update/manatees
Monday, July 29, 2002 10:57 a.m.
From: Jeb Bush

How can they stop a one day event?

Jeb

———

The issue was resolved, and I got this e-mail several weeks later from the Columbia Pictures team.

Subject: [None]
Wednesday, August 21, 2002 8:33 a.m.
From: Barry Waldman

On behalf of Jerry Bruckheimer, Michael Bay, and myself, I would like to thank you for your assistance in helping to swiftly resolve our Manatee problem and allow BAD BOYS 2 to film off the waters of Watson Island in Miami Beach.

As we begin our first few weeks of shooting, we are ever grateful for the support that the City of Miami, the City of Miami Beach, the Department of Transportation, and the State of Florida have shown, and are continuing to show, our production.

Should you or your family have the opportunity to come to Miami, please accept our invitation to visit us on set; you are more than welcome, and we would enjoy having you there.

————

A friend chastised me for a late-night e-mail exchange.

Subject: [None]
Tuesday, July 30, 2002 10:41 p.m.
From: Charles Davidson

alright now Gov, emails this late are supposed to come only from the worker bees

i tried to get kathleen one morning by sending her an email about 4:30am -- I got a reply at 4:45 am

DON'T WORK TOO HARD!

Subject: [None]
Tuesday, July 30, 2002 10:48 p.m.
From: Jeb Bush

I am one of the worker bees.

Jeb Bush

————

I had attended the Wausau Possum Festival, a fund-raising event in the Panhandle that was a favorite campaign stop for all office seekers. Given I was up for reelection, I happily participated and won the last possum auctioned off that evening for $500.

Suject: Possum
Tuesday, August 6, 2002 2:49 a.m.
From: Dinah Pulver

So, inquiring minds want to know. What happened to
that possum you bought over the weekend? As a sixth
generation native Florida cracker, I can happily
say that is one of the few wild animals I haven't
eaten. Armadillos, gopher tortoise, sea turtles and
manatees, but no possum.

Suject: Possum
Tuesday, August 6, 2002 6:55 a.m.
From: Jeb Bush

**My possum was returned. Kind of like catch and
release.…**

Jeb Bush

———

*Certainly there are things I wish I had done differently as
governor. That includes allowing a bill known as the "Scarlet
Letter" Adoption Bill to become law. Among its provisions
was requiring single women giving up their babies for adoption to make public, through newspaper ads, the names of all
potential fathers. It was intended to fix the problem of a biological father suing for custody after an adoption had taken
place, but this bill was deeply flawed. When it passed over-
whelmingly in both the Senate and House in 2001, I refused to
sign it—but I didn't veto it either. This meant it automatically
became law. Instead I directed the legislature—specifically its
author, Senator Skip Campbell—to fix the problems with the
bill.*

Senator Campbell broke his promise to fix the law during the 2002 legislative session, and the public outrage was fierce.

Subject: Adoption Law
Thursday, August 8, 2002 11:20 a.m.
From: Louise Palmier

Are you insane? You advocate adoption and then put all these stumbling blocks in the way. How would you like to publish in newspapers all the people you have slept with in your lifetime? I truly believe the Republicans are a disaster for this state and the entire nation. Havoc in this country has never been greater. Rich taking advantage of the poor has never been more rampant. A pox on all your houses. The fact that you have a department that cannot keep track of foster children should be a huge clue as to your pitiful management toward the children of Florida. And you want to make it more difficult for children to be adopted? I repeat, are you insane?

Subject: Adoption Law
Saturday, August 10, 2002 7:53 a.m.
From: Jeb Bush

No, Louise, I am not insane. the sponsor of the bill was Senator Skip Campbell a well regarded Democrat. I threatened to veto the bill for the provision you tried to describe and a few others. He agreed to take up the changes in another bill that would have made our adoption process more balanced but he failed to do so.

I hope you have a restful weekend. The tone of your emails are getting such that I think some rest might be helpful. I intend to do the same.

Jeb Bush

———

Subject: Skip Campbell's adoption bill
Tuesday, August 13, 2002 9:36 p.m.
From: [No name]

Is it safe to assume that you know you were lied to,
and you wish you had vetoed the adoption bill as you
had been asked to do by the real experts?

Subject: Skip Campbell's adoption bill
Tuesday, August 13, 2002 9:55 p.m.
From: Jeb Bush

yes.

Jeb Bush

Thankfully I signed its repeal in 2003.

———

This note of encouragement came from my film commissioner.

Subject: Thanks
Saturday, August 24, 2002 10:10 p.m.
From: Rebecca Mattingly

Please tell me how you are able to take media beatings
and unfair attacks for just doing your job. I know
you've been at this political thing a lot longer than
me and your skin is by far, thicker than mine.

Subject: Thanks

Saturday, August 24, 2002 10:38 p.m.
From: Jeb Bush

my faith, my principles and my wartime attitude.
Don't let the bastards get you down!

Jeb Bush

———

As the new school year got under way, I was delighted to get this letter of support from a second-grade teacher.

Subject: Education
Thursday, September 5, 2002 6:18 p.m.
From: Alleen Miller

This is my 42nd year of teaching, of which 38 years have been in the state of Florida. I wanted you to know how very proud I am of the educational programs that you initiated during your first term as governor.

Yes, the programs do require more of the people responsible for the improvement in learning but at the same time that is why we are here—to make certain that the children receive the ultimate education. I feel more emphasis is being placed on improving the skills necessary for the children to succeed in today's world.

Our teachers are no longer attending "frilly" workshops but are receiving powerful and informative workshops that will actually improve our children's reading, math and writing skills.

I have never seen such beautiful writers as I do today. I wish this skill had been emphasized when I was in school. Instead writing meant penmanship and not creative writing.

I am proud of being able to say that I teach at an A+ school and I have had parents tell me that they are using this instrument in helping them choose the school that their child/children will attend.

This is my last year of teaching, which is going to be hard to accept but I know that schools, under your leadership, will continue to reach new highs and remain an exciting part of the state of Florida!

Subject: Education
Thursday, September 5, 2002 7:49 p.m.
From: Jeb Bush

I cried reading your email. I have worked hard to change the system against much opposition that does not like change and reform. Your real world endorsement of our efforts is so very meaningful to me. God bless you for years of service to our students!

Jeb

PS iAm on my blackberry so please excuse any typo's.

———

The Florida primary election was on September 20—our first statewide election since I signed election reforms into law. At the request of the secretary of state, I ordered the polls to be extended by two hours as voters and local election officials adjusted to the new technology.

Of course, all was not perfect.

Subject: vote
Thursday, September 12, 2002 4:29 p.m.
From: [No name]

So, suddenly our voting machines are a priority with you? I really think that, if you had been on top of things, this would NOT have happened. This is America and our votes are supposed to COUNT. FIX IT, GOVERNOR.

Just sign me...
Horrified Republican

Subject: vote
Thursday, September 12, 2002 10:18 p.m.
From: Jeb Bush

If you live in Florida, you know that 65 of the 67 counties got it right. We have provided $30 million to implement the reforms. Local supervisors of election are in charge of making elections work. The fact that Dade and Broward Counties couldn't get it right if a local problem. Shame on them! We will provide support at the state level but it is there responsibility. Thank you for writing.

Jeb Bush

———

There were more threats not to vote for me in November if I didn't shape up. How did elected officials set the record straight before e-mail?

Subject: BUILDING SCHOOLS
Monday, September 23, 2002 7:19 p.m.
From: Anthony and Cynthia Ungaro

If I understand what I hear in the news you propose to float millions in bonds to build schools. The collateral for these bonds will be another TAX on cable TV. You must think we pretty damn stupid. Since January 96 cable has increased over 92% and you want to add to that!!!!!!!!!!!!!!! You better pick another gimick to pander to the voters. This is one Republican who will stay HOME in November.

Subject: BUILDING SCHOOLS
Tuesday, September 24, 2002 8:33 p.m.
From: Jeb Bush

No sir, you have it wrong. We are taking the growth in the communication tax revenues, not through a tax increase but through increase use of the communication services, to be bonded to build classrooms. I have cut taxes by $6 billion cummulatively in four years and will continue to defend against tax increases. My opponent is the one who has already said will raise your taxes!

I need your vote in November.

Jeb Bush

———

Keiko the whale was made famous when he starred in the movie Free Willy. *He eventually was released back into the wild, and at the writing of this e-mail, he had been spotted in a Norwegian fjord. I have no idea why this woman thought I had done something to Keiko. My guess is she didn't vote for me either.*

Subject: Please read
Sunday, September 22, 2002 8:23 p.m.
From: Kelsey

I want to say that I disagree with your reasons for stealing Keiko the Orca from its freedom, and have its family taken away from him. I request that you have Mr. Hertz letter withdrawn. Do you even care about Keiko? You may not, but some people do. Why put it in a little swimming pool anyway, theres no point. Please keep him how he is.

Subject: Please read
Sunday, September 22, 2002 9:09 p.m.
From: Jeb Bush

I have been accused of many things but I have not stolen Keiko from the ocean! Thank you for writing.

Jeb Bush

———

This e-mail is from David Lawrence, who retired as editor and publisher of the Miami Herald *to devote himself to early childhood education. He is a true hero.*

Subject: [None]
Monday, September 23, 2002 3:31 p.m.
From: Dave Lawrence Jr.

I am to introduce you, and a number of others, at
your Early Childhood Cognitive Development Summit
next week, and am trying to prepare something
earlier this week because am out of town most of the
week.

So…I am asking each person to tell me (a) the first
book they remember hearing or reading, and (b) maybe
an early and influential book. For instance, I might
say to (a) "The Little Engine That Could," and to
(b) "Dick and Jane," which was my first grade text.
Any thoughts you have, beyond titles, would be
welcomed.

Help me with this for you, please.

It will be good to see you.

Subject: [None]
Monday, September 23, 2002 9:33 p.m.
From: Jeb Bush

**Thank you David. I remember vividly my mom reading
the Babar books to me. I loved the pictures! I also
remember reading Zelda the Zebra while my mom toilet
trained me but that you can't mention.**

Jeb Bush

———

David Struhs, head of the state Department of Environmental Protection, was another great American.

Subject: Cabinet follow-up
Tuesday, September 24, 2002 8:20 p.m.
From: David Struhs

Good discussions today at the cabinet meeting.
Thanks.

Our message worked well:
Saving time = Saving money = Saving the environment.
Remember, Since you became Governor, we have:

91,000 new acres of state forest.

88,000 acres of new wildlife habitat

7 new state parks

120 miles of new trails

Subject: Cabinet follow-up
Tuesday, September 24, 2002 8:54 p.m.
From: Jeb Bush

**I am blessed to have such a talented steward of our
environment by my side. Thank you David.**

Jeb

———

E-mails like this made me very happy I was running for reelection.

Subject: Thank you
Wednesday, September 25, 2002 7:56 p.m.
From: David Williams

I would like to say thank you for giving so much of
your time to be our Governor. I am a Code Enforcement
Officer for St. Johns County Florida. I deal with all
types of situations daily, but for me my time stops
at 4:30 every day, and my weekends are my own. I
can't imagine what a day in your shoes are. So on
behalf of my family and myself I would like to say
thank you for the time you give. I've never written
a letter to a political person before. I just felt
a need to express a positive statement. This has
nothing to do with Republican or Democrat, it has
to do with the public recognizing the sacrifices a
individual and also that individuals family gives,
when he or she wants to make a difference in the
world. We think your doing a fine job. Thanks again

Subject: Thank you
Wednesday, September 25, 2002 9:07 p.m.
From: Jeb Bush

**thank you David. Your email has made my day! I work
hard but joyfully on behalf of the wonderful people
of our great State.**

Jeb Bush

———

*The legislative session ended without passing major medical mal-
practice reform, which had been one of my priorities. The trial bar*

was a powerful adversary, but if reelected I was not going to give up my quest to reduce the exorbitant costs of runaway lawsuits.

Subject: Medical malpractice reform.
Monday, September 30, 2002 2:41 p.m.
From: Sue Regala

We need your immediate help. My husband and I are worried that soon we will have to leave our home and business. Phil and I are very concerned that his malpractice policy will not renew next year. He will not stay in Florida to practice orthopedics without coverage and risk financial ruin from a lawsuit. We will find a state that has tort reform that supports the physician instead of trial attorneys in a fair manner, as some states already have done for years. Why has it taken Florida so long? California, Indiana, and recently Nevada have tort reform and their physicians are able to stay and practice in their states....My husband can't just raise his fees to make up his expenses. He is a participating provider for Medicare. His fees are capped.

There are breaking points for every practice and this seems to be affecting all the doctors in my community. Some have been hit harder than others. We have lost 3 general surgeons since January. Some have retired because that could not afford their new premiums and one could not obtain coverage. My husband spoke to a internist that said his 42 person group got a nonrenewal notice from their carrier Friday. Who will care for their patients this season if they can't get coverage?

My husband is 37 years old. He has been practicing
for only 5 years since graduating from the University
of Miami residency in orthopedics. I am an operating
room RN. Not only is he a good man and father, he is
a good doctor that cares and respects his patients.
Phil has 11 full time employees with his partner, who
is also an orthopedic surgeon. Their employees are
aware that their jobs are at risk in this malpractice
crisis....

Thank you very much for your time reading my letter of
concern about our malpractice crisis in our household.
It breaks my heart that our family will leave this
state next July if we can not continue to afford the
$125,000.00 premium or unable to retain coverage. We
have started to think about our options. In the end
everyone will pay the price for good healthcare.

Subject: Medical malpractice reform.
Monday, September 30, 2002 9:16 p.m.
From: Jeb Bush

**Sue, I understand your situation and am as equally
concerned as you and your husband are. I have asked
that a commission make serious recommendations for the
next legislative session. we need to act and I wish we
could have acted this year but I found little interest
in the legislature. There are many suggestions that we
need to pursue but the primary one is to place a cap
on non economic damages similar to the one that exists
in California. Unfortunately, our courts have ruled
that along with a cap, there must be a mitigating
benefit for patients and that is where the difficulty
exists. I pledge to you that I will fight for the cap
(as I have done so in the campaign) and a reasonable**

solution in the other areas. I am very frustrated that the legislature has not moved on this critical issue since it relates to patient quality.

As an aside, my opponent is opposed to caps and is really beholden to the trial lawyers that do well with the current system.

I will fight hard in the campaign and as governor to bring about meaningful reform.

Jeb Bush

———

On election night I won 56 percent of the vote against Democratic candidate Bill McBride (he had defeated Janet Reno in the Democratic primary), so there was great joy in my family and among my friends and staff. I was the first Republican governor in state history to be reelected.

I had run hard on my record of lifting student achievement, cutting taxes, reducing crime, protecting the environment, strengthening the economy, and providing assistance to Florida's most vulnerable citizens. I was grateful to be given the chance to continue the work we had started.

I also suffered a defeat on election night that caused me grief for the rest of my governorship, though. I opposed a constitutional amendment that mandated reduction in class sizes in Florida. I understood the desire for smaller class sizes, but I did not feel a constitutional mandate was the way to accomplish it. The biggest challenge was how to pay for it. Funds would come out of classroom instruction and teacher salaries to cover the costs of reduced class size. Yet no studies had shown convincingly that this one measure in and of itself would guarantee an increase in student learning. I wanted to continue to focus on the areas in which we were already achieving success—and I did not want to take away funds for teachers' salaries, despite the union's claim.

Unfortunately, Florida voters did not agree, and the amendment passed. A few months before election day, the polls were showing a whopping 80 percent of Floridians supported the amendment. I was the only statewide elected official who campaigned against it, and I got the winning margin down to 52 percent. It wasn't enough, though. It became law.

Lloyd Brown, the editorial page editor for the Florida Times-Union, *succinctly summed up the situation.*

Subject: Congratulations
Wednesday, November 6, 2002 8:23 a.m.
From: Lloyd Brown

...and condolences. I'm glad classroom size isn't MY problem.

"Constitutional compliance vouchers" might help.

Subject: Congratulations
Wednesday, November 6, 2002 10:13 p.m.
From: Jeb Bush

You have got that right! I am looking for ideas. You have any?

Jeb Bush

———

As much as I loved being governor of Florida, I had to make phone calls I had hoped were never necessary.

331

Subject: Tallahassee Police Officer Sgt. Dale Green Killed Tonight
Wednesday, November 13, 2002 10:27 p.m.
From: Tim Moore

Sgt Dale Green of Tallahassee PD was killed tonight while responding to a home invasion robbery call. Suspect shot and killed Green and suspect has since been located and taken into custody in north Tallahassee.

Sgt Green was the Team Leader for the TPD Sniper Team and did a lot of teaching for FDLE. He was married and has a wife and kids in Tallahassee.

Subject: Tallahassee Police Officer Sgt. Dale Green Killed Tonight
Wednesday, November 13, 2002 10:42 p.m.
From: Jeb Bush

Commish, you have a telephone number for his wife? How sad! These killings make my so angry and resolved to stay the course to never let up in the fight against crime.

Jeb Bush

———

Here's more on the new constitutional amendment mandating smaller class sizes.

Subject: Meeting with Senator Cowin
Friday, November 15, 2002 9:46 p.m.
From: Jack Keitzer

Education is a great concern of mine as well as many others.

The paper stated this morning that you had some thoughts of increasing gambling options in some form. I firmly believe this is the worst approach to our # 9[71] problem. I am convinced there will be a solution that will not break our backs financially. The position that you and the legislature have been put in is not to your liking nor to many thousands. Business people have problems to solve every day and could possibly be a source to tap. I have offered assistance to Anna [Cowin] in whatever form she or anyone might need in solving this problem.

Thank You for your time and if I'm not needed, that's OK, I'll still pray for Your success.

Subject: Meeting with Senator Cowin
Friday, November 15, 2002 9:49 p.m.
From: Jeb Bush

thank you Jack. All i said was that everything was on the table. I am opposed to tax increases. I am opposed to the expansion of gambling. I am opposed to bigs cuts in programs for the most needy. That is why I voted against amendment 9. it is a big gorilla that requires a big increase in revenue and or a big cut in expenses.

Jeb Bush

----

71 The Class Size Reduction Amendment to the Florida Constitution was the ninth constitutional amendment.

Questions were beginning to come in about what a second term might look like. There were indeed some issues I felt strongly about.

Subject: two budget questions
Thursday, December 5, 2002 12:06 p.m.
From: Joe Follick

Governor, this is Joe Follick with the Tampa Tribune. I know you're busy, I appreciate your time and thoughts.

Jon Shebel[72] told me yesterday that it's time for the state to begin talking about instituting a personal income tax with that revenue dedicated to providing a few critical needs: heatlh insurance for all public school children, prescription drugs for elderly, etc. He proposes implementing this - after years of discussion - with a constitutional amendment rather than going through the Legislature. Is this a feasible plan and one that would help the state, in your estimation?

Subject: two budget questions
Thursday, December 5, 2002 9:14 p.m.
From: Jeb Bush

An income tax? Over my dead body.…

Thanks for writing.

Jeb Bush

---

72 Jon Shebel was head of Associated Industries of Florida, a large business-lobbying association.

———

Election years sometimes are seen as not productive, but we had accomplished a great deal between the extended travel the campaign required. A few of the highlights follow:

- *I joined the president of the United States in the Oval Office to sign an agreement that ensured adequate water would be made available to save the Everglades. By "adequate" I mean 1.7 billion gallons, which was being diverted to the Gulf of Mexico and the Atlantic Ocean. The Everglades Restoration Project recaptured that water.*
- *I was the first governor to ask for and receive state funding for shelters for victims of domestic abuse, and we continued our push to reduce domestic violence in Florida.*
- *I signed into law tougher penalties for DUI. This included making the third conviction within ten years a third-degree felony, which is punishable by imprisonment of up to five years.*
- *I announced in November that the unemployment rate stood at 5.1 percent—the lowest it had been since 9/11. Of the ten largest states, Florida was the only one with positive job growth from September 2001 to September 2002. It was validation that our post-9/11 economic recovery plan had worked and was continuing to work.*

We will end with Rilya Wilson, whose story still does not have an ending. Her body was never found.

Her caretaker, Geralyn Graham, was arrested before the end of the year, but she was not convicted and sentenced until 2013 for kidnapping and child abuse. The jury deadlocked 11–1 on murder charges. She will spend the rest of her life in prison.

By the end of May, the blue-ribbon panel had come back with its interim recommendations to improve the foster-care system. The recommendations included moving to a community-based care system—an idea I had long advocated. They called for better oversight, better coordination with law enforcement agencies, and better training for caseworkers.

On May 15 I signed into law a bill that made falsification of child custody records a felony. "I sign this bill in her honor," I said at the ceremony. "We must ensure that what happened to Rilya never happens to any child again."

In August I accepted the resignation of Kathleen Kearney, head of the Department of Children and Families. Kathleen was a dear friend and dedicated public servant. She deeply cared about kids and to this day is a child advocate. However, I needed to make a change in leadership to usher in the new reforms needed to improve the system.

Rilya's disappearance put a very painful spotlight on the broken foster-care system in Florida. It had been neglected for years, and we began attempting to fix it the minute I took office. In her memory we put a number of additional reforms into place to better protect Florida's children.

We drove decisions out of Tallahassee and down into the communities where private-sector providers improved the quality of care provided to children. The number of children adopted into loving homes increased by 107 percent during my governorship, and the number of backlog cases needing investigation plummeted from more than two thousand in 2002 to fifteen by the last year of my governorship.

I was very proud of the improvements we made, but when it comes to children, it's never enough. Every child deserves a chance, a home, and love.

CHAPTER 5

"I Am Optimistic That
We Can Do It..."

And how will we realize our destiny? We will do it with the grace of God, a fierce determination, and the lessons we have learned.

—Inaugural Address, January 7, 2003

The New Year began with the excitement and pageantry of Inauguration Day. In many ways the second time around is even more special than the first.

I was humbled that Floridians trusted me to be their governor for four more years. I was grateful to my family—Columba, George P., Noelle, and Jebby—all of whom stood by my side during the campaign and on the day I was sworn in. As I said in my remarks that day, "They have sacrificed greatly for me, and I love them dearly."

I was determined not to let any of them down.

The minute the applause faded away, there was an immediate sense we had only four more years to finish what we had set out to do four years earlier. I felt good about what we had done so far with improving education, providing tax relief, strengthening the business climate, saving the Everglades, and taking care of the most vulnerable among us—the disabled, senior citizens, and at-risk children.

However, our to-do list was still long.

Perhaps my most ambitious goal was to provide an environment—strong economy, excellent schools and roads, good quality of life, and more—where Floridians of all backgrounds could rise. I wanted Florida to be a place where people would come from all over America to raise their children, pursue their dreams, and find success.

As a conservative, I believe strongly that faith, family, and friends are the drivers that change society—not government. I learned from my parents that accepting personal responsibility, working hard, and caring for others are much stronger predictors of success than a reliance on government. As governor I knew growing government bureaucracy often impeded opportunities for working families. I challenged everyone there that day to rethink how we lived our lives and how we thought about our government.

"In our most private moments alone," I said, "we should reflect on our unearned gifts and rededicate our lives to those around us. In a thousand ways, we can be more accepting, more giving, more compassionate. And if we are, we can embed in society a sense of caring that makes government less necessary. There would be no greater tribute to our maturity as a society than if we can make these buildings around us empty of workers—silent monuments to the time when government played a larger role than it deserved or could adequately fill."

Talking about empty buildings might have rattled some nerves in Tallahassee that day. Before the year was out, I would call the legislature back into five separate special sessions to get their work done—most importantly to deal with the growing medical liability crisis in our state. Skyrocketing insurance costs were causing a massive exodus of doctors in search of more affordable working conditions. With that debate came a lot of shouting, finger-pointing, and a great deal of tension.

The year 2003 was without a doubt my toughest legislative year. It was one in which I had to struggle to heed the advice of former Florida governor LeRoy Collins, who said the proper role of a governor is to steer the ship beyond the harbor "but not beyond the horizon, where it can no longer be seen by those onshore."

To add to the tension, the case of Terri Schiavo burst onto the national scene before the year's end—once again shining the national media spotlight on Florida.

Before we get down to some of the tougher issues of 2003, however, let's have some joy first. I loved this e-mail from Shelly Brantley, my new point person for improving the services provided to Floridians with developmental disabilities.

Subject: FAMILY CAFE child fup[73]
Monday, January 20, 2003 9:43 p.m.
From: Michelle Brantley

I have always known deep in my heart and soul that
I would devote my life to serving individuals
with disabilities. What I never expected was to
have Florida's most powerful Governor, who could
choose any cause or issue, to make individuals with
developmental disabilities one of his top priorities
and then ask me to assume a leadership role. I am so
humbled and grateful for this opportunity to serve
the most courageous and inspirational individuals and
families I have ever known. I plan to give this job
my very best.

---

73 For being the governor who declared he hated acronyms, I was famous for using "FUP" a lot. It's the shorthand version of "follow up please."

Subject: FAMILY CAFE child fup
Monday, January 20, 2003 10:00 p.m.
From: Jeb Bush

you make me cry. Maybe it is the long day. But I think it is your passion which I share. Let us make this work!

Here is what I believe. We are all divinely inspired as God's creatures.…Those with developmental disabilities are divinely inspired as well, but have an added protection and closeness with God. I have not consulted with divinity professors on this. I have not asked my priest. I just plain believe it. I just know that our Lord would protect them above all others.

So, acting on that belief, it is our obligation to make sure that they receive our support in His honor and in recognition of their dignity.

That is easier said than done. Their families are fiercely loyal and many times frustrated. They are angry after a near generation of hurt and betrayal. I have tried to rectify this with doubling of the funding in four years but have been betrayed myself by a beacuracry that is insensitive and incompetent.

Now you step in. Shelly, my hope is that you clean up the mess and shoot straight with our constituents. Tell them the truth and I will go to bat for you to the bitter end. No more empty promises. Only the truth and hope will prevail. I know that Secretary Regier[74] will support you and so will I!

---

74 Jerry Regier was secretary of the Department of Children and Families.

Thank you for agreeing to serve.

———

It's time to stop the presses for an urgent question from the Washington Post.

Subject: [None]
Wednesday, January 22, 2003 5:30 p.m.
From: Mark Leibovich

I realize (and respect) that you have no intention of cooperating with me for this story, so please forgive my intrusion.

But a question of such gravity has come up -- a question of such monumental import to the national interest -- that I have no choice but to ask you directly:

Is it true that your cat, Sugar, sleeps on your chest every night?

Subject: [None]
Wednesday, January 22, 2003 8:55 p.m.
From: Jeb Bush

Jeez. Sugar sleeps on a red blanket at Colu and my feet every night. this is going to be quite a profile. I am not worth it.

Jeb Bush

———

Then there was this from a state senator.

Subject: Stairs
Thursday, January 23, 2003 2:30 p.m.
From: Paula Dockery

Do you ever climb the stairs anymore? I'll bring my exercise shoes if you need a climbing buddy.

(You're looking thin, but I need the exercise)

Subject: Stairs
Thursday, January 23, 2003 2:45 p.m.
From: Jeb Bush

bigger suits make me look thin. I am really out of shape. I do walk to work and home every day.

———

I decided not to include family e-mails in this book, but I have to include this announcement of my mom's arrival into the twenty-first century.

Subject: [None]
Thursday, January 30, 2003 6:29 p.m.
From: Barbara Bush

We are in the car going to hear the Oaks[75] in Galveston and have a new toy. We love you. Mom
----
Sent from my BlackBerry Wireless Handheld

---

75 The Oak Ridge Boys—Mom and Dad's favorite country singing group.

Subject: [None]
Thursday, January 30, 2003 6:47 p.m.
From: Jeb Bush

a blackberry!!!!

Jeb Bush

Jim King was the new president of the Florida State Senate.
Jim was one of the larger-than-life members of the legislature.
His big laugh and constant jokes disguised a smart and fierce
opponent when on the opposite side of an issue. The editorial
page editor of the Florida Times-Union *apparently thought*
we were not getting along. This e-mail proved prophetic, as
Senator King and I clashed later in the year over my com-
mitment to impose reasonable caps on medical liability jury
awards.

Subject: House-senate
Thursday, January 30, 2003 9:45 a.m.
From: Lloyd Brown

Will counseling help Jim King or do you need an
exorcist?

Subject: House-senate
Thursday, January 30, 2003 9:17 p.m.
From: Jeb Bush

actually, Jim is acting like an adult which is good.
We have a difference of opinion on taxes and the size
and scope of government but I can work with him. I
would not be too harsh on him yet. He is

showing prudence, a good attribute in public leadership.

Jeb Bush

———

On February 1 the space shuttle Columbia *exploded over Texas upon reentry into the Earth's atmosphere. Because astronauts leave Earth from our soil, Floridians feel very connected to them and their families. I sent this e-mail to Pam Dana in the Office of Tourism, Trade, and Economic Development.*

Subject: [None]
Saturday, February 1, 2003 10:16 p.m.
From: Jeb Bush

we need to find a way for all floridians to help the families of the astronauts and the space program in general.

Jeb Bush

Subject: [None]
Sunday, February 2, 2003 1:47 p.m.
From: Pam Dana

I am in touch with NASA on a bi-daily manner. I will ask what they have in place to assist.

Also, here is the latest on the Memorials and NASA briefs.

1) Roy Bridges, KSC[76] Director, will hold an all hands meeting with his team at KSC during time frame of 10AM-12PM. This meeting is likely to be aired on NASA TV. Purpose is to apprised the KSC team of the situation at hand...and walking orders going forward.

2) A memorial is scheduled to be held in Houston on Tuesday. Date and venue, TBD.

3) KSC will hold its own memorial sometime this upcoming week, but NOT before Tuesday'smemorial in Houston. Protocol dictates that the Houston memorial outweigh/occur before all others. Florida's memorial will be hosted by the Astronauts Memorial Foundation at KSC. FYI, you have approved appropriations for the past few years to this Foundation....

As for the press, both Ed Gormel and I have fielded a number of press calls. The press are trying to find out the "economic impact" of this tragedy on the space program. My response has been as follows:...

It is premature to focus our attention to the impact on our economy. Instead, we are devoting our attention to thoughts and prayers for the families and lost ones.

————

Except for my youngest son, Jeb, I didn't know of any other Jeb Bushes. However, as it turned out, there was a Jeff Bush, who in 2003 was a graduate student in biochemistry at Florida State University. He apparently sometimes received phone calls intended for me.

---

76 Kennedy Space Center.

Subject: Endeavor science- Thank you
Wednesday, February 5, 2003 8:31 p.m.
From: Jeff Bush

I just wanted to say what an honor it was to have our
governor visit us today at Florida State. The fact
that you took time out of your very busy schedule to
make time to speak to the children really meant a lot.
You could see in their eyes the twinkle of wonderment
of how fascinated they were with the science that I
recall fostered an interest in science when I was in
their shoes. Also the fact that their governor has
championed and supported this noble cause of advancing
both science and our space program at the same time in
spite of the recent Columbia tragedy, is an ever more
appreciated display of solidarity and compassion. I
am proud to say that I am one of the few five hundred
and thirty some in 2000 in the state of Florida that
helped to send your brother to the White House. I am
a big fan of your politics and your compassion and it
was a real pleasure to meet you.

Subject: Endeavor science- Thank you
Wednesday, February 5, 2003 8:35 p.m.
From: Jeb Bush

**Thank you Jeff. I apologize in advance for all the
ugly calls and emails that you might get thinking you
are me! What will you do with your degree?**

Jeb Bush

Subject: Endeavor science- Thank you
Thursday, February 6, 2003 10:48 a.m.
From: Jeff Bush

346

No problem about the phone calls and emails, I think some of them on my answering machine are actually pretty funny. I eventually hope to possibly go to medical school and get into oncology so that I can help people and hopefully irradicate cancer and other diseases.

———

Apparently lightning hitting your airplane is a common occurrence if you are governor of Florida.

Subject: lightning-are you really okay?
Friday, February 28, 2003 9:21 p.m.
From: Trish Sullivan

The news report said you and the passengers were fine after the lightning struck the plane but is that really true? Are you really okay? I pray so.

(P.S. I was glad to see the AP report noted that Governor Chiles' plane was hit before too. I've heard too many jokes today about "someone up there not happy with our governor"!)

Subject: lightning-are you really okay?
Friday, February 28, 2003 9:24 p.m.
From: Jeb Bush

governor chiles was hit three times according to the veteran pilots!

Jeb Bush

———

Shortly after we won reelection, Frank Brogan told me he had been offered a job as president of Florida Atlantic University. Frank's life had been spent in public education—first as a high-school teacher, then as a principal, and ultimately as education commissioner and my lieutenant governor, where he worked to advance school choice and accountability. I was happy for Frank, but I would miss him. (He went on to be chancellor of the State University System of Florida, and today he heads higher education in Pennsylvania.)

That meant finding a new partner, though.

Many, including the media, were surprised when I chose Toni Jennings. She had served as president of the Senate from 1996 to 2000—the first senator to serve two successive terms as president. She had been both a strong partner and occasionally a formidable adversary. We didn't always agree, but she was smart. She was thoughtful, and she knew the legislative process better than anyone. I was confident we would make a great team.

We did. Toni was not only an outstanding lieutenant governor—the first woman to serve in this post in Florida—but she also remains a great friend.

Back to the "surprise" factor of my choice, though. Mike Griffin of the Orlando Sentinel *was perhaps the most descriptive.*

Subject: Good choice
Monday, March 3, 2003 3:54 p.m.
From: Mike Griffin

Toni will do a great job. She's the best person for the job.

But I think I just saw a pig fly by my window!

Subject: Good choice
March 3, 2003 8:47 p.m.
From: Jeb Bush

I don't get the pig thing but appreciate your kind email.

Jeb Bush

Subject: Good choice
Tuesday, March 4, 2003 8:18 a.m.
From: Mike Griffin

There was a time when I thought pigs would fly about the same time there's be a Lt. Gov. Jennings.

You're going to be a great team.

———

About the same time, we had a disagreement with Speaker of the House Johnnie Byrd. One of the key components of the A+ plan was giving cash awards to schools that improved their grades. It was a powerful incentive to help drive gains in student achievement. My legislative director, Jim Magill, sent an e-mail to key staffers sounding the alarm.

Subject: Speaker's Press conference on Teacher pay
Friday, March 14, 2003 4:54 p.m.
From: Jim Magill

PK from the Speaker's Office just called to 1) tell us that the Speaker is unveiling his teacher pay increase package on Tuesday Afternoon, and 2) invite the Governor or Lt. Governor to attend. She said our OPB[77] shop is aware of the details. What say y'all

---

77 Office of Policy and Budget.

This is what my director had to say.

Subject: Speaker's Press conference on Teacher pay
Friday, March 14, 2003 6:16 p.m.
From: Donna Arduin

the funds will come from the A+ school recognition
money

This is what I had to say.

Subject: Speaker's Press conference on Teacher pay
Friday, March 14, 2003 7:51 p.m.
From: Jeb Bush

I say that we will have to say that we will veto any
legislation that takes away the rewards for school
improvement.

Jeb Bush

I sent this note to members of the Orlando Regional Chamber of Commerce. They had visited Tallahassee the day before, and I wanted to enlist their support on some of the big issues before the legislature.

Subject: [None]
Thursday, March 20, 2003 6:44 p.m.
From: Jeb Bush

Thank you for taking the time travel from Orlando
to be in Tallahassee Wednesday. As you talk with
your legislators, I ask you to be a continued voice

of reason on the challenges I spoke of today THAT
ultimately we will face together.

First, the medical malpractice issue is about
everyone's fundamental right to the access of care.
This is an issue that has potential to implode, it is
a reality and not a political game.

Second, the workers comp issues touches us all and
should be a top priority of business.

Third, I urge you to encourage our legislature to
trust the marketplace and realize the easy answer of
more taxation will ultimately fail us. There seems to
be an attitude of doom and gloom here in Tallahassee,
while when I am in places like Orlando, Jacksonville,
and Miami people are continuing to be upbeat while
facing everyday challenges.

I thank you for your contribution to Orlando and to
the state of Florida. Please make your voice heard.

Jeb

———

*A hot-button issue in 2003—and still today—concerns col-
lege tuition costs for children of illegal immigrants. I think it
is wrong to punish children who are brought to America by
their parents through no fault of their own. The issue was
not resolved while I was governor. However, in 2014 House
Speaker Will Weatherford and Senate President Jack Latvala,
both Republicans, worked together to pass a bill, signed by
Governor Rick Scott, to allow undocumented students who
attended a Florida school for at least three years before*

graduation to pay in-state tuition rates at our public colleges and universities.

Subject: In-State College Tuition For Illegal Aliens?
Thursday, March 20, 2003 8:24 p.m.
From: Monica Corso

Have you seen this?

Hope all is well with you and your family.…

In-State College Tuition For Illegal Aliens?
Mar. 19, 2003
By Phyllis Schlafly

The officials of some state universities and colleges, and even some state legislators, seem to think they can get by with openly disobeying federal law. They are flagrantly violating the law that prohibits giving subsidized college tuition rates to illegal aliens.

Shouldn't our public officials, of all people, respect the rule of law? Texas, California, New York and Utah have legislatively thumbed their noses at the federal law by passing a state law that grants in-state tuition rates to people living in our country illegally.

Subject: In-State College Tuition For Illegal Aliens?
Friday, March 21, 2003 10:51 p.m.
From: Jeb Bush

thanks Monica. I support in state college tuition for residents irrespective of their status that have been here for a while. Not a year or two. It seems to me

that valedectorians should be treated fairly if for
no fault of their own, their parents came illegally
to our country.

Jeb Bush

———

On March 19 the president of the United States announced that
military operations—known as "Operation Iraqi Freedom"—had
commenced in Iraq. I immediately called a meeting of my top
security officials to discuss safety at home.

Subject: Follow-up question
Friday, March 21, 2003 4:16 p.m.
From: Jeff Burlew

My name is Jeff Burlew, and I'm a reporter with the
Tallahassee Democrat. I chatted with you briefly after
the domestic security meeting Thursday in Orlando. I
was just wondering whether you have talked to your
brother since then, and if so, what you told him. If
you want to share your conversation with me, that
would be great.

I'd like to take my journalism hat off for a moment
and let you know that my thoughts and prayers are
with your family.

Subject: Follow-up question
Monday, March 24, 2003 2:10 p.m.
From: Jeb Bush

I spoke to my brother the afternoon of the security
task force meeting. I told him a great majority of

Floridians were supportive of him and the troops. He said things were going well. I told him that I loved him and was proud of him. He seemed to be doing well given the pressures that I know he is facing.

Jeb Bush

―――――

If I am going to include an e-mail from my mom, I'd better include one from Dad too. He wrote this after I sent him an inauguration photo. (Gampy is what all his grandchildren call him, and sometimes my siblings and I do as well.)

Subject: photo
Friday, March 21, 2003 12:31 p.m.
From: President Bush

I love the photo of your swearing in. It is so good of you that I have gotten over my being cropped out by the photographer. Thanks a lot. .
Love to all ,says your devoted, DAD

Subject: photo
Friday, March 21, 2003 8:19 p.m.
From: Jeb Bush

thanks Gampy. I love you.

Jeb Bush

―――――

I hope you enjoy reading about medical liability tort reform, because it was one of my top priorities for 2003. Due to the inaction of past legislatures, we were in true crisis form. Doctors were leaving Florida because they couldn't afford liability insurance. The biggest losers were Floridians, whose health-care options were dwindling and whose insurance costs were rising because of outlandish lawsuits. We'll begin with this question from Joe Follick of the Tampa Tribune.

Subject: a question
Friday, March 28, 2003 9:38 p.m.
From: Joe Follick

The divide between the House and Senate seems more philosophically wide than any time in your tenure. Are you or Lt. Gov. Jennings or your staff actively working to get the two sides together or are you letting things play out a bit longer? It seems this was Lt. Gov. Brogan's strength. Do you miss him in that role?

A related question: Med Mal is widening that divide. And you and the Lt. Governor are doing a fly-around to discuss that topic Monday. Are you concerned that doing so will only further isolate the prickly Senate at this tender time?

Again, thank you very much for your time.

Subject: a question
Saturday, March 29, 2003 7:28 a.m.
From: Jeb Bush

Thank you Joe.

It is up to the legislature to do its job. I am confident that it will.

Lt. Governor Jennings and I support meaningful med mal reform to improve access to health care for Floridians. We will continue to press our case with the legislature and with the people of our state.

Jeb Bush

————

E-mails were always interesting during legislative sessions, as people began to panic that the legislature was on the brink of making a disastrous move. My great friend Al Cardenas, a future chairman of the American Conservative Union, was momentarily fearful I would give in regarding high standards for Florida's students. I didn't then, and I won't back down now. If we believe all students can learn, then we should hold all students to the same high expectations for achievement. We owe our students high standards. That is key to their future successes.

Subject: [None]
Wednesday, April 9, 2003 10:29 p.m.
From: Al Cardenas

Sorry to harp again on fcat.…Please don't agree to lower/substitute standards. Biggest damage to minority and inner city kids has been precisely that: lowering standards, easy way out culture.
Some teachers, parents, kids will be scared: good! That is precisely what is needed to redouble efforts and get results.

There will be a few heartbreaking dissappointments.… Give test in native tongue if kid doesn't pass it 3times in English.…Give free summer school tutoring after senior year...but make all kids jump through same hoops.

Gov, this is so important. Don't give in and tell me what to do to help.

Subject: [None]
Friday, April 11, 2003 7:38 a.m.
From: Jeb Bush

I won't give in.

Jeb Bush

————

I include this e-mail from a student in honor of my mom, who taught all my siblings and me the joy of reading at very early ages. You could say that's the best example of a gift that keeps on giving.

Subject: [None]
Thursday, April 17, 2003 12:39 p.m.
From: Hillary

A girl from my classs the other day asked you a question do you like to read! Well now I have a question for you

Why do <u>you</u> read!

Please explain clearly!

Subject: [None]
Thursday, April 17, 2003 6:08 p.m.
From: Jeb Bush

I read for enjoyment. I read to learn. I read to work.
I read to think. I read to reflect. I read to relax.

Thank you for writing.

Jeb Bush

———

*Then the very bumpy road that became 2003 began.
Much to my chagrin, the legislature's very fractious sixty-day
session was coming to a close without a budget being passed.
They also had not acted on any of my top priorities. The
House and the Senate could not agree on anything—or so it
seemed.*

*Donna Arduin called to give me an update from the chair-
man of the House Committee on Appropriations and to discuss
when and if to call the legislature back into special session. I
didn't want to waste the taxpayers' money if I thought they
would just bicker again. I sent Donna and other top staffers
this note.*

Subject: [None]
Wednesday, April 30, 2003 10:30 p.m.
From: Jeb Bush

I appreciate your calling tonight. If there is a
possible change of behavior and it is tangibly
evident, then I would consider starting on Monday
week if we still can finish with enough time to
prepare for the next fiscal year.

However, if there is no tangible change in attitude
on both sides, then I am resigned to allow for the
possibility of failure to increase the humiliation

that will be felt by the members for not being able
to do the one thing that they are supposed to do.
Pass a budget. A budget that they agreed to in the
broadest sense but for $5 million in appropriations
out of a $52 billion budget.

Based on today's actions, I see no tangible evidence
of a willingness to look out for the people we
serve...the thousands of small businesses impacted by
incredibly high premiums or non existant workers
comp insurance. No consideration of the even larger
number of workers who might lose their jobs because
of inaction that could easily be resolved. No
consideration of the millions of people potentially
impacted by the med mal insurance crisis which is
causing planned walkouts across the state by doctors.
The serious impact on school districts, our teacher
shortage and most importantly students throughout
the K 20 system since we can't achieve a budget.
No one has thought about the problems of straight
jacketing districts when the constitution requires
them to lower class sizes without flexibility. No
consideration for the medically needy recipients who
must be real confused since we are telling them that
they have two months more but the legislature can't
pass a bill to do so even though no one disagrees
with doing it. I could go on and on.

Culture change has to happen and it has to happen
now. If not, we will have four years of misery for no
reason.

Again, you did the right thing to call me. However,
unless there is some real changes in the attitude
inside the bubble, I am prepared for the worst

**and am prepared to take the grief for getting the
legislature to change.**

Jeb

———

*Then Donna called back with a tiny bit of good news. With one
hour left, the legislature passed an emergency measure extending
the Medically Needy program for two months. It was set to expire
the very next day.*

Subject: [None]
Wednesday, April 30, 2003 11:08 p.m.
From: Donna Arduin

house just passed the senate's clean medically
needy 2 month extension…one small step for the brat
pack

Subject: [None]
Wednesday, April 30, 2003 11:10 p.m.
From: Jeb Bush

praise the LORD.

Jeb Bush

———

*The media naturally had questions about what happened and
what would happen next time. Lucy Morgan worked for the* St.
Petersburg Times, *and Victor Epstein worked for Gannett News
Service* .

Subject: a question for you
Friday, May 2, 2003 2:48 p.m.
From: Lucy Morgan

Some House members say you told them ""this is the worst [expletive deleted] session I have ever seen" during a meeting in the house lounge yesterday. Is this true?
If not, what do you really think of this session?

Subject: a question for you
Friday, May 2, 2003 9:31 p.m.
From: Jeb Bush

I did not say that but I am very disappointed that we did not get done the people's business during the regular session. I am optimistic that we can do it over the summer.

———

Subject: VIctor Epstein/Gannett News Service: Legislation questions
Saturday, May 3, 2003 3:55 p.m.
From: Victor Epstein

Sorry to bother you on a weekend, but we're still working hard over here on assorted stories. I have two questions for you, if you have a minute.

1) Did the bickering between the House and Senate take the "fun" out of the Legislature for you?

2) Are you worried this could be the start of a trend brought about by the supermajority that will make

it more difficult for the executive and legislative branches to work together in the future ?

Subject: VIctor Epstein/Gannett News Service: Legislation questions
Saturday, May 3, 2003 7:58 p.m.
From: Jeb Bush

1. **It was not a fun session given the lack of action on the budget.**

2. **I believe we are at a crossroads in our state politically. If the Republican Majority works together to solve the bigger issues of the day, I believe we will see continued dominance. This means passing a budget and at a minimum passing meaningful medical malpractice and workers comp reforms.**

Jeb Bush

————

Then Floridians started weighing in with their thoughts.

Subject: News Article
Monday, May 5, 2003 7:17 p.m.
From: Chris Card[78]

The best quote I have seen this session is "I'm the Governor not a therapist". I just burst out laughing. How appropriate when those around you appear to be acting foolishly.

————

78 Chris Card is a friend who (at that time) ran the Sarasota YMCA. It had a unique community-based care system that we ultimately adopted state-wide to better deliver foster care and children's services at the state level.

Subject: News Article
Monday, May 5, 2003 10:15 p.m.
From: Jeb Bush

how sad that is the quote of the session!

Jeb Bush

———

Subject: disappointment
Wednesday, May 7, 2003 1:13 a.m.
From: Jeff Dolan

I am very disappointed in the disgrace that passed for the Florida legislature this year. Even though I am a registered Democrat in recent years I began leaning toward the Republican side and was excited when the Republicans took total control in Florida. I was even going to change my voters registration.

After watching the disgusting display this legislative session I can tell you I will not be changing my registration.

It was embarrassing to see that the only things that got passed are the bills the big money special interests wanted.

Wekiwa river basin protection- forget it! developers don't want it.

Everglades cleanup- HA! the sugar industry has DEEP pockets.

Class size amendment (which I voted against because it
should not be in the constitution)- nothing done on it.

Smoking amendment- all they had to do was READ the
amendment and it would of taken about 5 minutes to
create a new law but NO, the lobbyists stuck their
noses in and of course nothing can get down without
permission of the lobbyists so nothing has been done.

Medical malpractice?
Workers comp reform?

Of course we did get a new bill passed to raise our
phone bills. Like our phone bills will be lower! Once
again, the power of campaign contributions.

Can't anything get done that justs benefits the
average citizen even if it goes against the "big
money" donors? It sure doesn't seem that way.

Now because nothing was done in two months of petty
bickering we, the taxpayers, get to pay $40,000 to
have these people go back and start again. Instead of
making the taxpayers pay why not dock each legislator
one days pay for each day of the extra session. They
stay an extra week, they lose one weeks pay. That
would be incentive to finish on time!

I know we are stuck with these house and senate
"leaders" for another year. I just hope Florida can
survive another year of their "leadership".

A disgusted Floridian.

Subject: disappointment
Friday, May 9, 2003 1:47 p.m.
From: Jeb Bush

Jeff, I was disappointed with the work of the
legislature. Although some good bills passed, many
needed bills, including the budget did not. Having
said that, I will work hard to push the legislature
to pass some of the bills you mentioned and some
additional ones.

Jeb Bush

———

*It was time to quit whining and get to work. I sent this note to top
staff members on Sunday afternoon.*

Subject: non budget items
Sunday, May 11, 2003 6:28 p.m.
From: Jeb Bush

I would like an update on Monday regarding the non
budget bills that could be making it to the special
session agenda:

- workers comp
- med mal (are we prepared to go public with our
  plan? did you see the poll this weekend? have we
  vetted our proposal?)
- ammendment 9
- charter schools
- voters bill

- **article five**[79]
- **oxycontin**[80]
- **civil rights**
- **PIP**[81]
- **smoking**[82]

I think after this weekend's articles, the legislature will want to get these done. We need to provide them the discipline they will need to make them successful.

Jeb Bush

———

As the back-and-forth with the legislature continued, I did get some very good news from my friend Kirsty, who you will recall had trouble passing the FCAT.

Subject: FCAT, HB1739, graduation
Monday, May 5, 2003 5:28 p.m.
From: Kirsty

My walk into a brighter future would not have been possible without your help. Thank you for believing in me. I have sent you a personal invitation to attend my graduation on May 21, 2003. I would be so honored if you could attend the ceremony.

---

79 Article V of the Florida Constitution deals with the judiciary and addresses a number of funding issues. This includes the courts, state attorneys' offices, and public defenders.
80 Although OxyContin is a legal pain reliever, Florida was one of many states beginning to grapple with its illegal abuse.
81 PIP stands for "personal injury protection," which Florida requires be part of car-insurance coverage.
82 In 2002 the voters strongly supported a constitutional amendment to ban smoking in enclosed indoor workspaces. The legislature had to pass a bill to make this amendment a reality, which it did.

It is hard for me to believe that it was only May 14th last year when you came to my high school and I had the opportunity of a lifetime to meet with you to discuss my own needs and the needs of so many disabled students regarding the FCAT. I'll never forget how nervous I was, yet so excited to share my concerns. It has been an interesting year; one I won't soonforget. I can't wait to begin my journey into the future. Please join me and my family, as we celebrate a new beginning; my bright future!

Subject: FCAT, HB1739, graduation
Monday, May 5, 2003 10:00 p.m.
From: Jeb Bush

thank you Kirsty. I am proud of you. I don't know if I can make it but I will be there in spriit.

Jeb Bush

———

About this time controversy broke out regarding a severely mentally disabled woman who had been raped and became pregnant while living in a state-supervised group home. She had no family and lacked the mental capacity to make decisions for herself. With my full support, the Department of Children and Families sought separate guardians for the mother and unborn child. This was a tragic case, and I had great compassion for the mother and her well-being. However, I also believed the unborn baby deserved an advocate. This was given the pressure being applied for the mother to have a late-term abortion.

Although the courts denied our efforts to appoint a guardian for the baby, a circuit judge, based on the recommendation of the court-appointed guardian for the mother, ultimately ruled she should carry the baby to term. The baby girl was born and adopted.

The protection of the unborn is a very important part of my deeply held faith and my belief in the sanctity of life. It is not always easy, as this incredibly sad situation evidences.

Subject: Question about some news I read
Wednesday, May 14, 2003 10:22 a.m.
From: Jessica Frick

I just read an article that says the state is forcing a handicapped rape victim to have an appointed guardian for her fetus.…

The article also says that the state coerced her into continuing her pregnancy term.

Is this true? Why are you choosing this option?

Is there ever a time that you feel an abortion is an option?

I hope to hear back from you when you get a chance.

Subject: Question about some news I read
Thursday, May 15, 2003 10:13 a.m.
From: Jeb Bush

Thank you for writing. If the article said that the state coerced her into continuing her pregnancy to term, it is incorrect. This mother is severely developmentally disabled and cannot make decisions for herself or her child. Having a guardian for each of them is more than appropriate given the uniqueness of this tragic case.

Jeb Bush

———

Although the legislature was already in special session to pass a budget and other pending legislation, I called for a second special session in June to deal with the huge unresolved issue of medical malpractice reform. The mostly liberal trial lawyers were one of the state's most powerful and politically connected lobbying groups. They even had sway with Republican legislators. I was determined to stand up to the trial bar, as this issue was driving up health-care costs and driving doctors out of our state.

Subject: $250,000 cap on non-economic damages
Sunday, May 18, 2003 6:10 p.m.
From: Troy Tippett

I am writing first to thank you for your strong stance on a $250k cap on non-economic damages and your calling a special session of the legislature to deal with the medical liability insurance crisis. As we approach what we hope will be a long term solution, I can't help but reflect upon the other states that have recently gone through this same process. On virtually every occasion there was a great hue and cry initially, at least in the medical press, about the success of the physicians in obtaining tort reform. But on every occasion -Pennsylvania-Nevada-Mississippi-and now most recently West Virginia when the details become apparent we find that the doctors have made some regrettable compromise and did not end up with anything that we think would be acceptable in Florida. I think it is crucial that we hold to our position=an across the board $250k cap on non-economic damages per incident. The proposals I see

floated by Sen. King and others would either totally
release the cap or increase it based on death,
coma, paraplegia,(you fill in the next condition
or possibly the legislature can next year) and
so on. If we agree to this expansion we are again
talking about giving out more money for certain
bad outcomes not because the alleged or agreed to
malpractice was any more blatant but because of the
bad outcome. Furthermore we have no indication from
the insurance companies as to how these additional
expansions might eventually affect rates. California
continues to do well with an across the board cap.
This has been our battle cry to do like California
because they have the experience and success. I
don't think we should bow to Sen. King but continue
to stand tall for what has worked for 28 years in
California. I very much appreciate your continuing
to lead the charge for a $250,000 cap on non-
economic damages as the "Heart and Soul" of any
acceptable outcome.

Subject: $250,000 cap on non-economic damages
Sunday, May 18, 2003 6:29 p.m.
From: Jeb Bush

thank you Troy. I will not accept anything that
doesn't reduce insurance rates immediatly and
then has the potential for further reductions. We
will work with the health care professionals and
institutions this week to unveil our plan. Yes, there
will be a special session.

Jeb Bush

———

In the meantime there was a lot of frustration with the current special session. The legislators were not happy. They felt they needed a cooling-off period. I felt the people of Florida needed and deserved a budget. I sent this note to the legislative team.

```
Subject: [None]
Saturday, May 24, 2003 8:00 p.m.
From: Jeb Bush


We need to pass…

* a budget
* workers comp
PIP
Board of Governors
amendment 9
Charter schools
Quinones Arza bill[83]
Everglades
VACA
Primary date change bill

Anything else?

How can all of this get done? Especially if Byrd
won't take up any bills until the budget passes?

Jeb
```

———

83 This bill dealt with high-school students who moved to Florida during their junior or senior years and whose previous states of residence had different graduation requirements than ours.

Although all the issues were important, workers' compensation reform topped my list. The current system was crumbling under the huge weight of runaway costs, endless litigation, and fraud. The problem was so severe that it not only was keeping business out of Florida, but it also was driving businesses away. Finally the legislature came through.

Subject: Big Problem -WORKERS COMP INS
Friday, May 30, 2003 6:00 p.m.
From: Rose Robbins

My husband, Clarence Manz and I opened a new corporation, in November 2002. Once all the paper work, etc. was done, the building rented, orders put in to buy the necessary equipment and opening our doors in January, we came to find that it was impossible for us to get Worker's Compensation Insurance. Further, as owners of the company, we are no longer exempt. Therefore after months of trying, I finally had to resort to go to a staff leasing company and become employees of the company. As we had to have a minimum payroll to get accepted by the company, we were paying 2019.00 per week, which now has decreased to 2003.50 per week. This may not seem a lot, however, it increase our monthly budget by $ 4000.00. Due to this we are looking at one month left of company funds and 1 month of personal savings to carry this company for these additional 2 months. After which we will be jobless, and penniless. We started the company with 100,000.00. Now, after six months, this is the situation we find ourselves in. We have meet so many people who have not been able to get Worker's Comp Insurance and have decided to work under someone elses name, or not bother and risk losing everything or going back to their old companies instead of starting their own. We are very worried about the situation. Further, my husband, whose expertise is what we built the company on, has 30 years experience in the business. I have 30 + years experience in business management, financials, marketing and contracts. Yet we are about to fold. The added cost of employment versus Worker's Comp Insurance at an affordable price has taken months of business/personal cost away from us. PLEASE, LOOK AT THIS, HELP US AND THE OTHERS TRYING TO GROW AND BECOME BUSINESS OWNERS IN FLORIDA.

Subject: Big Problem -WORKERS COMP INS
Saturday, May 31, 2003 8:48 p.m.
From: Jeb Bush

Rose, my heart goes out to you. I have tried for two years to get the legislature to reform our workers comp laws. This year, they did so. I will sign the bill into law in the next two weeks. It will help you when it is implemented. Did you look at the JUA option.[84] It may be too expensive but it might be helpful. I am passing on your email to our workers comp team to see if they can be of help to you. thank you for writing.

Jeb Bush

———

I was very happy to take a break from legislative-related e-mails to provide some advice for a new graduate.

———————

84 Florida Workers' Compensation Joint Underwriting Association.

Subject: Advice to 18 year old
Wednesday, May 28, 2003 4:04 p.m.
From: Susan Norton

Our son Rush is graduating from High School and off
to college in the Fall. One ensuing question is what
gift will mean something now and later to an 18 year
old that "has everything". One thing that no one has
enough of is the advantage of hindsight…also called
wisdom. I thought what better source than those who
not only survived but thrived. Therefore would you
be kind enough to respond as to a) what you wish
you knew then; b)what you would do differently or c)
advice to an 18 year old male or to any or all of the
above.

Thank you very much.

Subject: Advice to 18 year old
Wednesday, May 28, 2003 10:09 p.m.
From: Jeb Bush

**Wow, mom, thank you for asking such a provocative set
of questions.**

**First of all Rush, congratulations on graduating from
high school. I am glad you passed the FCAT (smile) if
you went to public school.**

**I wish I knew when I was young that life was so full
of so many variables and twists and turns that my
frets were not worth it. All of the things that I
thought I wanted to be became less and less relevant
with each turn of the corner. I have now learned
that the key to a successful life is to be prepared**

to take advantage of life's opportunities and to avoid as many of the pitfalls that are always there. It is OK to take a risk or two. If you fall in love and you know it is the real thing, pull the trigger even though you haven't figured out how to pay the mortgage. Don't worry so much about the perils of becoming a dad because all of the i's aren't dotted and t's crossed, than your peers seem to do. It will work out and, as a sidebar, you will make your mom a happy Grandmother!

I guess I am saying...LIVE LARGE. TAKE RISKS. RECOGNIZE THAT THE WORLD IS A DYNAMIC PLACE WITH MORE OPPORTUNITIES THAN YOU CAN EVER IMAGINE. When you were a kid, you thought you were going to be a fireman or a baseball player. Don't be constrained by your old dreams. Be liberated by your new ones.

Jeb Bush

———

Among the businesses I worked hard to promote in Florida was the film industry. So this e-mail was good news indeed.

Subject: Thanks from Australian Film Crew in Florida
Tuesday, June 10, 2003 1:33 p.m.
From: Glenn Wilkinson

I would like to compliment the Florida Film Commission for an outstanding effort in helping us to co-ordinate our filming requirements in Florida. Our television production company Instinct Television Australia, produces the wildlife documentary series "Killer Instinct with Rob Bredl". Aside from the sensationalism of the title, this 39 episode television series examines the challenging survival techniques and environmental importance of many Australian and World animal species. The TV series adheres strongly to the philosophy that we contribute to the education of people, the awareness and appreciation of the environment and preservation of species. We do this in an entertaining way and reach a broad demographic.

The programme is hosted by Rob Bredl, also known as the "Barefoot Bushman", and currently rates number one on the Outdoor Life Network USA www.olntv.com and also runs primetime on the UK Horizons Network, BBC Discovery, RTL2 Germany, and in Italy, Scandinavia and New Zealand.

We were invited to the USA to film five episodes of the current series by our American distributors Associated Television International and The Outdoor Life Network. I made contact with Susan Simms, your Los Angeles Liaison several months ago from Australia. Susan has proven to be an invaluable source of information an strongly influenced our decision to film in Florida. I had approached several other States with the animals which met our criteria for filming and received very little response, the Florida Film Commission and associated Counties were quick to respond with an incredible diversity of animals and locations for our filming needs.

Our film crew is currently filming in Jupiter today at the BUSCH Wildlife Sanctuary and moves to Palmdale on Wednesday for three days of filming at Gatorland Alligator Farm. The owner, Allen Register and his wife Patty are great fans of our show and are looking

forward to working with Rob Bredl and the Killer
Instinct crew.

Thank you again to the Palm Beach Film Commission, we
believe we will produce two outstanding episodes of
the series in Florida and special thanks to Susan (whom
I met with on Monday) for her incredible commitment
in helping to coordinate our filming requirements from
across the Pacific and on the ground here in the USA.

**Subject: Thanks from Australian Film Crew in Florida
Thursday, June 12, 2003 9:29 p.m.
From: Jeb Bush**

**Wow, thank you Glenn. It is not a regular occurance
that I get an email like this one. we are proud of
our environment for motion pictures and filming. I
will pass on your kudos.**

Jeb Bush

———

*Although I was in my second term and continued to give out my
e-mail address at events, there were still some people in Florida
who didn't believe I answered my own e-mail.*

Subject: [None]
Friday, June 13, 2003 12:19 p.m.
From: Alan Gimlin

I am writing this email for two reasons. One is I heard
you on the "Sean Hannity" radio show when you said that
you answered all of your emails. My second reason for
writing gave me the opportunity to see if it is true.

My son Nathan plays on the West Florida Young Guns
Baseball Club. This is an AAU 13 and under team.
Two weekends ago they finished second in the State
Tournament. They lost to the Orlando Blast. The
second place finish along with there winning the
International Tournament at Disney World entitiles
them to play for the National Titile in Kinston N.C.
the end of July.

The biggest obstacle to the boys is the cost of going
to the tournament. For the team to go with the proper
amount of chaperones will cost about ten thousand
dollars. The kids are determined to raise the money
and have raised almost have of it to this point. They
have had "tag days", washed cars and sponsored a golf
tournament. We are looking for 30 people to become
"Platinum Partners". For one hundred dollars they
would receive a plaqued with the team picture and
there name on a 4'x6' banner that will be displayed
behind the dugout for each game at nationals. I am
sure you can see where this is going. I don't really
expect that you will do it, I am sure you get these
request by the bucket loads for all sorts of great
causes. These are good kids. To be on the team you
must maintain a 3.0 gpa. Many of these kids come from
families that have not been as fortunate as most and
a couple of them are in the Big Brother program and
have sponsors that bring them to games and practices.
I don't want to sound like they will not go without
your help. There are alot of cars that can be washed
between now and the end of July and somehow we
will manage. For some of these kids this wiill be
there first time out of Florida and may be the most
important thing to them that has ever happened. I
will see to it that they will go.

I did want you to know that these kids existed and that they were something that you could be proud of. They display the values that have made our country great. If you need my address to send me a check, email me back and I will get you the info.

p.s. I voted twice for you and your dad and once for your brother. keep up the good work. we need you

Subject: [None]
Saturday, June 14, 2003 5:57 p.m.
From: Jeb Bush

Alan, thank you for writing. I get requests like this all of the time and try to help. I will write a check but it can't be that much. You should be proud of Nathan and his team members. What is your address?

Jeb Bush

———

Subject: Fewer F schools = More A and B schools
Tuesday, June 17, 2003 10:06 p.m.
From: John Baker[85]

A couple of times, I've overheard Lucy Morgan telling someone, "The Governor emailed me last night, blah blah blah." So, I figured this must be the email address and decided to take a crack at it (along with every member of this year's Girls State). Not sure if you noticed or not, but you should've seen their notebooks fly open and their pens furiously writing

85 John Baker was the bureau chief for the Florida Public Radio Network.

down the address when you gave it to them. The scent of burning ink filled the old House Chamber.…:-)

Meanwhile, I'm going to spend the next few hours reminding myself that fewer F schools do indeed mean more A and B schools. See you at tomorrow morning's press conference.

Subject: Fewer F schools = More A and B schools
Tuesday, June 17, 2003 10:07 p.m.
From: Jeb Bush

I love giving out my email address to young people. they are inpsirational. Girls State and Boys State participants are the best. yes, I expect fewer F schools and hope that there are more a and b schools. Onward.

Jeb Bush

———

I was thrilled on June 18 to announce that the number of Florida schools receiving A grades was six times as many as in 1999, while the number of failing schools had dropped by more than half. It was further proof A+ was working. Florida's children were receiving better educations. This inquiry came from Lori Horvitz of the Orlando Sentinel. *She might have been trying to stir the pot, but I loved her question.*

Subject: education reporter seeking comments for a story related to school grades
Friday, June 20, 2003 3:56 p.m.
From: Lori Horvitz

Demographic information shows that a disproportionately large number of poor schools continue to receive D's and F's, while the more affluent schools continue to receive the largest share of A's. As you know, plenty of high-poverty schools are earning A's. The principals say the efforts necessary to help their schools attain the high marks have been huge, requiring a lot of money and ongoing, intensive training. Do you think these efforts can be sustained and replicated at every high-poverty school in Florida?

Could you please respond today, June 20?

Subject: education reporter seeking comments for a story related to school grades
Friday, June 20, 2003 9:29 p.m.
From: Jeb Bush

Yes, I believe the results can be sustained if the school districts believe it to be important. Are you saying that D and F schools get more money than A and B schools? You will be the first reporter to recognize that fact. It is worth reporting.

Jeb Bush

———

Why was I obsessed with helping small businesses by lessening their tax burdens, reforming workers' compensation, and generally trying to reduce regulation? It was because of people like the owner of the Marinated Mushroom restaurant in Tallahassee.

Subject: small business owner exhausted, you can buy business for the right price
Sunday, June 22, 2003 5:06 p.m.
From: Melinda McDaniel

Let me give you an example of what goes on with the politics of owning a small business. When I did this expansion I met with my inspector from DPBR[86] and told him of the plans. This was prior to doing anything but talking about it. Now, someone in Panama City that works for DPBR (a person that has never seen the place) tells me that I have to have two bathrooms. I requested that he come out and look at the place and informed him that the construction was finished and the way it was set up, one bathroom was sufficient. Well, I have now been told that if I send in another $150.00 they will give me a variance. That means that it is okay to have only one bathroom, as long as I pay the $150.00 to DPBR. That seems like extortion to me. But, what is my choice? If I don't pay it they will close me down.

Then, I had a $6,000.00 plumbing leak in my home. I filed for insurance coverage and they assisted with approximately $2,000.00. And then, guess what, they dropped me. I have been in my home for 15 years, never filed for anything from that company, paid all the premiums and on time and they cancel my policy. That isn't right. So, I called the insurance commissioners office and I was told that it is perfectly legal for a company to do that. The company gave some flimsy excuse of "hurricane risk". Why is it that they can get away with running a business like that?

---

86 The acronym actually is DBPR—Florida Department of Business and Professional Regulation.

There are a couple of examples of what I deal with
on a regular basis. I guess I could go back to
teaching school, but I don't want to. Why is it
always so difficult? All I am trying to do is earn a
living and get my son through college, pay my bills
and maybe have a little fun. I know I have severe
burnout but I just have to deal with that. It
just seems to me that there should be some
recourse somewhere. It seems that some problems
should be able to have solutions that don't involve
money.

I just don't see anything changing that truly affects
my bottom line. What can you and your brother do to
make a difference for the regular people?

Thanks again for at least taking the time to read my
emails and respond. It means a great deal.

PS: Would you like to buy my business and I will work
for you?

**Subject: small business owner exhausted, you can buy
business for the right price fup**
Sunday, June 22, 2003 5:24 p.m.
From: Jeb Bush

**I can't buy your business cause I have lost much
of my net worth in public service. However, we are
striving to help small businesses and your example is
a good one that I might be able to help. Did you get
a building permit to have one bathroom and the state
came in after the fact and said you needed to pay
$150 to get a variance to have one? If that is true,
then that is wrong. Either you should be told that**

you need one or you should be told you need two up
front. I will look into that.

Jeb Bush

––––––

Having finally passed a budget and workers' compensa-
tion reform, the legislature was back in session and debat-
ing medical malpractice reform again. I was committed to
bringing them back until the issue was resolved. Tension was
mounting.

Subject: Malpractice- No compromise
Tuesday, June 24, 2003 11:55 a.m.
From: Julian Belisle

Please don't compromise on the Medical Malpractice
issue. It is an impending crises of tremendous
consequences. As a practicing CV Surgeon, I can
tell you that we are mad as hell and we aren't
going to take it anymore. The Senate and all of
their proposals are only going to make matters
worse. We have not been as vocal as we should,
and the Trial attornys have more money, but it is
the PEOPLE who will suffer. Ultimately, people need
their Doctors more than they need self serving
attornys.

So please don't compromise. Polls show that the
Doctors are supported by the voters. We need
a 250K cap and also, all MD's that testify in
malpractice cases should be required to have a
Florida Medical license, so there veracity can be
monitored.

Subject: Malpractice- No compromise
Tuesday, June 24, 2003 3:01 p.m.
From: Jeb Bush

thank you for writing. I am grateful for your email.
We will stay the course.

Jeb Bush

———

Subject: Med Mal
Tuesday, July 08, 2003 9:17 a.m.
From: Judie Budnick

I want to congratulate you for fighting to change this
law. It must be capped and capped NOW!

My son is his in third year of med school in Nova
Southeastern Medical School in Davie, Florida.
Virtually none of his classmates are planning on
practicing medicine in our state. Oh very sad! We
educate them here and then they leave to practice
their profession elsewhere. We become "home" to
thousands of new citizens annually and fewer
physicians. This will lead to a very "sick" state!

Once again, thank you for your brave position to
"take on" the Republican lead Senate. Just know,
there are millions of Floridians who strongly support
your vision and guts.

Subject: Med Mal
Saturday, July 12, 2003 3:08 p.m.
From: Jeb Bush

thank you Judie. We will prevail.

Jeb Bush

———

Alan Levine, my deputy chief of staff who later served as secretary of the Agency for Health Care Administration, wrote an e-mail outlining our proposed medical malpractice reforms. It ended up in the Miami Herald. *I received an e-mail from a reader of the op-ed. I would mark him down as not a fan.*

Subject: Your email communications
Friday, July 11, 2003 9:59 a.m.
From: Michael B. Feiler

I read Mr. Levine's communication in the Miami Herald this morning. It is amazing to me that you are part of the large group of people blinded by the need for politifcal retribution and utterly ignorant of the real cause of this crisis -- insurance company greed. Why does the governor not support the use of subpoenas? What is wrong with forcing the insurers to tell the truth? Why are you so hell bent on eliminating bad faith law -- the ONLY law, by the way, that PROTECTS your doctors and hospitals from the avarice of their carriers?

Do you have wives and children? Are their lives meaningless to you? Is it for the greater good to protect the wrongdoer that harms them so that the insurance companies can have more record profits?

Lost in all of this hubbub is basic human compassion. Your conduct, Mr. Governor, is an affront to

Republican principles and indeed, human decency.
You won. The trial lawyers lost. Get over it and do
what's right.

You know, I was a Republican from the time I was
eighteen until just a few years ago. I voted for
Bob Martinez; I voted for Daddy Bush (but not W).
But the party has so strayed from the philosophical
libertarian roots laid down by Lincoln and fallen so
in line with those who put profit above people, that I
could take it no longer. And now you have proven that
you don't care either.

This is not about trial lawyers. This is
about people who are being squeezed -- doctors
who can't afford overpriced insurance, and patients
that are being denied helathcare. The facts are
indisputable -- only the most severely affected
get awards that go above the proposed caps --
and for those cases, a cap already exists in the
arbitration system.

Yet, facts aside, you seem unwilling to even thinik
about the fact that greedy insurance companies are
manipulating the system yet again to fatten their
pockets.

There is an insurance crisis. Fix it by attacking
the problem -- the insurance industry. And do it
before it's too late, and YOU are the one (God
forbid) missing a loved one while the wrongdoer
skates and the insurance company walks away
laughing.

Shame on all of you.

Subject: Your email communications
Friday, July 11, 2003 8:56 p.m.
From: Jeb Bush

With all due respect, as a libertarian, you should understand how markets work. Several years ago, there were 15 companies writing med mal insurance in our state. Now there are two with many restrictions. The companies that left were losing money and anticipated losing much more. The ones that remain are losing money. If premiums earned are less than claims, they lose money. That is what is happening because we have had an increase in claims and suits. Those are the facts.

Our system is flawed and it needs reform. Surely you don't want to have the Government to become the insurer? That is in essence what the Senate has proposed.

If you have read the papers, you have noticed that we have continued to make major concessions. Now it is time for the Senate to respond and I believe they will.

The access to care has been already jeopordized by the climate that we are in. Many have already suffered. I will stay the course because it is the right thing to do.

Thank you for writing.

Jeb Bush

———

Now it's time for a more important question of the day.

Subject: Name
Monday, July 21, 2003 8:37 p.m.
From: Tom Stevens

My wife asked me what Governor's Jeb Bush's "first" name is. What does Jeb stand for? I told her Jeb was his first name and Jeb was his name and it doesn't stand for any thing. It's his name.

Being a stanch Liberal Democrat she is sure there must be a cover up somewhere. (Strangely she has never questioned General Jeb "Stuart" as having any reason or perpetuating any cover-up.)

Please, is there any third party that I can contact that will provide "the Truth" so I can get on to other earth saving matters.

Subject: Name
Monday, July 21, 2003 9:02 p.m.
From: Jeb Bush

Thank you tom. John Ellis Bush is my name. J.E.B. It has been that way since i was born. No coverup that I am aware of. Jeb Stuart, the great military man was James Ewall Brown Stuart.

Please move on to the earth saving matters for the sake of the country. :)

Jeb Bush

———

In 1999 I signed a parental notification law that required parents to be notified if their minor daughter was seeking an abortion. The Florida Supreme Court had ruled it unconstitutional, so there was a proposal to make it a constitutional amendment. I very much supported it. So did Floridians, who approved the amendment in 2004 by more than 60 percent of the vote.

Subject: Parental Notification
Monday, July 28, 2003 2:18 p.m.
From: Jeff Frisco

As a Father of 6 (soon to be seven) I believe firmly in the parent's responsibility and authority concerning all matters with respect to their minor aged children. This is a God given right. To make an exception for abortion defies logic as well as principle and I believe is a concept only supported by a small group of radical pro-abortion advocates. I fully support a constitutional amendment which would make parental notification the law of the land in Florida.

Please provide your full support to those pursuing this goal.

Subject: Parental Notification
Monday, July 28, 2003 8:50 p.m.
From: Jeb Bush

I will do so!

Jeb Bush

Here's more on medical malpractice, which was dominating the conversation that summer—as it should have. It was an issue that affected all Floridians.

Subject: Name 3 docs who are leaving the State...
Thursday, July 31, 2003 2:44 p.m.
From: James Terrell

...because they can't pay thrie malpractice premiums !!!
You can't,because there aren't any!!!They just want
to keep more of the money they make!!! I don't blame
them for trying,but DON'T let their greed drive your
ambition to curtail the rights of Florida's citizens
who have their lives devastated by medical negligence.

Subject: Name 3 docs who are leaving the State...
Thursday, July 31, 2003 3:52 p.m.
From: Jeb Bush

I have met three doctors in the last month that have
left because of their med mal insurance premiums.
A pediatric neurosurgeon in Jacksonville and a
neurosurgeon and ER doctor husband and wife team from
Tampa. Thanks for writing.

Jeb Bush

———

Subject: Request from Pat Williams of Orlando Magic
Tuesday, July 29, 2003 10:05 p.m.
From: Alan Florez[87]

---

87 Alan Florez was one of several young men who served as my personal
assistants and travel aides while I was governor. I could not have survived
without them.

Pat Williams Sr. Vice President of Orlando Magic has requested that you contribute to a book for Warner Books called *Coaching Your Kids to Become Leaders* that he is writing.

Here are the four questions:

1. When did you first realize you had the ability to lead and when did you begin receiving those opportunities?

2. Who were the key people who helped you develop as a leader and what contribution did they make?

3. Do you have an interesting story or anecdote concerning your start as a young leader?

4. What advice do you have for adults on how to recognize leadership potential in youngsters and then nurture it?

Subject: Request from Pat Williams of Orlando Magic
Sunday, August 3, 2003 11:49 a.m.
From: Jeb Bush

1. **I was sent to Caracas Venezuela at the age of 24 to open a representative office. I was ten years younger than the next youngest bank rep. It was a very difficult challenge since our two children were 18 months and three months and there were shortages of every kind. Our bank did well and that is when I knew that I could do more than I thought I could. The fear of the unkown subsided!**

2. My dad is my hero and the best role model anyone could have. Just watching him live his life has been my inspiration for success.

3. In 1979, I took a leave of absence from my job to work in my father's campaign. My first speech I had to give as a surrogate was in front of 2000 Puerto Ricans in San Juan...in spanish. I was so nervous but go through the speech and learned again to overcome fear and anxioty and communicate with sincerity and from the heart. It has been a lesson that has served me well over time.

4. I think it is important to listen to people, particularly young people. By listening, it is easier to encourage which all young people need!

Jeb Bush

———

We finally had a deal. I did not get everything I wanted, but the reforms would go a long way toward solving the medical malpractice crisis in our state. It included capping jury awards, stabilizing the insurance market, and providing insurance relief for doctors. All these provisions would help meet the most important end goal: protecting access to quality, affordable health care for all Floridians.

I appreciated this e-mail from my good friend Tony Villamil, who had left my team to head up the Washington Economics Group.

Subject: Malpractice insurance/ Thank you!
Saturday, August 9, 2003 10:17 a.m.
From: Tony Villamil

The agreement with the senate is a significant and positive step in improving our business climate, and should be looked at from the perspective of bringing much more certainty to a chaotic health insurance market. The "no piercing" provisions are the key to increase the supply overtime of insurance providers and policies, reducing premiums overtime and incresing choice. Florida citizens and their employers are the winners.

Today's Herald article misses ther key point of the certainty brought to a chaotic market place and the importance of the certainty in increasing future supply of insurance and choice. To me this is where the victory lies and where we should be informing our residents. I also think we, your communications team, should do a summary of the important victories we have gained, taken as a system and not piecemeal, on behalf of Florida. Four key areas from a business climate perspective stand out:

1. Workers insurance reform

2. Malpractice reform

3. Keeping taxes low.

Supply side economics works. Last time I took a look at state corporate income revenues they were significantly above projections. Compare us to the big tax states.

We are doing fine in a very difficult US and global environment. People and employers are coming to

Florida, not leaving! Thank you and your team for great leadership! Lets go on the offensive now!

Subject: Malpractice insurance/ Thank you!
Saturday, August 9, 2003 11:40 a.m.
From: Jeb Bush

I wish we could have done a little better.

Jeb

———

Mike Thomas with the Sentinel *wrote a column I didn't particularly like about the relationship between Senate President Jim King, the legislature, and me. My frustration was not really with him. It was with what had been a very tough legislative year. There were huge disagreements and some very tough compromises. There was also lots of bickering and name-calling. We had powered through it, though. That was what the people had elected us to do—to get it done. In 2003 it had not been easy.*

Subject: Jimmy vs Jeb
Tuesday, August 12, 2003 8:51 p.m.
From: Jeb Bush

Mike, I didn't agree with the thesis of your column. I am sure that is not a surprise for you. Getting along is important. Doing what is right is important as well. I compromised on the med mal issue to about where you proposed and that was in the works for several weeks. Without the public posture (with caveats to be willing to compromise as I did over and over again), the compromise wouldn't have occurred. Trust me, without the threat of consequences, there would be no bill at all. It was important to get this done and if it needs improvement, then we will go to work again.

I can assure you I am not aloof or arrogant regarding my relationship with the legislature. Sometimes, we disagree. So what? Isn't that part of living in a democracy? I respect those who don't agree with me but that does not mean I will bend to the point of abandoning principle.

I have noticed an interesting dynamic in the politics up here. The political press is exclusively focused on the horse race aspects of life in the bubble. They don't write what they hear said if it doesn't fit their template. Then this is read by the editorial page writers who don't do much more, it seems to me, than to read their own paper to validate their already established views which for but one paper is slanted to the left.

I count on the handful of columnists who actually seem to get information from more than one source to have a chance to get my side of the issue out. You are one of those and I really appreciate your openness to hear the other side. I only hope you keep challenging the conventional wisdom of the opinion leadership that fits the cycle that I described above to be a contrarian from time to time.

During my tenure as Governor, had I not reached further than the conventional, the A plus plan would have been watered down and the achievement results we have achieved would not have occurred. We would not have eliminated race as a criteria of admissions to

universities and procurement and would have had the
stagnant results that symbolized the past. Instead,
we have increases in opportunities in both areas.
We would not have eliminated the ugly aspects of
career civil service and not moved to a system where
public employees are obliged to serve and they are
rewarded for doing so. We would not have sucked out
some of the excesses of government largess. there are
scores of examples never reported in this regard.
We wouldn't have cut taxes for the first time in a
generation to improve our business climate and keep
government from growing faster than folks ability
to pay for it. There wouldn't have been a better
selection process for Governors to select judges.
ETC. ETC. ETC.

You get my drift? I don't expect you to agree with
all of my actions but I hope you respect my desire
to change the things that I have believed needed to
be changed and without my leadership, even though
it might have been perceived to ruffle feathers, it
wouldn't have happened. If I had run the two times
that I got elected saying something different than I
have acted as Governor, then I think I should meet
the wrath of Kahn. I think I have been pretty true to
my pledges as a candidate.

You are a good man and I appreciate your interest in
what I am striving to do.

Jeb

Subject: Jimmy vs Jeb
Thursday, August 14, 2003 11:21 a.m.
From: Mike Thomas

Just saw this. Was out yesterday. Wouldn't be a real pregnancy without at least one middle-of-the-night rush to the hospital. Wife Laurie (25 weeks) got sick and dehydrated, which put fetus/unborn child/ impending daughter in some distress.

Do you mind if I excerpt some of this for tomorrow's column. I suppose it's "public record" but I regard e-mails as off-the-record unless they obviously were written as an official response.…

Would probably leave out most of first graff because it's pretty insider. Same with columnists and "good man" material. But I like your points about the press and editorials, and accomplishments.…

Let me know.

Subject: Jimmy vs Jeb
Saturday, August 16, 2003 8:31 a.m.
From: Jeb Bush

I am sorry, like you, that I just got to this. My intention wasn't to make news with this but I know that I created a public record. I get a kick that press folks always worry about the insider stuff since that is the the "stuff" that I fret about. Same with columnist and "good man" material. I leave it up to you.

On a much more important note, I hope your wife and precious daughter are doing well. Nothing is more important.

Jeb

Subject: Jimmy vs Jeb
Monday, August 18, 2003 8:50 a.m.
From: Mike Thomas

I want you to feel free to complain without me
tossing it in the public domain. I happen to agree
with a lot of what you said about political press.
They're a lot like sports reporters (except for Mr.
Silva, of course!)

As for editorial boards, i was on our's for a couple
months and went bonkers.

Laurie and daughter are doing fine. Unfortunately,
this means I'll have to work another 18 years. (Don't
abolish Bright Future scholarships!!!)

———

*During this same time, I participated in a student shadow pro-
gram. Nothing makes you feel better about the future of our country than spending time with kids.*

Subject: Shadow date
Wednesday, August 13, 2003 9:22 a.m.
From: Amber

"Big Bad Governor" Bush, First of all, I can't
thank you enough for allowing me the opportunity to
shadow you yesterday. The day was very eventful and
exciting. I am so appreciative that you allowed me
to partake in such an experience. I am extremely
fortunate to have such a personable Governor who
truly does care (not to mention one with your great
personality). You have inspired me to reach for my

dreams as well as make a difference. Seeing that it
is possible to be an honest and genuine person in a
high political office conveys a positive message for
tomorrow's leaders.

I hope that I will be surrounded by people like
you when I become heavily involved in the political
arena. Meeting your staff today proved that what you
said was true. Surrounding yourself with brilliant
and wise thinkers, only makes you a stronger
person and leader. I learned a tremendous amount of
information while shadowing you. I can only hope
to be as successful and collected as you have shown
to be.

Thank you once again for all you do. I truly enjoyed
my time with you and the choir of protesters. My
only regret was that there weren't more hours in the
day. I hope that our paths continue to cross in many
future endeavors. Keep me in mind after you fire all
of your employees and need replacements! It would be
an honor to work for you, much less, follow in your
footsteps any time. I hope to stay in contact with
you. Thank you for going out of your way to meet
my mother. I know it meant the world to her. Best
wishes.

~We were on the news last night!

Subject: Shadow date
Wednesday, August 13, 2003 9:59 p.m.
From: Jeb Bush

**Thank you Amber. You are one cool kid. I was really
impressed with your presence. Wow. You are going**

places. If you want to intern with our office one of these days let me know.…

Now you have to kick butt and do well in school!

Jeb

———

The execution of a man named Paul Jennings Hill was drawing close. It was nine years after he had killed an abortion doctor and a volunteer outside a Pensacola clinic. Passions ran high. There were the usual protests against the death penalty, but in Hill's case his supporters considered him a martyr. Some of the more extreme supporters even sent death threats.

Subject: the paul hill story
Wednesday, August 20, 2003 8:49 p.m.
From: Lesley Clark

It's Lesley at the Herald. We are hearing that you were threatened in one of the death threat letters that were sent to several officials, protesting the upcoming execution. Were you threatened in one of the letters? Your office has said you did not receive a letter. Is that the case? Some of the material I have seen threatens yourself and the president. Has the Secret Service been notified? And given the clamor about the execution, are you contemplating delaying the execution or do you believe it should go forward, and if so, why?

Subject: the paul hill story
Wednesday, August 20, 2003 9:42 p.m.
From: Jeb Bush

I get threatened all of the time. The execution goes on as planned.

Jeb

———

In 2003 the tragic case of Terri Schiavo began to attract more and more national attention. Her parents, Robert and Mary Schindler, had been battling her husband, Michael, since 1998 on whether Terri's feeding tube should be removed. Earlier in 2003 the Schindlers had hired a Right to Life spokesperson and activist, Randall Terry, to take their case to the public. They had lost their latest court battle on September 17, when a judge denied their petition. Her feeding tube was due to be removed any day. After meeting with the Schindlers, their profound love for their daughter moved me. As a father I decided it was time to try to do what I could to help them keep their daughter alive.

There were a few e-mails from people who felt the state should stay out of it. Here is one example.

Subject: Schiavo
Tuesday, October 7, 2003 4:24 p.m.
From: Phyllis Hayward

WHO is paying for the costs involved in YOUR intervention in this case? This is NOT something the government or tax payers should be involved in. If the parents wanted her to learn to eat they should have done that 13 years ago. God help you should you ever be in the situation that either Michael or his wife Terry are in.

However, the e-mail traffic asking me to intervene flooded my in-box. Here are a few examples of those.

Subject: Terri
Monday, October 13, 2003 7:31 a.m.
From: Pamela Hennessy

Sorry to bug you on your day off. Couldn't a simple executive order remove Michael Schiavo as Terri's guardian? Even temporarily? That would certainly solve some problems.…

There are people in Canada willing to care for her and trying to seek out asylum for her. Her family cannot legally move her, though, as long as Michael Schiavo is the guardian. Even something as short as 24 hours would clear the way.

I know I'm asking you for yet another favor, but removing Michael as her guardian would solve a boatload of problems in one fell swoop. You have the grounds to do so as he's not filed the required guardianship papers for a number of years. That alone should be enough.

Subject: Terri
Monday, October 13, 2003 7:38 a.m.
From: Jeb Bush

No. I don't have the power to issue an executive order to remove Mr. Schiavo as guardian. There are limits to what a governor can do.

Jeb Bush

———

Subject: MY one question for you/Fw: This is what they want to hear from you
Saturday, October 18, 2003 4:38 p.m.
From: Susan Alyn

Can you provide any measure of hope for a legal way to preserve this woman's life? To think that all her parents want to do is care for her and not see her starve to death, is, I think, not asking for a lot in this world. My own parents would feel the same way about me, I am sure, though I can not vouch for any husband's motives on this planet.

Subject: MY one question for you/Fw: This is what they want to hear from you
Saturday, October 18, 2003 4:41 p.m.
From: Jeb Bush

I cannot offer much hope. I am sickened by this situation and pray for her family. We have looked at every angle, every legal possibility and will continue to do so. It is clear that we need to make living wills the norm for families in our state. Too few people use them.

Jeb

———

At the same time the fate of Terri Schiavo was occupying my mind, I was dealing with a completely different issue—one I hoped would be a life-changing business coup for Florida.

After the major hit Florida's economy took following 9/11, I devoted a great deal of time to trying to lure businesses to Florida. Not only did I want to create more opportunities, but I also wanted a more diverse business base. Therefore, if one industry suffered a setback—such as tourism after 9/11—others would still thrive. The plan was to use the $500 million economic stimulus money that came from the federal government after 9/11. It was a one-time payment, and I was determined to use it for long-term growth.

After a great deal of lobbying, the Scripps Research Institute— one of the world's largest and most prominent nonprofit biomedical research institutes—announced it had chosen Palm Beach as the location for its second major research facility. It was a coup to convince Scripps to come to Florida, but the expectation was other companies would follow—an "industry clustering" around the Scripps Florida nucleus.

I called it a seminal moment in Florida's history. It put us at the forefront of biomedical research. I was hoping Scripps coming to Florida would be as big as the arrival of air conditioning and Walt Disney.

Part of the state's agreement with Scripps was to provide $310 million in seed money, which again would come from our federal stimulus fund. This was the amount Scripps projected it would need to pay for its operations and research for seven years while it ramped up its grant and philanthropic revenue. The state's support and job projections were premised in Palm Beach County, matching the state investment by providing Scripps with a 360,000-square-foot building and one hundred acres of land (room for future Scripps expansion) on a five-hundred-acre parcel that would be used to build the biotech cluster. Palm Beach County had already identified the location of the five hundred acres—an orange grove called Mecca Farms that was closing.

This e-mail, though I'm not sure I understood some of what he was hinting at, came from John Kennedy of the Orlando Sentinel.

Subject: With Scripps, next week you may be brought back to your old role...
Tuesday, October 14, 2003 7:34 p.m.
From: John Kennedy

as a business "closer," akin to what you used to do in your South Florida real estate days. Senate and others seem to need to hear from you to resolve some concerns.

I wonder if you might comment regarding how you feel in that closer's role? It's one you have some experience in. Likewise, this Scripps deal and the other proposals in the air are fairly intricate, leveraged with some, er...unconventional financing, etc. That seems to be another area you had some familiarity with in days past.

Anyway, I'm guessing that you're finding the crafting of this deal kind of fun. Would you say this one of the more pleasing chapters of your five years as governor?

Thanks for your comments. And congrats on all you've done in bringing Scripps this far.

Subject: FW: With Scripps, next week you may be brought back to your old role...
Wednesday, October 15, 2003 3:48 p.m.
From: Jeb Bush

While I certainly enjoyed my job in South Florida real estate, the Scripps opportunity can't be matched. Nothing compares with being Governor of this great state at this exciting time. People who run for office do so because they want to serve and make a difference. Changing the shape of Florida -- through the prestige of the Scripps brand name -- is one of those opportunities, and I look forward to working with the Legislature to revolutionize this state and create unparalleled growth, education, development. That is what will be fun and rewarding.

———

The two big issues of Terri Schiavo and Scripps oddly merged when the legislature once again went back into special session to approve the Scripps package.

Terri's feeding tube had been removed October 17—just days before the Scripps special session began. Despite popular belief she was not on artificial life support. She was receiving nutrition and hydration.

The special session on Scripps had just begun when the House introduced a bill to save Terri Schiavo. After working closely with the House and Senate leadership, we added Terri's Law to the call for a special session and negotiated language that would give me the authority to order a one-time reinsertion of her feeding tube. Had we not found a compromise, we would not have been able to do anything for Terri, and the Scripps special session was in danger of coming to a halt over the impasse.

I was grateful we were able to come together on these two important issues that had huge implications for the lives of Floridians. In less than twenty-four hours, the legislature passed what became known as Terri's Law, which authorized the governor to issue a one-time stay of the withholding of nutrition and hydration and required the courts to appoint a guardian ad litem. I signed the bill immediately into law. Terri's feeding tube was reinserted. Her husband immediately sued and challenged the constitutionality of the law. Thankfully the courts denied his motion to enjoin my order. Terri's story would continue.

The support poured in. Here are just a few samples.

Subject: Your finest hour
Tuesday, October 21, 2003 7:42 p.m.
From: [Name not included]

All of us who pleaded, begged, prayed and lashed out at you in despiration, will forever remember how you came to the rescue of this poor woman and her family who has been victimized by so many for so long. Unfortunately the fight is not over, but you have, for the moment, confounded the unholy alliance of her husband/lawyer/Judge Greer, and given hope to all who have been grieving over the inhumanity of this story.

Thank you Governor Bush.

Subject: Thank You...
Tuesday, October 21, 2003 11:10 p.m.
From: Raquel Pointer

I wish to thank you on behalf of every person that has suffered an injustice to their basic human rights due to 'letter of the law' justice, technicalities, or just plain apathy.

You have saved something more in America this day than just one simple human life.

I am both surprised and very proud that you, and the majority of our legislature, chose the more difficult route offered and didn't do the political side-step. Abraham Lincoln, among many of our forefathers, was faced with such an 'unfavorable' choice...but the

<u>rightness</u> of his decisions and actions far outlived
and outweighed the temporary backlash.

I am impressed that "of the people and for the
people" still holds some meaning when it truly
counts. You have shown great humanity and strength
in not washing your hands of this sad dilemma, nor
shirking your responsibility.

Thank you.

———

*During this very busy and complicated time, there were some
distractions from the more serious business of governing.
Floridians—especially the residents of Miami—were caught
up in the great sport of baseball. The Florida Marlins (now
the Miami Marlins) were headed to the World Series—thanks
partially to a Chicago Cubs fan. In a now-infamous incident
for all baseball fans, a Cubs fan grabbed a foul ball and prevented the Cubs outfielder from catching it for the second out
in the eighth inning of game six, which the Cubs were winning 3–0. If they won the game, they would be the National
League champions—and would be going to the World Series
for the first time since 1945. Instead the Marlins won the game
and eventually the series. This sent them to the World Series
against the Yankees. This query came from a* Miami Herald
reporter.

Subject: Marlins question from Jim DeFede
Wednesday, October 15, 2003 2:45 p.m.
From: Jim DeFede

I'm writing a column for tomorrow about the poor Cubs
fan who caused all of the commotion last night at the

Cubs-Marlins game. A Chicago Alderman said the young fan had beeter move out of Chicago.

I'm suggesting he should move to Miami. Can you offer any (humorous) incentives for the young man to relocate to Miami? Shula's Hotel and Steak House is offering him a free weekend at their hotel, the Latin Shriners are going to make him an honoraray Shriner and so on.…

As I said the tone is going to be light and humorous.

Any thoughts?

Subject: Marlins question from Jim DeFede
Wednesday, October 15, 2003 4:32 p.m.
From: Jeb Bush

He can apply for asylum in the Sunshine State and I promise we will expedite his safe passage.

The Marlins went on to win the World Series four games to two. As a result New York Governor George Pataki sent me twenty-six Coney Island hot dogs from Nathan's—one for each World Series the Yankees had won—and thirty-nine empire apples—one for each American League pennant the Yankees had won. My staff and I feasted. When I thanked Governor Pataki for paying off his bet, I did remind him the Yankees had been in existence for one hundred years, so twenty-six hot dogs did not compare to the Marlins' two World Series victories in twelve years.

––––––

My lieutenant governor and partner finally got a BlackBerry.

Subject: Technology
Monday, October 27, 2003 6:52 p.m.
From: Toni Jennings

Ok here I go from somewhere over Crestvie my first blackberry message but I can t see the punctuation marks. Better content in future communications. Signing off. TechnoToni

Subject: Technology
Monday, October 27, 2003 7:04 p.m.
From: Jeb Bush

Your language is bad but the intent is awesome, Techontoni!

Jeb

————

On Sunday, December 14, American soldiers captured Saddam Hussein and dragged him out of the hole where he was hiding. Mark Silva of the Orlando Sentinel *wanted to make it all about politics.*

Subject: good morning
Sunday, December 14, 2003 10:01 a.m.
From: Mark Silva

How I love working Sundays. I'm curious if you have some thoughts today on the capture of Saddam and just how far that may go in fulfilling the declaration made May 1 on the carrier: Mission Accomplished. And how much it could serve to quell the complaints of a Democratic crowd of contenders on the president's handling of the war. A comment or two is greatly appreciated on this day of rest. (Happy holidays, by the way!)

Subject: good morning
Sunday, December 14, 2003 10:22 a.m.
From: Jeb Bush

Today is a day to rejoice. It is a great day for freedom. No politics!

Jeb

———

We'll end this somewhat frustrating year with one of my favorite subjects. Thank heavens for this e-mail from Jackie Hallifax of the Associated Press.

Subject: Reading
Monday, December 22, 2003 12:59 p.m.
From: Jackie Hallifax

I'm working on a story about your reading initiative.

I know you're proud of the recent NAEP[88] scores, believing they measure the success of reading initiatives in Florida. But what about outside the classroom? Do you think that people are reading more because of the time and energy you have expended on the issue in the last couple of years?

———

88 National Assessment of Educational Progress.

If you think Florida is reading more, what makes you conclude that? If you don't know, when and how do you think that will be measured?

Finally, are you reading more? What are you in the middle of? Any recommendations?

Thanks. Hope your holidays are lovely.

Subject: Reading
Monday, December 22, 2003 8:56 p.m.
From: Jeb Bush

That is a good question. I hope more people are reading. I watch the media and there seems to be more reading talk going on. I am reading several books right now. I just finished "the future and its enemies"[89] which is very timely. I am reading a book about Barcelona and Love is the Killer App.[90] In 2003, I read more books than I did in the my adult life and hope that 2004 is even a better reading year! Merry Christmas.

Jeb

A postscript on Scripps is necessary.

   Unfortunately the institute got off to a bit of a rocky start through no fault of its own. Litigation by antigrowth advocates halted construction of the Scripps buildings at Mecca in 2004. The Palm Beach County Board of Commissioners later voted 4–3 to move Scripps to thirty acres on the Florida Atlantic University

---

89 *The Future and Its Enemies: The Growing Conflict over Creativity, Enterprise, and Progress* by Virginia Postrel.
90 *Love Is the Killer App: How to Win Business and Influence Friends* by Tim Sanders.

Jupiter campus. This abandoned plans for the creation of the five-hundred-acre cluster. The controversy over the location resulted in a four-year delay in Scripps's start.

Then came one of the worst recessions in US history, which meant a significant falloff in research grant funding from the National Institutes of Health and fewer philanthropic dollars, which has hurt life science research institutes' budgets.

However, contrary to some of what has been written about Scripps, I am thrilled to write in 2015 that the idea I had back in 2003 to build a life-sciences industry from scratch in Florida is already paying dividends—with many more to come.

We have seen some tremendous medical advances coming out of Scripps's Florida campus. This includes research regarding Alzheimer's and Parkinson's. As we had hoped, with Scripps as the motivating factor, a number of other research institutes and medical-related facilities either relocated or built facilities in Florida. Those included Sanford-Burnham, Torrey Pines Institute for Molecular Studies and Max Planck Florida Institute for Neuroscience, world-renowned, prestigious research institutions. Lake Nona Medical City, a 650-acre health and life sciences center located near Orlando, was established in 2005 and is becoming a destination for veterans, children, medical training, and medical investments. (As a nice bonus, thanks to the agreement we crafted back in 2003, the state is entitled to 20 percent of the net royalty income Scripps Florida receives from its intellectual property.)

More than 10 percent of the country's biotech firms now reside in Florida, and Florida's growth rate in related employment and venture capital funding are outpacing the nation as a whole.

Bringing Scripps to Florida is a classic case where patience was—and will continue to be—a virtue.

However, let's get back to 2003.

As I warned at the beginning of this chapter, it was a bumpy road. When the staff put together the year-end highlights, though,

I was thrilled to see the statistics showed we were on the right track on most of our initiatives. Floridians were safer and had more job opportunities, and their children were doing better in school.

For most Floridians—even if they didn't realize it immediately—getting both workers' compensation reform and medical malpractice reform passed would impact their futures and their families' well-being for years to come.

- *By the time I left office, the workers' compensation reform legislation provided a 40 percent decrease in insurance rates and saved employers in Florida $400 million. This was the equivalent of another big tax cut that strengthened businesses and made our business climate more conducive to job growth. We achieved this significant reduction in costs by reducing legal fees, eliminating exemptions, and providing alternative dispute resolution reforms. At the same time, eliminating fraud increased benefits to workers and improved access to quality care. The result was we led the nation in small-business growth—81,000 new businesses—while I was governor.*

- *The medical malpractice reform legislation set caps on noneconomic personal injury awards between $500,000 for physicians and $750,000 for hospitals and other health facilities. Our reforms helped prevent physicians from leaving our state. During my governorship the number of licensed doctors in Florida increased by 6,700, and in the ten years after adoption of my reforms, medical liability claims dropped by 60 percent, noneconomic damages fell by 28 percent, rates stabilized, and capacity returned to the insurance market.*

Even though the Florida Supreme Court recently overturned the caps on noneconomic damages in wrongful-death lawsuits, these tort reforms are one of my proudest achievements and are an example of why we need serious medical liability reform at the national level to help control health-care costs.

In the final days of December, I told Floridians that 2003 had been "a period of innovation, achievement, and growth in Florida."

Of course, being the optimist I am, I predicted that in 2004, "Floridians will continue to grow and build on our state's successes while overcoming the challenges life often brings."

We had no idea then that in 2004, Mother Nature would paint a bull's-eye on our beloved state in a way that would redefine the very meaning of the word "challenge."

Chapter 6

2004

"We Will Prevail."

Our recovery is going to be a long-term effort. It will not be easy. It will not be quick. And it will not be without pain. But it will happen.

—Address to the State of Florida on the last day of the 2004 hurricane season, November 30, 2004

This year, 2004, would test our mettle in Florida—you might even say our souls.

However, on January 1 we were still gloriously unaware of what was to come.

So I began the year by making lists. We had a lot of work to do, and I was anxious to get started. So I sent this list to Denver Stutler, who became my new chief of staff when Kathleen Shanahan decided to return to the corporate world. I missed Kathleen's friendship and advice—although she continues to supply an abundance of both—but I understood it was time for her to get on with her life.

So now lucky Denver got these interminable lists. Most items are self-explanatory, and for your sake I won't try to explain those that aren't. Eleven years later I'm not sure I remember all the details. However, on January 3 it all seemed important, and

417

I wanted my team to get going. Yes. I expected a lot of the people who served alongside me, but Floridians deserved nothing less.

Subject: [None]
Saturday, January 3, 2004 2:36 p.m.
From: Jeb Bush

We have a heap of things that can bite us in the rear or be good policy news if we are successful. To name a few:

Everglades rule legal contest
Everglades fed judge ruling
Public private partnerships at sfwmd
Cypress gardens
Coronet
Alternative energy proposal
Phosphate mining
Keys management plan
Growth management reform

Rural count initiative
BRAC
Scripps
Ftaa
Eco dev strategic plan
High speed rail

Just read
University funding reforms
Community college funding reform
School choice reform
Upk implementation

Class size repeal

Initiative and referendum reform

Faith based prisons
Outsourcing of prison medical
Djj management issues
Homeland defense
Perscription drug law changes

Kidcare
Dd reforms and waivers
Ess outsourcing
Dcf district reform
Perscription drug fraud
Perscription drug benefit
Mega med waiver
Health care reforms
Med mal reform

Service first
One florida lawsuit
Felons voting lawsuit
Myflorida marketplace
Convergys
Other outsourcing possibilities
Telecom bid for state
Other sto issues (incl management)

And a few others like victory 2004!
We need to talk about how to monitor these things
with a little more
intensity.

Happy new year!

Jeb

———

By this time we have established that I adore my dad, but I don't always think he's right. For example, I don't jump out of planes. When it comes to vegetables, though, there is no daylight between us. This exchange was with Mike Thomas of the Orlando Sentinel.

Subject: obesity
Thursday January 8, 2004 11:48 a.m.
From: Mike Thomas

I'm writing about obesity and highlighting your task force. Leadership comes from the top.

Do you know your BMI[91]?

Are you still working out or were the sessions on the Disney ship[92] an aberration?

Can you bench press as much as the president?
How about five fruits and vegetables a day?

Subject: obesity
Thursday, January 8, 2004 2:37 p.m.
From: Jeb Bush

I walk to work and back when in tallahassee. I workout on the weekendsbut don't lift weights. I enjoy a fine fruit buit draw the line with brocoli.

Jeb

———

91 Body mass index.
92 My parents took our entire family on a Disney cruise after Christmas in 2002. I assume Mike is referring to that trip.

———

Sticking to the food theme, I didn't know finding good chicken was part of my job description, but apparently it was. I considered that a perk.

Subject: Please Test Guatemala Chicken if you want my vote again for re-election
Friday, January 16, 2004 8:38 p.m.
From: Na and Jim Nash

While you are in Guatemala, could you or your wife please try some of the chicken from **Guatemala's Pollo Campero** (Guatemalan Chicken Chain) and tell us what is so good about it that people will wait in line for hours here in the US. If you think it is really great, could you convince them that we have a large Latin population in South Florida and they need to open restaurants here. Please also tell them to start in Boca Raton in the Palmetto Park and Powerline area so it will be easy for us to get some. I am not Latino, an old 45yr old farm boy from Iowa (what do I know about chicken anyway Ha ha), but my wife is from Thailand and is requesting an extra hot version, you know some that will make that thingy in the back of your throat curl. Make sure you let them know.…

We are anxiously waiting for your review of the chicken.

Subject: Please Test Guatemala Chicken if you want my vote again for re-election
Tuesday, January 20, 2004 7:12 p.m.
From: Jeb Bush

Thank you for writing. I heard of this amazing chicken and was told that there are plans to bring it to South Florida by the owners of the chain.

Jeb Bush

For the record, Columba and I went to Guatemala not in search of good chicken but to head the presidential delegation attending the inauguration of Óscar Berger Perdomo, the new president.

You know how sensitive I am about the state website and how hard we worked our first couple years to make all our different websites easy to navigate and helpful. So I got right on this complaint.

Subject: salt water fishing licenses
Sunday, March 14, 2004 1:46 p.m.
From: H. Brauer

Have tryed to re-new my salt water fishing license and foung out that the co. that did it before no longer holds the contract. Went to the Flporida Game comm. and found out that they to are no longer taking applications and are thinking of going to an out of state co. BUT, I could send an e-mail to your office and the Comm.s' office.

Had it returned because there is a problem with the address.

Come on Governer, lets have some one get there stuff together and get this up and runnung. Were starting to look like a second rate state.

Subject: salt water fishing licenses
Sunday, March 14, 2004 2:56 p.m.
From: Jeb Bush

I went online to the Florida Fish and Wildlife Conservation Commission and found the icon for licenses on the home page. http://www. floridaconservation.org/license.html. it doesn't seem that hard but maybe I am wrong so I am sending this email to Ken Haddad who runs the agency. I don't agree that Florida is a second rate state.

Jeb Bush

———

State Senator Ken Pruitt made my day with this brief e-mail exchange. I was very proud of our healthy pension system, which was a major challenge for many of my fellow governors.

Subject: Public Pension Gap Grows
Thursday, March 25, 2004 7:23 p.m.
From: Ken Pruitt

Congratulations - that rate stabilization mechanism has worked wonders (-: Ken

Public Pension Gap Grows
Article published on March 17, 2004

The underfunding of public pension funds in the U.S. continued to grow in 2003. So reports Bloomberg News.

Together, the funds studied by **Wilshire Associates** saw their shortfall grow to $366 billion. For California alone, the difference between assets and liabilities grew to $25.6 billion. Illinois has a $43.1 billion shortfall; Ohio's is $29.7 billion; and New York's is $28.3 billion.

Only two states have pension assets that currently exceed their plan's liabilities. They are **Florida** and North Carolina.

Subject: Public Pension Gap Grows
Thursday, March 25, 2004 8:44 p.m.
From: Jeb Bush

Amazing that only two state pensions have surpluses.

Jeb

———

This e-mail also meant a great deal to me, since school choice was at the heart of my A+ education plan. Coming from two leaders in the field meant even more: Patrick Heffernan of Floridians for School Choice and Tina Dupree of FloridaChild. I, of course, also loved the Wall Street Journal *article.*

Subject: WSJ Florida Schools -- Gov. Bush
Thursday, March 25, 2004 4:08 p.m.
From: Universal Pre-K

As an appreciative organization of families privileged to work with Florida's lawmakers on the passage of the Opportunity, McKay and Corporate Tax Credit scholarships, we know that you are the leaders responsible for the Wall Street Journal article below. You are getting the national credit that you deserve.

Thank you for setting a great example for government leaders everywhere on what it takes - and what it means - to give families the simple freedom to choose where their children will learn. Next month I hope America will be reading about scholarships for Florida's four year-olds and the GI Bill for Children!

With sincere thanks for your vision, courage and conviction.

Wall Street Journal

Review & Outlook

Thursday, March 25, 2004

The Empire Strikes Back

Florida's school-choice success terrifies the establishment.

"Florida will be a pivotal battleground this November, but on the crucial subject of education reform the battle in that state is already joined.

"In the past five years Florida has delivered real school choice to more American schoolchildren than anywhere else in the country. Which is no doubt why Jesse Jackson was down in Tallahassee earlier this month calling Governor Jeb Bush's policies racist. He and his allies understand all too well that when poor

African-American and Latino children start getting the same shot at a decent education that the children of our politicians do, the bankrupt public education empire starts looking like the Berlin Wall.

"This is the backdrop to this week's wrangling in the Florida senate over a bill ostensibly aimed at bringing accountability to the state's vouchers programs but which is really aimed at regulating them to death. Yes, there have been embarrassments, notably a scholarship operator now being criminally investigated for siphoning off $268,000. As bad as this is, it is small beer compared to the glaring scandal of a public school system in which more than half the state's African-American and Latino teens will never see a high school diploma.

Ironically those fighting vouchers may have a keener appreciation of Florida's significance to the voucher wars than those defending them. With national attention having focused largely on Milwaukee, Cleveland and the District of Columbia, it's easy to forget that Florida now has three key programs. The first are called Opportunity Scholarships, which allow children to opt out of failing public schools. Second are McKay Scholarships, which provide full school choice to special-ed students.

But perhaps the most innovative is a corporate tax credit that allows businesses to take a dollar-for-dollar deduction for every contribution to a designated scholarship fund. Certainly in terms of sheer numbers this is the most far-reaching, with 13,000 low-income students now benefiting and 20,000 on a waiting list. Because these corporately funded

scholarships are capped at $3,500 per child in a
state where the average per pupil expenditure runs
around $7,500, each scholarship represents not only a
lifeline for the recipient but significant savings for
the taxpayer.…

Meanwhile, they regulate. The accountability bill
includes some reasonable provisions (especially in
the financial reporting and auditing realms). But its
real attraction, as this week's debate demonstrated,
was as a vehicle to be loaded up with the kind of
voucher-strangling amendments pushed by Democrats Ron
Klein and Debbie Wasserman Schultz.[93]

The good news is that despite this all-out effort
to frog-march poor kids back into miserable public
schools, the genie seems to be out of the bottle.
Even the liberal newspapers that oppose school
choice had to concede that a pro-voucher rally
in Tallahassee attracted more marchers (if not
more favorable media attention) than the Reverend
Jackson's protest that preceded it. And that's
precisely what has them so worried."

———

*About this time I managed to irritate some boaters—at least this
boater who felt I had picked the manatees' rights over boaters'
rights. Boat motors were responsible for the deaths of several manatees. I worked hard to balance the interests of boaters with my goal
of protecting the loveable manatees. It was a tricky balancing act.*

---

93 Debbie Wasserman Schultz is still a formidable opponent as chair of
the Democratic National Committee and a congresswoman from Florida's
twenty-third congressional district.

Subject: Manatees
Friday, April 9, 2004 8:25 a.m.
From: Patrick Keefe

someone told me the other day that JEB, stands for.
Just End Boating !
Is this true? If so go back to Texas, with this
mentality!
Florida is boater country! Love it or Leave it!

Subject: Manatees
Friday, April 9, 2004 8:33 a.m.
From: Jeb Bush

Wow. Have a wonderful easter!

Jeb Bush

Subject: Manatees
Friday, April 9, 2004 7:53 a.m.
From: Patrick Keefe

wow! thats your reply? wow? must be true then! boats
are more important to Floridians, than horses and
cattle to Texans. WOW! ?

*Patrick had copied on the e-mail Steven Webster, executive direc-
tor of the Florida Marine Contractors Association, of which
Patrick was a member. Steven's response follows.*

Subject: Apology
Monday, April 12, 2004 6:19 p.m.
From: Steven Webster

I was just shown a copy of an email sent to you by one of our members. Not the nicest email in the world. The author is a good guy; builds a heckuva dock. But his email to you sure didn't show off his plusses.

I told Pat never do that again.

Contractors, as you can imagine, can be a coarse crowd, but they're also honest and intelligent. This weekend, at our quarterly meeting, I'll remind all members that we can disagree or debate without being demeaning or stupid.

I apologize. You and your office have earned our respect (and our votes; I don't know a single admitted Democrat in the Association!).

These guys will mess up now and again. Don't be surprised if I occasionally must repeat this apology.

Subject: Apology
Monday, April 12, 2004 8:14 p.m.
From: Jeb Bush

No problem. We are trying to help and angry emails won't change that.

Jeb

———

This exchange about same-sex marriage was with a gay friend. I abhor discrimination of any kind. Because of my Catholic faith, I believe marriage is a sacrament best reserved for a man and woman. While I disagree with the decision made by the US Supreme Court, we now need to strike a balance between respecting the religious freedom of the American people and ensuring gay and lesbian families are not discriminated against in our society.

Subject: I have some personal insight on gay marriage that I think you will find useful
Wednesday, March 3, 2004 6:29 p.m.
From: Xavier Cortada

I just received an email (below) forwarding a letter sent by Bette Midler to the president about his support for a Constitutional Amendment to ban gay marriage. I understand you also support the proposed Amendment and ban.

The president's rationale (during the State of the Union address) is that "activist" judges are usurping the democratic process, but how would today's jurists be any different from those in the Brown v. Topeka Board of Education case you mentioned to in your State of the State speech yesterday? Fifty years ago, that "activist" Court did not just do right by those school children (who were being treated unequally); but the case was a blessing for the rest of our nation (which was being denied the right to live in a free and open society). When one of us is denied equality, then all of us are denied liberty.

Today, I am feeling particularly denied and particularly unequal. My life partner, Juan Carlos, and I have been together for eight years and are being denied rights afforded to others who can

legally marry. Worst, I feel suffocated -- living in
a society where liberty evaporates with every attack
on people who happen to be gay—and I see it can
only get worse as this debate rages on. The problem
is not just the homophobia and violence (remember
Matthew Shepard?) that this marginalization
generates, but also the image that is generated
in society at large: Gays and lesbians as second
class citizens. For our beloved Country this would
mean that "all are equal, but some are more equal
than others." Nothing can be more threatening to a
democracy.

When you have a chance, I'd like to talk to you—and
perhaps your brother --about this. Open dialogue is
always healthy.

Call me—or email me -- when you have a chance.

**Subject: I have some personal insight on gay marriage
that I think you will find useful
Saturday, April 24, 2004 6:58 p.m.
From: Jeb Bush**

**Thank you for writing and I apologize for not
responding earlier. The tyranny of the present has
gotten me!**

**I am sensitive to your point of view but respectfully
disagree. If there is discrimination, there are
remedies. The cases of violence against gay and
lesbians are unconscionable and the laws in Florida
exist to bring justice. Your relationship with Juan
Carlos can be made more permanent through contractual
obligations that set forth asset disposition and**

other issues. However, I don't believe that your
relationship should be afforded the same status in
the law as a man and a woman agreeing to marraige.
The institution of marraige is under attack in our
society and it needs to be strengthened. This does
not have to be at the expense of other kinds of
relationships but in support of the most important
institution in our society.

We can discuss this if you like and again, I am
expressing my opinion with the respect that you
deserve.

Jeb

———

*I was delighted when the state legislature agreed to pass a bill
creating the Agency for Persons with Disabilities—another very
important step toward giving the disabled in Florida a strong,
independent voice. I truly believe our society will be judged by
how we treat the most vulnerable.*

**Subject: Thank you for Supporting People with
Disabilities.**
Thursday, April 29, 2004 6:59 p.m.
From: Susan

Thank you for being the champion of people with
developmental disabilities and their families.

The new Agency for People with Disabilities will
continue your work that focuses on improving the
lives of Florida's most vulnerable citizens.

**Subject: Thank you for Supporting People with
Disabilities.
Thursday, April 29, 2004 8:34 p.m.
From: Jeb Bush**

I am very pleased.

jeb

---

*The state legislative session was not unlike that of 2003—a
little dysfunctional. This was what I meant to say to Senate
President Jim King. However, a lot of good things had been
accomplished as well. Most of what I mention below is self-
explanatory with two exceptions: the legislature passed and
I signed the Wekiva Parkway and Protection Act, which both
protected the beautiful Wekiva Springs and wildlife area in
Orlando and allowed for a beltway to be built to deal with
traffic issues in the area. Certificate-of-need (CON) reform
was designed to cut through red tape to modernize hospital
regulation.*

**Subject: [None]
Saturday, May 1, 2004 8:15 p.m.
From: Jeb Bush**

**In spite of the disfuntional nature of the session,
some good things were accomplished. Health care
reform, a new disabilities agency, campaign finance
reform, migrant worker reform, middle school reform,
a plan for the Wekeiva, a good budget (with some
largess that might be extracted), CON reform, and
a few other things. Almost 500 bills were passed**

believe it or not. You should be proud of the accomplishments. Well done, Mr President.

Jeb

———

With the new budget completed, it was time for the annual turkey hunt. I remained committed to removing wasteful spending from the budget. My friend State Representative Gaston Cantens had a very long list of favorite projects—eighteen to be exact. This was often the problem. Not all projects were wasteful, but sometimes there was just too much of a good thing.

Subject: [None]
Tuesday, May 25, 2004 8:58 p.m.
From: Gaston Cantens

Hope all is well with you and your family. Life is good in South Fla.

Thanks for doing the bill signing for the sexual predator bill in Miami. I will see you on Thursday at FIU.[94]

Speaking of FIU...I am hopeful that you will give due consideration to the historical lack of adequate funding at FIU in comparison to other universities. This year is no different. Please take notice of what happened with FIU: the actual PECO appropriation is actually less than what you had recommended.

---

94 Florida International University.

I have also listed other items that are very important to this community. While at first glance the St. Thomas dollars may appear to be some turkey, it is a very important, innovative program to ensure that we recruit and retain minority teachers in critical shortage areas. This is very important to Bruce, Planas, Quinones and myself.

The Tamiami Community Center dollars will finally provide west Miami-Dade with a facility for after school sports and tutoring programs. Historically, suburban areas have been slighted when it comes to facilities for teenagers. West Miami-Dade has NO similar facility. This is a nonrecurring investment in the children of West Miami-Dade that will provide recurring benefits. The County and the Fair are also putting up significant dollars for this project - approximately $4 million total.

The diabetes programs provide tremendous relief to those afflicted with the silent killer that is known as diabetes. The research program is making great strides and already has produced several individuals that are living insulin free as a result of the transplant. It is only a matter of time before individuals are able to free themselves of the multiple daily injections that prevent them from having normal lives.

I have never been a high maintenance member and do not want to change that now. These items, however, are very important to me and I hope that you will understand my plea. Unlike other years, I do not have another opportunity to get these things done; this is it - now or never - do or die.

Subject: [None]
Tuesday, May 25, 2004 9:55 p.m.
From: Jeb Bush

Yours is a long list and some will be vetoed and
some will not. here is my dilemma which I know given
your service, you understand. We have huge demands
on our state budget...schools, community colleges,
universities, Medicaid, social services, environmental
programs, transportation, corrections (adult and
juvenile). All of these grow each year and while we
fulfill the needs, we never fulfill the wants. Adding
new programs with such demands is easy to do, and
popular to do and politically correct to do if one
wants to gain points with the editorial boards, but it
is not the wise thing to do. I have strived to keep
taxes low and intend to continue to do so. The hard
working constituents that we share don't put pressure
up on Mt. Tallahassee but I know you respect them as
much as I do. We cannot allow the government to grow
faster than the tax producers ability to pay for it.
With high speed rail. UPK, Medicaid, the class size
initiative, the demands on infrastructure created by
our growth, there is no way we can not raise taxes
unless I am tough on the line items this year.

You have been a great legislator (and would have been
a great Speaker if it had worked out) and my respect
and admiration for you is apparent to all who ask me.
I cannot however approve all of these items based on
my respect for you and our friendship if they break my
commitment to limited government. I hope you understand.

Your friend,

Jeb

Subject: Budget Vetoes
Saturday, May 29, 2004 7:02 a.m.
From: Peggy Simone

Thank you, thank you, thank you!! Your budget vetoes are right on---the state has so many programs that are required by statute to be funded, that there won't ever be enough money to fund new ones, no matter how worthy.

I admire your strength and resolve to do the right thing for the right reason!

Subject: Budget Vetoes
Saturday, May 29, 2004 7:06 a.m.
From: Jeb Bush

Thank you Peggy. It is not fun but I believe it is the right thing to do.

Jeb

Here is a sampling of what was on the minds of Floridians as we neared the end of the school year and the beginning of summer.

Subject: Encouragement for you and your brother!
Sunday, May 30, 2004 6:54 p.m.
From: John R. Syfrett

Polk County Schoolteacher, here!

This morning,in the 5th. Grade Sunday School class, that I'm teaching, they had an interesting question.

"Do you think the Governor of Florida and the President of the United States pray about decisions that they have to make, in doing their job with our state and country?"

These students come from a variety of schools all over Lakeland. They are great kids! Curiousity, questions, strong faiths and more questions!

I told them that being a public servant is a tough job! I also told them that I believe our Governor and our President are led by, and consult with, a higher power - God!

I appreciate you always looking out for the citizens, visitors, and people of our great state, Florida. I appreciate your brother for his great ability to "stay the course" and to look after the best interests of our country, its residents, and the people of the world that appreciate freedom, and democracy. Thank you for being an excellent governor and being such a good brother, to our President!

Any words of encouragement, or comment, to these youngsters that are getting ready to become middle schoolers? I will relay any response or message to them next week in Sunday School class.

Have a productive and super week!

Subject: Encouragement for you and your brother!
Sunday, May 30, 2004 8:42 p.m.
From: Jeb Bush

Thank you John. I do pray over the big decisions.
I also pray for the military and their families,
the lonely and sick in our state and my own family
including my brother who needs everyone prayers.

I believe in the power of prayer!

I hope your students have a great summer (I also hope
that they read their summer reading books!) and a
great school year in the fall.

Jeb Bush

———

Subject: I am Scott Jackson From Boys state
Wednesday, June 2, 2004 9:50 p.m.
From: Scott Jackson

I want to remove the speed limiter on my car.
Do you can allow remove the speed limiter for my
car?

Subject: I am Scott Jackson From Boys state
Wednesday, June 2, 2004 11:53 p.m.
From: Jeb Bush

what is a speed limiter?

Jeb

Subject: I am Scott Jackson From Boys state
Thursday, June 3, 2004 3:02 p.m.
From: Scott Jackson

Speed Limiter in (Engine Control Unit) computer chip. Speed Limiter make stop to 110mph and make waste of gas for car. I found records of my car. My car was race. My car is 2000 Honda Civic DX.

Subject: I am Scott Jackson From Boys state
Thursday, June 3, 2004 3:44 p.m.
From: Jeb Bush

why do you need to go 110 mph? The max speed limit is 70 mph.

Jeb

———

President Ronald Reagan died on June 5 after ten years living with Alzheimer's. Despite a sometimes-bruising primary campaign in 1980, my dad considered it a great honor to serve by his side as vice president. He also considered him a mentor and friend. He certainly was a hero of mine.

Subject: Hi, Governor
Sunday, June 6, 2004 7:24 p.m.
From: Marie Dinon

Below is a snip out of the 2004 Florida Kids Count. I thought it was interesting to see that the graduation rate continually declined while Lawton Chiles was Governor and has continually increased since you've been in office. I'll have to look up the most recent

years available. Even with higher standards, I'm sure
we are continually improving.

Your positive leadership has been great for Florida.
I'm thinking of you today as we reminisce about
President Reagan. Your leadership style reminds me
of him. He was always positive and believed in our
country as you are positive and believe in Floridians
even as you're always setting higher standards.

Another characteristic you share with President
Reagan is fearless determination to do what you
instinctively know is right.

Hope all is well. Thanks for being our Governor.

Subject: Hi, Governor
Monday, June 7, 2004 12:29 a.m.
From: Jeb Bush

thank you Marie. I can't think of kinder compliment
than to be compared to our beloved President Reagan.

Jeb

———

I received more praise for being Veto Corleone.

Subject: I appreciate all you do for Florida!
Monday, June 7, 2004 8:50 a.m.
From: Teresa L. Weaver

I truly appreciate all that you do for our wonderful
State of Florida. I saw what you did with your

fantastic "VETO" powers and I wanted to thank you personally.

I know that it takes a great deal of backbone to do what you do sometimes and you don't always get the recognition you should. I want you to know that some of us see and like what you are doing in Tallahassee.

Your a fine Governor, and I just wanted you to know how much we appreciate what have done for us Floridians.

You have the tax payer in mind when you do things and that is always a blessing. I also want to thank you for being so involved with the reading programs throughout Florida.

As a result of your desires, my daughter and son, who are involved with the Vanguard High School Key Club are very involved with a local library. They are helping with the reading programs at the Forest Branch of the Marion County Library, and are thrilled to be doing it as well.…You're the Greatest Governor, Jeb!

Subject: I appreciate all you do for Florida!
Monday, June 7, 2004 10:31 a.m.
From: Jeb Bush

thank you Teresa for your kind email. I am very appreciative.

Jeb

———

A year after the Florida Marlins won the World Series, the Tampa Bay Lightning brought hockey's Stanley Cup to Florida after beating the Calgary Flames. Oh, what fun it was to be the governor when our teams were the champions. In this case I had bet Alberta Premier Ralph Klein that if Tampa Bay won, I would send him a jersey to wear, and he would send me some of Alberta's world-famous Grade A beef. I received this note from one of my staffers in our Tampa office.

Subject: Stanley Cup is in FLORIDA!!!!!
Tuesday, June 8, 2004 12:30 a.m.
From: Kimberly Dale

We did it…We WON THE STANLEY CUP!!!!!!!!!!!!

Thank you for all of your support!!

So, when the Premier sends down the food, I am more than happy to make a trip to Tally to help eat it!

I am going to bring your jersey to the Forum tomorrow to get signed by the players before sending it to the Premier for him to wear- if that is okay with you??

Thank you again, for supporting the Lightning!!!

Subject: Stanley Cup is in FLORIDA!!!!!
Tuesday, June 8, 2004 9:33 a.m.
From: Jeb Bush

I might be able to give it to him in person.

Jeb

———

Matthew Green had been working for us as the state meteo-rologist but was leaving to take on a new position. If he knew then what was coming, I wonder if he would have changed his mind.

Subject: New opportunity with FEMA
Thursday, June 24, 2004 10:34 a.m.
From: Matthew Green

I would like to let you know that I have accepted a new opportunity with the Federal Emergency Management Agency at the National Hurricane Center in Miami.

Thank you for allowing me the opportunity to serve you and your administration. I appreciate your sincere interest in emergency management and the welfare of the people of Florida. These past six years have been both professionally and personally rewarding. It is an honor to have been bestowed a nickname by you, one that will undoubtedly stick with me for years to come.

I look forward to the day that our paths cross again.

Subject: New opportunity with FEMA
Thursday, June 24, 2004 6:47 p.m.
From: Jeb Bush

Stormboy, your job is to divert all the big ones away from paradise.

Good luck down in Miami.

Jeb

By now you know how much I loved hearing from Floridians who were benefiting from new policies or programs we had put into place. Promoting adoption was one of my top priorities. While I was governor, the number of annual adoptions increased 107.6 percent, and more than 16,000 adoptions were finalized.

Subject: thank you
Thursday, June 24, 2004 10:30 p.m.
From: Lori Geoffrey

I wrote you about 2 years ago regarding the frustration to adopt children in this state. Everyone is pushing the country to adopt but I understood why they get discouraged. I live in Miami-Dade County and was told after I was approved that there were no children up for adoption in Miami. I wrote you and was given some names to call. Less than a month and a half later I had two beautiful boys in my home. Brothers ages 9 and 12.(adopted in Ft Walton Beach)

Keep up the great work with supporting adoptions. My husband and I need to now move to a larger home because we would like another sibling group. I do not know what the answer is but I do know many go outside the country because of the system we have here.

I am an airline employee (American Airlines) and I could fly anywhere for next to nothing making my choices much broader and affordable than the average household but we chose to adopt within our state.

I feel the future is our children and we need to invest more finances into them. I understand the ratio of state workers to children in their care is scary. This is not a recent problem. My husband and I have

talked to many couples who gave up in the 70's and elected to go outside our country.
In closing thank you again for helping us get the most precious gift of all.

Subject: thank you
Friday, June 25, 2004 6:06 p.m.
From: Jeb Bush

Thank you so much for writing. We have had a huge increase in adoptions out of foster care and I am so appreciative that you have adopted two precious children from the Sunshine State.

Jeb Bush

———

In 2002 the people of Florida passed a constitutional amendment that created a voluntary, universal system of prekindergarten classes for four-year-olds. The idea was to better prepare our children for school. The new pre-K system, to be designed by the legislature, was to start with the 2005 school year. About this time I vetoed the bill the legislature passed regarding pre-K. It was a very weak bill with limited options for parents, low standards for teacher accreditation, and low education standards. The bill had many critics—many of whom called it "glorified day care."

Subject: Thanks for being a hero
Friday, July 9, 2004 9:52 p.m.
From: Bebe Fearnside

I want to thank you for standing up for quality for Florida's youngest citizens. You made a real stand

which shows the direction that you want Florida
to go as we begin an outstanding program for our
preschoolers. I began my teaching career 42 years ago
and have seen many changes through the years. I served
on the first advisory council for Prek[95] started in
1985 and have served every year since then. I started
as a member of the first Partnership Board and have
continued to this date. Your action stands out as one
of highlights in this long journey. Your commitment to
quality will be the hallmark for this program. Thanks
for putting the children and families first

Subject: Thanks for being a hero
Saturday, July 10, 2004 7:54 a.m.
From: Jeb Bush

you are most welcome.

Jeb

———

*By midsummer we had settled into something of a typical sum-
mer pattern. The legislative session was long over. With the budget signed, the turkey hunt season was over, and I could put away
my "Veto Corleone" pen. The opening of school was still a month
away. It was that time of year when most Floridians were thinking more about going to the beach with their families than what
was going on in Tallahassee.*

*I headed to Maine to visit my parents and celebrate the
wedding of our oldest son, George P., who married Amanda
Williams of San Angelo, Texas, at historic St. Ann's Church in*

---

95 I think "Prek" is a shortcut for "pre-K," which is a shortcut for "pre-
kindergarten." (And this was written before texting.)

Kennebunkport. It was a wonderful family celebration as we joy-fully welcomed Mandi into our family.

There was good news back home as well.

For the first time since 2001, we were able to give Floridians a sales-tax holiday. From July 24 through August 1, there was no sales tax on most back-to-school items. That included books and clothes valued at less than fifty dollars and other school supplies under ten dollars. We also cut the state gasoline tax by eight cents during the month of August. Estimated sales-tax savings for Floridians were more than $95 million.

We basically said to let the shopping begin!

Subject: Thanks Gov!
Monday, July 26, 2004 7:16 a.m.
From: Don Germaise

Thank you for your part in helping supplant the Germaise family budget....

My daughter and I took advantage of the sales tax holiday yesterday. We bought $60 worth of school supplies, seven school uniforms, a pair of new shoes and some work shirts for me. Not only did we stimulate the economy -- which made me feel like an red-blooded republican -- but we saved $9.54 in sales tax. Which was more than enough to cover the cost of two hot fudge sundaes at Baskin-Robbins!

BTW: The nay-sayers who trash the sales tax holiday are WRONG! As I went from store to store, a lot of fellow shoppers were raving about the sales tax savings. It works. These were working to middle class people who appreciate this tax break! Keep fighting the good fight.

Subject: Thanks Gov!
Monday, July 26, 2004 7:37 a.m.
From: Jeb Bush

Thanks Don. It is a great concept that has broad
appeal, best I can tell. Go buy some books!

Jeb

———

*About this time a tropical wave moved off the west coast of Africa
and started its journey across the Atlantic Ocean. Not many people paid attention.*

*The meteorologists did. I did too, along with the other Atlantic
and Gulf Coast governors. We knew some tropical waves grew up
to be hurricanes—not all but some.*

*Unfortunately this one did. This wave soon became Hurricane
Charley, the strongest storm to hit the United States since Andrew
hit Florida in 1992.*

*I flew back to Florida the day after the wedding. I was well
aware we might be in trouble. We prayed for the best but prepared for the worst.*

*On August 11 I declared a state of emergency and urged 1.9
million people along Florida's west coast to evacuate. Many chose
to board up their homes and ride out the storm, but many did
head for shelters. Cruise ships rerouted, Disney World shut down,
and the entire state braced itself.*

*The storm did some zigzagging in the Gulf of Mexico and sud-
denly went from a Category 2 to a Category 4. To make things just
a little more complicated, a day ahead of Charley was Tropical
Storm Bonnie, which made landfall just south of Apalachicola.
Damage was minimal. Twenty-two hours later, though, Charley
brushed the Dry Tortugas, a small group of islands off the coast
of the Florida Keys. It was the first time in history two tropical*

storms came ashore in the same state within a twenty-four-hour period. It's a record no state wants to claim.

Charley then took aim at Captiva Island with winds of 150 miles per hour.

My team was ready. That included Susan Pareigis, secretary of the Agency for Workforce Innovation, whose job was to help displaced workers.

Subject: Ready to go
Friday, August 13, 2004 10:18 p.m.
From: Susan Pareigis

Say the word and we're in SWF, Orlando, Daytona – where ever you want us to go first. Mobile One Stop is ready at daylight.

I've spoken with folks in Port Charlotte, Cape Coral, Fort Myers and Naples – <u>lots</u> of water and wind damage.

Subject: Ready to go
Friday, August 13, 2004 10:24 p.m.
From: Jeb Bush

Get ready to rumble.

———

Charley made landfall on the mainland near Punta Gorda. It devastated the counties of Charlotte, Hardee, and DeSoto in the southwest part of the state. It then barreled through the state like a tornado. It cut a narrow but destructive path, continued to the north-northeast along the Peace River corridor, and caused major wind damage and massive power outages. It passed *through Orlando as a hurricane and finally exited Florida on the Atlantic side—just south of Daytona Beach. Damage in the state was estimated at more than $20 billion. Tragically ten people died in Florida from the direct impact of the storm.*

I went to Charlotte County the next day to visit the emergency operations center and the special needs shelter. It was heartbreaking.

People wrote with questions, concerns, and encouragement.

———

Subject: Charley
Tuesday, August 24, 2004 5:59 p.m.
From: Susan van Hoek

I just had to say how proud I am of the remarkable job you all are doing re: Hurrican Charely. It seems nothing short of miraculous. I already gave to the Red Cross but will give to the Hurricane Charley Relief Effort too. I only wish I could be there to work and give aid and comfort in person.

Subject: Charley
Tuesday, August 24, 2004 6:58 p.m.
From: Jeb Bush

Thank you Susan. Your generosity is great!

Jeb

———

I heard from Barbara Sheen Todd, a former Pinellas County commissioner.

Subject: Hurricane information
Tuesday, August 24, 2004 9:37 a.m.
From: Barbara Sheen Todd

I was disappointed that our appointment was cancelled
this week. I do understand that you are quite
occupied with the aftermath of Hurricane Charley
and hope we can reschedule soon. I have some very
interesting concepts to share with you.

Regarding the hurricane...I have had a personal
encounter with Charley. My property in Hardee county
was totalled. Years of work...gone...and no sign of hope.I
had been unable to secure insurance....Others who live
there all the time are still trying to put things
together.

My brother lives on Pine Island....His home was
destroyed. He has received NO help from FEMA or
anyone else. His situation is not unique.

The story I am hearing from many folks who are going
through this devastation is that insurance companies
are **really dragging** there feet. FEMA is quiet slow to
respond...and in fact is telling people there is little
they can or will do.

Not a good thing. The system needs to be reviewed and
possibly overhauled.

On a positive note...the response from citizens is
uplifting. I am seeing people outreach to their
fellow Floridians with caring and genuine concern.

Thank you for all YOU do. May God continue to bless
you and guide you.

Subject: Hurricane information
Tuesday, August 24, 2004 10:29 p.m.
From: Jeb Bush

Sorry for the cancellation.

Why couldn't you receive insurance for your property
before the storm?

There is significant help for people that seek it. over
100,000 have already done so and checks are being
distributed as I write. FEMA has responded to this storm
far, far faster than any hurricane that I am aware of
and that has been confirmed by third party observers. I
will pass on your observation regarding the insurance
companies but again, all indications are that they have
been quicker to respond than in the past.

Having said all that, if you have specific examples
of where help is needed where there has been no
response, please don't hesitate to let me know and I
will go to work.

Jeb Bush

———

*I was committed to minimizing the economic impact of Hurricane
Charley. Ensuring small businesses got back on their feet quickly
was vital to protecting jobs and keeping our economy from fall-
ing into a recession. It was much like the days following 9/11.*

Subject: Injured Businesses May Qualify for Loans –
Lakeland Ledger
Thursday, August 26, 2004 9:30 a.m.
From: Pam Dana

Your bridge loan program is getting good press.

Subject: Injured Businesses May Qualify for Loans –
Lakeland Ledger
Thursday, August 26, 2004 10:03 a.m.
From: Jeb Bush

excellent

Published Thursday, August 26, 2004
Injured Businesses May Qualify for Loans

By Mary Toothman
The Ledger

"LAKELAND -- Polk County business owners in need of help after Hurricane Charley's wrath may be able to qualify for some of the $1.5 million available for short-term, interest-free loans to get them up and running again.

"Tom Patton, executive director of the Central Florida Development Council, said it's hoped the money will be doled out quickly so the economy can get a boost.

"We can process them right away, and we're shooting for a 72-hour turnaround," he said. "It gets you started so you can get going."

"Gov. Jeb Bush signed an executive order approving the loans. The Governor's Office said the "bridge loans" of up to $25,000 will be available to owners of small businesses (up to 100 employees) in counties most affected by Charley, including Polk. They come in

90-day or 180-day repayment terms. To be eligible, a business must have been operational for a year before Aug. 13 and have verifiable, physical damage to the property. The loans are not available for economic problems caused by decreased sales or temporary closure.…

"Patton said he expects a lot of response.

"I think it's going to get a number of people back on their feet," he said. "Our goal is to have $1.5 million out of here in a week to 10 days."

———

Subject: Hurricane shelters
Friday, August 27, 2004 11:05 p.m.
From: Dave Butcher

Hi Jeb (I hope it is ok to call you that…let me know),

I seem to remember hearing that this was your direct e-mail. I just wanted to express a concern about the hurricane shelters. I think we came a long way in hurricane response since Floyd. I moved down to east Polk county just before Floyd and ended up getting stuck in the I-4 parking lot mess during Floyd. I would like to suggest (if it hasn't already been done) that there be a certification process for structures to be considered for use as shelters during the storm.

The certification should show that the shelter has been built well enough to withstand a major hurricane like we had down here. To my knowledge there were two shelters that failed during Charley: the one in Desoto county and one in southeast Polk county (the Warner Southern College gym). A shelter should be the last resort for someone if they have no place else that is safe. I have a few other ideas that I think would be good for the people in the storm. Let me know if you are interested. Thanks for your time,

P.S. I'm a state employee…if that matters :)

Subject: Hurricane shelters
Saturday, August 28, 2004 8:39 a.m.
From: Jeb Bush

Thank you Dave. I appreciate your input. We will be reviewing all of our policies to improve what we do to prepare for hurricanes.

jeb

———

We had done a lot of things right, but we had room for improvement too. As we continued our efforts to help Floridians rebuild their homes, businesses, and lives, we hoped at some point to find the time to take a good look at lessons learned from Charley and how we could do better next time.

What we didn't expect was that "next time" was right now.

Hurricane Frances came off the coast of Africa as a tropical wave on August 21. We watched warily as it came across the Atlantic. It decreased then increased in intensity before it began bouncing around the Caribbean. It was a hard storm to predict.

State Meteorologist Ben Nelson sent this report to Denver Stutler; Deputy Chief of Staff Deirdre Finn, whose portfolio included emergency management; and me. You can see how hard it is to pinpoint exactly where these massive storms will come ashore.

Subject: Hurricane Frances - 11 AM Sunday update
Sunday, August 29, 2004 11:47 a.m.
From: Ben Nelson

At 11 AM Sunday, Frances' eye was located about 550 miles to the east of the northern Leeward Islands, or about 760 miles due east of San Juan, Puerto Rico. This position is also located about 1740 miles to the southeast of Miami. Frances strengthened to Category 4 status on Saturday afternoon and remains at that strength this morning. Maximum sustained winds are near 135 mph. Frances has taken a turn towards the west, although there have been some northward wobbles on satellite imagery during the past few hours. The current westward motion is near 9 mph. This motion is expected to continue during at least the next few days, with a gradual acceleration anticipated beginning tomorrow.

Frances is now close enough to the Lesser Antilles for a Hurricane Hunter reconnaissance plane investigation this afternoon. Since this will be the first plane into the hurricane, we will have better information on the hurricane's intensity and wind fields. This data will get plugged into tonight's run of the computer models. With the new data, the official forecast could change somewhat, especially during the 4 and 5 day periods.

Subject: Hurricane Frances - 11 AM Sunday update
Sunday, August 29, 2004 4:11 p.m.
From: Jeb Bush

Thank you Ben and Deidre. We will watch and pray.

Jeb

———

The Republican National Convention got under way in New York City on August 30, where my brother was officially nominated for a second term. Mark Silva, who was now the White House correspondent for the Chicago Tribune, *thought it odd I was not in New York. He was interested in politics. I was interested in the storms pounding my state.*

Subject: Where's Jeb
Monday, August 30, 2004 7:33 a.m.
From: Mark Silva

How's the relief effort going? And can you tell me, for publication, why you're not in New York? Is it just the storm, or is this not your game? There a chance you'll still come for a quick trip? I heard Wednesday.

Subject: Where's Jeb
Monday, August 30, 2004 7:42 p.m.
From: Jeb Bush

We have a lot of work to do. Tomorrow, I go to hardee, Polk and Seminole County to thank the educators for their incredible work to get schools and community colleges open yesterday. I will not be going to NYC but in no way should that be seen as a lack of fortitude to work for the Prez's reelection. Now, we have Frances approaching our shores so I will be doing double duty.

Jeb

———

This inquiry came from Dinah Voyles Pulver at the Daytona Beach News-Journal.

Subject: Frances
Tuesday, August 31, 2004 5:05 p.m.
From: Dinah Voyles Pulver

Aren't you doing some kind of statement today? I can't believe the full scale panic already. It's pretty serious.

The 5 p.m. track map has Daytona Beach right smack in the middle.

Subject: Frances
Tuesday, August 31, 2004 5:20 p.m.
From: Jeb Bush

it is too early to tell. no need to panic. Big need to prepare.

Jeb

———

The next day it became time to declare a state of emergency, as hurricane experts warned us Frances could come ashore as a Category 4 along Florida's heavily populated east coast. Eventually forty-one counties were put under evacuation orders. It affected 2.8 million residents—the largest evacuation order in state history. There were still a lot of uncertainties, but we could not put lives in danger. It was better to ask people to leave and listen to them complain later if the storm proved a nonevent.

We waited anxiously as the storm made up its mind about where to come ashore and at what strength. It finally made landfall on September 5 near Port St Lucie. At a Category 2, it was weaker than we had feared, and initial reports did not reveal catastrophic damage. Frances was just getting started, though.

Subject: Hello young man
Sunday, September 5, 2004 11:37 p.m.
From: Debby Sanderson[96]

Pete and I are fortunate to be safely at our home in the mountains of NC, but we've been watching the coverage closely throughout the past few days.

I'm very proud of the way you have handled yourself on TV during Charley, and now Frances. I watched you yesterday and again this morning on FOX. You came across in a very reassuring, cautiously optomistist, and a warm and complimentary manner regarding the grit and spirit of Floridians. Throwing in the comment about the football games was perfect, and it helped break the tension in the air. It was great![97]

It's hard to believe we have been under seige with back to back horrific storms, and now bracing for possibly a third to hit us!!!

It was so good of the President to come down and tour the destruction with you during Charley. The feedback I heard was extremely possitive from our Republican and Democrat friends.

---

96 Debby Sanderson was a state senator.
97 I wish I remember what I said about football, but unfortunately I do not.

My heart goes out to you and the good people of Florida. There will be so many challenges to help put their lives back into some semblance of order.

Thank you, Jeb, way to go!! please get some rest tonight.

Subject: Re: Hello young man
Monday, September 6, 2004 1:49 p.m.
From: Jeb Bush

Thank you Debby! Wow, what a three week period in our lives!

Jeb

———

Unfortunately, you did read that right in Debby's e-mail. There was a third storm on its way. Before we talk about Ivan, though, let's close the book on Frances.

After coming ashore it marched across Central Florida, went out into the Gulf, came ashore again in the Panhandle, and then traveled up the ridge of the Appalachian Mountains. It wreaked havoc the entire journey with torrential rains and widespread tornado breakouts.

Frances pretty well finished off Florida's citrus crop. What Charley had not destroyed, Frances did. Damage to the industry was estimated at $2 billion. Parts of Florida received up to thirteen inches of rain, and there was massive flooding along with widespread power outages—again. The US Army Corps of Engineers estimated they gave out more than forty thousand tarpaulins—called blue roofs—to cover damaged roofs. Many communities were short of water and gasoline. Kennedy Space Center, Cape Canaveral, and Patrick Air Force Base together took *about a $100 million hit. In total Frances caused an estimated $15.8 billion in damages.*

Now Ivan was on its way. It didn't seem possible, but as we assessed damages from Frances and continued cleanup from Charley, Florida braced itself for its third storm in a month.

Subject: more fun than we can stand
Thursday, September 9, 2004 12:04 p.m.
From: Matt

I think the man upstairs is testing us. Three in a row is more fun than we can stand. I know you have to be whipped…everybody is. Everywhere you turn…as you well know…people have lost roofs, all or part…some major home damage others little or none…a real hit and miss. People have generally great attitudes even in the face of this from talking to them at the local restaurants. FEMA has been a great help with $$ for several people we know and tarps etc. We were lucky with only downed trees and limbs…somehow missing the house We did a neighbors roof yesterday and folks know its due to your work and our Florida emergency groups. You and your teams may not be hearing it…but its appreciated.

we're hanging in in Palm Bay…now for chapter three…Ivan

be safe

Subject: more fun than we can stand
Thursday, September 9, 2004 12:41 p.m.
From: Jeb Bush

We are gearing up yet again.

Jeb

———

Subject: [None]
Wednesday, September 15, 2004 9:09 p.m.
From: Jeanne Stephens

I hope you and yours are safe while Ivan is passing nearby. I am keeping you all in my prayers. Hope all goes well for you and Florida.

Subject: [None]
Wednesday, September 15, 2004 9:32 p.m.
From: Jeb Bush

it is hitting hard and will wreck havoc.

Jeb

———

Like Frances before it, Ivan had a mind of its own as it meandered through the Caribbean and headed into the Gulf of Mexico. At one point in the Gulf, it was a Category 5 hurricane the size of Texas. When it came ashore in Alabama and Florida's Panhandle on September 16, it was a strong Category 3. It dumped torrential rain and spawned tornadoes all through the Panhandle. Before leaving our state, Ivan killed fourteen Floridians and left a part of Florida devastated. The total estimated price tag was $6.6 billion.

Subject: PRAYERS!!!!!!!!!!!!
Friday, September 17, 2004 5:33 p.m.
From: Kip Liles

I just want to say, as one native Floridian. that my prayers are with you during this time of devastation to our State and its many residents.

You look so weary on televisions, and I know you are - you certainly have every right to be!!!!!!! You must be completely drained emotionally; physically; and mentally. I wish I could offer more help than prayers; but we know that OUR God does answer prayers. May HE keep you safe in HIS hands, and give you the strength that you need in the massive job you have on your hands (and heart)!!!!!

Subject: Re: PRAYERS!!!!!!!!!!!!
Friday, September 17, 2004 5:51 p.m.
From: Jeb Bush

Thank yoiu for the encouraging words. We will prevail.

Jeb

———

This inquiry came from Paige St. John of Gannett News Service.

Subject: CAT Fund[98]
Monday, September 20, 2004 10:46 a.m.
From: Paige St. John

Who advises governors on how to comport themselves (and thereby a state) through disaster (i mean that both pragmatically and in principle…)

---

98 CAT was short for the Florida Hurricane Catastrophe Fund.

Subject: CAT Fund
Monday, September 20, 2004 5:30 p.m.
From: Jeb Bush

Come to think of it, I have not gotten any advice
on my job from outsiders.It has been from experience
dealing with past intense occasions (9-11, even
political campaigns),learning as I go and just
plan instincts. In addition, I have a great staff
of people who have worked very hard these last six
weeks.

Jeb Bush

Subject: CAT Fund
Monday, September 20, 2004 5:47 p.m.
From: Paige St. John

love for you to sing the praises of staff. some
have really stepped up. Also some key private
individuals?

as for instinct, i have to say, i've seen others
flub this kind of job. there's got to be some art in
visbility without self-promotion and silencing the
"it's-all-about-politics" crowd.

Subject: CAT Fund
Monday, September 20, 2004 6:43 p.m.
From: Jeb Bush

denver stutler, deidre finn, obviously craig fugate[99]
and his team, jill bratina[100] and many, many more are
doing great work.

I have learned a lot during my tenure as governor.
One is when to be partisan and when not to be. Storms
don't hit just r's or d's or independents, they all
floridians. As Governor it is essential that I respond
in the same way.

Jeb

———

*Please note the subject line of this next e-mail exchange is
"Hurricane Jeanne."*

Hurricane Jeanne? We couldn't believe it either.

*We thought we were free and clear, but Jeanne did a 360 in
the Atlantic Ocean. Hurricane number four was on its way.*

Subject: Hurricane Jeanne
Friday, September 17, 2004 11:44 a.m.
From: Audrey Davis

Looking at the path of Jeanne, I found myself
wondering if you are asking yourself, "When is enough
enough?"

Anyway, just wanted to let you know we finally go our
power back here in Palm Beach Gardens and I couldn't
be happier with lights and air conditioning again.
However, while the power was off in our neighborhood

---

99 Craig Fugate was director of the Division of Emergency Management.
He is now the director of FEMA.
100 Jill Bratina was director of communications.

I did notice that the children were outside playing in their yards, neighbors were talking to each other (which normally did not happen) and neighbors were helping neighbors cut trees and clean yards. It was a little like what I remember from my childhood. Now with the power on, life is getting back to the old pattern. We drive home, open the garage door and go into our homes to the TV and air conditioning. Some of us have decided not to let the communication die. We are planning a block party or some other kind of get together.

There is also a radio program down here where the disc jockeys are trying to match people in need with people who may have something they can do without or a service they could donate. Surprisingly, not too many people are calling to gouge the system and the program is a huge hit.

What I guess I am trying to say, as hard as these hurricanes have been on you and Florida, there is some good coming out of it.

Thanks for being a strong leader in a time of need and I will continue to try to be a strong constituent.

A loyal democrat but supporter of Jeb Bush.

Subject: Hurricane Jeanne
Monday, September 20, 2004 1:56 p.m.
From: Jeb Bush

Thank you Audrey. I really appreciate your kind email. This has been a test for our state and by and large, we have responded. I am so proud of the acts

of compassion and courage that is done below the radar. We will get through this and be stronger than we can ever imagine.

Jeb

————

Subject: GREAT JOB
Monday, September 20, 2004 2:22 p.m.
From: Don Quinn

JUST TO LET YOU KNOW I AN VERY PROUD TO BE A FLORIDIAN IN THE WAKE OF THE PROBLEMS WITH CHARLEY, FRANCES AND IVAN. I BELIEVE EVERYTHING WAS DONE TO WARN THE CITIZENS OF THE DANGER AND HOW TO BE PREPARED.

THE AFTERMATH WAS ALSO HANDLED VERY PROFESSIONALY.

PLEASE CONVEY MY APPRECIATION TO YOUR GREAT TEAM.

ON OCTOBER 31 MY CHURCH, RIMA RIDGE BAPTIST IN ORMOND BEACH, IS HAVING "INVITE A FRIEND TO CHURCH" SUNDAY. SO I THOUGHT I WOULD INVITE YOU AS MY FRIEND. I FIGURE YOU WOULD BE OUT AND ABOUT GETTING SUPPORT FOR YOUR BROTHER SO I THOUGHT IT WOULD NOT HURT TO ASK.

WE CONTINUE TO PRAY FOR YOU AND YOUR FAMILY.
GOD BLESS

Subject: GREAT JOB
Monday, September 20, 2004 7:58 p.m.
From: Jeb Bush

thank you Don. I will pass on to the scheduling
team. I have been amazed by the simple but profound
acts of kindness and compassion shown by our fellow
floridians.

Jeb

_____

*The overwhelming focus at this point was undoubtedly our
record-breaking and historic hurricane season. Other issues and
problems also needed to be addressed, though. About this time we
received bad news in the ongoing struggle to keep Terri Schiavo
alive. The Florida Supreme Court had ruled against Terri's Law.
This set off the sequence of events that would ultimately result in
her feeding tube being removed. This e-mail exchange was with
her brother.*

Subject: My sister Terri
Friday, September 24, 2004 2:54 p.m.
From: Bobby Schindler

I wish yesterday's decision would have been different,
nonetheless, I wanted you to know how grateful I am
for all that you have done to try and save mysister,
Terri's, life. My family will be forever indebted to
you for thecourage it took for you to intervene to
help.

I know that many in the media have been unfair and
mean-spirited with whatthey are writing and saying,
but throughout it all you have remained loyalwith
trying to get Terri back home where she belongs --
with my mom and dad.

Hopefully, because of your efforts defending Terri's law our family may nowhave an opportunity to be in a better position to save my sister's life.

Again, thank you Governor, you and your family will remain in my constant prayers.

Subject: Re: My sister Terri
Friday, September 24, 2004 3:11 p.m.
From: Jeb Bush

Thank you Bobby. What are your next steps.

Jeb

Terri's story continued into the next year.

———

Prayers were always welcomed.

Subject: You have our thoughts, prayers, and support
Friday, September 24, 2004 10:23 p.m.
From: Russell, Janet (wife), and Presley (daughter) Allen

Over the last few months Floridians have sustained significant property damage; and in some cases familial losses. As a consultant to the Intelligent Transportation Systems Section of the FDOT Traffic Engineering and Operations Office, I am also aware of the significant damages that the local and state government agencies have incurred. All of this, on top of many things that I'm sure I am not aware of, must be an unfathomable weight on your shoulders.

As a Christian, father, and republican, I am writing you to say, "Keep your head up, comfort all that you are surrounded by, and always remember to look to God for the right answers and direction."

Mr. Bush, I want you to know that our thoughts, prayers, and support are with you always, and that through faith, God's will will prevail.

Subject: You have our thoughts, prayers, and support
Saturday, September 25, 2004 7:18 a.m.
From: Jeb Bush

thank you Russell. I have found strength through God like never before these past weeks.…

jeb

———

Subject: [None]
Friday, September 24, 2004 11:08 p.m.
From: Jeanne Stephens

This hurricane season is incredulous! I hate that this one has my name. Have they ever had a Hurricane Jeb?

I heard you were in Bartow today. I would have loved to hear you speak but I had to work.

Keep up the good work. You are appreciated.

Subject: [None]
Saturday, September 25, 2004 7:21 a.m.
From: Jeb Bush

**no hurricane Jebs that I am aware of. Great ready for
Jeanne. She is now moving more inland.**

Jeb

———

*Nine days after Ivan, September 25, Jeanne came ashore as a
Category 3 hurricane near Port St. Lucie—almost exactly where
Hurricane Frances had made landfall three weeks earlier. Jeanne
killed four people and left millions without power for the third
time in a month. I was not amused to see one report state it was
hard in some places to determine what storm had caused what
damage. In some cases there was so much damage from previous
storms, there wasn't much left to damage. Yet Jeanne's final price
tag was put at $7.2 billion.*

*Sadly Jeanne is best known for triggering massive landslides
in Haiti. These killed more than three thousand people.*

Subject: hug from a democrat
Friday, September 24, 2004 11:52 a.m.
From: Barbara Czipri

I have to be perfectly honest and tell you upfront
that I have never been a great fan of yours, but
your leadership during this hurricane season has been
EXACTLY what Floridians need. Every day when I see you
at the 9 a.m. conference on TV, I wish that I could
reach through the screen to give you a BIG hug. I'm
sure you could use a lot of them about now. One thing
that we have very much in common is our love for this
state and the wonderful people who live here.

Yes, we will get through this. Above all, regardless
of our political views, we are Floridians first. I pray

that one positive outcome of the summer of 2004 will be that the upcoming legislative session will be free of the partisianship of recent years. We all need each other and we all need to work together in the best interests of our state. I hope that you will use your "bully pulpit" to help ensure that this happens.

In the meantime, please eat your veggies, get as much rest as you can, and get as many hugs as you can. We'll all pray together, and we WILL get through this--hopefully as stronger human beings than before, and more united as Floridians than before. Thanks for the great job that you're doing.

Subject: hug from a democrat
Monday, September 27, 2004 3:38 p.m.
From: Jeb Bush

thank you so much for your kind words. I really, really appreciate the sentiments expressed. This has been an emotional time for all of us. I have been truly inspired by people's patience, courage and resolve and I have been so saddened by the suffering of so many. Again, I appreciate the virtual hug.

Jeb Bush

———

Subject: Thank You.
Friday, September 24, 2004 5:49 p.m.
From: Grace Nicole

I just wanted to take a minute to say thank you for all of your hard work and effort through these last

weeks. I never do these things so I hope this doesn't
sound silly. You have just been doing a great job and
I am so glad that you are my Governor. There is no
other way to say it. I want you to know that there
are everyday people throughout the state who have
been comforted by your sincerity and presence in the
media.

I have found myself nervous and fearful as I watched
the news and within minutes of watching you on a news
brief have been calmed. I can't even explain it. You
just seem to make so much sense and frankly your more
to the point comments have often caused me to laugh
right out loud. Only moments before I had been scared
and upset and then you've got me laughing. Don't get
me wrong, I knew that you were being as serious as you
could be, but somehow I was amused right through my
fear by how much sense you make and how straight you
say it.

As I sit here waiting for yet another Hurricane
(Jeanne), I just wanted to thank you. I also want
to thank you for everything else you have been
doing that I don't get to see. I can't imagine how hard
you have been working. I want you to know
that you are appreciated. I am grateful for you and I
am grateful for the great men and women in your family.

Subject: FW: Thank You.
Monday, September 27, 2004 2:14 p.m.
From: Jeb Bush

**thank you Grace for your very kind and overly
generous email. I really appreciate your taking the
time to write.**

It has been a joy to be in service to the state
I love. I have been inspired by the courage and
compassion shown by so many. I am saddened by the
suffering as well.

Hang in there and stay safe!

Jeb

———

I took some time out after Jeanne to thank the best team in the history of emergencies. I don't think any other team had faced four storms in six weeks. They pulled through for our state and certainly for their governor. I started with the man at the top, Craig Fugate.

Subject: [None]
Tuesday, September 28, 2004 8:18 p.m.
From: Jeb Bush

words cannot express my deep felt admiration of how
you have handled your duties during these difficult
times. I am grateful beyond words.

Jeb

Raquel "Rocky" Rodriguez was my general counsel.

Subject: [None]
Tuesday, September 28, 2004 8:26 p.m.
From: Jeb Bush

I am lucky to have the best legal team in America. Thank
you for leading a tremendous team that could be doing other
stuff for a lot more pay and helping our state in ways that

are never acknowledged. Rocky, I am so fortunate to have you and your great lawyers doing such incredible work.

Jeb

Jill Bratina was the communications director.

Subject: [None]
Tuesday, September 28, 2004 8:31 p.m.
From: Jeb Bush

How can I express my appreciation to you and your team during these tough times? I can't really, but know that I am so appreciative of the great work of our communications team. You have been stellar and so have been all the unsong heroes. Onward,

Jeb

Pam Dana was head of the Office of Tourism, Trade, and Economic Development.

Subject: [None]
Tuesday, September 28, 2004 8:34 p.m.
From: Jeb Bush

thank you to you and your team for the hard work during these difficult times. I really appreciate the beyond the call efforts by all.

Jeb

I loved this exchange with my appointments secretary, Celeste Lewis. I called her "Red" because she was a self-proclaimed redneck from Quincy, Florida, one of the most Southern small towns in the Florida Panhandle. Her Southern drawl and quick wit always kept us laughing—even in the midst of the challenges.

Subject: [None]
Tuesday, September 28, 2004
From: Jeb Bush

thank you for your great work during these tough times. I appreciate you, Red!

Jeb Bush

Subject: [None]
Wednesday, September 29, 2004 7:49 a.m.
From: Celeste Lewis

You made me cry. I had to pull over--I just hope I'm doing the right thing.

I adore you and appreciate this e-mail more than you know.

Red

Subject: [None]
Wednesday, September 29, 2004 7:55 a.m.
From: Jeb Bush

Drive safely

———

The power of humor never ceases to amaze me. I loved this e-mail, which lifted my spirits at a time of never-ending exhaustion.

Subject: An amusing story for you
Tuesday, September 28, 2004 11:48 a.m.
From: Robert Olsen

My daughter Emily was watching the press conferences
with me prior to hurricane Jeanne making landfall
and she was asking typical three year old questions.
Is there another storm coming, Daddy? Why is it
coming? I fielded all of these questions as well as I
could, waiting for you to address the State. When you
stepped up to the podium, my daughter looked at me
and asked, "Is that the Storm Governor, Daddy?"

I laughed and said, "Honey, I think he feels that way."

Just thought you might appreciate this story.

Subject: An amusing story for you
Wednesday, September 29, 2004 7:16 p.m.
From: Jeb Bush

:) :)

Jeb

————

There were mounting issues over insurance claims that were
eventually resolved in a special legislative session in December.
This e-mail will give you just an idea of the kinds of complaints,
concerns, and accusations being made.

Subject: Hurricane help
Tuesday, October 26, 2004 10:45 a.m.
From: Bettie Cooney

Today's paper indicates some people with over $8K
deductible are trying to get tax money to revuild.
Anyone with over $8K deductible is
shoe stringing" and paying very low premiums
for insurance. Do you think it fair they do not
carry adequate insurance and stick the taxpayers
with their replacement costs I don't. Nor do I
believe in tax subsidized insurance for oceanfront
property--it is past time we make everyone realize
there are just some places you should not try to
build and live--if you still choose to, then tax
monies should not revbuild it for you!!! People
must begin taking responsibility for actions and
this is a good start.

Subject: Hurricane help
Tuesday, October 26, 2004 7:06 p.m.
From: Jeb Bush

what I think is unfair is to have multiple
deductibles for some and not for others. That is why
we are going to help in a thoughtful way the folks
that have been hit twice or three times.

Jeb Bush

———

Not many might have heard it, but there was a collective sigh of
relief that came from Florida when the hurricane season officially
ended on November 30. We had a lot of work to do. People were
still trying to put their lives back together, and that began with
their houses. The economy had taken a huge hit. The schools were
playing catch-up.
Too many people were mourning the losses of loved ones.

We also felt a little like the survivors of a shipwreck, though. The worst had happened, and we were still there.

I took the time to answer these questions for the St. Petersburg Times.

Subject: from St. Petersburg Times reporter
Wednesday, November 24, 2004 10:57 p.m.
From: Jamie Thompson

Hope all is well. Sorry to pester you over the holidays. We're working on a story about the end of hurricane season, featuring Max Mayfield, Wayne Sallade[101] and (hopefully) you. We're basically trying to revisit some of the key players during the season, hear how you made it through.

Do you have time to answer some questions via e-mail? (I didn't get a call back on my interview request, so thought I'd try you here.) If you have time to answer by Saturday, would be great.

1. What's the #1 thing you learned this hurricane season?

2. With the hurricanes and the election,[102] did you have any time to rest?

3. What, if anything, did you do to decompress after all the storms? Take a mini vacation? Rest at home?

---

101 Max Mayfield was director of the National Hurricane Center, and Wayne Sallade was head of emergency management in Charlotte County, Florida.
102 My brother was reelected president of the United States on November 2.

4. Are you planning a vacation to relax in coming weeks/months, and if so, where?

5. Did you have a long stretch, or several long stretches, when you weren't able to see your wife or talk to your kids? Did you do something special with them after the storms stopped coming? Are they understanding about your absence, or do they get annoyed?

6. Do you think hurricane amnesia is still a concern, or taken care of for the time being?

7. Can the state afford to have another active hurricane season next year?

8. For you, what was the worst moment during hurricane season?

9. The most dramatic moment?

10. Are you superstitious at all about the weather? Were you superstitious about the hurricanes?

11. Of all the places you visited to survey storm damage, can you recall one or two moments that stick in your mind? People you met, things you saw?

12. Did you hear any good jokes about Florida's hurricane season?

And anything else interesting you'd like to say about the season...

Thanks again!

Subject: from St. Petersburg Times reporter
Thursday, November 25, 2004 6:05 p.m.
From: Jeb Bush

1. I learned that whatever successes we have had, they are never final. We need to learn from the experiences of the hurricanes to be better prepared for next season and the ones after that.

2. Nope

3. I rest at home with my precious wife on Sundays and sometimes the whole weekend!

4. I will be going to Boca Grande with my family after Christmas.

5. My wife was very understanding and gave me comfort.

6. Hurricane amenesia is over for the short run!

7. Yes, we can withstand other storms but it would not be my first choice of options.

8. the worst part of each storm was meeting people in the special needs shelter that had nothing and were really hurting. We focused on helping them since they were the most vulnerable.

9. there were many.

10. nope

11. The shelters I visited in Port Charlotte, the Ft
Pierce and Pensacola come to mind. In addition,
meeting the County Commissioners of Santa Rosa at
the Emergency Operations Center the day after Ivan
hit shore was very emotional since three of them
had their homes destroyed but they were focused on
helping their consituents. To be honest with you,
I could give you a hundred stories of courage,
emotion, strength and compassion.

12. there were a few interenet jokes I saw that made
me laugh. the best was the one under the heading
"We have moved" that showed a map of the states and
Florida was tucked in between Montana and Idaho.

Jeb Bush

———

*Meanwhile I was trying to convince the state legislators we
needed a special session to deal with the multitude of issues facing
Floridians and our state after four major hurricanes in six weeks.
Our emergency teams had done incredible jobs in the immediate aftermath of each and every storm. In every natural disaster, though, it was sometimes the long-term problems that were
the most overwhelming. How could we help people get their lives
back to where they had been before Charley?*

Subject: Re: Special Session
Monday, November 29, 2004 8:24 a.m.
From Lisa Perrone

I apologize for being a " pest" but is there going
to be a special session dealing with the hurricane
issues?...

I hope you and your family had a wonderful holiday. I know mine did as we had a lot to be thankful for this year.

Subject: Special Session fup
Monday, November 29, 2004 8:41 a.m.
From: Jeb Bush

We are still trying to get the leadership of the Legislature to agree to the need for this. It is hard to get data from the insurance companies for the multiple deductible issue but we are pressing hard.

Subject: Special Session fup
Tuesday, November 30, 2004 12:57 p.m.
From: Lisa Perrone

Please, do not give up on these ideas/proposals. We all want help. I am asked almost daily if I know anything new or if Tallahassee is doing anything about the hurricane issues. There is still a need for relief.

People have had to go back to work, children have gone back to school, people have had to move forward with their lives but the daily issues of how to get your home fixed whether it is the financial end or the contractor end, still exists. Many people are just too tired and frustrated to keep fighting with the insurance companies or contractors. They are giving up because they do not see the light at the end of the tunnel. It should not be this difficult. I know many, including myself, are afraid they will not have their homes repaired by next hurricane season. Never mind the people who were renters and have been kicked out of their dwellings and cannot find another place to live. The list of issues continues. Please do not give up on this.

Subject: Re: RE: Special Session fup
Tuesday, November 30, 2004 1:48 p.m.
From: Jeb Bush

I will not give up.

Jeb

———

Subject: hurricane assistance
Friday, December 3, 2004 3:28 p.m.
From: Steve Windhaus

Jeb, I have just read the column in today's local paper about your initiative to help victims of insurance deductibles. However, I am a little confused. The column didn't clearly explain this initiative, at least as it relates to someone like me.

I had two hurricanes, two deductibles, total damages (from Frances and Jeanne) of about $12,000, total deductibles of $16,712 and all the costs to repair will be mine to personally finance.

Business has picked up for my firm in the last month, and the bills are getting paid. It is such a relief (for the first time since August), but the cash flow is insufficient to begin serious repairs.

The good news is that what repairs I have made are about 30% of what State Farm estimated would be required. In the end, with $2,000 I could probably repair everything on my own. I have come to realize the greatest cost factor is labor, but I am quite capable of dealing with this, with the help of some very good friends.

Given that scenario, how would your initiative benefit someone like me?

Subject: hurricane assistance
Friday, December 3, 2004 7:39 p.m.
From: Jeb Bush

Our proposal to the legislature is to pay for amounts above the first deductible (minus a $250 amount) with a cap of $10,000. So I guess you would pay your first deductible, plus $250 and we would pay the rest. Make sure your views are known to your elected officials in the legislature. I am glad the business is picking up.

Jeb

———

The state legislature did go into special session in mid-December and passed some very key measures that went a long way in helping Floridians get back on their feet.

- *A reimbursement of up to $10,000 for the second insurance deductible because of multiple storms and up to $20,000 if one had to pay three or more deductibles.*
- *Property tax rebates of up to $1,500 to those whose homes the storms destroyed.*

- *An approved $68 million to restore beaches and dune systems the storms eroded, which was key to the tourism industry.*

Much to my delight, the legislators also fixed the pre-K education bill to make it worthy of all four-year-olds in Florida and something I could sign. The bill passed was essentially a voucher program that provided parents with a wide variety of education choices for their little ones.

Linda Kleindienst of the Sun-Sentinel *asked me what I thought.*

Subject: Your reaction to the special session
Thursday, December 16, 2004 11:02 a.m.
From: Linda Kleindienst

In writing a story about how this week's session has gone, I'd like to get a reaction from you on how smooth it has been and how Speaker Bense and President Lee[103] have worked together.

Are you relieved to be dealing with legislative leaders who have left the rancor of the past several years behind - and does this give you hope for smoother sailing during your last two years as governor? And are you now satisfied with the pre-K bill?

Thanks for any reply you can send.

Subject: Your reaction to the special session
Thursday, December 16, 2004 9:59 p.m.
From: Jeb Bush

---

103   State Senator Tom Lee was president of the Senate, and State Representative Allan Bense was speaker of the House.

They did a great job. The session was collegial. They got the work done. They did it on time. Floridians will benefit greatly and I am very thankful.

Jeb

PS the Pre K bill is a fine piece of legislation and I will proudly sign it into law. It fulfilled my suggestions in the veto letter and we will get to work.

———

Eleven years later it still does not seem possible that four major storms slammed into our state in six weeks. They did, though, and we got through it.

How bad was it?

- *Total estimated damage by November 30 was $42 billion. To put that in perspective, the state budget for the entire year—to educate our children, fund social services programs, keep our citizens safe, build and maintain roads and bridges, maintain prisons, take care of parkland, and so much more—was $57.3 billion. Four hurricanes came dangerously close to matching that in just six weeks.*
- *Floridians filed 1.66 million insurance claims to reclaim $20.9 billion in insured losses.*
- *Seven hundred thousand homes were damaged or destroyed.*
- *More than 140,000 volunteers donated six million hours. They served fourteen million meals and delivered twenty-seven million bottles of water and more than a million bags of ice.*
- *A state of emergency was declared in every single county in Florida at least once.*

- *Every single school in Florida was closed at least one day.*
- *Hurricane Ivan is number six on the list of costliest Atlantic hurricanes; Charley is number eight; Frances is number ten; Jeanne is number thirteen.*
- *My favorite statistic is the $10.4 million in donations that poured into the Florida Hurricane Relief Fund that I set up after Charley. The money came from all over the United States and the world—from individuals and corporations. I wish I could list them all. The smallest donation was from a little girl who emptied her piggy bank and sent seventy cents. It counted as much as the generous corporations who sent us millions. All these years later, I am still grateful.*

As any Floridian would tell you, though, it is not the statistics we remembered at the end of the day but the stories of courage, generosity, and perseverance.

All these years later, I wish I had kept a journal to document all that happened during those six weeks. Many of the memories are seared into my brain, though.

- *The sight of the eighteen-wheeler dangling over the side of the collapsed bridge on Interstate 10 in Pensacola, which split the community in half. (We managed to put up a temporary bridge in just seventeen days.)*
- *The emergency operations center in Charlotte County, which had lost its roof but where people were still working.*
- *The chaos of the shelters where people desperately asked for help finding out about their loved ones, homes, or pets. We tried to help every single one at least find answers to their questions—no matter how bad the answers were. In all cases we gave out hugs.*
- *Many bumpy helicopter rides through gathering or passing storms as we tried to get to the scene of the latest devastation as quickly as possible. I am surprised the staff hung in there, but they all did.*

- *How grateful I was when the president of the United States came down to help give out water and hugs.*
- *Making sure people could vote in the primary election, which was less than three weeks after Charley. This was despite most of the polling places in three counties having been destroyed. We got it done, though.*
- *The woman in Brevard County who had a generator, so she got up at 4:00 a.m. every day to make enough coffee to fill twenty thermoses. She then left them on the doorsteps of her neighbors so they could at least start their days with hot cups of coffee.*

One of my happier moments was attending the annual football showdown between Port Charlotte and Charlotte High Schools. It is a fierce rivalry, and there is no love lost between the schools or teams. Peace River draws the battle line.

In 2004 Charley took out Charlotte High School (located in Punta Gorda), so all the students were attending Port Charlotte High School in split shifts. The twenty-fourth edition of "The Rumble by the River" was played October 30 in a stadium rimmed by wind-torn buildings and huge mounds of rubble. I flipped the coin to start the game, sat with fans from both teams, and wore a T-shirt that said, "Divided by a river and united by a storm." Yes. The tears flowed.

Here are some excerpts from my remarks on the last day of the hurricane season.

As we braced for each storm, I asked for your attention, your patience, and prayers. As we move forward, I ask that we hold on to the generosity of spirit, the creative collaboration, and the compassionate character that have defined our state through this trying season....

We each carry images from the storms that will stay with us forever. I have many from my travels around the state. There's the woman in Barefoot Bay who wrapped her arms around me because she needed a hug. She'd lost everything and was sorting her life out in a shelter. She was wearing a Salvation Army T-shirt and told me about the volunteer work she was doing with that organization to help other storm victims despite her own situation.

At a community center, I spoke with a tiny, elderly woman with a single foam curler on the top her forehead. She introduced me to her daughter, also a senior citizen, who had come to Florida to help her mom repair her home and put her life back together.

In Santa Rose County, I remember the tears in the eyes of a local official who had lost everything. His tears weren't for himself but for the pain of his friends and neighbors who had evacuated to safety and had not seen the damage Ivan had left behind. He didn't have the words to describe the devastation, and he wept at the heartbreak he knew would find them and hundreds of others when they returned to homes that didn't exist anymore....

I have never been prouder to be governor of Florida. It has been a gift of extreme privilege to witness the strength of so many people who look beyond the rubble with hope and resolve and who extend hands to help others share that view.

I thank you all for your tenacity, determination, hard work, and faith.

We are redefining Florida's future as a place of unlimited promise created by the strength of seventeen million people who are forever connected by this experience.

God bless the great state of Florida.

Chapter 7

"I Don't Know What Lame Duck Means."

This is the not the time for timid tweaks to the status quo. This is the time for bold, brave ideas in Florida that will shape our future and define us as dreamers, builders, and problem solvers.

—State of the State Address, March 8, 2005

As difficult as 2004 had been for Floridians, a natural disaster of historic proportions shocked and grieved the world before the year ended.

On December 26 an earthquake in the Indian Ocean triggered a series of tsunamis along the coastlines that sent waves of more than one hundred feet slamming into the shore. Before it was over, 230,000 people in fourteen countries died. Indonesia was hardest hit, followed by Sri Lanka, India, and Thailand. My brother asked Secretary of State Colin Powell and me to head up a US delegation to assess the damages and begin organizing the American relief effort.

I thought I had seen everything after Charley, Frances, Ivan, and Jeanne, but I was not prepared for what we found. Entire towns were flattened, and many people who lived there had disappeared. Secretary Powell, who had seen the aftermath of war, felt the same. I was honored to go, represent my country and the American people, and let the people living in the countries hit by the tsunami know America stood with them. I came home humbled and grateful—especially to be an American and the governor of the great state of Florida.

More than ever I was ready to go back to work to make our state even better. By this point I had a clock on my desk that counted down the days until my governorship was over. I wanted to make every last second I had to serve the people of Florida count. The clock was ticking.

A top priority for 2005 was Medicaid reform. The state-federal partnership program designed to provide health care for the poor, elderly, and disabled was in desperate need of an overhaul. Runaway costs were threatening to bankrupt the system. Combined federal and state spending had grown by 112 percent since 1999, and a disastrous maze of paperwork and red tape had made navigating the system nearly impossible for both patients and doctors. There were no incentives to get people well or keep them that way.

My plan gave participants and providers more choices and flexibility—including opting out of Medicaid—all of which would provide better care at reduced costs. I had support from at least one state senator.

Subject: [None]
Tuesday, January 11, 2005 10:06 a.m.
From: Ken Pruitt

I am so proud of your efforts on Medicaid - I don't know when you found the time to formulate it, but it sounds awesome.

Subject: [None]
Tuesday, January 11, 2005 7:53 p.m.
From: Jeb Bush

Thank you Ken. The kudos go to the OPB team and Alan Levine and the Medicaid folks. The Senate staff has been helpful as well. Much work to do.

Jeb

————

Support came from another important source—Bob Sharpe, president and CEO of the Florida Council for Community Mental Health.

Subject: Medicaid Reform
Wednesday, January 12, 2005 11:39 a.m.
From: Bob Sharpe

Congratulations on a bold, thoughtful, 'outside of the box' proposal. Very well articulated. We look forward to working with you and the Agency on the details of Medicaid reform related to people with disabilities.

Subject: Medicaid Reform
Wednesday, January 12, 2005 7:26 p.m.
From: Jeb Bush

thank you bob. I would love to have your suggestions for true reform.

Jeb

————

I sent this note to Alan Levine; Deputy Chief of Staff Carol Gormley, whose portfolio included overseeing health-care agencies; and Nina Oviedo in our Washington, DC, office.

Subject: [None]
Tuesday, January 11, 2005 8:35 p.m.
From: Jeb Bush

great work on the rollout today. This is the beginning but we are off to a good start. thank you and to your teams.

Jeb

Subject: [None]
Tuesday, January 11, 2005 10:58 p.m.
From: Alan Levine

Thank you for the confidence you have placed in your team.

I have never felt more of a purpose, and consider myself fortunate to be working alongside such great people.

Thank you, Governor.

———

About this time Florida received terrific news. Moody's Investors Service upgraded our bond rating from Aa2 to Aa1. This made us only the eleventh state in the nation to reach that level. The upgrade was not only a testament to our fiscal discipline and good health but would mean a real cost savings to the state (and thus to taxpayers) through lower interest expenses. I was ecstatic and often teased about my efforts to prod the media into sharing my excitement. This note of congratulations came from Marvin Dejean, vice president of business development for Minority Development & Empowerment, Inc.

Subject: GOVERNOR BUSH CELEBRATES RATINGS UPGRADE BY MOODY'S
INVESTORS SERVICE
Thursday, January 13, 2005 12:37 p.m.
From: Marvin Dejean

Please allow me to congratulate you on your
sound fiscal policies. Your leadership and strong
commitment to sound policies are the main reason
that we South Floridians continue to enjoy a great
lifestyle while other states struggled through
the recession. You make the rest of us fiscal
conservatives proud to live in the State. Keep up
the good work.

Subject: GOVERNOR BUSH CELEBRATES RATINGS UPGRADE BY MOODY'S
INVESTORS SERVICE
Saturday, January 15, 2005 3:58 p.m.
From: Jeb Bush

Thank you marvin!

jeb

———

It was year seven of my governorship, and we were still trying to perfect the state website. Simone Marstiller, who played a variety of roles in my administration, was state chief information officer at the time.

Subject: MyFlorida.com in Spanish
Wednesday, January 26, 2005 9:32 a.m.
From: Simone Marstiller

Governor, the MyFlorida.com team has been working on a project to translate the web site into Spanish. The translation's done and ready to go live. But, before doing so, I wanted to give you the opportunity to tool around the site. Please let me know what you think.

Click on the following link to get to the test site: http://216.251.249.130/myfl/enes/?24;http://www.myflorida.com

When we go live it will be http://www.espanol.myflorida.com

Subject: MyFlorida.com in Spanish
Wednesday, January 26, 2005 10:02 p.m.
From: Jeb Bush

all of the back pages are in English. what is the benefit? How would this work? will there be a spanish box for people to see the first page?

Jeb

———

Even when you are confident you are on the right path, it's nice to get validation from an organization you respect. In this case it was the Wall Street Journal.

Subject: Kudos on the Medicaid article in the Wall St. Journal!
Wednesday, February 2, 2005 9:33 a.m.
From: John Noble

Source: The Wall Street Journal
Date: February 02, 2005
Section: REVIEW & OUTLOOK (Editorial)
Page: A14

"All 50 states agree: Medicaid, the federal-state partnership to provide health care for the poor, is a fiscal and moral mess. The question is, what are our politicians going to do about it?

"By far the most promising answer to date comes from Florida, where Governor Jeb Bush is proposing a radical restructuring of the program that serves 2.2 million low-income people at an expected cost this year of $14.7 billion. The aim is twofold -- to provide incentives for better service by putting more choice in the hands of the consumer and to rein in the rate of growth in spending.

"If it succeeds, the Sunshine State's vision could serve as a template for reforms in other states. And in the best case, it could lead to a remaking of Medicaid in the same way that reforms in the early 1990s in Wisconsin and elsewhere paved the way for an historic and hugely successful national welfare reform."

Subject: Kudos on the Medicaid article in the Wall St. Journal!
Wednesday, February 2, 2005 10:28 a.m.
From: Jeb Bush

Thanks

Jeb Bush

———

I sent this note to Senate President Tom Lee along with a long e-mail exchange between Alan Levine and a newspaper reporter about the Medicaid reform bill. Alan had done an outstanding job clarifying some of the misconceptions about the bill. I needed Senator Lee on board if we were going to get the bill passed.

Subject: myths vs. realities
Wednesday, February 2, 2005 8:09 p.m.
From: Jeb Bush

If we work together, we will improve health care outcomes, fix costs and be a leader in the country. If we blink, we will be part of the slow steady decline of government's relationship with the people we serve.

Jeb

———

Earlier in February I had led a delegation of senior business and retired military leaders to Washington to meet with top Pentagon officials. They argued that none of Florida's military bases should be closed. The Department of Defense was in the final stages of its federal Base Realignment and Closure (BRAC) process. Protecting our state's twenty-one military installations was one of my top economic priorities.

Subject: Thanks
Wednesday, February 16, 2005 8:20 a.m.
From: Dianne

Thanks for trying to keep our military bases and
the ships here in FL. Most of us retiree's try to
move close to a base where we can at least get our
benefits. Me, I just love the military, the uniforms,
the ships, what they do for our country. So thanks
for fighting to keep our bases and ships here. I
learned one thing that the bigger the military
strength the longer we stay No. 1. The less we have
the more chance we have of war on our land. Americans
born here have no idea what seeing a barbed wire
fence across the street, machine guns in banks,
stores, airports and phones tapped, also your dollars
in the bank you can only with draw so much or they
ask questions. They take too much for granted.

Subject: Thanks
Thursday, February 17, 2005 6:41 a.m.
From: Jeb Bush

we will fight on.

jeb

———

*During my governorship I signed many pieces of legislation into
law to strengthen the Second Amendment rights of law-abiding
gun owners. I am proud to have earned an A-plus rating from the
National Rifle Association.*

*This e-mail exchange with Marion Hammer—the chief lob-
byist for the NRA in Florida—was about pending legislation*

regarding what is popularly known as a stand-your-ground law. The Florida law later became famous during the Trayvon Martin/George Zimmerman trial. The media wrongly fixated on this law, as Zimmerman argued self-defense—not stand-your-ground law—at his trial. Stand-your-ground law is important. It enables people, including gun owners, to stand their ground and defend themselves without obligation to flee attackers.

Subject: NRA backed bill makes law favor victims NOT criminals
Tuesday, February 22, 2005 11:20 a.m.
From: Marion Hammer

The Attorney General has given us a letter of support for the bill. The Police Benevolent Association has given us a strong letter of support for the bill. The Police Chiefs are supporting the bill and are preparing a letter of support. The Sheriffs have given us a letter saying they are not opposed to the bill. The State Attorneys have signed off on the bill. A survey by a Pensacola TV station shows 89% of the people support the bill.

There are currently 25 Senate sponsors (and growing). (Including Senators Lawson, Bullard, Campbell & Smith)

There are current 61 House sponsors (and growing). (including Reps. Chris Smith, Greenstein, Sands, Taylor, Stansel, Kendrick, McInvale)

I am attaching a copy of the amended version of the bill that all of the law enforcement groups have signed off on.

Further, I will also email you a copy of my testimony on the bill from the Senate Criminal Justice Committee where it passed UNANIMOUSLY (8-0) (Including Senators Ron Klein and Fredericka Wilson)

This is a strong bipartisan bill with which I'm sure you will have no problem.

Subject: NRA backed bill makes law favor victims NOT criminals
Tuesday, February 22, 2005 5:16 p.m.
From: Jeb Bush

Thank you for writing. It is always better to not have any surprises. thank you for passing on this information.

Jeb

Seriously? I felt as if I was just getting started!

Subject: requesting a definition
Wednesday, February 23, 2005 9:36 a.m.
From: Joe Follick

this is Joe Follick with the New York Times Florida papers. My editors asked for the "lame duck" story. I was interested in how you would define "lame duck?"

Thanks for your time, Joe

Subject: requesting a definition
Thursday, February 24, 2005 7:01 a.m.
From: Jeb Bush

I don't know what lame duck means.

Jeb

———

On February 24 Lieutenant Governor Toni Jennings and I announced the next step in our mission to overhaul education in Florida. The newest reform bill, designed to be a follow-up to the A+ education plan, focused mainly on reading and teachers. Included in the bill were provisions to ensure the state maintained the priority of early literacy. After all, if children can't read, they will not have chances for success. It also included options to increase teachers' salaries and provide better training opportunities. The increases in teachers' pay were tied to successfully changing the constitutionally mandated caps on classroom sizes. I felt strongly that the billions the state was being forced to spend on shrinking classroom sizes would be better spent on teacher salaries. I sent this note to Deputy Chief of Staff Patricia Levesque, who was the lead education adviser on my staff.

Subject: [None]
Thursday, February 24, 2005 7:58 a.m.
From: Jeb Bush

Great work on a plus plus. I am revved up. Thank you for all you do.

Jeb

———

About this time I ran into Grover Norquist. Palm Beach Post *reporter Shirish Dáte then inquired about this. Grover and I have an interesting relationship. Even though I never signed his tax pledge during any of my campaigns for the governorship, he still praised my record of cutting taxes and limiting the size of government. Grover even called me the best governor in America and said he used my record to shame other governors. We saw eye to eye on the need for limited government and lower taxes in 2005. We still do today, but I am not going to sign any pledge. My commitment to lower taxes is resolute, and my record of fighting for taxpayers speaks for itself.*

Subject: grover
Thursday, February 24, 2005 3:54 p.m.
From: S.V. Dáte

So what did you and Mr. Norquist talk about?

Subject: grover
Thursday, February 24, 2005 4:11 p.m.
From: Jeb Bush

Freedom and limited government.

Jeb

———

Standard & Poor's Ratings Services upgraded Florida's general obligation debt rating from AA+ to AAA based on the state's conservative financial and budget management practices, budget reserves, and economic trends. Most e-mails on the topic contained one word: "awesome." This article in the Tallahassee Democrat *said it all.*

State bond rating increases to AAA
By Nancy Cook Lauer
DEMOCRAT CAPITOL BUREAU CHIEF

Florida hit the "gold standard" for the first time
Friday, when Standard & Poor's Ratings Services
raised its rating of state bonds to AAA.

This is good news for taxpayers and investors alike,
said Ben Watkins, director of the state Division of
Bond Finance. Investors who hold state bonds will see
their value increase, and taxpayers will save tens of
millions in interest payments on state debt in the
coming decade.

"We've never had a triple-A before,"
Watkins said. "We've finally broken through the glass
ceiling, as it were. We're the gold standard."

Subject: Florida's Bond Rating Upgraded
Monday, February 28, 2005 4:43 p.m.
From: David Biddulph

Today's WSJ (page C-5) states that due to
conservative fiscal management, the state's general
obligation bonds have been upgraded by S&P to AAA.

Do you think the other team would have been inclined
to cut taxes, control spending and improve a states
credit standing while recovering from a "perfect
storm"?

Nice going.

```
Subject: Florida's Bond Rating Upgraded
Monday, February 28, 2005 5:13 p.m.
From: Jeb Bush
```

```
thank you David. No, I don't think so!
```

```
Jeb
```

———

One of the most difficult and saddest chapters of my governorship was coming to a close as the family of Terri Schiavo was very close to running out of legal options, as was I in my support of their efforts. A judge ruled her feeding tube should be removed by 1:00 p.m. on March 18. A flurry of legal and legislative activity took place for a few weeks—including in Washington, where Congress passed a bipartisan habeas corpus law (with support from two notable Democratic senators, Barack Obama and Hillary Clinton) to allow Terri's family to seek federal court review. At one point civil-rights activist Jesse Jackson even came to Tallahassee to support efforts for a bill to save Terri. We met for about thirty minutes in my office.

The most heated part of the court battle took place on March 23. The Department of Children and Families filed a petition to intervene in Terri's case to investigate allegations of abuse and failure of her guardian to provide adequate medical care and to take protective custody of Terri. The sworn declaration of a prominent neurologist, Dr. William Cheshire, supported the petition. He concluded after observing Terri (her husband refused to permit a full examination) and reviewing the records of her care that there was sufficient doubt about her diagnosis, and her nutrition and hydration in good conscience could not be withdrawn. The judge denied the petition. At a tense press conference that afternoon, I was asked if my goal was to take protective custody of Terri. I asked my general counsel, Rocky Rodriguez, to step up to the podium. "DCF could take protective custody of Ms. Schiavo. I'll leave it at that," she said.

DCF Secretary Lucy Hadi added that DCF's goal was to stabilize her. "We don't have immediate plans to take protective custody of Terri Schiavo."

Attorneys for Michael Schindler, Terri's husband, immediately ran to court to ask the judge to prohibit DCF from taking any action. The judge entered a restraining order prohibiting DCF or anyone else (presumably me) under penalty of contempt from taking custody of her or attempting to reinsert her feeding tube. This effectively ended our ability to take action unless an appellate court reversed the order, but all our appellate efforts also were rejected.

Thousands of calls from people begging me to do more flooded our offices, and I received more e-mails in March 2005 than any other month of my governorship—more than sixteen thousand. The courts had spoken, though. There was nothing more we could do. At the end of the day, I knew in my heart I had done absolutely everything I could to save Terri.

I would like to share a very small sampling of some of the incoming e-mails—only to demonstrate how hot the passions were on both sides of this issue.

Subject: Hello from Boca
Thursday, March 17, 2005 11:19 p.m.
From: Bonnie McGee

This is just my opinion....

I would like to see a video shot of Terry Shivo (?sp)
taken "today". I need to see her in a vegetative
state, and I am sure most Americans do, to determine
whether to pull her feeding tube. I was a registered
nurse, and have seen it all. IF, it were me in a coma
or vegetative state I would expect my son to PULL THE
PLUG, TUBE, or whatever to end my life with dignity!!

You need to put your foot down Jeb. You wouldn't want that, and am sure you would instruct George P. and Nichole to fulfill your wish to stop all heroics. I need to see her in her present state to confirm in my mind that she really has no life.

Okay. I said what I have been holding in for to long. Hope you are not upset with me, nor think I am evil. Just calling a spade, a spade.

By the way, I am going to miss you when you have to leave office. Am I going to be able to keep in touch with you by email when your term is over??? I have really enjoyed our brief emails.

———

This e-mail came from Poland.

Subject: Poland asks you to spare Terri Schiavo's life
Sunday, March 20, 2005 1:26 p.m.
From: Anna Foltanska

We thank you for standing up for Terri but words are not enough. You have the power to save her. Please, act immediately. The world is watching.

———

Subject: Teri
Friday, March 25, 2005 12:11 p.m.
From: Robert Cowart

As I know that you want what is best for our state and it's residents, but I can not sit back

and watch you try and step in on such a personal
family matter. I respectfully ask you to please
stop any interference and let her husband do what
was asked by his wife. I voted for you as well as
President Bush but I must say that if our govenor
continues to try and resolve a family matter then
this will be the last time I will ever support
any member of the bush family in any politcal
election.

I ask you to let her imeadiate family (husband) make
these decisions, not our government.

Thank you and god bless.

———

Subject: Terri Schiavo
Saturday, March 26, 2005 1:44 a.m.
From: CAROLE KAYLOR

I am very happy to see your efforts to intervene in
Terri's case. I admire your strength of character to
take this stance. Please

Know that you are in my prayers. I ask that you
continue your efforts to protect people that are in
this state. From what I have seen of Terri online and
on television, she is not a patient in a persistent
vegetative state. I am a nurse who has cared for
patients who are similar to Terri, and they all
brought joy in my life. This is not a "religious"
issue, it is one of humaneness and compassion. The
fact that this case has been reduced to it's current
state tells me that our society is in a decline. I
hope we can recover.

———

Subject: Terry Shiavo
Tuesday, March 29, 2005 3:38 p.m.
From: Wendy Snow

We appreciate all we've heard about your leadership
and pray that God continues to grant you wisdom in
your position as Governor of Florida. We're praying for
Terry Shiavo and her family during this difficult time.

Our culture is definitely on a downward spiral when
we allow someone who is mentally handicapped to be
systematically killed via starvation. If there is
anything you can do within your powers as Govenor,
please make a difference in the life of this lady by
allowing her to have food and water.

"If we are going to err let it be on the side of
life"

Thank you for your work on behalf of the people of
Florida. May your number increase.

———

*Terri died on March 31. What I said ten years ago is still in my
heart.*

    Statement by
    GOVERNOR JEB BUSH
    Regarding the death of Terri Schiavo

    After an extraordinarily difficult and tragic
    journey, Terri Schiavo is at rest. Columba and I
    offer our condolences to Mr. and Mrs. Schindler,

Bobby Schindler, Suzanne Vitadamo, and to all those who offered their prayers and support to Terri's family over these past weeks, months, and years. These prayers were not in vain.

Many across our state and around the world are deeply grieved by the way Terri died. I feel that grief very sharply as well. I remain convinced, however, that Terri's death is a window through which we can see the many issues left unresolved in our families and in our society. For that, we can be thankful for all that the life of Terri Schiavo has taught us.

I still firmly believe that human life is a gift and a mystery and that its mystery is most evident at its beginning and ending. May all of us whose hearts were moved during the life of Terri Schiavo grow in wisdom at its ending.

———

While Terri's saga weighed heavily on my heart and mind during the last few weeks of March, the usual business of governing went on. I made time to chide Mike Thomas at the Orlando Sentinel *for writing what I felt was a misleading column about my Medicaid reform proposals. I might add that one reason politicians are scared to death to overhaul entitlement programs—most of which need reforming to make them fiscally sound—is that every time someone mentions the word "reform," the media claims the programs are being cut and recipients will lose benefits. This is not only not true; it's irresponsible, dangerous, and a major reason the nation is now $18 trillion in debt.*

Subject: [None]
Sunday, March 20, 2005 3:18 p.m.
From: Jeb Bush

So I am reading your column. You used the word
cut quite a bit. Mike, there is no proposed cut
in the Medicaid budget. Only curbs in the growth.
Our proposal calls close to two billion dollars
more spending next year over this year. that is an
increase, not a cut. I hope you are having a great
sunday. Go Gators.

Jeb

————

*We also got great news about Florida's employment rate. Florida
was leading the nation in job creation. Donna Arduin weighed in
from California, where she was now budget director for Governor
Arnold Schwarzenegger.*

**Subject: GOVERNOR BUSH HERALDS FLORIDA'S STRONG
EMPLOYMENT REPORT**
Friday, March 25, 2005 10:50 a.m.
From: Donna Arduin

Employment growth, rating upgrades…good thing you cut
taxes and did not raise them!

GOVERNOR BUSH HERALDS FLORIDA'S STRONG EMPLOYMENT
REPORT

"TALLAHASSEE - Governor Jeb Bush today praised the
most recent employment report, highlighting that
Florida once again leads the nation in job creation.
Statistics released today by the Agency for Workforce
Innovation show Florida added 257,300 jobs (seasonally
adjusted) from February 2004 to February 2005.
Florida's unemployment rate was 4.5 percent, nearly a
full percentage point below the national rate."

**Subject: GOVERNOR BUSH HERALDS FLORIDA'S STRONG
EMPLOYMENT REPORT**
Friday, March 25, 2005 12:14 p.m.
From: Jeb Bush

:)

———

When a soldier from Florida was killed in combat, I called the family. I made this call on the day before Terri died and got this e-mail from his wife.

Subject: Thanks for sympathy about my husband
Wednesday, March 30, 2005 11:56 p.m.
From: Dawn Armstrong

I want to thank you for the time you took out of your busy day to express your sorrow for the loss of my husband, SSG Robert Armstrong. I fear that I may have not come across right when I said that I tried to take care of him and then the Army got him. I meant that my turn at taking care of him was transferred temporarily to the Army taking care of him. What a stupid way I chose to say that.

I hope it came across to you, from my heart, how much Robert loved serving America and also Florida in all the efforts that you have spearheaded during devastating hurricanes and such events.

I'm so devastated at losing his precious mind, body and soul in my presence, that I'm almost too exhausted to speak what I truly feel. I've long appreciated all you do as Governor, and want you to know that, in spite my selfish feelings in wanting

Robert back, I know he died doing exactly what he wanted to be doing. He believes fully in the war against terror and felt good about playing a role in that.

Subject: Thanks for sympathy about my husband
Thursday, March 31, 2005 6:29 a.m.
From: Jeb Bush

Bless you, Dawn. Please let me know if I can be of assistance to you.

Jeb Bush

Subject: Thanks for sympathy about my husband
Thursday, March 31, 2005 12:31 p.m.
From: Dawn Armstrong

Thank you so much. You are a comfort, and knowing where Rob is now is also a comfort.

I will be deriving strength from many sources -- one source of strength is from you, Governor. We have witnessed your steadfastness in the face of many challenges for a very long time now, since your first campaign for Governor. I still have the videotapes of your early debates and feel the stirring of pride and amazement at how you handled that old salt, Governor Lawton Chiles. I was actually pumping my hand with "Yes, Yes" while watching in wonder at your strengths, and the amazement has never stopped through all the hurricanes, conflicts and battles that have been brought your way.

May God grant us all the peace we so long for, in His perfect timing. Take care. I'll be praying for you and your administration.

Subject: Thanks for sympathy about my husband
Thursday, March 31, 2005 8:59 p.m.
From: Jeb Bush

you are making me cry. Maybe it is the day with Terri's death. I don't know but the fact that you would write what you did given your loss, makes me thank God Almighty that there are people like yourself. I am nothing.

Let me know how I can ever be of help to you and your family.

Jeb

———

As we got into April, we also got into the heart of the legislative session. This e-mail exchange concerned a bill that would fill a major gap in medical safety standards by requiring regulation of abortion clinics to improve patient safety. After years of trying, we finally got the bill passed this session.

Subject: [None]
Wednesday, April 6, 2005 5:55 p.m.
From: Paula Dockery

Thank you for your sweet note. I'm so relieved we got it out of committee.

Paula

I'm heading up to the 22nd floor for the Gator reception. Want to come?

Subject: [None]
Wednesday, April 6, 2005 8:50 p.m.
From: Jeb Bush

believe it or not I hiccuped again and missed telling you that thousands of pro choice and pro life women will be protected by your leadership. I am so appreciative. It breaks my heart that we have 90,000 abortions that occur each year in Florida. that is roughly one third of all live births in our state and women have no protections with our current laws. Our bill will do much to help to deal with the trauma of losing a child without the medical complications.

thank you. We will keep working with you to get it to the floor and make it law.

Jeb

———

Of course, I was always pushing tort reform and encouraging our friends in the legislature such as Representative Don Brown.

Subject: Tort Reform
Friday, April 8, 2005 2:39 p.m.
From: Donald Brown

Nationally, total tort costs today exceed $200 Billion annually, or more than 2% of America's Gross Domestic Product — a significantly higher percentage than in any other developed nation.

Trial lawyers are now hauling in fees that can range as high as an astounding $30,000. an hour, turning some plaintiff's attorneys into overnight Billionaires.

Tort Reform is need NOW!! ***Please join me in co-sponsoring HB 1513***.

If we don't do tort reform now you might just find yourself being sued by **Santa Claus**.

Subject: Tort Reform
Friday, April 8, 2005 3:30 p.m.
From: Jeb Bush

count me in! Joint and several and the rest.

Jeb

———

On February 24 a horrific crime focused attention on the need to protect our children from predators. A convicted sex offender abducted Jessica Lunsford, age nine, from her home in Homosassa. He held her captive, raped her, and murdered her. A bill had already been introduced to protect other children from similar fates.

Subject: bracelets
Wednesday, April 13, 2005 10:57 p.m.
From: Sherry McCalin

As a teacher, mom and Republican citizen with 6 registered Republican voters living in my household, I implore you to protect the children of this state by starting legislation requiring location bracelets for released sex offenders. Jessica Lunsford would be alive today if we had a law like this in place.

Subject: bracelets
Friday, April 15, 2005 6:51 a.m.
From: Jeb Bush

thank you. the Jessica Lunsford bill is working its way through the legislature and I will sign it into law.

Jeb Bush

––––––

Subject: repeat sexual offenders
Sunday, April 17, 2005 10:39 p.m.
From: Jeff Burke

Please help push legislation that would keep sexual offenders off the streets. Personally, I would pay higher taxes to keep my family safer. I have a teenage daughter and am in the process of adopting a baby from China.

I live in Citrus County. We need a nationwide tracking system. Under the present system these people can drift from state to state undetected and many states have a lot of privacy protection for these offenders. Thank You for considering my opinion.

Subject: repeat sexual offenders
Tuesday, April 19, 2005 4:57 p.m.
From: Jeb Bush

I hope to sign into law tougher penalties and a larger budget to deal with this tragic issue. I appreciate your writing.

Jeb Bush

———

Children are meant to bring joy and levity into our lives. This includes Kayla, who apparently collected snakes. Sadly she never answered my question about the snakes. I really did want to know. In her defense she did sound very busy.

Subject: Hi Mr.Jeb
Friday, April 22, 2005 6:31 p.m.
From: Kayla

You've probably heard of my school, NorthLake Park Community School.I'm Kayla, and I have a little brother named, Cesar and a little sister named, Isabel.I'm 10.Cesar is 9.Isabel is 7. My hobbies are; #1Snakes#2 football #3listening to Jesse McCartney#4 basketball#5 SCHOOL! Sorry I'm out of time I can email you later to tell Cesar and Isabel's hobby. Right now I've got to go see some teachers dancing and singing at the School Faculty Show.Bye for now.

Subject: Hi Mr.Jeb
Sunday, April 24, 2005 6:47 p.m.
From: Jeb Bush

thank you Kayla. Your favorite hobby is snakes? What do you do with them?

Jeb Bush

———

In April I signed into law the Stand Your Ground bill, which expanded people's rights to defend themselves by eliminating any duty to retreat in the face of aggressors before people used or threatened to use deadly force.

As a result of this and other measures, violent crime decreased in Florida by 25 percent while I was governor.

Subject: Gun Law
Wednesday, April 27, 2005 7:55 p.m.
From: Tag

Shazam! A wrong has been righted. Thank you for doing the right thing!

A person once said that a man is known by his friends; I say he is known by his enemeies. When you review all those grousing and carping about your decision, you know you are in good standing.

Subject: Gun Law
Thursday, April 28, 2005 2:46 p.m.
From: Tag

Thank you Tag.

jeb

———

I was carefully watching the Senate debate on my latest educa-tion reform bill. I sent this plan of action to Patricia Levesque and Chris Flack, who was director of legislative affairs. For the sake of not overdoing the footnotes, I won't overexplain my notes, but I think you can tell I wanted to pull out all the stops and get every-one on board.

Subject: [Subject]
Saturday, April 30, 2005 7:26 a.m.
From: Jeb Bush

We need a paln of action for the senatevfor A plus plus and class size referndum. Here are a few suggestions:

1. We need to get al cardenas his ammo and we need public support from school district to get the three senators to support.

Maybe marco can call them and I will do the same over the weekend.

2. Patricia, can you call Ben Wilcox to go through the plan with him, show him the benefits and see if he could publicly support the plan and call Jones?

3. Maybe the super or chair of polk cty school board can call paula?

4. We need to get evelyn not to cave on vouchers just yet. Can someone call her on this? I will do the same.

5. Can kirtly help?

6. We may need bob ward and the speaker's help.

7. Any way we can reach agreement with the union?

Jeb Bush

Unfortunately the bill did not pass. My top education adviser was crushed. So was I.

Subject: [None]
Thursday, May 5, 2005 9:32 p.m.
From: Patricia Levesque

I couldn't say this to you face to face because
I didn't want to start crying. I'm so honored to
serve you. I'm so thankful you are an honorable and
principled man. I guess it's human nature to always
think of the what ifs. What if we had done a press
conference on the $1 billion maybe that would have
squelched the south florida equity issues before the
media and others perpetuated the misinformation.
What if we hadn't put a voucher in, maybe we would
have gotten more vocal support from the supts and
sb folks. What if we had done fly arounds. What if
I had just gotten you the names of the members to
call last night instead of today -- too late.

I want to say I'm sorry. I'm sorry we lost. But
I know we did the right thing putting forth the
proposal. And after I have a good cry tonight I will
also do what Villalobos said and in good conscience
sleep like a baby.[104]

Subject: [None]
Friday, May 6, 2005 7:14 a.m.
From: Jeb bush

---

104 When Senator Alex Villalobos spoke on the floor about his decision
to vote against my class-size proposal, he said he would sleep like a baby
afterward.

```
You are a great team member. It was a great idea
that would have helped teachers, parents and
students. I am the one who is osrry that I didn't
do enough.

Jeb
```

———

Governing, like politics, is a roller coaster. On the heels of the bad news that further education reform had gone down came the very good news that another top priority had passed—a series of bills to ensure infrastructure kept pace with growth. I understood why people wanted to live and raise families in Florida. It was a great place to live. With the rapid growth, though, we needed to protect our standard of living and environment. The new laws required communities to ensure adequate roads, schools, and water supplies for new development.

Not to leave you hanging, the Medicaid reform bill also passed—or at least a version of it. The reforms would be tested in Broward and Duval Counties, our pilot counties.

———

I don't even want to use the h *word, but the time has come.*

The beginning of the hurricane season is June 1. Given what had happened in 2004, we didn't want to take any chances. To make sure Floridians were as ready as they possibly could be, we worked with the legislature to pass the same kind of sales-tax holiday on hurricane supplies as we sometimes did on school supplies. We wanted everyone to go out and get flashlights, batteries, storm shutters, and whatever else they needed to batten down the hatches.

My deputy chief of staff overseeing disaster management sent me this e-mail.

Subject: Hurricane issues
Monday, May 9, 2005 13:21 p.m.
From: Deirdre Finn

Dept. of Revenue is asking for the go-ahead to begin rules for the hurricane tax holiday, which exempts sales tax from June 1 to June 12 on the items to prepare for hurricane season, including flashlights, radios, tarps,first-aid kits, tie down kits, batteries, coolers and generators. The bill briefing is scheduled for tomorrow. Shall we wait until then or should we give Revenue the green light?

Subject: Hurricane issues
Monday, May 9, 2005 3:41 p.m.
From: Jeb Bush

Go forth and begin work!

Jeb Bush

————

On May 11 Education Commissioner John Winn and I announced the best news: the newest FCAT scores showed more than two-thirds of Floridian third graders were reading at or above grade level. That was the highest number in state history. We were ecstatic. These were the first of several "good news" education numbers we received over the next few weeks that showed our early education reforms were indeed working.

Subject: GOVERNOR BUSH AND COMMISSIONER WINN ANNOUNCE FCAT RESULTS FOR 3RD AND 12TH GRADE
Wednesday, May 11, 2005 11:01 p.m.
From: Mark Maxwell

Governor, these results are awesome! You should
be very proud of what has happened with student
achievement. You took a lot of heat, but you have
proven all the naysayers wrong! I am honored to have
been a part of something that history will judge as a
defining moment for education.

**Subject: RE: GOVERNOR BUSH AND COMMISSIONER WINN
ANNOUNCE FCAT RESULTS FOR 3RD AND 12TH GRADE
Thursday, May 12, 2005 7:23 a.m.
From: Jeb Bush**

it was a good day.

Jeb

———

*Bills to consider signing or vetoing piled high on my desk. Yes.
It was turkey-hunting season. I appreciated this note from one
of my appointees to Florida's Supreme Court. He was thanking
me for signing a bill that gave a much-needed pay boost to the
judiciary branch.*

Subject: THANK YOU
Friday, May 27, 2005 12:21 p.m.
From: Justice Kenneth B. Bell

It must be interesting to simultaneously experience
how Santa Claus and the Grinch feel! ;)

Seriously, thanks! Your signing of the bill that
approved our pay plan is greatly appreciated. This
court has been experiencing severe personnel problems
associated with the inadequacy of pay. This new
allocation will be a much needed boon.…

Have a great vacation!

Ken

Subject: THANK YOU
Friday, May 27,2005 7:31 p.m.
From: Jeb Bush

it is tough being a conservative and acting on your beliefs. It is easy to always say yes and let government grow faster than folks' ability to pay for our generosity with their money. I know you understand my plight. that is all from the equal and independent executive branch! :)

Jeb

PS No vacations yet. I have 300 bills to analyze and much work to do.

———

It's nice as governor when you can tell your constituents you hear them and you are already doing something about their concerns.

Subject: Key Question
Wednesday, June 8, 2005 12:50 p.m.
From: Gary Altpeter

After a newspaper printed your E-mail address saying that you try to answer all you receive, I suspect you might be swamped.

Anyway, if you should read this, I have a question for you. First, I must tell you of my perception of the Bush "clan." I love your father, I think he is a kind, compassionate man who defines moderation. Your brother, however, is cut from a different mold, and frankly with his "my way, or the highway" attitude, scares the heck out of me! You, I see as somewhere in between them in your thinking. You will probably not agree, but that is not the point.

The purpose of saying all that, is to set up my question. That is, where do you stand on controlling the alarming growth afflicting our State? Central Florida is a particular example, and specifically central Brevard is cited. Our infrastructure cannot support it. Our water and sewage services, our police and fire protection, our roads, and our medical care are already strained to the breaking point. This year, when our "snowbirds" visited us, our hospitals were in a genuine crisis mode.

We have four county commissioners who deny it, but never saw a bulldozer they did not like. Unfortunately, most of the city council members in this area seem to feel the same way.

I believe that if you and our legislature do not take action to control development, the entire State is in deep trouble.

I invite your input.

Subject: Key Question
Wednesday, June 8, 2005 12:59 p.m.
From: Jeb Bush

I am very concerned about how uncontrolled growth
will severely impact our quality of life. This
year, we have passed real growth management reform
which puts teeth into concurrency (infrastructure
must be committed to with capital identified when
land use decisions which increase density or when
comprehensive plan ammendments are made) and backs
it up with a dramatic increase in state funding for
schools, water and roads.

I appreciate your writing.

Jeb Bush

———

*It's time to talk about some of the more serious topics of the
day.*

Subject: thank you?
Thursday, June 9, 2005 9:23 a.m.
From: A.J. Borromeo

Do I have you to thank for Florida getting
"whataburgers?"

I was just curious because I always thought it was a
Texas monopoly!!!

thank you, I love whataburger,

Subject: thank you?
Thursday, June 9, 2005 4:37 p.m.
From: Jeb Bush

I can't take credit but they are tasty aren't they?

jeb

I loved this Florida businessman's sales pitch. I can't remember if we bought his pens or not, but he made an impression.

Subject: Bill Signing?
Thursday, June 9, 2005 2:42 p.m.
From: Jim Smith

I was recently watching my local news channel here in the Tampa Bay area and one of the news segments featured your signing of a new bill. I also noticed that you appeared to be signing the bills with generic pens that appear to be from a national supplier that makes them by the millions. Many of the bills that you sign are significant to the sponsors and the people involved and I think should be commemorated as lasting tributes to those present.

Although I am a woodturner, it appears that more politically correct term is now ' word artist ', none the less, one of the items that I make are pens and pencils from rare and exotic woods. I make these pens uniquely by hand from woods from around the world and they make wonderful gifts. The pens, and associated cases, would appear to me to perfectly suited to such things as bill signing and other special occasions. Each pen can be laser engraved with almost any inscription that could identify the bill signed, the date, etc. The case, if selected, could also be engraved with the Florida State Seal or other image of your choosing.

I would very much like the opportunity to send you, or your designated representative, a few sample pens and cases for your review and consideration for future bill signings or other events. Please give my idea some consideration and let me know your thoughts.

Subject: Bill Signing?
Thursday, June 9, 2005 5:12 p.m.
From: Jeb Bush

thank you Mr. Smith. you are correct, I am a Sharpie man. the pens have the state seal and my signature on them. I am asking William Piferrer to followup with you to discuss your product. He will call you.

Jeb

———

I sent Nancy Argenziano, a state senator from Citrus County, this e-mail after I read an interview she gave the Citrus County Chronicle.

Argenziano chaired a government oversight committee that passed legislation regarding procurement contracts. The law requires government contracts to go before legislative budget review.

"Gov. Jeb Bush opposes the law because he believes it interferes with the executive branch,"

Argenziano said. She and the governor had a spirited conversation about it.

"He cursed at me that day. I cursed at him back," she said during an interview last week with the Chronicle Editorial Board. "He was being the governor, and I had to make him know I didn't work for him."

She also opposed attempts by Bush and the House to reform Medicaid by privatizing it.

"That was a very frightening idea," she said. "The House bill was a total giveaway."

Subject: DMS Newsclips for 6/20/05—Executive
Monday, June 20, 2005 9:14 p.m.
From: Jeb Bush

Nancy, Nancy, Nancy, I don't remember cursing at you. I know it helps you with the image you want to have, the feisty independent minded politician, but I didn't curse at you. I probably cursed with you, but not at you. And yes, I know and appreciate that you don't work for me.

As it relates to Medicaid, which tax do you want to raise to keep up with a program that has been growing by 13.5% a year? Or which service should be cut? Or which provider should have its rates cut again? Medicaid is privatized already, with over 80,000 private providers. The question is how do we get better health care outcomes, less fraud and abuse and a sustainable growth in the program.

I hope you are having a fine summer.

Jeb

———

Suddenly the summer was speeding by. I made time to go to the launch of the space shuttle Discovery, *the first since the* Columbia *tragedy two years earlier.*

Subject: launch
Tuesday, July 26, 2005 12:16 p.m.
From: Matt Conroy

Jeb---Now how did ya' like that!?

I will never tire of watching a launch…especially a shuttle. What a great kick off to a new school year getting underway shortly too! The opportunities our kids have is phenomenal…and today's launch is one more step to deeper space exploration and inspiration to our kids.

Subject: launch
Tuesday, July 26, 2005 5:28 p.m.
From: Jeb Bush

It made me cry with joy. what a powerful testament to ingenuity and determination!

Jeb

———

About this time I appointed Denver Stutler as the new secretary of transportation. My new chief of staff was Mark Kaplan, who had been part of my team in various key roles since the beginning. Most recently he had been Lieutenant Governor Toni Jennings's chief of staff. He would stay on board until I left office. I received this e-mail from Denver shortly after he began his new job.

Subject: Update from the field
Thursday, July 28, 2005 1:03 p.m.
From: Denver Stutler

Hurricane Dennis provided an opportunity to see our team work in concert with the other responders and one observation that I have shared with Craig is they set up a call center manned by personnel on 12 hour shifts with real time data so that motorists can get information on roads 24 hours a day. They had 26,000 calls in eleven days after Ivan. It was idea by one of the District Three employees they implemented.

I had already shared with Deirdre that the Executive (senior management) Board gathers ten times a year for two days to go through every performance measure. This past meeting we updated what we are going to measure. More than 96% of the $2.8 Billion worth of contract lettings were delivered on time. And an even higher percentage of $800 Million worth of consulting work.

My visit to District Seven this week provided me an opportunity to meet staff, and get briefed on all their major projects in the Tampa Bay area. I

also surprised Jose[105] at the Airports meeting where
he received an award for his work on the hurricane
response last year.…

Thank you Governor for the opportunity.

Subject: Update from the field
Thursday, July 28, 2005 10:06 p.m.
From: Jeb Bush

**isn't it cool to be large and in charge? Continue to
seek out the team's thoughts and suggestions. Well
done, Denver.**

Jeb

———

*Did you notice the very nonchalant way I introduced that our first
hurricane of 2005 had come and gone? After slamming Cuba as a
Category 4 storm, Dennis came ashore in the Florida Panhandle
on July 10 as a Category 3. It was compact and moved fast.
Although Dennis did have a powerful storm surge, it did not have
nearly the impact of the 2004 storms. Practice often makes perfect, so the evacuation of seven hundred thousand people in the
Panhandle had gone fairly smoothly. However, one report about
Dennis said the damage was minimal ($600 million) because the
area was still recovering from Ivan.*

*That was true of all Florida. As we braced for the new season,
we were still recovering from the old. That is why I loved this next
e-mail.*

---

105 José Abreu, the previous secretary of transportation, who was now
director of Miami International Airport.

Subject: Thank you one year later from the girl in Port Charlotte:)
Thursday, August 4, 2005 8:26 p.m.
From: Natalie Collins

I'm sure this email does not go directly to the Governor. I do hope that maybe this short message could be passed on to him. My name is Natalie Collins I'm 24 years old. I live in Port Charlotte, FL. I work for Kix country 92.9 (Clear Channel) the radio station were I met the governor. He stopped by and informed the public over the air about what he was going to do to help with the recovery from hurricane Charley. With as hot and stinky as it was at that radio station, governor Bush still smiled and shook everybody's hands. I remember him specifically asking how we as individuals made out through the storm. That amazed me. I just want to thank the governor One year later for all the tremendous work and time he pored into our precious little communities. Our whole town (Punta Gorda and Port Charlotte) would have never made it through as well as we did without such a wonderful leader. I mean that from the bottom of my heart. My husband, children, and I are doing well one year after the storm. We are blessed that our home is now finished and back to the way it was before the storm. We will never forget the true genuine dedication that Governor Jeb Bush showed in the most scary time in our lives. So I just want to say a great BIG THANK YOU!

Subject: Thank you one year later from the girl in Port Charlotte:)
Friday, August 5, 2005 7:20 p.m.
From: Jeb Bush

Wow! your email warms my heart. I am so pleased that you and your family are doing well. Punta gorda still has a way to go to completely recover but there has been pretty good progress. I remember the radio station was pretty hot but I don't remember stinky! :)

Jeb Bush

———

It's time to check in again on the dog days of summer musings of Floridians.

Subject: Illegal Immigrants
Friday, August 19, 2005 8:57 p.m.
From: Heather Craft

I would like to say that I think that the illegal immigrants has gone wild in this country. I would like for you to do something about it in this state. It has gotten worse it seems like every where my family and I go there are Mexicans. I have noticed how people are now having to put things in english and spanish to cater to the immigrants. I feel that if you want to come to the country you should do it legally and you should learn the language of that country. I would like to see something done to cover our borders and to find and get rid of the immigrants. I don't feel that they should be allowed to get the benefits of financial assistance like the people who are here legally. I would be happy to for my tax dollars to go and supply border agents in Florida. By the way thanks for the tax break last year we would really appreciate another one this year. It is getting expense to just go to work and back. If everything goes up b/c of gas going up but does everyone realize that our wages are not going up.

Subject: Illegal Immigrants
Saturday, August 20, 2005 7:00 a.m.
From: Jeb Bush

thank you for writing. The illegal immigrant issue is getting worse and I agree with you that we should increase the number of border patrol agents. By law, illegal immigrants cannot receive government benefits but nonetheless, we should control our borders.

We will certainly consider another tax holiday on gasoline.

Jeb Bush

———

Subject: Taxes
Saturday, August 20, 2005 11:32 a.m.
From: N. Paul Gurski

Just read a piece in the paper about citizens in florida not appreciating any tax breaks they receive. Anyways I and my friends sure do appreciate any breaks we get rather it be in taxes or anything else. Want to thank you from the bottom of our hearts and keep doing a good job.

Subject: Taxes
Saturday, August 20, 2005 11:46 a.m.
From: Jeb Bush

I believe that floridians appreciate tax cuts. I just think that few floridians knew we cut 90 million in gas taxes last year. We are striving to providing relief this year as well.

Jeb

———

Subject: ERA proclamation.
Tuesday, August 23, 2005 8:55 p.m.
From: H K "Petey" Kaletta

It is my understanding that you have declined to sign the proclamation honoring the 85th anniversary of the 18th Amendment.[106]

This is very disappointing to me. I am a 67 year old woman and a staunch Republican. If you do not feel that our cause, the ERA and other issues relating to women's rights are important enough for you to make a firm public statement to that effect, I may have to look elsewhere for support. That means I will give my support to those who recognize that women have made and will continue to make important contributions to this county. Please be aware that I am NOT a single issue voter. I just feel that this is an issue that should not be shoved under the rug any more, by you or anyone.

Subject: ERA proclamation.
Wednesday, August 24, 2005 9:46 a.m.
From: Jeb Bush

---

106 I believe she meant the Nineteenth Amendment, which gives women the right to vote. The Eighteenth Amendment was prohibition.

You are incorrect. I did sign a proclamation
regarding Women's Equality this week.

My record as it relates to the appointment of
women to boards and commissions, to positions of
responsibility in state government and the judiciary
is unmatched by any of my predecessors. I fully
support women's equality and have acted on my belief.

Thanks for writing.

Jeb Bush

———

*Just to prove you can't please all the people all the time, my friend
Steve MacNamara sent me this e-mail about comments one of his
colleagues at Florida State University made regarding shrinking
the size of government.*

**Subject: Now how are you supposed to take his study
seriously???**
Saturday, August 27, 2005 7:47 p.m.
From: Stephen MacNamara

**FSU prof says Bush made civil service smaller, not
necessarily better**

"Research by a Florida State University professor
compares Florida's "Service First" reform of state
employment to Goldilocks' taste-testing the three
bears' porridge.

"Seeking a "just right" compromise between lifetime
job security and cut-throat capitalism, Gov. Jeb Bush

has made state government smaller, but not necessarily more efficient, says Professor Jim Bowman. And in a paper presented to the American Society for Public Administration, the human-resources teacher said employee attitudes toward Service First break down on fairly predictable lines between bosses and workers.

Personnel administrators tend to like the four-year-old system, especially the ability to fill vacancies quickly. But Bowman's test-sampling of employees in three big agencies indicates that - among the 16,300 employees who were moved from Career Service to Selected Exempt - there is a widespread suspicion that Bush's intention was to shrink state payrolls."

For the full story, read Sunday's *Tallahassee Democrat*

Subject: Now how are you supposed to take his study seriously???
Saturday, August 27, 2005 7:57 p.m.
From: Jeb Bush

shrink the beast.

Jeb

About this time we were watching a storm over the Bahamas. I declared a state of emergency on August 24 as we warily watched the storm's track. Its name was Katrina.

Subject: PRAYING...
Thursday, August 25, 2005 9:07 p.m.
From: Toni Eade

I know, you must feel, your being tested in
Florida…but WE ARE ALL PRAYING FLORIDA
WILL BE SAFE & KATRINA WILL MISS.…

KEEP UP THE GREAT JOB.

Subject: PRAYING…
Thursday, August 25, 2005 9:13 p.m.
From: Jeb Bush

thank you toni. we are being tested.

Jeb

*Katrina came ashore and dumped up to sixteen inches of rain
in the Miami area, spawned a tornado, and brought down
power lines in the Keys. Damage from flooding and tornadoes
in South Florida was estimated at more than $1.7 billion, and
nearly 1.5 million people were left in the dark. It then moved
over land into the Gulf, and it became a monster. At one time
Katrina was a Category 5 and the largest storm ever recorded
in the Gulf of Mexico. Although it was a Category 3 by the time
it came ashore in Mississippi and Louisiana, the storm surge
caused historic damage. This included the tragic breaching of
the levees in New Orleans that flooded 80 percent of the city. To
the east of the eye wall, waves pushed inland as far as twenty
miles in Mississippi, Alabama, and even the Florida Panhandle.*

*I asked our team to start preparing to reach out to our neigh-
bors. I received this e-mail from Major General Douglas Burnett
of the Florida National Guard.*

Subject: Katrina/New Orleans
Sunday, August 28, 2005 12:10 a.m.
From: Douglas Burnett

I have approved this list of capabilities of the
Florida Nat'l Guard which we will send to the Adjutant
General of Louisiana. I have again talked with General
Landreneau and he is aware of our plan to support.
Mississippi Nat'l Guard has very large numbers of
Army Guardsmen, but the mix of capabilities is
different than ours. Both combined is pretty significant
capability. The biggest challenge they face, as I
recall from Hurricanes of the sixties (Betsy/Camille),
is extensive flooding and lilttle way to drain the city
after storm passage. The search and rescue piece will
take on a whole new meaning for New Orleans and will
present orders of magnitude for rescue that will be
beyond anything we have seen in years.

Subject: Katrina/New Orleans
Sunday, August 28, 2005 6:31 a.m.
From: Jeb Bush

thank you Doug. this is a scary, scary storm.

Jeb

———

Subject: Gulf coast disaster
Wednesday, August 31, 2005 1:11 p.m.
From: Ed

Jeb--Is there anything the State of Florida can do to
help those people in the hurricane area?

Subject: Gulf coast disaster
Wednesday, August 31, 2005 1:54 p.m.
From: Jeb Bush

we are! we have 500 emergency responders at least in the area. we have sent convoys of food, water and ice. we have the guard activated and blackhawks[107] in the impacted area.

Jeb

———

Just as other states had come to our aid in 2004, we came to the aid of our neighbors after this horrific storm. It made sense for us to focus on Mississippi while Texas focused on Louisiana. By September 1 we had just over one thousand emergency and law enforcement personnel on the ground. My chief of staff, Mark Kaplan, called Governor Haley Barbour's chief of staff and told him we were at the border and ready to start search and rescue missions, but we needed permission to enter. Haley's beleaguered chief of staff said they had no idea how to make a formal request. Mark suggested he just say "OK." We would worry about the paperwork later. He agreed, and across the border came the Florida National Guard, search and rescue teams, medical teams, ambulances, emergency equipment and operators, bridge inspectors, trucks of water, flashlights, and generators. Part of our handshake deal was the understanding FEMA would reimburse Florida for the cost, but at that point in time, we did not care. My budget director, Mike Hansen, had gotten legislative approval for us to take $14 million out of our reserve fund. Again there was no time for red tape. (FEMA eventually did reimburse us.)

I believe nearly 2,500 Floridians ended up going to Mississippi to help. We knew how to do hurricanes.

———

107 Black Hawk helicopters.

In late August the final report came out from the BRAC Commission regarding military base closures. Florida did very well. We were ecstatic, as military bases are an important part of Florida's economy and culture.

Subject: very impressive article
Friday, August 26, 2005 8:58 p.m.
From: [No name]

I read an article in the TU about the expansion of Eglin Air Force Base in Pensecola, that was very impressive. I didn't realize that. So NAS, Pensecola had gains and a big maybe for Cecil Field.[108] The AP wire reported that Florida had come away with the most. I e-mailed a former staffer that predicted your hard work w/BRAC would pay off and was very important. I said, you were right, look at this article. I got a cute email back that read "who can resist our governor?" What wit. I think she set me up on that one! I read with interest the article about Oceana which stated that eminent domain issue would not apply as that had already been addressed and denied (as far as a crash zone acquisition). It appears as though it is only a matter of time. Way to go! Very good news during a stressful time for Florida.

Subject: very impressive article
Friday, August 26, 2005 9:17 p.m.
From: Jeb Bush

For seven years we have been preparing and I think we have achieved a huge victory for our state. I am proud of the efforts of many.

---

108 There was hope US Naval Air Station (NAS) Cecil Field, closed by an earlier BRAC team, would reopen. That never materialized.

Our year of great economic news continued. This e-mail came from our friend Brewser Brown, who had gone back to the private sector.

Subject: [None]
Friday, September 16, 2005 2:33 p.m.
From: Brewser Brown

Congratulations on the 3.6% unemployment. I guess tax cuts aren't so bad after all…I will await the media's mea culpa.

Subject: [None]
Saturday, September 17, 2005 4:36 p.m.
From: Jeb Bush

thanks Brewser.

Jeb

The term "broken record" comes to mind as I tell you about the time another monster storm was out in the Gulf of Mexico. Hurricane Rita likely never got the respect it deserved since Katrina swallowed all the media's attention in 2005. However, Rita is on record as being the most intense tropical cyclone ever recorded in the Gulf of Mexico. It resulted in a massive evacuation of the Gulf Coast, including the city of Houston. By the time it came ashore close to the Louisiana-Texas border, Rita was a Category 3. Nevertheless, it devastated a number of counties along the Louisiana-Texas coastline.

Rita came close enough to Florida to trigger yet another evacuation of the Florida Keys and South Florida—a total of 340,000 people. Thankfully, damage from the hurricane-force winds and flooding was considered moderate—a mere $50 million. Although, I am sure the people whose homes and businesses the storm battered would disagree with that description.

One of my favorite stories about my dad relates to Hurricane Rita. He and President Clinton were raising tens of millions of dollars for the victims of Hurricane Katrina— about $150 million total when they were done. However, Dad had a special relationship with Cameron, Louisiana, dating back to his offshore oil days. When Rita flattened the town, he reached out to them to see what he could do to help. They asked if he could help raise money to build an emergency room. The hospital was gone, and they would rebuild that later, but an emergency room would be very helpful sooner rather than later. So Dad raised $1 million for a new ER. He was going to deliver the check in person, but he wanted to do something a little extra special for the town. (Apparently he thought $1 million was not special enough.) He suggested to his staff he should bring with him the star of "that ER show"—George Clooney. He thought it would be a perfect fit. By this time George Clooney was a big movie star and long gone from NBC's ER. Dad was a bit behind. He was watching the show's reruns on cable TV. His staff felt it unlikely Clooney would make the trip to Cameron. To make an already long story short, Dad tracked George Clooney down with the help of his friend and Hollywood producer Jerry Weintraub. George said yes, and the three of them (Jerry came along too) went to Cameron. Dad and George have been friends ever since.

Now back to the story. We were evacuating the Keys.

Subject: adjective 'minimal'
Monday, September 19, 2005 7:20 p.m.
From: Matt Conroy

Just wanted to wish you well--you have some long hours ahead. I hope your counterparts on the Gulf Coast watch and listen how you plan and prepare (They need to). If anyone has stayed in Keys with this potential large surge they are nuts==but some will stay.

Wish the media would stop saying "minimal" level one Hurricane---that's like your wife whispering in your ear--"honey, I'm 'minimally' pregnant, or hearing "a minimal nuclear warhead was just launched."...The adjective 'minimal'--just doesn't work in some cases and a hurricane is one :-)

Good luck and take care.

Subject: adjective 'minimal'
Monday, September 19, 2005 7:33 p.m.
From: Jeb Bush

you have that right. a hurricane is a hurricane is a hurricane.

Jeb

———

Subject: [None]
Monday, September 19, 2005 6:42 p.m.
From: Tom Knibbs

I was in a nice comfy hotel room in DFW[109] this morning...and I came home for this?!!

————————

109 Dallas-Fort Worth.

You should have some pull by now with the guy upstairs...after all...we're hurricane experts now, or aren't we?

Wishing us all good luck and good fortune...for the 7th time in a year!

Subject: [None]
Monday, September 19, 2005 7:43 p.m.
From: Jeb Bush

thanks tom. we are prepared and ready to help those that are hurt by rita.

Jeb

———

Subject: fema
Monday, September 19, 2005 8:51 p.m.
From: marsha crist

I am from the Phila.,Pa. area. I have watched the disasters in your area, and the ones in the Gulf. To my amazement, the question has come to mind, Why haven't you been elected to Head FEMA. It is sheer compassion and the fastness in which you take control during the Hurricanes and other emergencies that is the bases of my statements. It is also amazing, that you make sure the people are safe,and evacuated in a safe, and fast way, and that they do have a place.

Subject: fema
Tuesday, September 20, 2005 9:32 p.m.
From: Jeb Bush

thank you.I have the best job in the world, being governor of the best of the 50 states. Nothing would take me from it. I will continue to do my job with passion and enthusiasm.

Jeb

Subject: Thanks for Your Leadership During these Times of Emergencies
Tuesday, September 20, 2005 9:40 p.m.
From: Roberto Martinez

Jeb: We seem to take your leadership during times of emergency for granted because you do it very well. However, we should not overlook the fact that six hurricanes have hit Florida in the past 13 months alone, inlcuding some of the most damaging ever on record, and you have led us through these crises with a distnguished record of effective leadership. You didn't stop the storms, but we weathered them as well as we could substantially because of your hard work and effort.

Thanks!

Subject: Thanks for Your Leadership During these Times of Emergencies
Tuesday, September 20, 2005 9:51 p.m.
From: Jeb Bush

Thank you Bobby. Let us hope we get a respite for the rest of the season and let us hope south florida

upgrades its preparation and response which is good but can always do better.

Jeb

———

I loved this e-mail exchange between Rocky Rodriguez and Judge Angel Cortinas. My first priority in appointing new judges in Florida was to find highly qualified men and women who adhered to a judicial philosophy of enforcing the state's constitution rather than making new laws from the bench. I was also proud that the number of minority judges in the state judiciary grew significantly during my tenure. I had made it a point to ensure we appointed men and women to our bench who not only were high-quality jurists but also reflected Florida's rich diversity.

Subject: First All-Hispanic Panel in Florida's History
Wednesday, September 21, 2005 3:15 p.m.
From: Judge Angel A. Cortinas

Rocky,

I hope all is well with you. You asked that I give you advance notice of the first all-Hispanic panel of the Third District Court of Appeal. It is scheduled for Monday, October 3, 2005 at 9:00 a.m. and will consist of Judges Ramirez, Suarez and myself—all three appointed by Governor Bush. This milestone, which reflects the progress of Hispanic-Americans in our State and our judiciary, was made possible by the Governor's appointments.

It is fitting that this historic event will take place during Hispanic Heritage Month.

Since adoptions were a top priority of mine, I was indeed thrilled with this news from Carol Gormley and Lucy Hadi.

Subject: Adoption bonus
Friday, September 23, 2005 6:51 p.m.
From: Carol Gormley

Lucy wanted me to let you know that Florida has received (for the 3rd year in a row) an adoption bonus from the feds because we exceeded goals for permanent placements. Florida's award of $3.5 million is the largest in the country (NY is 2nd with a $1.9 m award). The money will be distributed to CBCs[110] that are responsible for the increases. One of the reasons Fla earned this amount was because of our success in placing older children.

There is likely to be a story about this over the weekend.

Subject: Adoption bonus
Friday, September 23, 2005 7:27 p.m.
From: Jeb Bush

we need to let the world know. this is great news.

Jeb

_____

I sent this random note to a couple staffers:

---

110 CBC stands for Community-Based Care, a network of agencies on the front lines of placing children for adoption.

Subject: [None]
Monday, October 3, 2005 8:09 a.m.
From: Jeb Bush

I need to get a sword for marco.

———

You might ask why. It was because the Florida House of Representatives was about to designate Marco Rubio as its incoming speaker. This would make him the first Hispanic to hold that post when it became official after the 2006 elections. As I had been a huge supporter of his election to the House and his election as speaker, I was thrilled. I wanted to present to him a Chinese sword, since I was known to say from time to time, "I am going to unleash Chang." This meant I wanted to unleash a mythical power for conservative causes. I did indeed find and give him a sword.

———

Who can resist answering questions from a reporter writing about a "media diet" that includes Hulk Hogan? Eric Deggans wrote for the St. Petersburg Times.

Subject: interview request fro St. Petersburg Times
Monday, October 10, 2005 4:23 p.m.
From: Erick Deggans

I'm Eric Deggans, Media Critic for the Times, and I'm assembling a piece on the concept of a media diet -- that we each traditionally consume an amount of media that is regular and fuels our worldview in the way food fuels our body's energy.

I'm hoping you might be willing to take a few moments to lay out what your media diet is. I'm going to be listing about four or five people as a sidebar to the story -- i'm shooting for everyone from MSNBC news anchor Keith Olbermann to Tampa Bay area resident Hulk Hogan, in hopes of pulling together a fun, eclectic mix.

Here's a few questions to spark the process:

1) Can you give a quick chronological lineup of the top media sources you access in a day (not counting blogs you access sporadically, for example), starting from when you wake up to when you go to sleep?

2) If you can think of your media consumption in terms of healthy/unhealthy, what is your best habit or healthiest source, excluding your current employer? What is your worst?

3) Have you ever discontinued accessing any media outlets because you felt their influence might be unhealthy? Can you say which outlet and why?

4) From your perspective, what makes a healthy or positive source, as opposed to an unhealthy one?

I know these questions may seem a bit odd, but I think many consumers fall into a media diet of sorts with little awareness of how such consumption might affect their worldview. And I'm very interested in what a leading public official consumes by way of news and even entertainment media in an average day.

Anyway, I hope this doesn't seem too strange and you can find some time to answer. If it would be more convenient for me to call so we can do it over the phone, I'd be happy to ring you up. And if you decide not to answer, thanks for considering it, anyway.

Subject: interview request fro St. Petersburg Times
Monday, October 10, 2005 6:35 p.m.
From: Jeb Bush

1.Usually at 6 am, I scan the st pete times, the Herald and the Orlando Sentinel every morning on line. I usually scan the other papers like the Tribune, The Sun Sentinel, the Times Union as well on line if I wake up early which I normally do.…I read the Sayfie Review if it is up before I leave for work. I do all of this while watching Fox and Friends with my wife.

I listen to public radio on the way to work unless I walk to work. I read the NY Times, the WSJ during the day and the US Today Sports Page. I listen to public radio on the way home unless I get to walk home. I watch the 6 pm Hume hour on Fox News and sometimes MSNBC or Fox in the evening. While watching the evening news, I read the clips from the day but only the articles that are important to me which are typically education stories. After that, I try to watch movies or sports. Enough news already!

2/3/4 I don't view any media outlets as unhealthy. Sometimes I think their approach is wrong but I think knowing of different points of view is important. In my job, it is important to know how reporters are covering stories and how editorial writers are thinking. I enjoy human interest stories as well. I get a ton of news from emailers who send me articles with their comments asking for my opinion.

I hope this helps.

Jeb

———

Subject: RE: History of Arts
Wednesday, October 19, 2005 10:38 a.m.
From: James Bardsley

Just a note of congratulations to your wife for her efforts in promoting Art in Florida. We know the artist who has done the paintings in the House of Representatives. We are friends with the other two artists who paint Native Americans in a Florida setting. Between Chris Still, Herman Trappman, and Dean Quigley you have a vast well of talent to choose from if you need artists.

Saturday was the first time we had seen pictures of the Mansion, and knew that your wife was involved.

You and she are to be proud of what you have done . I am confident that you will not only continue to excell in your role as Governor, but will eventually become the first Family to have 3 Presidents .

Subject: RE: History of Arts
Wednesday, October 19, 2005 6:25 p.m.
From: Jeb Bush

I am very proud of my wife. She has worked very hard on her projects with great success.

Jeb

———

We got more good economic news. Now that was a broken record I could listen to over and over and over.

Subject: Florida leads U.S. in job growth!!!
Congratulations to you and your team!
Saturday, October 22, 2005 4:36 p.m.
From: Howard Leonhardt

Hats off to you and your team for creating the best job creating environment in our country!

Great job!

We need your successor to continue to build upon your administration's success. Let me know how I can help.

Subject: Florida leads U.S. in job growth!!!
Congratulations to you and your team!
Saturday, October 22, 2005 4:40 p.m.
From: Jeb Bush

thank you Howard. Low taxes, investment in education and infrastructure and better regulation will be the key over the long haul.

Jeb

———

Subject: [None]
Saturday, October 22 8:05 p.m.
From: Trish Walton

It just occurred to me that though we hear every year
when the President takes vacation, we never hear of
you actually getting time off for you and your family.
It seems like you are always on the job and available.

Anyway, I pray that you and your family do actually
get some time to relax during the year. And, to say
thank you for being the best governor in the U.S.

Subject: [None]
Saturday, October 22, 2005 8:25 p.m.
From: Jeb Bush

**That is so kind. I do take a week vacation in july
but this year it had to be cut short because of
dennis. After I am long gone as governor, I will take
more time off.**

Jeb

———

Just when we thought hurricane season was winding down,
Wilma appeared on the radar. It made landfall on the southwest
coast of Florida as a Category 3 and moved across the southern
peninsula to hit South Florida from the west.

Wilma caused widespread damage in South Florida due to
winds and flooding. This caused some to speculate that the warm

waters of the Everglades helped sustain its strength. A storm surge inundated the Lower Keys, the sugar crop was devastated, and there were massive power outages. Damage in Florida was estimated at more than $19 billion.

I sent this note to Pat Roberts, who was then (and still is) president of the Florida Association of Broadcasters.

Subject: [None]
Thursday, October 27, 2005 10:00 a.m.
From: Jeb Bush

I hope you might share with the Florida Broadcasters my appreciation of their willingness to consider airing the PSA promoting the Florida Hurricane Relief Fund.

As you know, Wilma's wide swath across our state has devastated not only our coastal communities, but our rural interior neighborhoods as well, heavily impacting our poorer residents. Established last year to help fill the many gaps in recovery funding that government and insurance cannot cover, this Fund is proving crucial in helping Florida rise and rebuild. Funds are allocated by local unmet needs committees, and the overhead associated with the fund is less than 3%. While many large donations last year were made to the fund by corporate donors, we expect that due to Katrina, we will need to more aggressively reach out to the compassionate neighbors in our state.

I understand that many of the towers were damaged or destroyed from this hurricane, and that many of you may have damage to your private residences. Please know that my wishes and prayers are with all of you during the rebuilding process.

———

Subject: [None]
Thursday, October 27, 2005 7:15 p.m.
From: Paul Mitchell

never before have I been so proud of a leader as I have
been with your performance as Florida's leader over the
past 16 months. Anyone can lead 17 million people when
the sun is shining, but it takes a unique person, say
one in 17 million, to lead a state through 4 natural
disasters in one year, to be followed up by three more
the following year, and still hold that state together.
Thank you for what you have done during the especially
difficult times for Florida, Governor. For each crisis
we as a state have faced over the last 7 years, you and
your team have found a way to get us through it. I am
just one of many, many grateful Floridians.

Subject: [None]
Thursday, October 27, 2005 7:24 p.m.
From: Jeb Bush

**Thanks Paul. It is a joy to be in service. After 8
canes and 2 trop storms, we are doing ok.**

Jeb

———

Questions from students were still the most fun.

Subject: Thanks
Monday, October 31, 2005 4:41 p.m.
From: Lucas

I met you today in Clewiston at the Wal-Mart. I wanted to say thank you for the card. My teachers understood that it was important to meet you.

I also have two questions to ask you: How did you learn to speak Spanish so well? And do you have any suggestions for how I could learn? There are no Spanish classes in the LaBelle schools.…It was such a thrill to meet you!

Subject: Thanks
Monday, October 31, 2005 5:48 p.m.
From: Jeb Bush

I learned spanish by marrying a Mexican girl, by living in Venezuela and by taking spanish courses in school. The first two were the most important.

There are no spanish courses in Labelle?

Jeb

PS it was nice meeting you today.

———

As 2005 drew to a close, hurricanes dominated my thinking. The 2005 storms had not come close to the monster storms of 2004, but the combined price tag for eight hurricanes in four years for the people of Florida was more than $70 billion.

I wanted to leave behind for my successors a plan from lessons learned. Although, hopefully no other team would ever have to face back-to-back record-breaking hurricane seasons. However, I wanted us to explore every option about how to save more lives, protect more property, and be more cost-efficient.

I sent this first note to a group of staffers. An exchange of e-mails with Deirdre Finn follows.

Subject: random thoughts
Saturday, October 29, 2005 7:59 p.m.
From: Jeb Bush

I have been thinking about the next hurricane season and the ones that are after that I won't have the privilege to deal with.

It seems to me that we need to really focus on a creating a culture of preparedness. that means that all important public and private institutions should be prepared. Why shouldn't Broward County have generators on site to deal with its water system? And all of the other systems as well? Why shouldn't school districts have generators to run schools if that is appropriate? We demand this of nursing homes don't we?

Gas stations are clearly important. We need to know what the cost is to power up (even minimally) a gas station? what is the obligation of the oil companies and their retailers to provide service in emergencies? What role should the state play?

How can we make sure businesses have a post hurricane plan? Shouldn't we spend money to train small businesses through chamber of commerces to be ready and prepared?

How can we implement the neighborhood relief centers concept recently proposed?

How can we make the sales tax holiday for hurricane preparation a bigger deal. I envision the WallMarts of the world selling several packages all at once to encourage preparation. We need to do much more in this regard. Schools, chambers, not for profits, local governments, Medicaid offices, etc etc.

Jeb

Subject: Culture of Preparedness
Wednesday, November 30, 2005 7:35 p.m.
From: Deirdre Finn

I am going to draft a traditional campaign plan for this project - budget, timeline, grassroots strategy, communications (press) plan, startegies for targeted constituencies including businesses, hispanic and haitian communities, migrant workers, elderly, disabled, the poor. Identifying specific goals and needs will help us enlist the help of others - whether it is government agencies or the private sector. It will also make good use of our funding. I will have a draft by end of next week.

Subject: fup
Wednesday, November 30, 2005 12:52 p.m.
From: Jeb Bush

is there anyway to get some polling done on citizens attitudes regarding hurricanes, preparedness, whether people plan to leave, etc etc? It would be helpful in preparing a plan for preparedness.

Do you think it makes sense to have a business element to the hurricane conference or a separate meeting of all chamber / business group directors to get them involved in the preparedness process? Maybe we can invite CEO's of major companies to explain what they do for their employees and customers. We could do ask the trade associations (hotel and motel, restaurants, gas companies, retailers, etc) at their annual meetings to add a hurricane component. If we want to change the culture, it will take a ton of effort.

I spoke to the CEO of Home Depot and he said he would help us with advice on how to "harden" existing housing stock. I will followup with him.

Finally, we need a plan for gas companies getting powered up after storms.

Jeb

———

Despite our second hurricane dance in 2005, I ended the year very excited about the progress we had made since January 1.

- *We had a new Medicaid reform law in place, which had been expanded in a special session in December.*
- *We finally had a growth-management plan that meant roads, schools, and the infrastructure could keep up with our rapid population growth.*
- *Our students' test scores were higher than ever before.*

- *Crime rates were the lowest in thirty-four years.*
- *Economic figures were through the roof. Unemployment was down. New jobs were up—255,100 created in the last year—and credit ratings were high. Even the hurricanes had not slowed us down much, thanks to a healthy reserve fund and a robust tax base.*

I was ready to begin my last year as the governor of Florida with a full heart, a long to-do list, but a slight sense of dread that the best job in the world was coming to an end.

Chapter 8
2006

"This Job Gives Me Great Joy!"

This is not a year for rest or caution. It's not a year for legacy. This is a year for taking our progress to the next level to build an even bigger future for Florida. This is the year we do even more.

—State of the State Address, March 7, 2006

We were sprinting toward the finish line.

I was determined to make the final year no different from any other. I wanted a "business as usual" kind of year. In my last State of the State address, I gave the legislature my long to-do list, and I hoped we could work together to pass the legislation to make the list reality. If they were hoping for a lame duck kind of year, they were about to be disappointed.

And we did get a lot done. It was one of the few years of my governorship when life did not choose an unexpected path for us. There were no hurricanes. No hanging chads. No horrific events like 9/11. No Elian Gonzalez or Terri Schiavo who stole our hearts but also dominated the headlines and incited passions.

I think it was what's called "normal."

Throughout the year, however, it was hard to get away from the pervasive feeling it was indeed our final year in office. Everything we did, we knew we were doing for the last time: our last budget, our last legislative session, our last turkey shoot, and our last school year. The time seemed to fly by—more so than usual.

So it seems only appropriate this last chapter about my last year be a little different too. For you hardy souls who are still hanging in there and reading this book, this chapter is going to fly by too, as I am going to share just a few of my favorite e-mails from my last year in office.

Ironically we will begin with Shirish Daté at the Palm Beach Post, *who possibly was the most critical reporter during my administration. He already was writing a book about my governorship. It seemed he should at least wait until we were done. I hope Shirish enjoyed our sparring as much as I did.*

Subject: questions
Monday, January 2, 2006 8:58 p.m.
From: S.V. Dáte

As you are aware, I am writing a book about your two terms as Florida governor. I have finished most of my research, and have some questions I'd like to ask you in person.

I would like as much time as you are able and willing to afford. A cumulative eight hours ought to cover it.

Is this possible in the next two months before the start of legislative session?

Thanks.

Subject: questions
Tuesday, January 3, 2006 6:54 a.m.
From: Jeb Bush

You are kidding, correct? No, I won't sit for 8 hours to discuss my tenure as Governor. If I felt you would be fair, I might do it, but you have proven yourself to be the least fair of all the journalists in Tallahassee.

Here is hoping you and your family have a healthy 2006.

Jeb Bush

Subject: questions
Wednesday, January 4, 2006 8:44 a.m.
From: S.V. Dáte

Eight hours…but not all in a row. There. That makes it seem less painful, no?

I sense that at this moment you are leaning against giving me interview time. I'll let you mull it over for a while and get back to you.

As to my fairness/unfairness -- that will have to be an area where we agree to disagree. (Although I must say: "least fair of *all* journalists in Tallahassee"? Surely even you agree that's a stretch…)

Thanks, governor, for the new year's wishes, and I hope you, Columba and your children and daughter-in-law have a happy and healthy new year, as well.

Subject: questions
Wednesday, January 4, 2006 8:20 p.m.
From: Jeb Bush

Nope. In all honesty, I don't think it is a
stretch. I think many would agree with me that
you are the least fair of all journalists in
Tallahassee. In fact, we could do a poll of opinion
leaders in our realm and I would venture to say
that you would win. Maybe I am wrong, but I don't
think so. Maybe we should do an objective survey
to determine who is right about this. As I said, I
could be wrong.

Please don't mark me down as neutral regarding the
eight hours or any hours. No can do.

In spite of your unfairness as a journalist and your
evil ways, I like your spunk! :)

Jeb

PS I am sending this email to all past communications
directors for the enjoyment.

———

*Tenacity pays off! After seven years of hounding my team to
make the Florida State websites among the best in the nation,* we
were there. *Lucy Hadi gave us this good news about the website
at the Department of Children and Families.*

Subject: Update on ACCESS Florida
Wednesday, January 4, 2006 4:49 p.m.
From: Lucy Hadi

I am truly amazed that statewide we are at nearly 80% of all initial applications for assistance being submitted via the web, and a majority of those are coming to us via the internet! This means that our customers are submitting most of their applications from some place OTHER than one of our offices. Please note, also, the results of our on-line, voluntary customer satisfaction survey. Looks like we are on the right track if 90% of customers would use the web application again.

As a point of reference, the only other state that has done much with internet applications--Pennsylvania--has set an "aspirational goal" of 7% but thus far has reached only 4% of applications for assistance submitted electronically. Texas has just started down the internet road and has set their goal at 20-30%. Here is another example of the successful leadership of our "E-Governor" in revolutionizing the delivery of government services!

I am not embarrassed to admit I wanted the whole world to know.

Subject: **Update on ACCESS Florida**
Wednesday, January 4, 2006 8:22 p.m.
From: **Jeb Bush**

Why don't we do an op ed nationally and statewide to let the world know. Also, governing magazine should know and the NgA.[111] Great work, Lucy.

Jeb

---

111 National Governors Association.

———

I still loved hearing about what was on Floridians' minds—especially when they had ideas on what should be done with their tax dollars.

Subject: Golden Goose?
Sunday, February 19, 2006 11:32 a.m.
From: William J. Roberts

Governor: I read about our whopping $8 billion reserve fund today; that's money stashed away, no? If the state could invest that money in tax-free municipals yielding a modest 4% it would earn $380 million dollars per year while maintaining its emergency money. That's a lot of money to fund education, low-income housing, etc. no?

Subject: Golden Goose?
Sunday, February 19, 2006 3:49 p.m.
From: Jeb Bush

some of the money will be reserved. Some will be given back to people who gave it to government. Some will be invested in affordable and workforce housing. Some will be invested in economic development projects that will create more economic activity. At least that is my recommendation. Thanks for writing.

Jeb

———

Even if I tried to forget the end was near, reporters would not let me. Jim Ash was with the Tallahassee Democrat.

Subject: The "L" Word
Tuesday, February 21, 2006 12:02 p.m.
From: James Ash

You are understandably squeamish about the use of the
term "legacy" in connection with your administration.
Please forgive us reporter types for giving in to the
temptation. Underneath our chrome hearts we are a
sentimental lot.

However, as the pages on the calender fall away,
and the clock ticks down toward a final legislative
session, we can't resist looking back and taking an
emotional GPS reading, as it were. So indulge me,
just this once.

What legislation or policy initiatives do you
consider the most significant of your administration?

How would you like your tenure to be remembered?

Has it really been as much fun as you make it seem?

Subject: The "L" Word
Tuesday, February 21, 2006 2:49 p.m.
From: Jeb Bush

**The most significant policy initiatives have been in
the education arena.**

**The A Plus plan, the School code rewrite bill,
the command focus on reading, ending third grade
social promotion, making the high school graduation
requirements more rigorous, expanding minority
enrollment in our universities with[out]using race**

as a criteria for admissions, the implementation of
the Universal Pre K constitutional amendment, the
college board partnership, the mentoring initiative,
the family literacy initiative, the PASS program,
the expansion of school choice programs are examples
of our strategic and systemic approach to education
enhancements and reform.

My hope is that this year (no time to be
sentimental!) the legislature will allow us to tackle
substantive middle school and high school reform.
We hope to get a teacher recruitment and retention
package developed with the legislature. We will work
with the school districts in implementing our one
of a kind teacher performance pay plan. We want to
stregthen our technical/career education programs
including implementing our ready to work initiative.

This job gives me great joy!

Jeb

———

*I still loved debating the issues of the day—one of which in 2006
was immigration. My brother tried but failed to get immigration
reform passed through a Republican Congress. I feel as passionately about the need to fix our broken immigration system today
as I did in 2006. This e-mail exchange was with Peter Wallsten,
now of the* Washington Post.

Subject: your birth home
Tuesday, April 4, 2006 6:59 p.m.
From: Peter Wallsten

I was in your old bedroom a few days ago, in Midland
to do an immigration story. Now I'm also writing
about the project to turn the house on Ohio Ave. into
a museum. Your parents lived there from 52-56, so I
suspect you have no memory of the place. But if you
had any thoughts on how Midland might have shaped
your ideas or values, I'd love to hear them for the
story.

Subject: RE: your birth home
Tuesday, April 4, 2006 9:07 p.m.
From: Jeb Bush

You wrote a good piece. I am responding to you with
some trepidation since I trust you will be fair about
my comments.

I don't have much recollection of Midland but I know
that the President is totally committed to keeping
one of most amazing American values of a more open
immigration system alive. In my opinion, it is why
we don't have riots like they have in Europe, why
won't don't see the ethnic strife of many parts of
the world and why we continue to lead the world in
innovation and economic progress. Allowing immigrants
to come with dreams to pursue them with commitment
has created a better, more prosperous USA.

Don't get me wrong, securing the border is very, very
important. the President correctly leads in the this
regard and there seems to be a consensus on this in
DC. That is a good and it is about time! A more secure
Southern border (and a Northern one as well) will help
us protect safe, legal and open immigration.

But the notion that we would felonize folks that have been here and that are contributing to our progress is just plain wrong. The House Republicans have realized their mistake and tried to get this out of their bill. Penalizing the children of illegal immigrants by denying US citizenship is wrong. The focus should be on protecting our borders rather than these piling on provisions that are punitive to many who have made a great contribution to our country. Along with that, the focus should be on a guest worker program and a means to deal with the millions of long term undocumented workers that have to be dealt with. Frankly, I also believe we should open up legal immigration to the qualified scientists, innovators, entrepreneurs and others who can additionally add value to our great country.

The policy issues are complex and they deserve a fair, transparent hearing in DC. However, the tone of the debate is important as well. I know that my brother will continue to show the sensitivity that is necessary to find the proper balance. Tone matters a lot in this debate and he has been a true leader in this regard. Your article gives some of the reasons why he is showing more sensitivity than others are in our Nation's Capitol.

The cumulative effect of some politicians pounding their chests about immigration is hurtful to both of us. I fear they do so for current political gain at the expense of thoughtful policy over the long term. Pete Wilson, a good man in many, many ways, fell prey to this as well. I know he felt he was doing the right thing but matters are worse now and the Republican Party is now the minority party in California.

Columba and I watch the news early in the morning and in the evenings. The cummulative effect of the coverage is that immigrants are bad and hurting our country. The coverage is black and white, good and bad, without the nuances that the coverage deserves. My wife came here legally but it hurts her just as it hurts me when people give the perception that all immigrants are bad. That becomes the impression by the press accounts. It is crazy and wrong. In Florida, immigrants have been part of the reason why we lead the nation in job growth, part of the reason why we are in our ascendancy and part of the reason of why we are a model in many ways about what America, in all its greatness, is going to be. Don't get me wrong. We have many challenges but our embrace of immigrants and our tolerance towards them is a positive not a negative in the Sunshine State. I was impressed reading the NYTimes article today about Senators Dominici, Specter and Martinez and their personal immigration experiences. Their stories symbolize our uniqueness in all of the world. We should never lose that spirit and we won't because we have a President who won't demagogue this issue and won't tolerate others to do so.

Jeb

———

As part of a Department of Defense-sponsored bipartisan mission, I joined three other governors on a trip to visit Iraq, Kuwait, and Afghanistan. We met with our military leaders and heads of state, but I particularly enjoyed time spent with the troops—especially the men and women from Florida. In Iraq I had a chance to attend Easter services with the troops.

It was an important visit for me to be able to see firsthand the heavy burdens our soldiers, sailors, airmen, and marines—and their families—carried for America and the world. At the same time, I saw the incredible pride and professionalism our troops have in carrying out their mission. They know our country is exceptional and bears special responsibilities.

When I got back, I thanked God I was born in America and felt an even greater sense of responsibility to do all I could to improve the lives and opportunities of families who produced such great representatives and protectors of America and the world.

I wrote every family member I could. Here are just a few examples:

```
Subject: [None]
Sunday, April 16, 2006 9:46 a.m.
From: Jeb Bush


I had the opportunity to visit with John in Iraq. He
is doing well.


Regards,


Jeb Bush


Subject: [None]
Sunday, April 16, 2006 9:47 a.m.
From: Jeb Bush


I had the chance to visit with your husband, Lt.
Hoppe, during my visit to Iraq. He is doing well.
Regards,


Jeb Bush
```

———

I still felt Florida was the best place to live, and I loved when others thought so too. This e-mail made me proud of our state.

Subject: Florida loves small business—thanks
Friday, April 21, 2006 11:21 a.m.
From: Martha Roberts

Florida loves small business, and I'm writing to thank you. My background is in Washington (BQ '88, President Bush's Administration, BQ '92) and I've started businesses in Virginia, New York and for several years lived and worked as an expat overseas. My husband left the UN last summer, and with all of America before us, we chose to bring our family and our business to Florida.

We can file our annual report witout a tax attorney; we changed our corporate address with an email instead of an Amendment to our Articles of Incorporation; and the customer service rep in your Revenue Dept. gave us her name and direct number for any follow-up. Simplicity. Efficiency. Accountability. Building a business is hard enough; thanks for clearing the bureacratic hurdles.

Subject: Florida loves small business—thanks
Friday, April 21, 2006 1:54 p.m.
From: Jeb Bush

Thanks for writing. Small business is our lifeblood!

Jeb

———

Speaking of my team, Shelly Brantley's e-mail illustrates why we all wanted to be public servants in the first place.

Subject: HI
Wednesday, April 26, 2006 9:07 p.m.
From: Shelly Brantley

Governor- 2 years ago I met this family at the family CAFE and set a personal goal that Brandon would be served by the waiver before I left office. Everytime I thought about serving new people -this little boy and his infectious smile flooded my mind and heart. I have kept his picture taped to my computer ever since. There was a part of me 2 years ago that thought this may never happen as Brandon's. waitlist number was over 8,000. His mom sent this e-mail to me this week that Brandon received a waiver offer letter. The advances to cerebral palsy are incredible and Brandon is still very young. He is striving with early intervention therapies. His parents both work full-time and have some insurance, but barely enough to pay for the treatment Brandon's needs. Today Bradon and his family have hope and supports. I have other goals I'd like to achieve between now and the end of my term, but I don't know that any of them compare to serving Brandon and his family.

Brandon's mom, Heather, wrote this e-mail to Shelly:

Hello Shelly,

guess what!?@

we finally are registered for the medicaid medwaiver pgram!!!!

I feel like you had a lot to do with it, so I would like to THANK YOU SHELLY! I just can't tell you how happy Barry and I are. WE will be able to have a life as well once the respid people start helping out at the house as well. I will actually be able to have time to cook dinner, a real nice dinner, instead of having no time and throwing things together because of the constant care that Brandon needs…not requires - but he needs.…

We are so thankful. It will save us so so so so much money per year that we can now do other things with that money such as vacations with Brandon etc…I hope you are doing well Shelly-We still would like for you to have the opportunity to meet Brandon, and for him to give you a huge hug!

Take care,

Thank your for everything!

———

Then, just like that, my last legislative session was over.

Subject: GOVERNOR BUSH APPLAUDS THE FLORIDA LEGISLATURE ON A SUCCESSFUL 2006 SESSION
Monday, May 8, 2006 11:19 a.m.
From: Chris Hart

Another great session!

You came in like a lion…and went out like…well, a lion.

Subject: GOVERNOR BUSH APPLAUDS THE FLORIDA LEGISLATURE ON A SUCCESSFUL 2006 SESSION
Monday, May 8, 2006 12:47 p.m.
From: Jeb Bush

Thank you Chris.

jeb

I did feel good about all we had accomplished in our last session, and I was grateful to Tom Lee and Alan Bense for their leadership in the Senate and House in getting important legislation passed. We had made some major steps forward on behalf of all Floridians on education, tort reform, economic development, and hurricane preparedness. We were even going to get rid of intangible taxes. Hallelujah! Could more have been done? Always. Was I happy with this list? Absolutely.

I sent Mike Thomas of the Orlando Sentinel *my thoughts about the session.*

Subject: [None]
Tuesday, May 9, 2006 8:12 a.m.
From: Jeb Bush

On the agenda front, I humbly suggest that we had a great session:

On the positive front:

1. a plus plus bill which is far reaching for education reform.
2. First Generation Matching Grant Program to help first in family students go to college.

3. a 20 plus percent increase in needs based aid.
4. the multiple authorizer bill for charter schools to make it easier to create charter schools
5. statutory fix on the opportunity scholarship program and accountability for all our choice programs
6. 21st century tech enhancement act which will increase research in our universities
7. a comprehensive energy bill
8. a slew of good hurricane preparedness bills
9. getting rid of the ingangibles tax
10. about $400 million in tax relief (less than we proposed but 8th straight year of some tax relief for floridians)
11. elimination of the doctrine of joint and several liability
12. reorganization of our space promotion effort
13. innovation incentive fund for $200 million to attract big high impact investments
14. real restriction on eminent domain for private use
15. the first step in reforming our property insurance system and relief for the rising assessments due to Citizens losses.
16. a tax break that will help us secure a multi thousand job investment in Orlando!
and a few other things.…

I would rank this session as the best or second best!

Again, thanks for the kind column.

Jeb

———

I set a record for turkeys killed in 2006—$448 million of them. As usual it did not make me popular with everyone. However, I confess I was going to miss Veto Corleone. During my two terms, I used my line-item veto authority 2,500 times and cut more than $2 billion from the state budget.

Subject: Horse Park 2 Million
Tuesday, May 23, 2006 8:17 p.m.
From: Carol Dover

I am very sad to have just learned you are planning to veto the Florida Horse Park revenue. Please forgive me for taking one last chance at trying to save what I know would be valuable to the entire State of Florida.

With this 2 million we can build the equestrian stalls that would meet the requirements of an olympic site. When completed we will be in line for the next 4 star competition that has been granted to the U.S. The only other 4 Star competition is Rolex in Kentucky - and this competition brings over 110 million in one week to the State of Kentucky. Captain Mark Phillips (the US Olympic Coach) also is working on the Florida Horse Park becoming the next Qualifier for the Pan Am Games. This would have a huge economic impact to the State as well.…

Thank you for considering my request.

Subject: Horse Park 2 Million
Thursday, May 25, 2006 9:38 p.m.
From: Jeb Bush

Carol, I know you are disappointed but I strive to adhere to principle on these matters and it is not easy. I just don't believe that this is a statewide issue that the state taxpayers should subsidize. I may be wrong but it is my belief. Maybe the next governor will support it if the next legislature approves it.

Jeb

———

I sent a note to my staff thanking them for being the best team ever and for making this possibly the most successful legislative session in my eight years.

Then I sent them this to-do list. In an effort not to overdo footnotes, I won't explain too much. I suspect the team exchanged a few e-mails after they read this list. "Is he crazy?"

Subject: unfinished business
Monday, May 29, 2006 4:21 p.m.
From: Jeb Bush

We have a lot of it. here is a list in no particular order of 30 of them:

1.   closing our economic development deals
2.   developing the strategy for the Haiti project
3.   completing the 8 year record
4.   implementing the hurricane preparedness spending with a timeline
5.   implementing the energy bill with timelines
6.   implementing the $250 million hardening plan
7.   implementing the insurance reforms and developing new items for consideration

8. developing the transition plans for the next governor
9. getting all of the appointments done from the recent bills
10. everglades consent decree
11. Lake O evacuation plans
12. implementing the growth management plans of 2005 bill
13. CSX agreement
14. FEC agreement
15. FDLE commissioner appointment
16. Space initiative implementation
17. A plus plus implementation
18. Charter school alternative chartering implementation
19. Guiness book for world records reading implemenation
20. No Child Left Behind changes advocacy
21. Teacher pay national data plan
22. rule making for BOG for centers of excellence et al bill
23. Ready to work initiative implementation
24. Wounded vets program
25. Procurement cleanup through DMS
26. Budget reform (listing line items in the base budget)
27. Abortion clinic rules
28. Implementation of crisis pregnancy center funding
29. MEDICAID reform implementation
30. Corporate governance advocacy

Yet another reporter was working on a "last year in office" story. These questions came from Fred Barnes of the Weekly Standard.

Subject: two questions
Thursday, June 1, 2006 2:21 p.m.
From: Fred Barnes

Sorry to both you. At the moment, I'm writing my piece about you for the Weekly Standard. I suspect you'll like it. Anyway, I have two questions I should have asked when I was in Tallahassee. 1) When other governors call for advice on emergency management, what do you tell them? And 2) I'm told you have doubts about political dynasties. Do you and, if so, what are they?

Subject: two questions
Thursday, June 1, 2006 6:59 p.m.
From: Jeb Bush

My advice has been to be humble but strong. Emergencies are not about politics so be humble is important. However, giving transparent clear information on a timely basis is expected because people are expecting strong leadership. I also have suggested that it is important to act decisively and worry about filling out the forms later.

I don't think Americans buy into the dynasty scenario. I think you might be hearing that I am not big on talking about dynasties since I don't think they reflect the service of my granddad, father and brother's public service. It is not the motivating factor. There are no dinner table talks about it.

There are no emails about it. There are [no] calls about it. It is not who we are.

Jeb

———

*I really appreciated this note from a Democratic state represen-
tative. I would miss the back-and-forth of a good philosophical
argument. I was beginning to get sentimental too.*

Subject: [None]
Friday, June 2, 2006 3:38 p.m.
From: Ron Greenstein

As you may be aware I, too, am serving my last year
representing the people of Florida. I wanted to take
this opportunity to let you know that I have enjoyed
working with you over the past eight years.

In spite of our philosophical differences as to
how some issues affecting our citizens should be
addressed, and in spite of our differences as to some
issues that shouldn't have been addressed, overall
I have found you open-minded enough to listen to
opposing points of view (I didn't say you changed
your mind, but you did listen).

We have watched our population grow, our budget grow,
and our needs grow. We have weathered devastating
storms, we have weathered hanging chads, and we have
weathered 9/11 and its affect on our state's security.

I am pleased to have worked with you on Florida
Forever plan, on your A+ plan (well, not the voucher

portion) and recently on the hurricane sales tax
holiday.

Although we have approached issues from different
sides of the aisle, we both have done our best to
serve those who elected us to be part of the process
and, hopefully, history will look kindly at our
actions.

I hope our paths continue to cross in the future.

Subject: [None]
Saturday, June 3, 2006 1:55 p.m.
From: Jeb Bush

**thank you Ron. You have been a fine legislator and I
have thouroughly enjoyed working with you.**

Jeb

———

*I was beginning to wonder what some of my staff might do after
our term ended. So I sent a note to my outstanding deputy chiefs
of staff: Patricia Levesque, Carol Gormley, Carol Bracy, Nina
Oviedo, and Deirdre Finn. I cc'd Mark Kaplan and Toni Jennings.*

Subject: [None]
Wednesday, June 14, 2006 11:08 p.m.
From: Jeb Bush

**How can a person be so fortunate? I am truly blessed
to have such an incredible group of illustrious
deputy chief of staffs. You all do the dirty work
(you too, Mark!) and you do it well. I appreciate**

your passion, loyalty, intelligence, insight and
intensity. As I begin to think that my time as
Governor is ending, I count my blessings more
and more. You all are at the top of the list of
blessing to be recognized. So here is the deal that
I propose. Let me help each of you, if you need it,
for the next step in your journey. In return, I get
to celebrate your continued success watching from
the sidelines.

Jeb

———

*This is one of the more interesting student inquiries I had in eight
years. I am glad she asked so I could answer.*

Subject: Student Inquiry
Thursday, June 22, 2006 4:55 p.m.
From: Michelle McCormick

I am finishing up my masters in journalism at USF and
am working on my final paper. I am researching the
attitude behind natural disasters and how poeple feel
it my be God passing judgment on his creation.

Here is my question for you, since you have been
to many places that have been hit. When you visit
these areas that have been hit do you often hear the
victims blaming God? How do they deal with such a
tragedy?

Thank you for your help, I look foward to hearing
from you,

Subject: Student Inquiry
Monday, June 26, 2006 8:01 a.m.
From: Jeb Bush

Thank you for writing and asking such an interesting question.

In my travels visiting with people after the storms of the last two years, I have not had anyone say that they blame God. I have had people (including myself) pray to God for strength and safety before, during and after storms. Many people have said that they are thankful to God for being alive after the storm's passing in spite of the hardships that came their way.

People deal with natural disasters in different ways. The great majority are thankful to be safe and alive. Some are angry. Some go into a depression. All in all, I am proud how Floridians have responded to help their fellow man and rebuild their lives quickly.

Jeb Bush

———

I sent another to-do list—this one to my education and communications teams. It contained ideas for op-eds we could write for the new school year. We had only one more opening day to promote what we had done in school reform.

Subject: Research Alerts
Wednesday, July 12, 2006 5:03 p.m.
From; Jeb Bush

possible topics for back to school op editorials:

- sales tax holiday week. "and while you are out there shopping for your kid, here are some of the things that will help your child this school year beyond supplies…go to the parent's night, meet your teachers, set expectations for homework, go to www.xyz.org to see what the standards are , etc, etc.
- Pay for performance. this year, school districts are giving raises of 8%(list several of the counties), in addition to that, if history is a guide, 50% of the $x million in school recognition money will go to teachers and $150 million will go to an unique bonus program for teachers , here is how it will work.
- A school that showed progress in every media market with the following template. Next week, xyz middle will receive $xxx or $100 per student in school recognition money for earning a B and improvement of two grades from the previous year. this was achieved by 1. more discipline in the classroom, 2 a more focused approach to reading, etc etc Statewide, x number of schools improved their grades last year, yyy,yyy students are now reading at grade level or higher than they were five years ago. Members of the legislature could do these, or the superintendents, or principals (or me for Miami). The a plus plan is working. There are newspapers for almost every school district and several for some of them.
- teacher pay comparisons
- is there enough data on the social promotion policy now to write about it?
- no child left behind changes

- **publicizing the hoover book**
- **an oped specifically about charter schools**
- **an oped specifically about career academies and ready to work.**
- **an oped about majors for high school**
- **an oped about the reforms for middle schools.**

I think we need to strive to hit the papers hard between now and October.

Has anyone developed a data base of opinion leaders? they could be mailed once a week on a new topic.

———

Here's one last e-mail from our friend Kirsty. She did pass the FCAT, and she did graduate from high school, and I rejoiced when she sent me this note.

Subject: Kirsty
Sunday, August 20, 2006 2:50 p.m.
From: Christine

I am so excited! I graduated from VCC[112] last semester with my A.A. degree in Psychology and am now starting at UCF[113] to pursue my bachelor's degree in Criminal Justice! I start classes on Monday and I am ecstatic! Words cannot describe the sheer elation and joy that I feel. I am becoming even closer to realizing my dreams and I know it is due in part to your help. Without your aid, I would not be able to pursue my dreams and there are not enough thank you's in the world to show my gratitude. I sincerely hope that

———

112   Valencia Community College.
113   University of Central Florida.

someday I'll be able to share a cup of coffee with you at the courthouse or FBI headquarters. =0) Take care and God bless.

Subject: Kirsty
Sunday, August 20, 2006 2:57 p.m.
From: Jeb Bush

great work, Kirsty. I am proud of you.

Jeb

———

I couldn't resist ribbing my friend Marco Rubio just a little. I forwarded him an e-mail I thought would be of interest to him. This is what I got back.

Subject: Thank you for your email
Friday, August 25, 2006 1:29 p.m.
From: Marco Rubio

Thank you for emailing my Legislative Office. I have always appreciated hearing the opinions of my constituents regarding issues we debate in the Florida Legislature.

As you can imagine, my district office receives significant amounts of emails on a daily basis, due to the high volume and because I personally respond to as many emails as possible, your response may take a minimum of one week. Please be sure to include your mailing address in your email communications and I will properly and directly respond to you.

Again, thank you for sharing your views. Please rest assure that I will keep your concerns in mind should I have the opportunity to work on these important issues during the next legislative session. If there is anything my staff can do to assist you, please feel free to contact us.

Subject: Thank you for your email
Friday, August 25, 2006 1:31 p.m.
From: Jeb Bush

Auto response!!!!!!!!!!!!!!!!!!!!!!!!!!!!!!!!

Jeb Bush

In his defense he did e-mail me back.

Subject: Thank you for your email
Saturday, August 26, 2006 7:32 a.m.
From: Marco Rubio

Even the most innovative among us need time to make dramatic changes like getting rid of the auto response!

———

I promise not to share too many of these nostalgic e-mails. Surprisingly I was not getting any "can't wait until you are gone" messages. I know there were people out there thinking that. Maybe they decided to leave me in peace for my last few months. This one came from a state representative.

Subject: fiscal conservatism
Thursday, September 21, 2006 9:43 p.m.
From: Rob Wallace

I sure am going to miss you rolling out pretty lean budget proposals only to have them bloated up by the Legislature. But I always liked your veto pen. Even still the growth in spending since 1994 has been phenomenal. I'm glad the fiscal conservatives have been in charge. Hope to see you soon.

Subject: fiscal conservatism
Saturday, September 23, 2006 5:27 p.m.
From: Jeb Bush

thank you rob. State government has done better than local or federal but we could have done better!

Jeb

Although we were hurricane-free in 2006, that didn't mean Floridians weren't still hurting from two years of hurricane hell, and it didn't mean we weren't still trying to help.

Subject: Homeowner's Insurance
Tuesday, October 10, 2006 6:22 p.m.
From: Brent Sylvester

I am writing to ask if there is anything going on at State level to help us residents with the outrageous Homeowner's Insurance rates? Sir, I am a totally disabled veteran and of coarse live on a shallow budget. My Insurance rate tripled and I have never filed a claim in my life with this type of insurance. My income has never tripled! Tell me sir, is it true that the plan is for the wealthy to squeeze the rest of us out? It is sure heading in that direction. All my life I dreamed of living

on water in Florida and that dream came true in
1999. I guess that all good things DO come to an
end because now there is a very good chance that I
will lose my home but NOT without a fight! I laid
my life on the line for my country once and I'll
do it again to save my home. With all due respect
Sir, the lower and middle class citizens here are
being raped right before your eyes! It wasn't our
ideas to build cities fifteen feet below sea level!
It wasn't our idea for the wealthy to build plush
beach homes on hurricane alley only to have them
replaced by Insurance companies time and time
again. Well, the cost has rolled downhill to us
now. What these insurance companies have done to
us is absolutely barbaric. The only comfort to me
is the fact that we all have our "Judgement Day"!
Please step in and do something about this because
in doing so, you will be respected in the highest
regard. Thank You For Your Time!

Subject: Homeowner's Insurance
Tuesday, October 10, 2006 7:24 p.m.
From: Jeb Bush

**we are trying to deal with 8 hurricanes and $38
billion of claims in the last two years. It has
created a crisis and we are working on solutions.
This year, the legislature allocated 1.3 billion
dollars to provide relief in different ways and i hope
we will have a special session to do more. I know
that this is a huge problem for you and many, many
others.**

Jeb

More and more I was seeing the phrase "the last time" in e-mails. Peggy was a supervisor in the Office of Citizen Services and a great public servant.

Subject: Question from student
Monday, November 13, 2006 11:47 a.m.
From: Peggy Kassees

one of the last few times I will be asking you information for kids:

This child asks who was your favorite teacher and what did that teacher do that has had a lasting impact on you personally or professionally.

Thank you so much, and thanks for the priviledge of working for you the past eight years.

Subject: Question from student
Monday, November 13, 2006 1:24 p.m.
From: Jeb Bush

I had many fine teachers but the one that has had the most lasting impact is Angel Rubio, my high school Spanish teacher. He made me read the great works of Spanish language literature. He pushed me further than I ever could have imagined going in terms of Spanish language knowledge.

Jeb

A huge disappointment in 2006 was the battering the Opportunity Scholarship program was taking despite its very successful record. More than seven hundred students—64 percent of whom were African American and 30 percent of whom were Hispanic— had received scholarships to attend better public and private schools of their choice. The scholarships gave all students chances to get the education they deserved.

Nevertheless, the Florida Supreme Court ruled in January that the program was unconstitutional because it used taxpayers' money to send students to religiously affiliated schools. I then asked the state legislature to put a referendum on the ballot in the next statewide race to let the voters decide whether to make the voucher program part of the state constitution. They failed to do so.

You might remember, though, we already had created the Florida Tax Credit Scholarship program. This allowed businesses to receive tax credits when they donated money to a nonprofit to fund scholarships for low-income students. So even though the courts had ruled against the Opportunity Scholarships, the scholarship recipients would not be kicked out of the schools they had chosen and could continue through this other fine program.

Although my time was almost up, that didn't mean I was going to quit trying to protect and promote Florida's voucher system. After all, it was working—a point I felt was often lost on the people who opposed it.

I found an unlikely ally in Robert Reich, secretary of labor under President Clinton and a professor at the University of California Berkley in 2006.

Subject: [None]
Monday, November 13, 2006 10:36 a.m.
From: Jeb Bush

this is Jeb Bush from Tallahassee (soon to be Miami), communicating with you.

I recently learned of your support for vouchers in education. Florida has the most extensive voucher programs in the country and I believe those programs have helped not hindered public education.

If you are ever down in Florida, I would enjoy discussing the subject with you. If not in person, then by phone if that works for you.

Jeb Bush

Subject: [None]
Tuesday, November 14, 2006 1:20 p.m.
From: Robert Reich

I've been supportive of the idea of "progressive" vouchers whose value vary inversely with family income. I don't know if you've tried this in Florida but I'd be happy to talk with you about this. I've left your staff person my telephone numbers.

Subject: [None]
Thursday, November 16, 2006 3:49 a.m.
From: Jeb Bush

i left word to speak to you.

In Florida, we had three voucher programs. One for students in underperforming public schools (90 plus % were near or under the poverty level) called opportunity scholarships. this one was ruled unconstitutional this year. Another using corporate tax credits for lower income students which has around 16000 students and another for ESE[114] students

---

114 Exceptional Student Education.

in public schools whose parents believe their IEP[115]
is not being carried out (if memory serves me right,
their are 14000 students in the McKay scholarship
program). Suffice to say, we are on the cutting edge of
the school choice movement and it is not a surprise
to me that we also are a national leader in rising
student achievement as measured by the NAEP[116]. There
is a renewed focus on dealing with students that have
been left behind and it is working.

I would hope one day that the right and left could get
together on this. Interestingly, the first advocates of
vouchers came from the left in the sixties.

How can we take advantage of the window of bi
partianship that will be short lived to create a
"Nixon to China" opportunity for a new approach in
education?

I think it is worth exploring. what say you?

Jeb

Subject: [None]
Thursday, November 16, 2006 2:03 p.m.
From: Robert Reich

Yes, I think it worth exploring, although I'd love
it if you were right in your assessment that we had a
window of bipartisanship right now. I'm attaching (and
pasting below) a piece I did several years ago for the
Wall Street Journal, advocating a progressive voucher
system. The right hated it because it gave lots of

---

115 Individual Education Plan.
116 National Assessment of Educational Progress.

money to the poor and took it away from the rich. The left hated it because it was a voucher system. So I guess you could say the response was bipartisan.

Looking forward to talking with you.

———

After the heartbreak of Rilya Wilson, this story was much appreciated.

Subject: Thankful for You
Tuesday, November 21, 2006 8:40 a.m.
From: Jacinta

I want to make you smile.

DCF worked and many people teamed together to redirect the lives of four children, giving them hope and a future. They were three, four, five and seven years old when DCF put them in foster care. The mother of three of the children had been killed in a drug deal gone bad in Atlanta. The grandmother of three of the children and the mother of one child was a drug addict who has been in and out of drug treatment programs for over twenty years. In three days I was able to have all four children placed with my family. The children are my nephew, two great nephews and great niece.

DCF worked with us to provide care and healing for these four sweethearts. Less than two years later my nephew has been united with his father, whom he did not know and the other three sweethearts have a new Mom and Dad. They were adopted by a wonderful young couple through DCF's efforts to place them as a sibling group. We still get to be aunt and uncle. The system worked. The safety net for our most vulnerable worked and work well. Many lives have been impacted for the better.

You have accomplished many wonderful things as Governor and I admire and respect you. I appreciate your statesmanship and I continue to pray that you and your family be blessed tremendously.

Subject: Thankful for You
Wednesday, November 22, 2006 7:47 a.m.
From: Jeb Bush

That is a wonderful holiday story! Happy thanksgiving!

Jeb

———

I asked my dad to come be the last speaker for our Leadership Forum, a speaker's series held in the House chamber. He tried unsuccessfully to choke back tears when telling a packed house how proud he was to be my dad. (I think I am more proud to be his son.) The video went viral, so I wasn't surprised to get this e-mail from Ohio.

Subject: The video of your father, President Bush
Tuesday, December 5, 2006 7:19 p.m.
From: Debbie Bedell

I'm not the type to write an email to someone I don't know, but I had to tell you how moved I was

by the beautiful display of love and pride your
father displayed for you recently. I have always
felt that your dad was not just one of the finest
presidents our country has had, he is also one of
the finest individuals to have held that office. When
I hear someone lament that there are no "Thomas
Jeffersons" anymore, I always point out your father
as an example of how that statement is not true.
His recent work with President Clinton regarding
the situation in Darfur is a great example of his
integrity and heart.

I don't know if you'll even get this but I was
inclined to write and tell you what a wonderful man
you have for a father. You are very fortunate!

**Subject: The video of your father, President Bush
Thursday, December 7, 2006 7:26 a.m.
From: Jeb Bush**

**thank you for writing. Simply put, he is the greatest
man I know!**

Jeb

———

*I miss e-mail exchanges with Floridians such as the following—
even if they could be frustrating. This one was such a mixed blessing, but I was grateful once again that e-mail gave me a chance
to set the record straight. It made me sad I was ending my term
as governor with her thinking I did not care about her. Yet I loved
the report about her children and their progress. That was more
important.*

Subject: The two terms you've been governor
Thursday, December 7, 2006 3:08 p.m.
From: Vanessa Clarke

I am a black, 32 year old, single mother of three
who resides in Broward County, Fl. I wanted to
acknowledge a job well done by you despite my not
being a political supporter of you or your family.
My daughter was held back when she was in the third
grade because she didn't pass the FCAT and I was
very unhappy about that. Nevertheless, I support
FCAT testing and I do believe that it is benefical.
You've made yourself very clear from your actions
through your Governship that black people aren't a
great deal of concern to you and that deeply saddens
me because I do believe that you should be viewed as
one of the BEST Governors in the history of Florida.
You've done a hell of a job with the issues of this
state and you proven to be very intelligent but I
can't imagine how much better you could have been
if RACE didn't matter to you or if everybody was
colorless. The world would be a much better place
if people could just be considered as people and
not as members of RACES because colors are just
mere characteristics of individual human beings.
You're obviously an educated and very rich man so
there's not much of anything that can really offer
you much of a challenge but I do have a challenge
for you that money can not buy or education won't
solve; try if you will to imagine that you were the
minority and the majority (your state's Governor)
never gave you any indication that your presence or
participation meant anything of value; how would you
feel? You were one of the best Governors that this

state has seen and that can't be changed. I only wish that I could have experience you at your very best "color blinded."

Subject: **The two terms you've been governor**
Thursday, December 7, 2006 9:16 p.m.
From: Jeb Bush

Thank you for writing. All people matter to me and I have tried as hard as i can to prove that. The achievement gap between black and white has narrowed in the last years thanks to our accountability programs. I have appointed more African Americans and minorities to the judiciary and positions in my administration than my predecessors because I passionately believe that government should reflect the diversity of the State. I believe that the proper policy is to be race conscious but have the same standards and expectations for all.

I really appreciate your kind comments and I want you to know that I care about your struggle and with you all the best.

Again, thank you for writing.

Jeb

———

I miss hearing from students the most. They really do say the darndest things. I still hear from some but not as many. Thank heavens I now have four grandchildren.

Subject: music lessons when you were young
Thursday, December 7, 2006 8:54 a.m.
From: Clare

My name is Clare and I'm 9. I live in Ormond beach
with my Mom and Dad and brother Charlie hes only
8. I play piano. Charlie does too but I think hes
tonedeaf. I hate going to lesson's becasue my teacher
smells of dead aligators. but my Mom says if I go
to my lessons and try hard someday I could be real
clever and become president, which would be neat.
But I dont believe her and she said I should write
to you and ask you, she bet you and George both had
lesson's.
Did you guys study music? What kind and for how
long?

Subject: music lessons when you were young
Friday, December 8, 2006 7:03 p.m.
From: Jeb Bush

thank you Clare Jane. yes, I had piano lessons. it
was tough and I didn't enjoy it. In fact, I wasn't
that good at it. But you know what? It gave me
discipline which helped me as an adult. So my advice
is to be obedient to your mom. She seems like a
pretty cool person and she knows best.

Merry Christmas and thanks for writing!

Jeb

———

I was inundated with e-mails during the last few weeks from constituents wanting last-minute appointments to boards and commissions, pardons, jobs, and other favors. I politely said, "I am deferring to the incoming governor." My time had come to an end. It was time to pack up and leave. Charlie Crist had won the election and would be sworn in as the next governor of Florida on January 4, 2007.

The people who wrote and thanked me for my service truly touched me, and to all of them I said the same thing: It was my honor.

It is perhaps ironic I end this chapter as I began it—an e-mail exchange with a reporter. Even when I pretend otherwise, I love mixing it up with the press. These questions came from Abby Goodnough, the New York Times *Miami bureau chief.*

Subject: a few questions
Friday, December 29, 2006 11:00 a.m.
From: Abby Goodnough

I'm writing an article about your leaving office, to run this weekend in The Times, and am hoping you might answer a few questions.

Is there any one accomplishment of your tenure that you are most proud of?

Do you hope to stay involved in government and policy after leaving

Tallahassee? And if so, how?

Is it true that you have no idea what you will do next? Are you thinking about it yet? What are your first priorities after Jan. 1?

When you told the Spanish-speaking press "No tengo futuro" earlier this month when they were asking the usual questions about your political aspirations, were you joking?

Grover Norquist and others continue to hope you will jump into the 2008 presidential race, even though you have repeatedly ruled it out. What do you think about the continued speculation (and hope, on the part of many) that you will run?

Subject: a few questions
Saturday, December 30, 2006 12:14 p.m.
From: Jeb Bush

Here is a go at your questions:

1. **Rising student achievement is the norm in Florida now and we are one of the few states that is closing the achievement gap.**
2. **I will stay involved in education policy but in a non intrusive way. Former Governors should take time off to let successors do their own thing.**
3. **I have no idea what I will be doing next. My priorities are to hang out with my beloved wife (until she can't take it anymore! :)), workout everyday and figure out what I will do next with my life.**
4. **I was misunderstood by a reporter.**
5. **I am flattered that all sorts of people are interested in what I am going to do and many have offerred advice as well.**

That will all subside soon.…

Jeb

Epilogue

Florida is my home. It has been my home for thirty-four years—ever since I moved here, like so many others, for a new job opportunity. Columba and I raised our children here, and our two oldest granddaughters, Georgia and Vivi, are growing up here. It is a diverse and dynamic state that looks a lot like America.

When I became governor of Florida, my goal was simple—to give every Floridian the same opportunities my family has had here.

So I will end where I began. I wanted Florida to be the best place in the world to live, work, and raise a family. I wanted every single child to have an opportunity to learn. I wanted everyone to feel safe. I wanted the most vulnerable, who had been pushed to the end of the line, to be at the front of the line. I wanted there to be good jobs for everyone who wanted to and could work. I wanted the government to spend less, and I wanted taxpayers to keep more of their hard-earned dollars. I wanted to protect our beautiful coastlines, crystal rivers, and wild spaces for generations to come.

To get there I stole a brilliant concept from one of the best books I've ever read: Built to Last: Successful Habits of Visionary Companies. *James Collins and Jerry Porras are the authors. Collins and Porras coined the phrase "BHAG," big hairy audacious goal. A BHAG is a visionary goal that companies and organizations can use to help their employees and team members strive for excellence in pursuit of future outcomes.*

During my governorship I governed by this principle. BHAGs became part of our vocabulary. I'm actually shocked we managed to get through eight years of e-mails without seeing it in writing. Even before taking office, I outlined the BHAGs to my team I felt could get us to that one singular goal. We were committed to making a difference in the lives of Floridians, and we never lost sight of why we were in office. When faced with a challenge, rather than ask "why," we asked "why not." We pushed the limits of state government to serve people, and we made it a point to stay connected to the people we were serving.

We had our share of bumps and bruises—some not of our own doing and some self-inflicted. However, when we sat down at our desks in the morning or traded e-mails late into the night, there was no confusion about what we were working to achieve. When I left office, I know life was better for more Floridians than when I came.

Thanks to an outstanding team; a good working relationship with the state legislature, who agreed with the need to move our state in a new direction; and the people of Florida themselves, whose support, encouragement, and good advice I always appreciated and needed, we succeeded.

I was proud of what we had accomplished in improving education. Although, I wanted to do more.

I was proud we also improved the lives of the disabled, made our streets safer, built better roads and bridges, and protected the Everglades. We even cut taxes, grew the state's rainy day fund, and cut wasteful spending. We proved you can be a fiscal conservative but still improve the quality of life for everyone.

To prove the point, Florida's population grew by a whopping three million people—more than the combined populations of Alaska, South Dakota, Montana, and Wyoming. Yet state spending as a percentage of our economy actually declined during my governorship. Middle-class incomes grew, and unemployment fell.

Don't panic. Here is the place where I could bury you with facts and figures of declining crime rates, job growth, credit ratings, tax cuts, graduation rates, and reading scores—but I won't. If that disappoints you, there is an appendix with a few statistics about my governorship.

I would rather highlight a few people I worked alongside to make Florida a better place.

- *Berthy De La Rosa-Aponte, who is the reason we are better serving the developmentally disabled in Florida. I still correspond with this feisty mom who told me she was a Democrat but would give me a week to teach me about her daughter, Lucy, and the needs of so many other families who raise and support these precious gifts from God.*
- *Willard Fair, a civil rights legend from Miami who joined forces with a future conservative governor to open the first charter school in the state and prove that every child could learn. Fair's purple leather attire still makes me smile, and I can still hear his deep voice saying to me, "Jeb, we're gonna open a school for kids who have no chance at success. We are going to prove everyone wrong about these kids." And we did.*
- *Tracy Richardson, whose daughter, Kahliah, was eight years old and stood by my side when I signed the A+ Plan in 1999. Tracy told me then she was "in turmoil" about her daughter's education and not happy with anything about her school. She made sure Kahliah received an Opportunity Scholarship. Kahliah is now working on her bachelor's degree while raising a son of her own.*
- *The tens of thousands of Floridians who rebuilt our state after our seasons of hurricanes. I hesitate to single anyone out, but I think all Floridians would approve my saluting the Florida Department of Transportation, who oversaw the rebuilding of the Interstate 10/Escambia Bay Bridge in Pensacola. I reopened with great ceremony just the eastbound lanes right before I left office. If you remember, Hurricane Ivan broke that bridge in half and broke*

Pensacola in half. That broken bridge came to symbolize our broken hearts in 2004. It was rebuilt and reopened in record time. When it was done, we felt whole again.

I will say it again: I loved being the governor of Florida. It was an honor and a privilege.

Now I feel strongly there is a better way forward in America.

I know in my heart America's best days are ahead of us if we have the courage to tackle our problems head on. If we work together to change a few big things, the future will be bright for every American who wants a chance to achieve earned success.

My eyes, however, are open to the challenges we face.

We need Washington to work again. It needs to be a place where listening to different ideas—and, yes, sometimes negotiating—are not lost arts.

We need leaders who know how to make tough decisions and who know how to close the deal.

We need a strong, confident America that is respected on the world stage—an America that leads rather than follows.

We need bold leadership. Optimism. An unwavering belief in the goodness of the American people.

We can achieve great things together. We did it in Florida. We can do it in America too.

I'm ready. Are you?

Appendix: Governor Jeb Bush's Accomplishments

Issue	Accomplishment
Economy	Cut taxes every year - $19 billion total Led nation in job creation from Jan. 2000-Jan. 2007 Led nation in small business creation 1.3 million jobs created over 8 years
Budget	Balanced eight budgets Grew state budget reserves by $8 billion Eliminated 2,500 earmarks, saving $2 billion Reduced state bureaucracy by 13,000 positions Earned AAA bond rating upgrade
Education	Number of A-B schools increased from 21 percent in 1999 to 74 percent in 2006 Nearly tripled the number of charter schools Number of Florida students in school choice programs today exceeds 300,000 Graduation rates have increased by nearly 50 percent
Public Safety	Crime rate fell to 35-year low Domestic violence reduced by 24 percent

Acknowledgments

There are so many people to thank who were instrumental in putting this book together. I am not sure where to begin.

First, there was the team of people who volunteered to sort through 250,000 e-mails. Then, during the course of their reviews, they convinced me the e-mails told stories about the importance of staying connected to the people we served.

Then there was another team of people, mostly former staffers, whose memories we picked clean to help fill in the holes of what all these e-mails meant and to connect the dots of eight years of governing.

Next came a team of wordsmiths who helped me piece all this together.

Then there were all the fact-checkers, proofreaders, and advisers—former staff, current staff, friends, friends of friends, Mom...everyone who gave us their advice and support regarding what we put on paper.

All of you were a part of this huge undertaking. You know who you are. Just know I am deeply grateful to you. This book never would have happened without you.

I am grateful to the technical people at Amazon for turning what we gave them into an e-book and making it available to the public.

Trent Wisecup was nicknamed "the foreman." He was not only a member of all these teams, but he also somehow managed to keep the teams organized and more or less on deadline. Jean

Becker, one of the most talented writers I know, provided sage advice in helping me with the narrative and the organization of the e-mails so they really did tell the story of my governorship.

We also shouldn't forget the people who wrote all those e-mails all those years ago. You really are the coauthors of this book. Thank you. I think if you knew then what you know now, you probably would have used spell check. I know I would have.

Made in the USA
Lexington, KY
04 October 2016